Studies of the causes of war generally presuppose a 'Realist' account of motivation: when statesmen choose to wage war, they do so for purposes of self-preservation or self-aggrandizement. In this book, however, David Welch argues that leaders are often motivated by normative concerns, the pursuit of which may result in behavior inconsistent with self-interest. He examines the effect of one particular type of normative motivation – the justice motive – in the outbreak of five Great Power wars: the Crimean war, the Franco-Prussian war, World War I, World War II, and the Falklands/Malvinas war. Realist theory would suggest that these wars would be among the *least* likely to be influenced by considerations other than power and interest, but the author demonstrates that the justice motive played an important role in the genesis of war, and that its neglect by theorists of international politics is a major oversight.

Since states are often led to war by the perceived demands of justice, Welch concludes the book by examining the meaning of justice across borders with an eye to clarify its relationship to international order. He argues that there is room for creative institution-building in the pursuit of a just world order, but that the current gap between empirical and normative political science makes progress toward this goal difficult.

D1427226

JUSTICE AND THE GENESIS OF WAR

CAMBRIDGE STUDIES IN INTERNATIONAL RELATIONS

JUSTICE AND THE GENESIS OF WAR

DAVID A. WELCH
University of Toronto

CAMBRIDGE
UNIVERSITY PRESS

Published by the Press Syndicate of the University of Cambridge
The Pitt Building, Trumpington Street, Cambridge CB2 1RP
40 West 20th Street, New York, NY 10011–4211, USA
10 Stamford Road, Oakleigh Melbourne 3166, Australia

First published 1993
First paperback edition 1995

Printed in Great Britain at the University Press, Cambridge

A catalogue record for this book is available from the British Library

Library of Congress cataloguing in publication data
Welch, David A.
Justice and the genesis of war / David A. Welch.
    p.   cm. – (Cambridge studies in international relations; 29)
Includes bibliographical references.
ISBN 0 521 44462 4
1. War. 2. Justice. I. Title. II. Series.
U21.2.W39   1993
355.02 – dc20   92–43110   CIP

ISBN 0 521 44462 4 hardback
ISBN 0 521 55868 9 paperback

CE

For my mother, Katharin Lindsay Welch,
and in memory of my father, Dr. Gene Armour Welch;
with love and gratitude

If morality had naturally no influence on human passions and actions, it were in vain to take such pains to inculcate it; and nothing would be more fruitless than that multitude of rules and precepts with which all moralists abound. Philosophy is commonly divided into *speculative* and *practical*; and as morality is always comprehended under the latter division, it is supposed to influence our passions and actions, and to go beyond the calm and indolent judgments of the understanding. And this is confirmed by common experience, which informs us that men are often governed by their duties, and are deterred from some actions by the opinion of injustice, and impelled to others by that of obligation.

Since morals, therefore, have an influence on the actions and affections, it follows that they cannot be derived from reason, and that because reason alone, as we have already proved, can never have any such influence. Morals excite passions, and produce or prevent actions. Reason of itself is utterly impotent in this particular. The rules of morality, therefore, are not conclusions of our reason.

David Hume, *A Treatise of Human Nature*, III, I, §I;
in Henry D. Aiken, ed., *Hume's Moral and Political Philosophy*
(New York: Hafner Press, 1948), 32–3

CONTENTS

LIST OF TABLES

FOREWORD

David Welch's book is a welcome contribution to a field – the study of international relations – that all too often degenerates into scholasticism, or develops theories on far too slender an empirical base, or provokes heated debates on arcane questions. Here we have solid academic analysis that is also relevant to the world of policy.

Professor Welch's careful and lucid examination of the role played by considerations of justice in the outbreak of wars has many merits. One of the most obvious is that it is written without jargon, and therefore suggests that even complex issues can be presented in such a way that not only initiates understand them. Another merit is the empirical research he has done in a domain – history – that has been neglected far too often by model-builders on the one hand, and on the other by students who seem to believe that the world, and the study of its politics, began around 1945.

Even more important is Welch's criticism of the kind of "Realism" that has tended to dominate the field, and which rational choice analysis reinforces: a truncated and desiccated view of reality that singles out state interests and calculations of power, and leaves out all the passions and emotions that shape the definition of interests, the hierarchy of preferences, and the objectives of power. The emotion that Welch studies, and whose weight in decision-making he tries to ascertain, is what he calls the justice motive, "the drive to correct a perceived discrepancy between entitlements and benefits." He rightly criticizes theories that either discard the consideration of motives because the nature of the international system is assumed to dictate state goals and strategies, whatever the leaders' motives, or else develop hypotheses on the basis of assumed "rational" motivations. Students of history – beginning with Thucydides – have always known better, even if they have not always been explicit about their underlying assumptions. Welch, who is both systematic and explicit, does a fine job in bringing history back into the political science of international relations.

Finally, he does an equally fine job bringing empirical and normative concerns together, and in showing the ethical implications of his findings about claims of justice. Those who believe that, in international affairs, the need for order will always come before considerations of justice, tend to forget what happens when the momentary scheme of order, based merely on power relations, offends the sense of justice of important actors. International relations is always a contest among various conceptions of justice, as well as a competition among holders of power. It was one of Judith Shklar's many insights that theories of justice need to be complemented by studies of political *injustice*, and Welch helps us understand why the shock of perceived injustice fuels so many violent conflicts. He cannot be accused of being too optimistic about the possibility of a clear and universal "code of justice" all states would accept. Is he too hopeful about what he calls a "patchwork of conceptions of justice" that could nonetheless "regulate international behavior"? Perhaps; but what matters is his eloquent and well-reasoned argument against moral skepticism. In a post-cold war world fraught with regional and ethnic conflicts, his careful normative analysis will be welcome.

Because of his awareness both of the "normative dimension of human behavior" and of the tragic clashes which conflicting "parochial conceptions of justice" breed, David Welch has written a book that every kind of political scientist, every citizen interested in the moral world of politics, and even practical policy-makers will find useful to read and endlessly thought-provoking.

Stanley Hoffmann
Joseph S. Nye, Jr.
Harvard University
December 1992

ACKNOWLEDGMENTS

Like most wars, this book began as an affair of the heart rather than of the mind. As a doctoral student of international relations in the early 1980s, I developed a keen interest in the causes of wars, because I – like many of my contemporaries – feared that the United States and the Soviet Union were stumbling down the path to nuclear destruction. It was little comfort that Herman Kahn assured us that nuclear war was unthinkable and, hence, impossible; any child knew that adult human beings are far from fully rational.

Coming from a background in philosophy, I was particularly sensitive to the importance of ideas and convictions in human behavior. I considered ideas and convictions to be chief among the things that made life worth living; but I also thought them dangerous and held them in awe. It seemed obvious to me that they were powerful historical forces that had led to innumerable wars in the past, and would do so again. Indeed, the Cold War was a product of those very forces, and an era of great danger. Yet as I began to steep myself in the literature on international conflict, I felt as though political science was either unaware of the importance of ideas and convictions in human behavior, or actively denied it. The dominant image of the human being in the study of war was of a narrow, self-interested, calculating, unsentimental creature, who held principle worth nothing, and felt nothing worth dying for. It was as though political science had cut away and discarded the human soul.

It was a long and circuitous journey from that initial disconcerting impression to this book, whose genesis – like that of most wars – was haphazard, unpredictable, and surprising. A great many people helped along the way with insights, suggestions, and thoughtful criticisms. In particular, I am indebted to Emanuel Adler, Charles Beitz, Robert Beschel, James Blight, Avner Cohen, Michael Doyle, Peter Feaver, Andreas Føllesdal, David Fott, John Lewis Gaddis, Alexander George, Kalevi J. Holsti, Veronica Jarek-Prinz, William Jarosz, Victoria Kamsler, Robert Keohane, Ana Margheritis, Laurence McFalls, Andrew

Moravcsik, Timothy Prinz, Edward Rhodes, Scott Sagan, Judith Shklar, Debora Spar, Allison Stanger, Janice Gross Stein, Fareed Zakaria, and one anonymous reviewer. Special thanks are due to Stanley Hoffmann and Joseph Nye, who heroically waded through the entire manuscript, not once, but several times. The greatest debt of all I owe to my wife, Melissa Williams, my toughest critic and strongest supporter.

I would like also to acknowledge the invaluable financial and institutional support of the Social Sciences and Humanities Research Council of Canada; the Center for Science and International Affairs, Harvard University; the Carnegie Corporation of New York (through Harvard's Project on Avoiding Nuclear War at the John F. Kennedy School of Government); the Harvard–MacArthur pre-doctoral fellowship program; and the Connaught Fund, University of Toronto. Needless to say, the views expressed herein are my own, not necessarily those of the organizations that have supported this project over the years.

INTRODUCTION

In this book I argue that the behavior of states in international politics does not merely reflect a concern for power and interest, but often a concern for the perceived demands of justice. This is not a novel claim; it may be found, for example, in the works of writers as diverse as Hugo Grotius and Alfred Thayer Mahan.[1] Yet its significance has been utterly lost on contemporary international relations theory.

Students of international politics readily acknowledge that states use the language of justice and injustice in their relations with one another, but are generally skeptical that this fact could be analytically useful. Some dismiss the use of such language as rationalization, deliberate misrepresentation, or propaganda, and assume that it masks a more basic opportunism or pursuit of self-interest. They therefore question the *sincerity* of states' claims to justice. Others credit the sincerity of these claims, but tend to deny that the justice motive can be useful in explaining state behavior on the ground that what states perceive to be *just* is materially indistinguishable from what serves their interest, or on the ground that, since states *always* use the language of justice and injustice, the justice motive is a constant and cannot explain variations in state behavior or help identify the conditions under which states are more or less likely to act in particular ways. The net result of both forms of skepticism is that the justice motive plays no significant role in international relations theory today.

I hope to show that the skeptics are mistaken and the omission regrettable. National leaders very often *do* see the world through normative lenses, and very often act in accordance with their perceptions of what is right or just. While some national leaders may indeed use the language of justice insincerely, many – in my view, most – do not. Moreover, while there is often a considerable degree of overlap between the things leaders claim for their states as a matter of justice and those things that would serve their national interests, the sense of injustice can engage powerful emotions that prevent dispassionate deliberation, hinder the careful weighing of costs and

1

benefits, frustrate negotiated settlements of differences, and increase the likelihood of pernicious misperceptions and misjudgments, with deleterious effects on leaders' abilities to serve their national interests effectively. Furthermore, while the justice motive may well be a "constant" of international politics, in the sense that national leaders are always vigilant in the defense of their perceived entitlements, they do not perceive *everything* that would serve their nations' interests to be theirs by right, and do not describe all of their interests in the language of entitlement. Only those issues that touch their perceived entitlements succeed in engaging their senses of justice.

Thus the omission is regrettable in the first instance because the justice motive has considerable analytic value that students of international politics hitherto have overlooked. By attending to the justice motive, we can craft better explanations not only of particularly important events in international politics, but also of broad patterns of state behavior. We may also manage to improve our ability to predict future events – something at which international relations theory has proven woefully inept to date – by refining our understanding of the relationship between what states seek and how they behave.

But, in addition to its analytical gains, an appreciation of the role of the justice motive in international affairs can have practical value. In the chapters that follow, I attempt to show that while national leaders are keenly aware of their own concern for justice, they are often insensitive to the role of the justice motive in the behavior of others, with the result that they seriously misjudge their protagonists' interests, objectives, and resolve. If national leaders were more attentive to the normative claims of others – and more circumspect about their own – they could better anticipate and manage conflicts, and in some cases avoid them altogether. As long as they are not, there is little hope of progress toward the elusive goal of a well-ordered international society in which conflicting claims of justice are resolved peacefully as a matter of course.

These are sweeping claims best treated by an ambitious research program rather than a single book. Nevertheless, I attempt to demonstrate the plausibility of these claims, and to show that these are researchable propositions. I do so by exploring the agency of the justice motive in the outbreak of five Great Power wars; by using the histories of those wars to probe the plausibility of a number of hypotheses about the role of the justice motive in state behavior; and by examining some of the central philosophical issues these cases raise to suggest that normative political theory has a crucial role to play in translating empirical findings into useful policy prescriptions.

I have, so to speak, three targets. The first is what I call the "Realist" account of motivation that undergirds the edifice both of classical Realism and its modern descendant, "neorealism" or "structural realism."[2] This is the view that states are motivated overwhelmingly either by self-preservation or self-aggrandizement. It is in Great Power wars that we would expect to find Realist motivations most powerfully at work because Great Powers are thought to be most concerned with the international distribution of power, and it is only in such wars that their status as Great Powers – and sometimes their very existence as states – is immediately put at risk. By demonstrating that the justice motive plays a crucial role in the genesis of Great Power wars, and by contending that an appeal to the justice motive can explain several aspects of the outbreak of these wars that seem counterintuitive from a Realist perspective, I hope to make the strongest possible case for the plausibility of the claim that the justice motive plays an important role in state behavior generally.

My second target is the conception of human nature – and thus of national leaders – upon which Realism is founded: egoistic, calculating, untrusting, and, above all, fearful. I do not claim that this conception of human nature is *false*; merely that it is woefully incomplete. To read the classic texts of international relations theory, one would never suspect that human beings have right brains as well as left; that in addition to being selfish, they also love, hate, hope, and despair; that they sometimes act not out of interest, but out of courage, politeness, or rage; and, that in addition to seeking to do *well*, they often seek to do *right*. One would also tend to forget that the Hitlers and the Stalins of this world are the exceptions, not the norms. More typical are the Herbert Hoovers and the Neville Chamberlains, men who operated within the full domain of human experience and whose foreign policies reflected that fact. In short, international relations theory needs to rediscover the human soul.

My third target is the "empirical-normative gap" within political science itself, which both results from and perpetuates the hegemony of power-political analysis, and which prevents communication and cross-fertilization between those who attempt to understand the nature and causes of state behavior, and those who are concerned with the philosophical dimensions of international politics. Nowhere is this gap more apparent or more unfortunate than in the study of war. The logic of many theories of war is deterministic: wars are the products of inexorable forces or laws that leaders obey but are powerless to control. But normative theories are essentially non-deterministic. Just war theory, for example, specifies a set of conditions under which

3

resort to war may be morally justified, assuming (on the principle "ought" implies "can") that states can *choose* whether or not to wage war, and that the choice may be influenced by calculations of right and wrong, not merely by calculations of power and interest. If the empirical-normative gap is intellectually mistaken, then it will have a pernicious effect both on our understanding of the causes of war and on our understanding of international morality. On the one hand, an appreciation of the *empirical* relevance of moral notions will lead to a better understanding of the forces that shape world politics; on the other hand, an appreciation of the *actual* moral claims states make can lead to less parochial (and hence more prescriptively useful) theories of international morality. Moreover, at a practical level, if perceptions of injustice are an important and neglected source of international conflict, then a reconsideration of the meaning of a concept such as "justice," when applied in an international and intercultural context, may lead to the creation and promotion of mechanisms and institutions better suited than existing ones (in certain respects, and in certain circumstances) to the tasks of conflict prevention and management.

Politics is an inherently normative pursuit that exhibits identifiable behavioral patterns. The institutional cohabitation of normative theory and empiricism within political science therefore seems natural. Why, then, should philosophers and empiricists have such difficulty speaking to each other? It is clearly not the result of confusion about the subject matter of political science itself. Rather, it would seem to be a function of deep hermeneutical and epistemological rifts that separate the humanities (for which political theory has a natural affinity) from the natural sciences (which empirical political science seeks in various ways to emulate). Social science is, after all, somewhat uncomfortably caught between the two. But this only makes it all the more important to try to bring them closer together. Bridging the empirical-normative gap at a particularly narrow point would seem to be a productive step in that direction; examining the role of the justice motive in the genesis of war presents just such an opportunity.

THE PLAN OF THE BOOK

While the foregoing discussion provides a glimmer of my concerns and my goals, it raises a number of important substantive, definitional, and methodological questions that require fuller treatment before the analysis itself can get under way. These are the subjects of Chapter 1, in which I elaborate and substantiate my characterization of the "Realist" account of motivation; I define and present an account of the justice motive, distinguishing it from mere self-interest; I attempt to demonstrate that, in addition to providing a corrective to the Realist account of motivation, the justice motive can play a crucial role in the elaboration and operationalization of other theories of decision, and that it accounts for certain discrepancies between the predictions of those theories and the historical record; I present a number of hypotheses about the supposed agency of the justice motive in international politics; I present the rationale for exploring that agency through particular historical case studies; and I address the relevant methodological issues, anticipating some obvious objections.

In Chapters 2 through 6, I examine the role of the justice motive in the outbreak of five Great Power wars. In each I attempt to gauge both the *importance* of the justice motive *vis-à-vis* other motivations in conditioning and triggering the conflict, and its *agency* – i.e., how it deflected the course of events in the direction of war rather than peace. These chapters are heavily interpretive, occasionally counter-factual, and (unavoidably) much briefer than the subject matter could permit. Accordingly, readers who see them as *histories* of these wars will find much in them that is objectionable. These chapters are intended to serve a very precise set of theoretical purposes, and I attempt to acknowledge their limitations by being circumspect in the conclusions I draw from each.

In Chapter 7, I turn to the philosophical issues raised by the supposition that states are motivated by concern for the perceived demands of justice in international affairs and that this can increase the likelihood of war. The central difficulty is that when states' conceptions of justice clash, the institutions and norms of international society may not be sufficiently developed, or may not enjoy sufficient legitimacy, to permit a peaceful resolution of the dispute. Where such a clash of conceptions may be traceable to deep cultural differences, we may expect the problem to be particularly acute. How are we to know what the "just" outcome is in such circumstances? Does it, in fact, make sense to say that there is one? What can "justice" mean in this context? These are among the issues I address in this final chapter. I argue that the term "justice" can have no meaning in the absence of norms and institutions capable of resolving disputes of this kind. Progress toward a "just" world order, I suggest, can only lie in the deliberate and piecemeal proliferation of regimes whose members agree to regard their arrangements as authoritative. While such progress is possible, it is undoubtedly slow. In the meantime, states as a matter of course will

5

project their particular conceptions of justice onto issues that fall outside the rubric of robust normative regimes, aggravating conflicts of interest by giving them an inappropriate moral tenor. True "realism," I argue, requires that we acknowledge this, and take it into account.

1 THE JUSTICE MOTIVE AND WAR

Students of international politics have devoted enormous effort to understanding the causes of war. There exists a rich literature on the correlates of war; on the war-proneness of various types of international systems, or of various types of regimes; on the influence of societal, domestic political, economic, bureaucratic, or military factors; on the impact of belief systems, operational codes, processes of cognition, affect, and personality; and on the effects of decision-making processes on decisions themselves.[1] Can we plausibly say that the causes of war are well understood? Certainly not as well as we would like.[2] Wars are, at present, largely unpredictable events. Yet few (if any) wars are entirely mysterious, at least in hindsight. We understand enough about the conditions under which wars are more or less likely to enable us to recognize with some degree of reliability moments of particular danger. In June 1914, hardly anyone suspected that the assassination of Austrian Archduke Francis Ferdinand would lead to a general war less than five weeks later; yet, as early as 1912, the common wisdom held that a major European war was likely within a few years.

Ideally, students of international conflict would like to specify the set of necessary and sufficient conditions for war. This goal is presently out of reach, and may well be unobtainable in principle. The fact that the journals are filled with papers reporting statistically significant correlations between the incidence of warfare and a wide variety of variables at different levels of analysis is a stark indication that the problem of war is an extremely complex one. Though not all statistically significant correlations reflect relationships of cause and effect, most theories of conflict advanced by students of international relations are accompanied by plausible arguments suggesting that there is more to the discovered patterns than interesting coincidences. War is clearly a phenomenon with multiple causality; that is to say, a wide array of factors at all levels of analysis may be needed to account for the outbreak of wars.[3] The set of necessary conditions for wars is very small, and probably includes little beyond the physical capacity of states to engage in conflict (the possession of weapons, the ability to get forces to the battlefield, and so forth). The set of sufficient conditions seems to be very large, but few if any factors are likely to be sufficient causes of war by themselves – only jointly, in fairly large numbers, and in a wide variety of permutations. In this respect, wars are like traffic accidents: the only prerequisite is that at least one vehicle be moving, but virtually any combination of bad weather, blinding sunshine, darkness, sharp curves, potholes, worn brakes, tread wear, intoxication, etc., may well be sufficient to cause an accident once that necessary condition is fulfilled. If this is an accurate way of conceiving the phenomenon of war, parsimonious theories are unlikely to be able to explain more than a handful of wars, and may have little predictive power.[4] As Bernard Brodie has written, "[A]ny theory of the causes of war in general or of any war in particular that is not inherently eclectic and comprehensive, that is, which does not take into account at the outset the relevance of all sorts of diverse factors, is bound for that very reason to be wrong."[5]

This intuition should not be taken as a paean to pessimism or agnosticism. Clearly, it would be a vain hope to explain traffic accidents in general merely by focussing solely on weather conditions, road conditions, or vehicle maintenance. Nor should we expect to be able to integrate these diverse factors neatly into a comprehensive, parsimonious general theory of accidents. Nevertheless, there is considerable merit in attempting to identify and explore the set of conditions – diverse as they may be – that make accidents more likely. There is no mystery, for example, in the claim that a driver with an elevated blood-alcohol level is more likely to have an accident (all other things being equal) than a driver who has not been drinking. While a campaign to crack down on drunken driving would not eliminate accidents altogether, it would nevertheless prevent some that otherwise might have occurred, and would save lives in the process.

By analogy, there is no reason *a priori* to despair of identifying from the historical record a number of important risk factors for war. Whether these may be fit into a larger theoretical whole is a question that can and should be left aside for the moment; indeed, it would be premature even to attempt to arrive at sweeping conclusions about *the* causes of wars until one is fairly confident that *all* important risk factors have been identified. Perhaps the most difficult aspect of this task is to remain open-minded at the outset about which risk factors are worth examining. In this chapter, I make the case for looking at one particular risk factor: the perception of injustice.

WAR AS A DECISION-MAKING PROBLEM

One way to approach the problem of the causes of war is to understand war as a decision-making problem, and to attend carefully to the components and processes of decision-making. While this is an intuitive approach, it characterizes only a small portion of the literature I alluded to above.

In 1960, C.P. Snow predicted that nuclear war within ten years was a mathematical certainty.[6] Fortunately, his prediction turned out to be incorrect. He was mistaken because wars are not random events; they are the products of decisions. Wars do not break out unless someone somewhere challenges a commitment, or refuses to yield in the face of a threat, or responds to a provocation, or escalates a skirmish, or launches a preemptive strike, or invades a neighbor, and so forth. These things do not happen by chance. This does not mean that wars cannot break out by *mistake* – the 1967 Six-Day war illustrates that they can: Israeli leaders mistakenly concluded that an Arab attack was imminent and launched a preemptive strike.[7] Nor does it mean that wars are always *deliberate*. The sequence of individual decisions that collectively lead to war may not be intended by national leaders at the outset, or may be made in an atmosphere of panic or desperation.[8] Wars are sometimes the unintended consequences of human actions, or the products of human failings. But it is useful to recognize that at all times, wars – like any other state action or policy – are the products of human decisions.[9]

Of any decision we can ask two questions: (1) what purpose (or set of purposes) was the decision meant to serve?; and (2) why did the relevant actor(s) believe that that decision was the appropriate one under the circumstances? The first question inquires about *motivations*, and the second about *calculations*. While these questions are logically distinct, they are interdependent in practice. To the extent that decision-makers engage in "wishful thinking," for example, their desires may lead them to overrate the likelihood of obtaining their goals.[10] Conversely, decision-makers' estimates of their capabilities – a crucial consideration in any rational calculation of the likelihood of achieving one's goals – may in turn influence that very set of goals. The desire of most people to own a Porsche, for instance, might intensify dramatically if they were to win a lottery. For this reason it would not be surprising to see German or Japanese leaders pressing today for permanent representation on the United Nations Security Council, when twenty or thirty years ago the thought would not have crossed their minds.

9

Students of international politics have devoted considerable effort to understanding the nature and limits of calculation, the result of which is an abundant literature on threat assessment, risk-taking, perception, misperception, cognition, and decision-making processes.[11] Yet very little effort has been devoted to the study of what national leaders seek, and how their goals affect the processes of calculation itself. If all states always acted on the basis of the same core set of motivations – or if there were no relationship at all between the nature of one's motivations and one's processes of calculation – then it would be perfectly appropriate to focus on the nature and limits of calculation in isolation from the motivations themselves. But neither of these conditions holds, and thus the cart has been put before the horse. Until we understand the relationship between the nature of states' motivations and their decision-making processes, the literature on the calculative dimensions of decision-making cannot proceed to the next level of theoretical generality. It can help us understand why decision-makers sometimes arrive at erroneous conclusions about the instrumentality of their actions (namely, when those calculations are founded upon serious misperceptions or misjudgments of the adversary's perceptions, beliefs, interests, needs, intentions, or likely responses to their own actions) – and this is an extremely valuable accomplishment. But it cannot help us identify in advance the full set of conditions under which specific decision-making pathologies are more or less likely.[12] To understand why miscalculations are important and when they are likely, it is necessary to understand what it is that leaders seek and why they seek it.[13]

REALISM AND MOTIVATION

The prevailing currents of international relations theory, informed by the Realist perspective, presuppose an account of state motivation, and treat it as a constant. Because a particular understanding of state motivation is built into the very foundations of the Realist paradigm, theorists who work within the tradition have so thoroughly internalized it that they are often unaware of the central role it plays in their understanding of international politics, and are rendered insensitive to alternative conceptions.

"Realism" is, unfortunately, vague and ill-defined.[14] There is enough variation among the approaches and substantive claims of those who consider themselves Realists to call into question any attempt to make sweeping general statements about what the concept does and does not admit. For present purposes, I shall employ a characterization of

Realism that I hope most students of international politics will recognize, and that few will consider a straw man. It is founded upon the following core set of claims:

1. States are the dominant actors in world affairs.
2. States may be treated as unitary, rational egoists.
3. International politics is anarchic (in the distribution of authority, though not in the distribution of power), and may be characterized as a Hobbesian state of nature.[15]

From these claims, suitably elaborated, may be deduced a series of descriptive, prescriptive, and theoretical propositions about state behavior captured or modeled by concepts and heuristics such as the balance of power (or balance of threat), the security dilemma, and relative-gains seeking.[16]

Realism's central insights into the nature of international politics are provided by Thucydides's analysis of the Peloponnesian war – in particular, his account of the fundamental cause of the war ("What made war inevitable was the growth of Athenian power and the fear which this caused in Sparta"[17]) and the doctrine propounded by the Athenian delegation to Melos (the strong do what they can and the weak what they must[18]). Thomas Hobbes – who began his career as a scholar translating Thucydides, and whose English version of *The Peloponnesian War* is perhaps the most elegant ever written – contributed to Thucydides's insights the state-of-nature metaphor and the conception of international politics as a "war of all against all."[19] The language of Realism has changed through the centuries – we now speak of anarchy, the Prisoner's Dilemma, and the Spiral Model rather than the state of nature – but these central themes have survived the process of modernization largely intact.

Critiques of Realism abound, and tend to concentrate on the claims that Realists (1) exaggerate the necessity and the harshness of international affairs; (2) underestimate the strength and number of interests states hold in common; and (3) overlook the role of institutions in regulating interstate interactions.[20] Indeed, if international politics were essentially a war of all against all, then it would be very difficult to explain why so many states enjoy harmonious relations marked to varying degrees by trust, honor, and good will. Indeed, in many parts of the world, the threat or use of force plays no role whatsoever in international affairs.[21] Realism suggests that the default relationship between states should be conflict, deviations from which constitute puzzles in need of explanations.[22] The infrequency of wars and the fact that the overwhelming majority of interstate relationships are peaceful and cooperative suggest a basic flaw in Realism's essential

11

characterization of the nature of international politics.[23] That basic flaw may well be Realism's account of motivation.

Within the Realist tradition, the answer to the question, "What do leaders seek?" is generally assumed: leaders (or, more commonly, "states") seek *power* for the purpose of self-preservation or self-aggrandizement. In so doing, they promote or defend "the national interest." As Robert Gilpin writes, Realism assumes "the primacy in all political life of power and security in human motivation."[24] There are important nuances in the ways in which different theorists understand this basic point. Self-preservation and self-aggrandizement, for instance, are logically distinct motivations. In addition, *power* may be conceived as an end (as Hans Morgenthau and "classical" Realists tended to view it), or as a means (as neorealists or structural Realists tend to understand it).[25] There are also important nuances in the implications for international politics that different theorists draw from the universal quest for power. What James Mayall calls "hard-line" Realists emphasize the Hobbesian war of all against all, while "soft-line" Realists accept that states may include the maintenance of order among their foreign policy objectives.[26] But, despite the nuances, there is, as Bruce Bueno de Mesquita remarks, a "common theme" running through the classics of international relations: "the self-interested pursuit of gain by national leaders on their own behalf and on behalf of their nations."[27]

The assumption that all states are motivated by self-aggrandizement or self-preservation has a powerful simplifying effect, and facilitates the formulation of parsimonious explanations of war. Gilpin puts it thus:

> Underlying Thucydides' view that he had discovered the basic mechanism of a great or hegemonic war was his conception of human nature. He believed that human nature was unchanging and therefore the events recounted in his history would be repeated in the future. Since human beings are driven by three fundamental passions – interest, pride, and, above all else, fear – they always seek to increase their wealth and power until other humans, driven by like passions, try to stop them.[28]

From here it is a short step – with a few additions – to explanations of war based on power transitions, long cycles of growth and decline, unstable balances, and so forth. Moreover, this particular vision of human nature enables scholars working within the Realist tradition to extend the analysis very easily to realms of state behavior other than the outbreak of war. It has been used, for example, to account for the difficulty states experience cooperating with one another in the economic sphere. As Joseph Grieco writes, "According to realists, states worry that today's friend may be tomorrow's enemy in war, and fear that the achievement of joint gains that advantage a friend in the present might produce a more dangerous *potential* foe in the future ... [S]tates in anarchy are preoccupied with power and security."[29] By holding motivations constant, analysts need not concern themselves with the superficial variety of goals states pursue and can quickly reduce international politics to its Hobbesian essentials.

Not all Realists are self-conscious about their motivational presuppositions. Martin Wight is a case in point. "The fundamental cause of war," Wight claimed, "is not historic rivalries, nor unjust peace settlements, nor nationalist grievances, nor competitions in armaments, nor imperialism, nor poverty, nor the economic struggle for markets and raw materials, nor the contradictions of capitalism nor the aggressiveness of Fascism or Communism; though some of these may have occasioned particular wars. The fundamental cause is the absence of international government; in other words, the anarchy of sovereign states."[30] In what sense can the anarchy of sovereign states be said to be "the fundamental cause of war"? Wight may have meant that anarchy is a necessary condition for war, but it is difficult to know how we would substantiate such a claim. As long as there have been nation states, the international system has been anarchic; we have no experience of a hierarchical system of nation states that would enable us to compare the incidence of conflict in the two types of systems. The claim would be trivially true, of course, if we were to define a hierarchical system in terms of the dominant authority's ability to control the use of force within it. But if we did not define hierarchy in this way, we would probably conclude that the claim is false – for if we defined a hierarchical system in terms of the distribution of *authority*, rather than in terms of the distribution of *coercive ability*, we would infer from our knowledge of domestic affairs that a body endowed with a monopoly on the legitimate use of force is nonetheless generally incapable of preventing violence among its subjects: more people die from domestic violence than interstate wars. Most tellingly, definitional problems aside, conflict has been present to a greater or lesser degree in all systems throughout history, be they anarchic or hierarchic, nation-state systems or other types of systems. Thus the anarchy of the system of sovereign states cannot be a necessary condition for war.

Wight must therefore have had in mind a weaker claim: that the condition of anarchy is particularly *conducive* to conflict.[31] This is an entirely plausible claim – but only on the basis of certain psychological presuppositions. Clearly, anarchy would be no obstacle to peace in a

13

world of angels. We must therefore suppose there to be certain ten-
dencies in human behavior that make violence more likely under
conditions of anarchy, such as a drive to dominate, or some combination of the self-preservation instinct and fear (born, perhaps, of
suspicion of others' motives) – precisely the dynamic captured so well
by the Prisoner's Dilemma. Wight, in short, relies upon an unstated
Realist understanding of motivation.

Consider also the following passage by Jean-Jacques Rousseau:

> It is quite true that it would be much better for all men to remain
> always at peace. But as long as there is no security for this, everyone,
> having no guarantee that he can avoid war, is anxious to begin it at
> the moment which suits his own interest and so forestall a neighbour,
> who would not fail to forestall the attack in his turn at any moment
> favourable to himself, so that many wars, even offensive wars, are
> rather in the nature of unjust precautions for the protection of the
> assailant's own possessions than a device for seizing those of others.
> However salutary it may be in theory to obey the dictates of public
> spirit, it is certain that, politically and even morally, those dictates are
> liable to prove fatal to the man who persists in observing them with
> all the world when no one thinks of observing them towards him.[32]

Anarchy and self-help are clearly responsible for the dilemma which
Rousseau believes leads states into conflict in precisely the same way
that it leads Locke's men in the state of nature, and Hobbes's in the
state of war, to seek refuge and security under a system of government. But the root evil in Rousseau's world view is not anarchy; it is
the pervasive fear of those who seek self-preservation and do not trust
others not to do them harm. Like Wight, Rousseau relies upon a Realist
account of motivation.

Given the centrality of motivation to the understanding of war, it is
curious that the topic has not been subjected to close and careful
scrutiny by students of international relations. The issue of motivation
is altogether missing, for instance, from Kenneth Waltz's seminal
discussion of the "first image" (the individual level of analysis) in *Man,
the State, and War*. "The evilness of men, or their improper behavior,
leads to war," Waltz writes; "individual goodness, if it could be univer-
salized, would mean peace: this is a summary statement of the first
image."[33] The question that arises from Waltz's statement is not
whether it is true – whether humanity is basically good or basically evil
is an intractable issue – but whether it is relevant. Why does Waltz omit
any discussion of motivation from his presentation of the individual
level of analysis? Certainly not because he has no views on the subject:
in his later work, he strongly affirms a Realist account of motivation.[34]

It seems reasonable to conjecture that it did not occur to Waltz in this path-breaking book even to ask the question of whether motivations might be of value in explaining variations in state behavior, because Realism treats motivations as axiomatic and invariant.

Similarly, Hans Morgenthau extols Realist theory for guarding against "two popular fallacies: the concern with motives and the concern with ideological preferences":

> To search for the clue to foreign policy exclusively in the motives of statesmen is both futile and deceptive. It is futile because motives are the most illusive of psychological data, distorted as they are, frequently beyond recognition, by the interests and emotions of actor and observer alike. Do we really know what our own motives are? And what do we know of the motives of others?
>
> Yet even if we had access to the real motives of statesmen, that knowledge would help us little in understanding foreign policies, and might well lead us astray. It is true that the knowledge of the statesman's motives may give us one among many clues as to what the direction of his foreign policy might be. It cannot give us, however, the one clue by which to predict his foreign policies. History shows us no exact and necessary correlation between the quality of motives and the quality of foreign policy. This is true in both moral and political terms.[35]

Morgenthau may be correct to suggest that it is futile to look *exclusively* to leaders' motivations to explain state behavior, but that does not mean that it is futile to look to them partially, or even largely, nor does it mean that a theory of the causes of war can neglect motivations and still lay claim to having isolated necessary or sufficient conditions for conflict. He is clearly correct to suggest that it is often difficult enough to ascertain our own motives, let alone those of national leaders; but while the search for motives may be difficult, it is evidently not fallacious, since there is nothing illogical in suggesting that motivations are related to behavior (in fact, by definition, quite the contrary). He is also correct to caution that knowledge of leaders' motives may not give us the ability to predict their foreign policies, since other factors, many of which are beyond a leader's control, are likely to be at work; but he cannot be correct for the reason he gives – "History shows us no exact and necessary correlation between the quality of motives and the quality of foreign policy" – because he has denied that we can know a leader's motives in the first place. And, finally, while he may also be correct to note that the (moral) quality of a leader's motives may be poorly correlated with the (moral) quality of his or her policies, he slips unnoticed from making empirical claims about the relationship between motivation and action to making ethically evaluative claims about it in a manner that suggests he is also denying any significant relationship between what leaders seek and what they do. In any case, the crucial claims Morgenthau makes, as they seem to emerge from a close look at this rather puzzling passage, are empirical claims for which he adduces no evidence. They are (1) that it is prohibitively difficult, if not impossible, to discern motivations from the historical record; and (2) that even if we could discern those motivations, they would be poor predictors of behavior. These claims are critically important, and I put them to the test in Chapters 2–6.

Morgenthau's views are complicated by a second passage several pages after the first, in which he writes, "International politics, like all politics, is a struggle for power. Whatever the ultimate aims of international politics, power is always the immediate aim. Statesmen and peoples may ultimately seek freedom, security, prosperity, or power itself. They may define their goals in terms of a religious, philosophic, economic, or social ideal ... But whenever they strive to realize their goal by means of international politics, they do so by striving for power."[36] This is, of course, a view of motivation. Why does Morgenthau repudiate a concern for statesmen's motives only to assert an account of motivation in the next breath? Precisely because Realism treats motives as given. They are assumed; they are not to be discovered.

From the perspective of international relations theory, we need not be concerned that our assumptions and axioms are *true*, only that they are *useful*. Newton assumed (wrongly) that mass concentrates at a point, but he could not have relinquished this assumption without jeopardizing his prodigious accomplishments in specifying theoretical relationships between physical objects. Similarly, the assumption that states are motivated by self-preservation or self-aggrandizement would be vindicated if theories built upon it proved more successful in explaining and predicting state behavior than theories presupposing a different account of motivation.[37] The burgeoning literature on the impact of organizational behavior, bureaucratic politics, state weakness, governmental weakness, domestic attributes and coalitions, lateral societal pressure, democratic and non-democratic institutions, capitalist and non-capitalist economic systems, timing of industrialization, and a variety of other factors suggests a certain level of dissatisfaction with the performance of Realist theories in general.[38] But political scientists rarely undertake direct and systematic comparisons of the performance of different paradigms.[39] In any case, many competing theories of state behavior do not challenge the Realist conception of human nature so much as merely disaggregate the

16

state.[40] To determine whether we can reap analytical gains by challenging the Realist account of motivation, we must begin by determining whether some other account of motivation can provide superior explanations of state behavior in precisely those cases where Realism would expect self-preservation or self-aggrandizement to be most salient.

Because of the ways in which many Realists formulate their understanding of state motivation, this is a difficult task, for reasons that become clear in the following passage by Geoffrey Blainey:

> One generalization about war aims can be offered with confidence. The aims are simply varieties of power. The vanity of nationalism, the will to spread an ideology, the protection of kinsmen in an adjacent land, the desire for more territory or commerce, the avenging of a defeat or insult, the craving for greater national strength or independence, the wish to impress or cement alliances – all these represent power in different wrappings. The conflicting aims of rival nations are always conflicts of power.[41]

This statement is unfalsifiable. If all war aims may be analyzed in terms of power by definition, the statement that states go to war to aggrandize or to protect their power is a tautology. If we substitute the word "interest" or "self-interest" for "power," the result is the same. To rescue Realism from pernicious circularity, we must specify in advance the general form of the goals that states acting in accordance with the Realist account of motivation would seek, and we must ensure that they do not exhaust the full range of possible goals.

It seems a reasonable interpretation both of classical Realism and its modern descendants to characterize the goals that states would seek if they acted on the basis of self-preservation or self-aggrandizement as those goods that enable the state to influence, or to resist the will of, other states. These goods fall into three categories: first, tangible goods such as arms, wealth, and – provided they are strategically or economically valuable – territory and resources; second, intangible goods such as credibility and reputation; and third, as necessary, allies. We would expect states acting on the basis of the Realist account of motivation to exhibit patterns of behavior predicted by Realist theories. All other things being equal, states should balance power; they should give high priority to defending or attempting to improve their positions in the international hierarchy; they should fight preventive or preemptive wars when they perceive threats to their position; they should avoid antagonizing more powerful states or coalitions; they should withdraw in the face of overwhelming might; they should assess threats and opportunities primarily in terms of relative trends in capability; and they should make decisions on the basis of prospective

17

costs and benefits. If the Realist account of motivation were false, glaringly incomplete, or grossly oversimplified, then we would expect to observe rather different types of behavior, perhaps even actions and policies that seem to be wholly irrational from a Realist perspective.

In fact, the historical record is mixed. There are several examples of textbook "Realist wars," which were fought for Realist reasons, and which satisfy the expectations of Realist theories of state behavior. I present one of these in detail in Chapter 3 – the Franco-Prussian war of 1870–1871. Thus the Realist account of motivation cannot be said to be *incorrect*. Yet there are many other wars that are anomalous from the Realist perspective, including several involving Great Powers that Realist theories would least expect to be deviant.[42] This is because some national leaders think and act like Realists, while others do not. If the wars examined in the following chapters constitute a representative sample, it would be difficult to argue that Realist leaders constitute the majority.

THE JUSTICE MOTIVE

Human beings – and thus national leaders – may be motivated by concerns other than, or in addition to, self-preservation or self-aggrandizement. These motivations may even be inconsistent with self-preservation and self-aggrandizement, at least under certain circumstances. Among them is a class of normative motivations, whose members include (for example) altruism, samaritanism, and supererogation. These motivations may be conceived of as elements of philosophic psychology more broadly understood – the domain of human experience governed by the concepts of the true, the beautiful, the right, and the good. The justice motive falls within this class. It is one aspect of a natural human moral faculty.[43]

In the infancy of both psychology and philosophy, normative motivations were given center stage in the elucidation of human behavior. Aristotle considered them the distinguishing characteristic of humanity. "[I]t is peculiar to man as compared to the other animals," he wrote in *The Politics*, "that he alone has a perception of good and bad and just and unjust and other things [of this sort] ... "[44] But the study of the sense of injustice as a spur to action is a relatively new subfield of modern social psychology, dating only from the 1960s. To grow and flourish, it had to overcome the resistance of more traditional psychological paradigms that dismissed normative motivations altogether or analyzed them in terms of more "basic" drives.[45] Only the demonstrated inability of traditional psychology to account for certain types of human behavior permitted the study of specifically moral psychology to establish itself as a serious enterprise.[46] Following the parallel, we might observe that political science lags behind psychology by two or three decades.

What exactly is the justice motive? One of the pioneers in the field, Melvin Lerner, characterizes the sense of injustice as "a reaction to a perceived discrepancy between entitlements and benefits."[47] Lerner writes:

> [P]eople are not aware of the constant monitor they maintain on whether their fate and the fate of others correspond with their entitlements, what they deserve. There is, nevertheless, every reason to believe, given the sensitivity and responsiveness to incidents of perceived injustice, that the monitoring process is ever vigilant – for most people. Although there may be some slight differences in nuances in the way people have construed judgments of deserving fairness, entitlement, justice, rights, "equity," it is probably safe to consider them all equivalent in terms of social-psychological processes.[48]

Lerner argues that the process of judging states of affairs as either just or unjust "occurs at a preconscious level and is revealed indirectly in the person's reactions to a given event."[49] Lerner notes that most people are evidently "capable of being moved to extremes of self-sacrifice in order to promote justice," and that "sometimes we do not act out of raw self-interest but try to do what is fair and just, regardless of the 'cost' to ourselves."[50] We have all experienced the unique sense of moral outrage associated with the perception that we have been unjustly treated; the phenomenon of which Lerner speaks should not, therefore, be understood as anything mysterious or otherworldly. It is as much a feature of normal human experience as is hunger, anger, sympathy, sadness, or joy.[51]

The justice motive may thus be defined as *the drive to correct a perceived discrepancy between entitlements and benefits*. The word *perceived* is crucial. For the justice motive to lead to action, it is necessary that the agent (1) believes that an entitlement exists, and (2) believes that that entitlement is not being fulfilled or respected. Whether or not those beliefs are accurate is an entirely unrelated issue; as we shall see in the next chapter, even an unfounded belief may trigger the justice motive, with devastating consequences. The *content* of those beliefs is also immaterial. It matters not what it is to which the agent believes she is entitled; what matters is that she conceives it to be hers as a matter of right, rather than as something she merely desires.

The demand for justice can only be satisfied by rectifying the

19

perceived discrepancy. This may be done in one of two ways: by providing the agent with the benefits to which she feels entitled; or by convincing her that she has misconceived the scope or content of her entitlements.[52] The latter requires the existence of a *procedure* that she regards as legitimate for resolving conflicting claims (i.e., due process). Thus the justice motive may be said to have both content and process components, and we would intuitively expect the justice motive to lead to conflict more readily in cases where procedures for resolving conflicting claims of entitlement are weak or nonexistent than where they are robust and authoritative. Consequently, we would expect the justice motive to lead to conflict more readily in international politics than in domestic society, since institutions and procedures for managing disputes are comparatively underdeveloped.[53]

It is important not to confuse the justice motive with self-interest, although there is no necessary contradiction between them; the attainment of "morally acceptable results" may be understood as a valued good similar to other types of goods, in which case someone who relentlessly pursues justice – even at great material cost – may nonetheless be said to be acting out of self-interest.[54] Moreover, when someone perceives a discrepancy between entitlements and benefits, she may often also feel that she is suffering a material penalty. Correcting her perceived injustice would *ipso facto* increase her material welfare. But it is important to note that the justice motive cannot be reduced simply to an aversion to loss and an appetite for gain.

The sense of injustice differs from an aversion to loss and an appetite for gain in three crucial respects. First, the sense of injustice differs *phenomenologically*; the subjective experience of the justice motive is not the same as the subjective experience of simple aversion to loss or desire for gain. The sense of injustice triggers a unique emotional response.[55] It engages powerful passions that have the effect of increasing the stridency of demands, amplifying intransigence, reducing sensitivity to threats and value trade-offs, increasing the willingness to run risks, and increasing the likelihood of violent behavior.[56] We are all familiar with the power of the sense of moral outrage that accompanies perceptions of injustice, and most people can readily identify examples in their own personal experiences when that sense of outrage has overridden prudence, diminished risk-aversion, or led to outright violence.

Second, the justice motive differs from loss aversion or appetite for gain *prescriptively*; the desire to do justice and to see justice done leads to a different net pattern of behavior than we would observe if people simply attempted to avoid losses or secure gains. Controlled studies have shown, for example, that subjects are willing to suffer economic penalties in order to enforce fairness as they perceive it.[57] Most of us can recall at least one occasion in our lives when a sales clerk has given us too much change; the justice motive – not an aversion to loss or appetite for gain – is what leads us to return the difference between what the clerk gives us and what we are owed. The very fact that we may feel a temptation to pocket the change and walk away illustrates that the justice motive and the desire for gain are distinct motivations that can conflict in certain circumstances – and the fact that some of us *do* quietly pocket the change and walk away demonstrates that the justice motive is not always the more powerful of the two.

Third, the justice motive differs from loss aversion or appetite for gain *extensively*. It extends only to those benefits that people actually conceive as entitlements. People do not consider everything that they would like to have theirs as a matter of right, and often consider to be theirs as a matter of right things that are utterly useless. Moreover, people have firm views of their entitlements, and tend to be categorical in their defense. They will often tolerate nothing short of their full satisfaction. In contrast, people are much more willing to trade off goods that they do not consider entitlements, or to forebear pursuing them if doing so requires great effort or cost. In short, the mode of reasoning involved in the defense of one's entitlements differs fundamentally from the mode of reasoning involved in the pursuit of other goods: it tends to be categorical and deontological rather than utilitarian.

The behavior of states, of course, reflects the decisions of state leaders. State leaders are human beings with innate moral faculties. Sometimes these faculties are highly developed, and at other times they are severely stunted. As we shall see in Chapter 5, this very difference undercut Neville Chamberlain's ability to understand and to forestall Adolf Hitler prior to World War II. Yet if the Adolf Hitlers of this world are the exception, and the Neville Chamberlains the rule, international relations theory ought to pay considerable attention to the unique characteristics of the justice motive, because it stands to reason that it plays an important part in shaping state behavior.

It is easy to demonstrate that normative motivations in general, and the justice motive in particular, have largely been neglected in the study of interstate conflict, even by scholars who have been sensitive to the issue of motivation itself.[58] Amos Yoder, for example, analyzed twenty-five possible motives for aggression and attempted to identify the ones at work in conflicts since 1914; none of his twenty-five categories fit the description of a normative motivation. The closest

21

was a category called "frustration about conditions," which Yoder conceived in terms of basic human needs rather than unresolved grievances.[59] Even more revealingly, in a book ostensibly about the relationship between justice and conflict, Robert Osgood and Robert Tucker listed a number of political motives for war, but left justice off the list altogether.[60] Only one major study of which I am aware even credits the possibility that the justice motive may have distinctive effects on the behavior of states – Northedge and Donelan's *International Disputes* (1971).[61] "In the most common form of dispute between states," Northedge and Donelan write, "one or both of them believes that the thing at issue is not something that they merely want but something that is 'theirs'. The conflict is not simply one of interest but one of justice." In such cases, Northedge and Donelan surmise, the "infusion of the conflict with a sense of legitimacy" gives a "special character" to these conflicts, "and makes comprehensible the value that the states attached to the things contended for."[62] It is regrettable that no one has followed up this insightful lead to explore the broader implications of the justice motive for international relations theory.

THE POTENTIAL CONTRIBUTION OF THE JUSTICE MOTIVE TO DECISION THEORY

This study represents a challenge only to what I call the Realist account of motivation. Among its constructive goals is to illuminate the ways in which the justice motive may improve our understanding of decision-making generally. In the first instance, the justice motive can help us operationalize theories of decision-making, improving their performance when applied to a naturalistic setting such as international politics. Second, it can help us account for certain discrepancies between the expectations of decision-making theories and real-world observations, enabling us to refine the theories themselves.[63] These are large claims worthy of much more elaborate and much more careful attention than I can give them here; but my aim in this section is to make the case that these are subjects worthy of further investigation by illustrating the potential contribution of the justice motive to a selection of approaches, issues, and topics in decision-making theory.

Expected utility theory. Analysts of international politics often rely upon the assumption that decision-makers are rational. Expected utility theory formalizes this assumption, and rests upon the following five postulates:

22

1. Individual decision-makers are rational in the sense that they can order alternatives in terms of their preferences.
2. The order of preferences is transitive so that if an individual prefers A to B and B to C, then she prefers A to C.
3. Individuals know the intensity of their preferences, which may be characterized as their utility.
4. Individuals consider alternative means of achieving desirable ends in terms of the product of the probability of achieving alternative outcomes and the utility associated with those outcomes.
5. Decision-makers always select the strategy that yields the highest expected utility.[64]

There is, at present, no theory of preference formation. To operationalize expected utility theory, the analyst must ascertain individuals' preferences, and estimate their intensities. Here the justice motive may be of considerable use. Since people constantly monitor the status of what they perceive to be their entitlements, and since reactions to perceived discrepancies between those entitlements and people's assets are especially intense, we might expect subjective conceptions of entitlements to provide a particularly useful indicator of utility when we come to apply expected utility theory in practice, provided that we can identify the content of people's conceptions of their entitlements. This is not particularly difficult; normally, individuals broadcast their conceptions of their entitlements for all the world to hear.[65]

The different intensities of preferences for perceived entitlements and for goods not conceived as entitlements can help rational-actor analysis explain, for example, why conflicts involving transfers of "home" territory are far more violent than conflicts involving other territory.[66] A neighboring province may be far more valuable economically or strategically than a province of one's own; but attachments to home territory are stronger by far, and its loss is much more likely to be perceived as a violation of right. Thus it is rational for states to pay higher costs in defense of home territory, because the fact that it is conceived as an entitlement amplifies its utility.[67]

Behavioral decision theory. Behavioral decision theory has mounted a strong challenge to expected utility theory in recent years, demonstrating experimentally that subjects routinely violate the assumptions of rational-actor analysis under certain circumstances and in systematic ways.[68] Among the crucial insights of behavioral decision theory are the claims that people assess alternatives not on the basis of their prospective net assets (i.e., their expected utilities), but in relation to a

23

reference point; that their crucial desideratum is prospective losses and gains as defined from this reference point; that they consider losses more painful than they consider gains pleasurable; and that they will accept poor gambles in order to avoid certain losses, but shun uncertain prospects of large gains in favor of smaller sure gains even though the risky choice might have a higher expected utility.[69]

According to behavioral decision theory, the selection of a reference point is central to the subsequent assessment of options and the choices people make. But just as there is at present no theory of preference-formation, there is no theory for predicting which reference points people will choose. Psychologists and economists consider the status quo an obvious point of salience, and have identified a number of processes that systematically bias people in favor of the status quo, such as the "endowment effect": people demand more to give up an object than they would be willing to pay to acquire it in the first place. Foregone gains are less painful than perceived losses, and therefore, over the long run, people's expectations will tend to converge on the status quo.[70] In addition, behavioral decision theory suggests that people will normalize (i.e., adjust their reference points) more quickly for gains than for losses, reinforcing the status-quo bias. Yet the status quo does not always serve as a decision-maker's reference point. People who are dissatisfied with a status quo will often take great risks to reach what they consider an acceptable state of affairs. In many cases, this may follow a loss from a previous reference point for which they have not normalized; they therefore strive to restore an earlier (acceptable) status quo. In other cases, people's *aspirations* or *expectations* may provide the appropriate frame of reference for understanding their risk-taking behavior.[71]

Since the sense of justice inclines people to evaluate states of affairs either as *just* or *unjust*, it seems reasonable to suggest that subjective conceptions of their entitlements could provide a crucial clue to understanding the reference points national leaders actually employ when they assess alternative choices in international politics.[72] Indeed, the implications of the phenomenological and prescriptive dimensions of the justice motive fit naturally with many core elements of behavioral decision theory – the willingness to take bad gambles to avoid losses; the unwillingness to gamble in the domain of gains; and the endowment effect (the fact that I consider something *mine by right* will make it more difficult for me to give it up). As we shall see in Chapter 2, in the period leading up to the Crimean war, Tsar Nicholas did not normalize for the perceived derogation of his right to represent Orthodox subjects of the Ottoman empire, and the burning moral outrage he felt over this perceived injustice led him to take significant risks to restore the status quo ante – a pattern of behavior fully consistent with the expectations of behavioral decision theory. And, as we shall see in Chapter 6, Argentina likewise failed to normalize for the loss of the Falkland/Malvinas Islands in 1833, and embarked upon a risky venture to recover them in 1982 when the discrepancy between entitlements and assets became too painful to bear. This behavior, too, is consistent with the expectations of behavioral decision theory. In both cases, by focusing on perceived entitlements, we can render intelligible behavior that simply would not make sense in view of the negligible strategic or economic value of the actual stakes.

But the justice motive can do more than simply help us understand the fit between the behavior of states and the expectations of behavioral decision theory; it can help us explain patterns of behavior that are *inconsistent* with those expectations. Behavioral decision theory would lead us to expect states to normalize quickly for territorial gains, and only slowly for territorial losses. But as we shall see in Chapters 3 and 4, Germany did not normalize for the gain of Alsace-Lorraine in 1871 and quickly normalized for the loss in 1918. France, on the other hand, did not normalize for the loss and quickly normalized for the gain. This pattern of behavior may be explained by appeal to the justice motive. France perceived a *moral entitlement* to Alsace-Lorraine that Germany simply did not share, and that even the most energetic of German polemicists, such as Heinrich von Treitschke, could not inspire.

Perception, misperception, and cognitive errors. In addition to helping us operationalize and refine formal theories of decision, the justice motive may help us understand the role of cognitive and affective processes in explaining state behavior.

Since the 1976 publication of Robert Jervis's pioneering work, *Perception and Misperception in International Politics*, students of international politics have come to recognize that decisions of national leaders may be powerfully influenced by psychological processes. While the theories Jervis brought to bear on the study of international politics – such as cognitive dissonance theory, theories of cognitive consistency, and attribution theory – are all controversial within the psychology community,[73] there is no question that the concepts these theories employ have improved our ability to understand state behavior, particularly in cases of crisis and war.[74] The approach has yet to produce general theories of state behavior, and very often it can only help us see *that* leaders make important errors in judgment, rather

25

than *why* they do so; but as I suggested earlier in this chapter, the justice motive may help us enrich our understanding of misperceptions, misjudgments, and decision-making pathologies, and move it to a higher level of generality.

Consider, for example, the perception of threat. Leaders frequently fail to perceive serious threats to their interests, or perceive illusory threats. While the misperception of threat may have a variety of causes, the recognition that leaders filter information through normative lenses may render many misperceptions intelligible. Raymond Cohen found, for example, that a major source of the perception of threat is the belief that another state has broken the rules of international politics. "[T]he actual gains the other makes – or the losses it inflicts on the state – are often less troublesome than the methods by which they were pursued. A state is likely to be seen as a threat if it displays a willingness to ignore accepted procedure, a disregard of what are usually considered the legitimate rights of others, and an exceptionally high propensity to accept risks in order to improve its position."[75] In short, claims or behavior that we are inclined to see as *unjust* lead us to impute menacing intent. Likewise, claims and behavior that we are inclined to see as *just* incline us *not* to impute menacing intent. Respect for entitlements may therefore provide a crucial bench mark for assessing the danger posed by other states. In retrospect, for example, it seems quite clear that Soviet policy during the Cold War was essentially defensive in nature. Stalin, Khrushchev, and Brezhnev were all preoccupied with domestic politics, and did not count among their priorities the conquest of Western Europe or the spread of socialism worldwide as American policy-makers feared. Yet a major reason why American policy-makers feared this was their perception that the Soviet Union did not respect the entitlements of other states, and did not behave according to the accepted norms of international behavior.[76] By the same token, as we shall see in Chapter 5, Neville Chamberlain *failed* to see that Adolf Hitler represented a threat to the repose of Europe until *after* Hitler abandoned the pretense of being motivated in his foreign policy solely by a concern for justice. The claims to entitlements that Hitler asserted until the spring of 1939 were claims that Chamberlain was inclined to credit.[77] Just as lack of empathy can lead to the misperception of threat,[78] too much empathy, or inappropriate empathy, can do likewise. The justice motive is a powerful source of empathy.

Estimating threats, gauging the intentions of other states, assessing their goals, and predicting their likely behavior are processes that are susceptible to a number of cognitive biases and errors. These biases and errors are a function of the fact that the goals, intentions, and calculations of others are rarely obvious, and must be inferred. Inferences of this kind involve *interpretations*, often based on confusing or modest behavioral clues. Such interpretations face important hermeneutical barriers. Philosophers have long observed that one can interpret the behavior of others only on the basis of some prior understanding of their behavior, courting infinite regress.[79] But psychologists have suggested that people invoke a number of shorthands or surrogates to compensate for the difficulties of interpretation. One of these is the "availability heuristic": we interpret the actions of others in the light of our own concerns, needs, and values, because these are readily available to us.[80] Projecting our own values or goals upon another actor can lead to serious misjudgments when that other actor is motivated by different values or goals, as Chamberlain's misjudgment of Hitler readily attests.[81] Another source of misperception is the "evoked set." When ambiguous information may be interpreted in a number of disparate ways, we tend to interpret it in accordance with whatever is in the forefront of our minds at that moment. Thus my interpretation of a bump in the night will depend heavily upon whether I have been reading a crime novel (I will fear that someone has broken into the house) or a ghost story (I will fear the house is haunted).[82]

Chapter 2 provides a number of specific examples of these dynamics at work, and illustrates how they can greatly increase the difficulty of crisis management when they engage the justice motive. In 1853, Tsar Nicholas had in the forefront of his mind his rights as protector of the Orthodox church in the Ottoman dominions. He therefore interpreted every British, French, and Turkish action that did not tend toward the satisfaction of his claims as *deliberate attempts* to deny him his entitlements, increasing the stridency of his demands and his intransigence in negotiations.[83] British officials did not understand the Tsar's true concerns. The strategic importance of the Dardanelles was in the forefront of their minds, and they dismissed the substance of the Tsar's claims as dissimulation masking geopolitical objectives. Their deliberate pursuit of coercive diplomacy was based upon a misdiagnosis of the Tsar's motivations, and succeeded only in aggravating the confrontation.[84] Similarly, in the period leading up to the Falklands/Malvinas war, Argentine leaders had in the forefront of their minds the looming 150th anniversary of the British seizure of the islands, which became a self-imposed deadline for the number one priority of Argentine foreign policy: the "recovery" of the islands. Because the sovereignty issue figured so heavily in their own evoked set,

Argentine leaders tended to interpret British actions – such as the withdrawal of naval forces from the South Atlantic (in reality determined by budgetary considerations) – as deliberate signals on the sovereignty question. For this reason, among others, Argentina miscalculated British resolve to resist a seizure of the islands. The British government, meanwhile, did not appreciate the strength and sincerity of the Argentine sense of injustice over the continuing British occupation; they did not appreciate the importance of the sesquicentennial to Argentina; they did not consider the Falklands a priority in their own policy; and – perhaps most importantly – they did not believe that the Argentine claim was legitimate. They therefore underestimated Argentine resolve, and dismissed Argentine noises about the islands as attempts to divert the attention of the Argentine people from the country's dire economic straits (possibly because economic difficulties were in the forefront of their own minds). In order to understand why this series of misperceptions and misjudgments occurred, it is necessary to appreciate the intensity of the Argentine perception of injustice, and the British conviction that Argentina's claims were unfounded.

The justice motive may also help us understand the important role of cognitive simplicity vs. cognitive complexity in decision-making. Cognitive complexity is a measure of "the number of logically distinct arguments or considerations that a policy-maker takes into account in judging an event or arriving at a decision."[85] Cognitively simple people are less circumspect in their analyses of a given situation; they are less open to new or discrepant information (in part because they deem fewer considerations significant); and they are more difficult to persuade (because they have fewer points of leverage upon which to exert pressure). Consequently, negotiating or managing a crisis with a cognitively simple protagonist should prove more difficult than with someone who is cognitively complex, all other things being equal. It would seem that cognitively simple leaders will therefore be more war-prone.

Scholars who employ the concept of cognitive complexity to explain political behavior disagree about the relative importance of situational and dispositional factors in determining the degree of cognitive complexity decision-makers will exhibit.[86] The justice motive can illuminate both the debate and the cognitive complexity of responses to events. Decision-makers who act on the basis of the justice motive should be expected to exhibit cognitive structures significantly *simpler* than those who do not. The phenomenology of the justice motive suggests that, all other things being equal, decision-makers motivated

28

by the perceived demands of justice will focus overwhelmingly on the categorical satisfaction of their demands, to the exclusion of other concerns. They will consider the demands of justice to be a consideration of such cogency that they will not easily be persuaded to modify their demands or reframe their understanding of the situation, nor will they tend to seek out, assimilate, or even notice relevant information on value trade-offs. The fact that some people have stronger senses of justice than others may help explain the extent to which cognitive complexity is dispositional; the fact that some issues touch people's perceptions of their entitlements, while others do not, may help explain the extent to which cognitive complexity is situational.

Before leaving the topic of cognition, it is worth noticing that the foregoing discussion strongly suggests that the justice motive holds great promise of helping us refine our understanding of the connection between affect and cognition on the one hand, and affect and behavior on the other. As Robert Mandel remarks, "In international relations there appears at the moment to be a far greater comprehension of the cognitive aspects of human interaction ... than of the affective aspects of human interaction – often involving reckless, daredevil, and passionate attitudes and behavior."[87] To the extent that analysts have explored the role of affect on decision-making, they have concentrated on the effects of fear, anxiety, stress, and wishful thinking.[88] We now understand, for example, that leaders' emotional needs can lead to a variety of biases and errors in processing information.[89] The justice motive may help us refine that understanding, because its affective component has cognitive and behavioral consequences, and the connections between these appear to be systematic. For example, an inflamed sense of justice may increase the likelihood of cognitive errors because of its simplifying effect on cognitive structures. That simplifying effect is a function of the unique – and uniquely intense – passions associated with the perception that one is being treated unjustly. One aspect of those passions is a sense of urgency, which may lead to premature, reflexive, or desperate behavior. Whether the connections between affect and cognition or behavior evident in cases involving the justice motive may be generalized theoretically and extended to embrace other emotions and other motivations is, of course, an open question at present; but it is also intuitively plausible.[90]

If indeed the justice motive can help us better understand decision-making in these various ways, the lack of attention it has received in the empirical study of state behavior would appear to represent a

29

significant oversight. Indeed, it may prove beneficial to the operationalization and articulation of a wide variety of theories of state behavior, not merely those that focus on individual decision-making. To understand the distinctive behavior of democratic regimes, for example – in particular, the remarkable fact that liberal democracies do not fight each other[91] – it may be helpful to notice that many democracies share conceptions of entitlements, of just procedures for apportioning them, and of just procedures for resolving disputes. Consequently, the justice motive should be less likely to lead to wars between democracies, and conflicts that do arise between democracies should be more likely to prove susceptible of peaceful resolution. In turn, various unit-level theories may help us better understand the effects of the justice motive on policy. Some may suspect that mass publics, for example, are more likely to perceive injustices, and to experience them with greater degrees of intensity, than officials and elites (although, as I shall explain in a moment, I am skeptical of this claim). If so, we would expect the policies of weak states to reflect those perceptions more powerfully than strong states, and democracies to reflect them more powerfully than authoritarian states.[92] The full exploration of these issues is beyond the scope of this volume, but the following chapters provide ample food for thought.

SOME HYPOTHESES ON THE AGENCY OF THE JUSTICE MOTIVE

As I discuss below, the cases I examine in this study were chosen primarily to provide an acid test of the Realist account of motivation. Rather different cases – indeed, rather different methods – would be needed to "test" many of the propositions I explore in the previous section. No doubt many of them would not withstand the appropriate tests. To take the last simply as an example: if the cases I examine here are representative, then there would appear to be no discernible difference between the propensities of publics, elites, and officials to perceive injustices, or to experience them with different degrees of intensity. In the Crimean war, for example, the Tsar was well ahead of Russian public opinion in perceiving Turkish injustices, while Lord Aberdeen and many members of his cabinet (most notably, Lord Palmerston) were well behind British public opinion in perceiving *Russian* injustices. The British public also appear to have been rather more sensitive to the perceived injustices of German policy in 1914 than was the Asquith government; but, in 1982, the Thatcher government appears to have given at least as much weight as the

British people to the moral stakes involved in the Argentine invasion of the Falklands. No discernible pattern emerges from these and the other cases I examine.

Although the following chapters cannot provide rigorous tests of such propositions, they nevertheless enable us to probe the plausibility of a number of hypotheses about the agency of the justice motive and its likely effects on international politics. Among them are the following:

Valuation

1. If an actor views a good as an entitlement, he or she will value it more highly than its strategic or economic worth warrants.

Process

2. If an actor's justice motive is engaged, he or she will accept poor gambles to restore the balance between perceived entitlements and assets.
3. If an actor's sense of injustice is engaged, he or she will exhibit insensitivity to new information and value trade-offs, and will be less amenable to negotiation and suasion through the application of carrots and sticks.
4. The justice motive will increase the likelihood of cognitive errors because of its influence on interpretation, its simplifying effect on cognitive structures, and its affective potency.

Behavior

5. An actor operating on the basis of the justice motive will be less willing to compromise in finding solutions to disputes, since the demand that entitlements be respected is a categorical one.
6. An actor operating on the basis of the justice motive will be *more* tolerant of other states' gains if they are perceived to be legitimate entitlements, and *less* tolerant of other states' gains if they are perceived to violate entitlements.

The net effect of these dynamics is that – all other things being equal – states motivated by a concern for justice should be more likely to go to war than states that do not perceive a discrepancy between entitlements and assets, under specific circumstances: namely, when other states challenge their subjective conceptions of entitlements, and when institutions and procedures for resolving international disputes enjoy insufficient legitimacy to permit a peaceful adjustment of those differences. Under these circumstances, the justice motive should be a significant risk factor for war.

This is not to suggest, of course, that the justice motive will always incline states toward war. Indeed, on balance, the justice motive may well be a more powerful force for peace than it is for war. If two states share a conception of their entitlements, or if they agree upon the legitimacy of certain procedures for resolving conflicting interpretations of their entitlements, the justice motive should facilitate the peaceful resolution of their disputes. The more international politics comes to resemble a "society" with shared norms, consistent conceptions of entitlements, and robust dispute-resolution institutions and procedures, the stronger this tendency will become.[93] But when wars *do* break out, we can often see how the justice motive led to that outcome, and we can plausibly argue counterfactually in many circumstances that states would have avoided or resolved their conflicts peacefully in the absence of perceived injustices.

PROBING THE AGENCY AND RELATIVE IMPORTANCE OF THE JUSTICE MOTIVE

Bearing witness to the effects of the justice motive requires observing it closely in real-life situations, simply because it is impossible to recreate the crucial affective components of the justice motive in the laboratory. Gauging the relative importance of the justice motive *vis-à-vis* Realist motivations requires that we carefully trace decision-making processes in well-documented historical events in which we ought to expect Realist motivations to dominate. If the justice motive can compete on Realism's home turf, as it were, and still perform relatively well, we can infer that it will also have analytic value in other cases. These dual tasks, then – probing the agency of the justice motive and assessing its relative importance *vis-à-vis* Realist motivations – require, as a first cut, that we examine a number of critical cases, treating them as heuristic case studies and plausibility probes.[94]

Which are the appropriate cases to examine? There are strong methodological reasons for looking at wars involving Great Powers. Great Powers are thought to be particularly sensitive to their relative positions in the international distribution of power, and in war their relative positions – and sometimes their status as Great Powers, or even their very existence as states – are immediately at stake. Realism would lead us to believe that Great Powers as a class should be the *least* influenced by normative motivations (*realpolitik*, after all, is a repudiation of those very motivations), and never more so than when faced with the prospect of war.[95]

There are also strong theoretical reasons to limit the scope of the study to the relatively recent past. In the early years of the system of sovereign states – the sixteenth, seventeenth, and eighteenth centuries – wars were waged by monarchs largely isolated from public opinion; they were typically fought by small professional or mercenary armies; and they rarely involved serious economic dislocation or physical destruction. In short, war had a significantly different complexion than it has today. A study including a large sample of wars conducted under conditions that no longer obtain would run the risk of generating obsolete conclusions. It would be less than useful today, for example, to find that contested royal successions frequently led to Great Power wars.

We must strike a balance, therefore, between confining the temporal scope of the historical survey to a past that resembles the present and foreseeable future in important respects, and providing a large enough sample of wars involving Great Powers to discern meaningful patterns of causes. We must strike a further balance between the need to keep the number of cases down, so that each can be treated in sufficient depth to establish often fairly subtle but vital interpretations, and the importance of ensuring that the cases studied are representative of a variety of contexts. These balances are nicely satisfied by looking at a subset of wars involving Great Powers in the post-Napoleonic era. It was Napoleon who first wielded the *nation en armes* in interstate conflict; it was during the Napoleonic wars that certain characteristic features of modern warfare emerged, such as massed artillery barrages and economic blockades; and it was during the Napoleonic wars that nationalism rose to the top of the international hierarchy of values, where it has arguably remained ever since. The period from 1789 to 1815 was an important watershed in international politics – politically, ideologically, militarily, socially, and economically. The world that emerged from it was, in its general form, the world that is still with us today.[96]

Since 1815, thirty-three wars have occurred in which at least one Great Power was a belligerent. Of these, two were general wars.[97] While this represents a sample diverse enough to identify patterns of causes and effects with confidence, it is too large to allow each case to be examined in more than cursory detail. We must therefore choose a smaller set from this sample.

The first criterion that we should employ in selecting from this list is

33

Table 1.1. *The Great Powers since 1815*

Great Power	Period
Britain	1815–present
France	1815–present
Austria-Hungary	1815–1918
Russia/Soviet Union	1815–present
Prussia/Germany/Federal Republic of Germany	1815–present
Italy	1861–1943
United States	1898–present
Japan	1905–1945
People's Republic of China	1949–present

Adapted from Levy, *War in the Modern Great Power System, 1495–1975*, 47.

that the subset chosen should include the "crucial cases" – those where we should intuitively expect the justice motive to be weakest, because *realpolitik* considerations ought to be strongest. We should therefore look at both general wars: World Wars I and II. In addition, to control as much as possible for variations in externalities, we should ensure that our sample includes wars from each major geopolitical context in the post-Napoleonic era.

The first identifiable geopolitical context is the Concert of Europe period. No single hegemon dominated Europe in this period of time, although Britain enjoyed unchallenged naval supremacy. The Concert of Europe was followed by a period of nation-building in Italy and Germany (the latter of which experienced spectacular economic growth), the rapid modernization of Japan, and, at the turn of the century, the rise of the United States to Great Power status. This "rising powers" period was, in contrast to the Concert of Europe, geopolitically dynamic; the older European Great Powers faced new, strong challengers, and were forced to retrench. Twice in the succeeding decades, Germany threatened to dominate Europe, resulting in spasmodic upheaval (the "great wars" period). The bipolar postwar order emerged from the ruins of World War II, and persisted at least until the end of the 1980s. It is notable not only for the rise of the superpowers as leaders of two rigid, ideologically antithetical blocs, but also for the advent of nuclear weapons.[98]

World Wars I and II will more than suffice as representatives of the great wars period; one war from each of the remaining three periods will provide ample grist for our mill. The Crimean war (1853–1856) was the largest and most destructive Great Power war between the Napoleonic wars and World War I, and it signaled the end of the Concert of Europe; it will serve as an excellent representative of the

Table 1.2. *Great Power wars since 1815* *(n = 33)*

War	Year(s)	Great Power participant(s)
Franco-Spanish	1823	France
Navarino Bay	1827	France, Britain, Russia
Russo-Turkish	1828–1829	Russia
Austro-Sardinian	1848–1849	Austria-Hungary
First Schleswig-Holstein	1849	Prussia
Roman Republic	1849	France, Austria-Hungary
Crimean*	1853–1856	France, Britain, Russia
Anglo-Persian	1856–1857	Britain
War of Italian Unification	1859	France, Austria-Hungary
Franco-Mexican	1862–1867	France
Second Schleswig-Holstein	1864	Austria-Hungary, Prussia
Austro-Prussian*	1866	Austria-Hungary, Prussia, Italy
Franco-Prussian*	1870–1871	France, Prussia
Russo-Turkish	1877–1878	Russia
Sino-French	1884–1885	France
Russo-Japanese	1904–1905	Russia
Italo-Turkish	1911–1912	Italy
World War I†	1914–1918	France, Britain, Austria-Hungary, Russia, Germany, Italy, United States, Japan
Russian civil war*	1918–1921	France, Britain, Soviet Union, United States, Japan
Manchurian	1931–1933	Japan
Italo-Ethiopian	1935–1936	Italy
Sino-Japanese	1937–1941	Japan
Russo-Japanese*	1939	Soviet Union, Japan
Winter war	1939–1940	Soviet Union
World War II†	1939–1945	France, Britain, Soviet Union, Germany, Italy, United States, Japan
Korean war*	1950–1953	France, Britain, United States, China
Hungarian Intervention	1956	Soviet Union
Sinai	1956	France, Britain
Sino-Indian	1962	China
Vietnam	1965–1973	United States
Afghanistan	1979–1989	Soviet Union
Falklands/Malvinas	1982	Britain
Persian Gulf	1991	Britain, France, United States

* Denotes wars between Great Powers (*n* = 6)
† Denotes general wars (*n* = 2)
Adapted from Levy, *War in the Modern Great Power System, 1495–1975*, Table 3.1, p. 73.

Concert period, because it is the closest approximation to a general war available. The Franco-Prussian war (1870–1871), which established Germany as the dominant state in central Europe, was the second most destructive Great Power war between 1815 and 1900, and for similar reasons will suffice as our representative of the rising powers period.

There is no post–1945 case of direct Great Power conflict that will suit our requirements. The Korean war (1950–1953) would be a suitable candidate in view of the fact that it resulted in combat between the regular armed forces of China and the United States, but a dearth of material prevents us from drawing reliable conclusions about North Korean and Chinese motivations.[99] Other plausible candidates include the Sinai, Vietnam, Falklands/Malvinas, and Persian Gulf wars. Each of these has its advantages and disadvantages as a case study. While information about French and British motivations is relatively plentiful for Suez, the operation lasted but a week and did not involve them in serious combat; hence it may hardly be considered a Great Power war.[100] The Vietnam war has the opposite strengths and weaknesses. While there is no question of the scope and intensity of Great Power involvement, the war was the result of an evolving policy and a very gradual military escalation that make it difficult to discuss the participants' motivations while at the same time maintaining parity of form with the other four cases. Of necessity, the Vietnam war would require a rather different type of analysis. The recent Persian Gulf war would undoubtedly make a fascinating study; but it is too recent to allow an objective dissection of its causes, because its principals (as of the time of writing) still hold office. Moreover, we may legitimately wonder whether it is best classified as having occurred in the "postwar" period.[101] By process of elimination, we are left with the 1982 Falklands/Malvinas war. Its only drawback as a case study (though not as a war) is its relative bloodlessness; with just over 900 battle deaths, it misses Levy's (and Small and Singer's) minimum 1,000 battle-death criterion for inclusion. This seems a trivially small margin, given its virtues as a case study: the clarity of the issues, the adequacy of the available record, and, as may be appreciated in retrospect, the fascinating light it sheds on the topic at hand.[102]

For each case examined, I will attempt to assess the relative contribution of the justice motive to the outbreak of war. It is useful in this regard to bear in mind the distinction introduced by Thucydides between the underlying and immediate causes of war, because perceptions of injustice could operate at either level. The underlying causes of war are those factors that condition a conflict by ripening the climate for it, and the immediate causes are those factors that trigger a conflict if the climate is ripe.[103] According to the Realist tradition, for example, the climate was ripe for a war between the United States and the Soviet Union at least from 1945 to 1989. The two superpowers' material and ideological interests conflicted directly; thus they both sat on a powder keg which needed but the appropriate spark to explode.

Table 1.3. *Selected cases*

Period	Geopolitical context	Chapter(s)	War(s)
Concert of Europe	Multipolar (stable)	2	Crimean (1853–1856)
Rising powers	Multipolar (unstable, diffusing)	3	Franco-Prussian (1870–1871)
Great wars	Multipolar (unstable, concentrating)	4 5	World War I (1914–1918) World War II (1939–1945)
Postwar	Bipolar (stable)	6	Falklands/Malvinas (1982)

The great political accomplishment of the postwar era, according to those who subscribe to this understanding of superpower relations, was successful fire prevention.

Five types of evidence can be useful for determining which motivations are at work in an historical event, although not all five will necessarily be present (or helpful if present) in every case. These are (1) the public statements of decision-makers and public documents; (2) the private statements of decision-makers (in letters, diaries, or reports of conversations) and internal documents; (3) published accounts from contemporary journals; (4) the judgments of historians; and (5) circumstantial considerations that permit relevant *post hoc* inferences. Each of these types of evidence has characteristic strengths and weaknesses.

Public statements by decision-makers or other governmental officials, such as speeches, debates, diplomatic notes, or policy declarations, are probably the least reliable source of evidence, since they may be intended to serve a variety of purposes for which sincerity is not always an asset, such as motivating domestic support, forestalling certain types of criticism, and masking base or unpopular motivations. However, while public statements alone cannot help us discriminate between sincere appeals to the demands of justice and rationalizations intended to legitimize or mobilize domestic support for a policy motivated by other considerations, certain types of arguments made in public statements to justify a given policy or action should be taken very seriously when considered in context. For example, to the extent that circumstances suggest that a decision to go to war would be contrary to the national interest, a public justification of that decision given in terms of the perceived demands of justice must carry some weight.

Private statements by officials – in letters, diaries, secret communications between governments, and so forth – should be taken as reliable indicators of motivations, all other things being equal. Such statements are less frequently designed to serve ulterior motives, because they are less frequently intended for public consumption. Again, circumstantial considerations in any given case may require that they be received with either more or less skepticism, but these must be confronted on an ad hoc basis.

Contemporaneous publications may or may not shed light on motivations, depending in part upon the relationship between the government and the media in a given case, the importance of public opinion in the formulation of high policy, and various publications' reputations for accuracy and insight. Stories and editorials in controlled or censored journals in authoritarian states should be treated in precisely the same fashion as statements by public officials; on the other hand, if the ways in which newspapers portray a situation help shape public opinion in a democracy, or accurately reflect the considerations taken most seriously by the populace, they may be taken as fairly reliable guides of the main currents of public or official thought. Here again, sensitivity to context is important in determining how evidence from the contemporaneous record should be handled.

Historians write extensively on the causes of wars, and their judgments can be of considerable value, for two reasons. First, professional historians may be said to be among those who most deeply and most profoundly understand the events they study. The standards of academic history require extensive familiarity with the documentary record, and historians' evaluations of events can therefore represent extremely well-informed opinions that political scientists should feel free to rely upon. Second, and perhaps no less importantly, "traditional" academic history is largely free of the encumbrances of paradigmatic political science. Since the present study represents a challenge to Realism, and since traditional academic history offers us a vantage point biased neither toward nor against it, we can aspire to a considerable degree of objectivity by relying on this particular source of insight.[104]

Last, but not least, are circumstantial considerations. For example, we may be able to infer motivations by attending to the ways in which leaders structure their decision problems, respond to stimuli, and search for and process information. For instance, we may be justified in suspecting that a leader preoccupied with ascertaining an adversary's *offensive* military capability is motivated by self-preservation, all other things being equal. We may also be justified in suspecting that a leader preoccupied with ascertaining an adversary's *defensive* military capability is motivated by self-aggrandizement. Similarly, we may be justified in suspecting that a leader preoccupied with construing the terms of treaties – to the exclusion, say, of information on enemy military capabilities and troop movements – is motivated by a concern for entitlements. Such inferences may often be little more than suggestive; but when used judiciously in concert with other indicators, they may provide powerful reinforcement to an otherwise precarious case. Only by looking at a variety of types of evidence is it possible to build a case about the relative strengths of various motivations that warrants our confidence, and circumstantial considerations may indeed tip the balance in favor of one interpretation and against another.

Ideally, it would be desirable to quantify the importance of the justice motive both in conditioning a given conflict, and in triggering it. The goal would be (a) to identify the factors that collectively contributed to the explosiveness of a given situation, and to assign the appropriate relative weight to those that can be traced to the perceived demands of justice; and (b) to determine which specific issues ignited the powder keg and the extent to which the aims of those whose decisions led to war can accurately be described in terms of the justice motive. Unfortunately, no quantifiable indicators are available. A second-best is to devise a *qualitative* system of discriminations that can usefully distinguish relative magnitudes without giving an unwarranted impression of precision. I describe such a system in Table 1.4.

In determining which category a particular case falls under, it will be necessary to ask whose motivations mattered, and to be clear about the confidence we can place in the evidence available. Both of these will vary from case to case. Where the evidence is less than conclusive, or where categorizations seem particularly debatable, I take care to note the controversy and to err on the side of caution in the assignment of labels. If there is to be a systematic bias in my evaluation of the roles played by the justice motive, it must be a bias against – not for – the supposition at hand.

Notwithstanding the intricacies, subtleties, and ambiguities of historical interpretation, the following five chapters demonstrate quite clearly the power of the justice motive as an explanatory tool even in cases where Realism would lead us least to expect it. They also reveal a wide diversity both in the types of issues that can give rise to perceptions of injustice, and in the ways in which the justice motive can influence the unfolding of events. In two of the five cases, the justice motive is clearly much more important than considerations of self-

Table 1.4. *The justice motive – qualitative measures of importance*

Category	Description
Conclusive	The justice motive seems to have been overwhelming in conditioning or triggering war. No other motive can plausibly be said to have influenced the outbreak of war significantly in the relevant respect.
Very strong	The justice motive was the most important factor among a few motivations, and seems to have been at least as significant as the other motivations combined.
Strong	The justice motive was no less important than any other motive, and the number of relevant motives is small.
Moderate	The justice motive was one important motive among a few, but other motives may have been more important.
Weak	The justice motive appears to have been a factor, but other motives appear to have been considerably more important.
Very weak	Some evidence can be found of the justice motive, but it appears to have played very little role in the outbreak of war.
Imperceptible	No evidence can be found of the justice motive.

preservation or self-aggrandizement; in two others, the justice motive played a crucial role, to the point where we may legitimately wonder whether Realist motivations – though present – would have been sufficient to lead to war. Only in one case – the Franco-Prussian war – are Realist motivations unambiguously dominant.

SOME OBJECTIONS ANTICIPATED

Before I turn to the case studies themselves, I would like to anticipate a few conceptual, epistemological, and methodological objections.

1. How do we distinguish the justice motive from rational self-interest, particularly when, in many cases, the satisfaction of an actor's claim to justice will result in a tangible gain? How do we know that the justice motive is responsible for the demand, rather than the prospect of the gain itself? How do we know that perceptions of injustice are not simply epiphenomenal?
The essence of this objection is that normative motivation cannot be understood apart from the self-interest of the agent; the real motor behind human action is desire for gain and aversion to loss, and the sense of injustice may be understood simply as an effect of that more basic human tendency. Indeed, several historically prominent ethical theories (such as egoism and non-cognitivism) have asserted as much themselves.

Earlier in this chapter I argued that the justice motive cannot simply be reduced to an aversion to loss and a desire for gain, because these two motivations differ phenomenologically, prescriptively, and extensively. We can observe these motivations in tension with one another from time to time, indicating that they are not identical. Nevertheless, there are many cases when they are not in tension with one another, and it may be a difficult task to decide which of the two is the more important influence on behavior. One way to make that discrimination is to observe the behavior closely and to see whether it reflects the unique phenomenology of the sense of injustice. Sometimes this will not be possible. As the following chapters illustrate, there are circumstances in which the exigencies of self-preservation and the demands of justice point in the same direction, and in which the evidence does not permit a reliable discrimination between the relative importance of the two motivations. In these circumstances, I assume that self-preservation is the primary concern, so as not to risk overstating the case for the justice motive.

2. *Is it not possible that states could claim virtually anything as theirs by right? If the claims that states advance as a matter of justice cannot be circumscribed in advance, then is not the justice motive too elastic a concept to be analytically useful?*
This objection rightly reminds us that the hypotheses I presented earlier do not specify in advance the content of the claims that states could advance as a matter of justice. I faulted Blainey for an unfalsifiable statement about motivation, and rescued his claim that "all states seek power" from tautology by specifying the general form of the goals that states seeking power should be expected to pursue. But I have not specified the goals that states motivated by a concern for justice should be expected to pursue. Have I myself fallen into a falsifiability trap?

It is true that states could, without logical contradiction, claim absolutely anything as a matter of justice. However, *they do not*. As long as they do not, the hypotheses I advanced about the agency of the justice motive are testable in principle. Moreover, although I have not specified the *content* of the goals that states motivated by a concern for justice should be expected to pursue, I have specified their general form: rectification of disparities between perceived entitlements and assets. Not just any grievance can count as a perception of injustice, for then the hypothesis that perceptions of injustice can lead to war would be trivially true. On the other hand, Lerner's characterization of the justice motive with which we are working – the drive to correct a perceived discrepancy between entitlements and benefits – is purely formal and subjective, and does not circumscribe *a priori* the instances and manifestations of perceived violations. Indeed, they cannot be completely circumscribed in advance. The *sincerity* of a perception of injustice is what counts, not its *content*, and not its *validity* (wars can result from sincere but unfounded grievances). We are not looking for any *particular* perception from a predetermined list of possibilities.

While we cannot circumscribe the content of the justice motive in advance, we can at least provide an illustrative list of issues that intuition and experience will tell us are most likely to generate perceptions of injustice, and classify the claims that might be asserted to rectify them. Among the issues that might be expected to trigger the sense of injustice most often in international affairs are disputes over territory, the legitimacy of governments, successions, interventions, freedom of navigation, access to the global commons, and the fulfillment of obligations. Perceptions of injustice on any of these issues might be *self-referential* (i.e., the actor perceiving the injustice would be the aggrieved party) or *other-referential* (the actor perceives an injustice suffered by someone else); and claims advanced to rectify the perceived injustice could be *performance-demanding* (requiring positive action by an offender, or by some other body charged with enforcement), and/or *forbearance-demanding* (requiring restraint or cessation of an offensive action or policy). A few hypothetical examples will help clarify these distinctions.

Disputes over territory may be among the most common historical triggers of the sense of injustice, if the frequency of irredentist claims is any indication. Generally, we would expect one or both of two issues to lie at the bottom of a territorial dispute expressed in normative terms: the first of these would be the assertion of title to control a given *geographic area*, based, for example, on historical occupation, discovery, or divine entitlement; the second would be the assertion of title to govern a given *population*, based, perhaps, on ethnicity, linguistic kinship, or popular will. It would not be surprising for one state to advance the first type of claim, and another to advance a conflicting claim of the second type; indeed, this is precisely the primary dynamic evident in Chapter 6. We must always be careful, however, not to be insensitive to possible ulterior motives when states make territorial claims by appeal to an entitlement. Where the real object of desire underlying a territorial claim is control of a valuable resource or an augmentation of prestige, then the appropriate explanation of a territorial conflict would lie in an appeal to power or self-interest.

Normally, we would expect a bona fide territorial dispute to arise from a clash of incompatible self-referential claims; we would not expect a disinterested state to go to the trouble of pursuing a territorial question on behalf of another in the normal course of events, simply because of the sensitivity of territorial questions and the ease with which they can become explosive. But other-referential territorial claims are not unheard of; they provided the *casus belli*, for example – and were arguably a crucial motivation – in the 1991 Persian Gulf war. Territorial claims can also be performance-demanding (one state may demand the evacuation of disputed territory by another) or for-bearance-demanding (for instance, a state may insist that a challenger curtail provocations, infiltrations, or incitements ultimately designed to further a transfer of control).

The legitimacy of governments is another question that one can easily imagine triggering the justice motive, since it raises explicit questions of entitlement. In democratic societies, norms governing entitlements to the exercise of political authority specify one pro-cedure for establishing legitimate governments (elections), and in monarchical or authoritarian societies, different norms specify differ-ent procedures. When the entitlements defined by social norms are violated, or when conflicting conceptions of entitlement clash, a war may follow. Most often, intuition tells us, a sense of injustice trig-gered by the conviction that a government is illegitimate will lead to civil war, if it leads to war at all; although instances of other-referen-tial claims of entitlement to exercise political authority are quite common (witness the frequency with which rigged elections are condemned around the globe), rarely do they lead to interstate war. Historically, those that have led to interstate war have often been associated with dynastic issues that blur the self- and other-referen-tial distinction.[105]

Successions raise explicit questions of entitlements and virtually invite conflicting claims, simply because most hereditary systems of government prescribe succession rules too abstract or indefinite to cover all contingencies. The list of wars fought over successions is very long indeed; but succession is decreasingly relevant as a cause of war in modern times, simply because relatively few modern governments are hereditary. More frequent are wars fought over interventions. Interventions trigger perceptions of injustice not only because they intrinsically violate norms of self-determination, self-government, and non-interference, but frequently also because of their effects. Interven-tions can change patterns of authority, distributions of rights and benefits, popular institutions, and processes of social and political decision-making. On each of these scores, interventions invite moral disapprobation – from those who bear them, those who suffer from

43

them indirectly, and even occasionally from their beneficiaries and perpetrators.

Freedom of navigation and access to the global commons are values historically cherished by states geographically disadvantaged from enjoying them, or economically dependent upon them. A variety of types of infringements could result in perceptions of injustice that lead to conflict: searches and seizures, impressments, piracy, extensions of territorial waters, and denials of fishing rights provide a few ready examples. As with other issues, these perceptions might be self-referential or other-referential, performance-demanding or for-bearance-demanding. Likewise with disputes over the fulfillment of obligations: conflicts might arise over payments of debts, reparations, deliveries of goods or services, non-observance of treaties, and so forth.

It would be premature at this point to attempt to provide historical illustrations of each of these types of grievances, because each would require justification against competing interpretations, especially those grounded in the Realist interpretation emphasizing self-preser-vation or self-aggrandizement. That is precisely the task of the next several chapters. The point here is simply that these are among the types of issues that could plausibly trigger the sense of injustice and contribute to the outbreak of wars, and that each can take on a variety of forms in specific circumstances.

3. How can we distinguish a sincere perception of injustice from an insincere claim?

Sometimes, we may suspect that leaders use the language of morality merely as cant.[106] As Kenneth Waltz correctly points out, it is not unusual for two states in conflict to wrap themselves equally in the mantle of justice.[107] How are we to tell from the historical record whether the language of justice is used sincerely, or whether it is merely a smoke screen for egoism? How would an observer, working solely from a written record, distinguish genuine moral outrage from rationalization?

The first point to bear in mind is that leaders do not always represent their claims as claims motivated by a concern for justice, as Chapter 3 clearly demonstrates.[108] This raises the possibility that, in general, leaders tend to report the nature of their concerns honestly. But from time to time they will dissimulate, and the only means of distin-guishing sincere from insincere perceptions is through careful use of the evidence. If leaders say one thing in private correspondence and another thing in public, for example, we can strongly suspect that the public statements are disingenuous. Context, circumstantial consider-ations, personal histories of the relevant actors, etc., can all be useful in assessing the sincerity of claims.

As a general point, it is no more difficult to assess the sincerity of an actor's perception of injustice than it is to assess his or her true subjective valuation of any particular good. The case studies in this book include clear examples of disingenuous claims, and clear examples of sincere ones, and give good reasons for making the necessary discriminations. Notice, however, that when leaders do *not* represent their claims as claims of justice, we are not inclined to suspect that their *real* motivations are moral in nature. This suggests that we are naturally inclined to interpret leaders' motives cynically, and we should be aware of this bias.

4.   *In some political systems (weak states and democracies), leaders may feel constrained by public opinion. If considerations of justice are salient to the domestic polity, but the leaders themselves are motivated (for example) by their desire to retain office, how are we to know whether the perceived demands of justice or the leaders' narrow political self-interests are the more important motive behind state action?*
We must be careful to distinguish two types of cases: (1) cases in which leaders themselves make disingenuous appeals to the demands of justice to legitimize or mobilize public support for their actions; and (2) cases in which an inflamed public sense of justice forces leaders to pursue a particular policy. In the former case, leaders *pull* public opinion; the motivation behind their policy, however, cannot accur-ately be described as a desire to rectify a perceived discrepancy between entitlements and benefits. In the latter case, public opinion *pushes* leaders; the desire to rectify a perceived discrepancy between entitlements and benefits is the driving force behind the policy itself. For present purposes, in the absence of a more elaborate and more refined domestic political model, it seems reasonable to treat the perception of injustice as motivational in the second case, but to dismiss it as instrumental in the first.

5.   *How can we know that perceptions of injustice are analytically important – e.g., that they are not constant, or that they are not spuriously correlated with conflict?*
The justice motive is not a constant; the Franco-Prussian war provides ample justification of this. More generally, people (and states) always make fairly specific claims, and always wittingly or unwittingly repre-sent them as claims founded upon justice or something else, such as

self-preservation. There is plenty of variation in the historical record. By carefully tracing the processes leading to the outbreak of particular wars, identifying causal paths, and documenting the role of the justice motive, we can see quite clearly how perceptions of injustice lead to war.

In the present study, I do not establish a statistical correlation between perceptions of injustice and conflict. Since I cannot say that there is such a correlation, I cannot judge whether it is spurious. But by demonstrating the importance of the justice motive in the outbreak of these particular wars, and by demonstrating the plausibility of a number of hypotheses about the agency of the justice motive that collectively suggest that there *should* be such a correlation, I provide at least *prima facie* grounds for suspecting both that there is, and that it is not spurious.

6. How can a study that selects cases on the dependent variable assess the importance of the justice motive as a cause of war?
In this study, I do not attempt to relate dependent and independent variables. Instead, I examine critical cases in order to provide a test of the Realist account of motivation, and to explore the agency of the justice motive. For these tasks, it is sufficient to look at cases in which the status of Great Powers is unambiguously at stake, and for which the documentary record is rich enough to allow detailed process-tracing. These requirements are satisfied by the five Great Power wars chosen. A number of propositions I posed earlier in this chapter as worthy of further investigation, however, could only be tested by a study relating dependent and independent variables. Proper tests of these would require, at a minimum, examining a further set of cases that did not escalate to war, to provide variation on the dependent variable.

7. How can we gauge the relative importance of the justice motive vis-à-vis other motivations without strength-of-association measures?
No statistical strength of association can establish causality. By tracing causal paths directly in critical cases, we can make far more reliable causal inferences than would be possible on the basis of a possibly spurious statistical correlation.[109] In any case, to gauge the relevant strengths of association, it would be necessary to have access to uncontroversial codings of a statistically useful number of events, roughly equally divided between wars and successfully resolved crises (for variance on the dependent variable). Since no such data set currently exists, one would have to be created. Presuming that we

could operationalize and measure the relevant independent variables (something the present study seeks to demonstrate in principle), and presuming that we could control for other factors, we would have to develop methods and standards to ensure inter-coder reliability, and intensively research a significant number of cases. At present, these tasks are overly ambitious.

At this point, readers may still have a number of queries about the possibilities and limits of the justice motive as an analytical concept, but these may be addressed satisfactorily in the course of applying it to the historical cases themselves. In the next five chapters, I attempt to gauge the agency and the relative importance of the justice motive *vis-à-vis* Realist concerns in the outbreak of five Great Power wars. These are enormously complex events, and I touch upon many controversial issues. Historical interpretation is controversial at the best of times, but all the more so in cases such as these. Nevertheless, I believe that the stories of these wars amply justify the view that the dominant tradition in the study of international relations has overlooked and failed to make sense of important dimensions of human experience. The vision of human nature upon which it is built, emphasizing fear, hostility, egocentrism, and absence of trust, does not capture the full reality of the men and women who led their nations into these wars. There is ample evidence of fear, hostility, egocentrism, and absence of trust, of course; but there is also ample evidence of higher and nobler sentiments. It is perhaps tragic that, in these cases, such sentiments led to war. But as I suggest in Chapter 7, in these sentiments lies our greatest hope for escaping the international state of nature that causes them to do so. Before I can make that case, however, the historical record must speak.

2 THE CRIMEAN WAR

Table 2.1. *The Crimean war*

Role of justice motive in conditioning conflict	Role of justice motive as proximate cause (by participant)	
Strong	Russia	Conclusive
	Turkey	Weak
	Britain	Moderate
	France	Very weak

The Crimean war was the largest and most consequential conflict in Europe between the Napoleonic Wars and World War I. It involved three of the five Great Powers, lasted two and a half years, resulted in more than a quarter of a million soldiers killed, and shattered the system that had maintained peace and order in Europe for almost forty years.[1] It was also, sadly, needless and avoidable. Disraeli considered it "a just but unnecessary war;" Sir Robert Morier called it "the only perfectly useless modern war that has been waged."[2] None of the major players desired a war, and at several points in the months leading up to it, peace seemed within reach only to be foiled by misperceptions, miscalculations, misunderstandings, ignorance, and plain bad luck.[3] Had the powers involved simply been able to communicate in a timely and effective way, war might well have been averted; but diplomacy was being conducted in each of the major capitals simultaneously, often at cross-purposes, and without a telegraph link to Constantinople; a crucial eight to twelve days would pass between the dispatch and receipt of communications to and from the Ottoman capital – the difference in some instances, perhaps, between successful and unsuccessful negotiation.[4]

Although circumstances conspired to defeat efforts at peacemaking, there would have been no need for those efforts in the absence of very tangible controversies. Historiographers of the event differ widely in their interpretations of those disputes but, as we shall see, they revolve

48

around one central issue: the perception of Tsar Nicholas I that France and Turkey had unjustly trampled on the legitimate entitlements both of the Orthodox Church in the Ottoman dominions, and of the Tsar as its spiritual head.

BACKGROUND

The Ottoman Empire was in many respects an anomalous political entity. Like Austria and Russia it was a multinational empire, but its central cleavage was religious, rather than linguistic or ethnic. Of a total population of some 36 million, more than 40 per cent, or 15 million, were Christians, and in most of the sultan's European possessions, Christians were in the majority. The Turks customarily granted Christian communities a considerable degree of autonomy, a practice that was generally expedient. The Turkish government referred to established Christian churches as "nations," and permitted them to live apart. Christians controlled most of their own affairs, were exempted from military duty, and had few legal relations with the state except those involving the payment of tribute.[5] Measures such as these minimized the incidence of politically explosive conflicts between Muslims and Christians, but they only amplified the centrifugal forces inherent in the empire itself; for the Turkish practice of permitting Christian churches to live apart from the rest of the polity gave these communities a degree of independence that only encouraged them to seek more. Their preferred mechanism was not to rise in arms against the Ottoman Empire, but to behave like independent states, appealing to foreign powers for protection. Austria, for example, claimed the right to protect Roman Catholic worship in European Turkey; France claimed a similar right in Palestine and Syria. Only the Armenian, Coptic, and Black Churches were without foreign patrons, but their members were small in number and widely scattered.

Certain Turkish diplomatic practices aggravated the instability of the sectarian *modus vivendi*. Even at the height of their power, the Turks generously allowed foreigners living in Turkey the protection of their own flags, and gave them immunities usually reserved for sovereigns and embassies in other European countries. They granted these privileges and immunities to the main European states through treaty devices known as "capitulations," which were so extensive that they generally exempted foreigners from all civil and almost all criminal laws. Even a Turkish subject could be exempted under the capitulations if he or she were taken into the service of a foreign embassy, or given a written grant of protection. The result was a high degree of

49

foreign penetration of Turkish domestic affairs, and constant pressure for more.

In general, Turkey could tolerate the penetration, and even benefitted from it in certain cases. Most foreign patrons interfered only occasionally and on the margins of Turkish affairs. Austria and France, for example, could at most claim a few hundred thousand clients. But the Orthodox in Turkey numbered 14 million, and the Porte could not acknowledge a Russian protectorate over the entire Orthodox Church in the Ottoman Empire without effectively transferring sovereignty over most of its European possessions to the tsar. Until the 1850s, the status of the tsar's rights in the Ottoman Empire remained benignly ambiguous; while Nicholas believed that he was entitled to represent the interests of the Orthodox Church at Constantinople, and while the Porte paid due attention to Russian representatives in matters affecting the Orthodox faith, the sultan had never actually acknowledged a Russian protectorate as such.[6]

France inadvertently forced the issue and exposed the ambiguity in 1850, when Prince-President Louis Napoleon instructed his representative in Constantinople, General Aupick, to press the Porte for a reaffirmation of the Capitulations of 1740, which placed all Christians visiting the Ottoman Empire under the protection of the French flag and granted Roman Catholic ecclesiastics certain rights at shrines in the Holy Lands. France's claim, as Harold Temperley notes, was sound in law but dangerous in practice. Her rights had been acquired at a time when Russia was weak, and she had allowed them to lapse in the interim. Austria and Russia had taken up the task of representing the interests of Christians in the Ottoman Empire, and Orthodox clergy had become accustomed to preeminence in the Holy Places.[7] Moreover, since 1740 the sultan had granted firmans confirming the new status quo in derogation of France's treaty rights. France had consistently acquiesced in these. Aupick's demand was therefore both unexpected and unwelcome in Constantinople and in St. Petersburg, and Russia lobbied the Porte heavily to resist it.

The coup of December 2, 1852, by which Louis Napoleon became Emperor Napoleon III, temporarily eased the pressure. But it was not long before Napoleon instructed his new ambassador, M. de Lavalette, to insist once again on a strict execution of the 1740 treaty. This forced the Sultan's hand; the Capitulations of 1740, unlike subsequent firmans, had the status of an international treaty and took precedence over them. On February 9, 1852, the Sultan issued a note confirming the treaty rights of the Latins in the Holy Land. In response to Russian pressure, however, the Sultan issued a firman several days later – the so-called "Greek firman" – confirming the status quo, flatly contradict-ing his concessions to the French.[8]

Caught between France and Russia, Sultan Abdul-Medjid wisely sought to duck his responsibilities. He neither ordered changes in the dispositions of the Holy Shrines, nor gave the Greek firman the public reading needed for it to take effect. France and Russia responded by increasing pressure on the Porte.[9] A settlement seemed within reach when de Lavalette proposed that all sacred buildings in the Holy Land be held jointly by Greek and Latin monks, an arrangement acceptable to the Turks; but the Tsar made a personal appeal for the status quo, and the Sultan rejected de Lavalette's compromise.[10]

The Sultan finally permitted a reading of the Greek firman on November 29, much to the satisfaction of Tsar Nicholas and the outrage of Napoleon. But, on December 22, Turkish authorities handed over the keys to the church of Bethlehem to the Latins, and permitted them to place a French silver star on the Holy Grotto. This delighted Napoleon and outraged the Tsar. Nicholas promptly mobi-lized two Russian Army corps near the Ottoman frontier. Count Nesselrode, the Russian foreign minister, wrote to Baron Brunnow, the Russian ambassador in London: "To the indignation of the whole people following the Greek ritual, the key of the Church of Bethlehem has been made over to the Latins, so as publicly to demonstrate their religious supremacy in the East. The mischief then is done, M. le Baron, and there is no longer any question of preventing it. It is now neces-sary to remedy it."[11]

It fell to the Tsar's special emissary to Constantinople, Prince Menshikov, to resolve Russia's grievances with the Porte. The Tsar instructed him to seek a new firman confirming the privileges of the Orthodox Church as of February 1852; to seek a second firman guaran-teeing future and full privileges to Greek Christians in the Ottoman Empire, and acknowledging Russia's right to protect them; and to seek repairs to the dome of the Church of the Sepulchre at Jerusalem. Russia's right of protection – the one truly intractable claim – was itself to be embodied in a Sened, or convention, having the force of a treaty.[12]

Russia represented Article 1 of the proposed convention as an elucidation and clarification of Articles VII, VIII, XIV, and XVI of the Treaty of Kutchuk-Kainardji (1774):

> The Imperial Court of Russia and the Ottoman Sublime Porte, desir-ing to prevent and to remove forever any reason for disagreement, for doubt, or for misunderstanding on the subject of the immunities, rights, and liberties accorded and assured *ab antiquo* by the Ottoman

emperors in their states to the Greek–Russian–Orthodox religion, professed by all Russia, as by all the inhabitants of the principalities of Moldavia, Wallachia, and Serbia and by various other Christian populations of Turkey of different provinces, agree and stipulate by the present convention that the Christian Orthodox religion will be constantly protected in all its churches, and that the ministers of the Imperial Court of Russia will have, as in the past, the right to make representations on behalf of the churches of Constantinople and of other places and cities, as also on behalf of the clergy, and that these remonstrances will be received as coming in the name of a neighboring and sincerely friendly power.[13]

What the Tsar did not realize was that this "clarification" overstated the actual terms of the Treaty of Kutchuk-Kainardji, the crucial article of which, Article VII, required the Porte "at all times to protect the Christian religion and its churches" and allowed Russian ministers "to make representations in regard to the new church at Constantinople." Article XIV required the Porte to respect "the completely free profession of the Christian faith as well as the building of churches new as well as old." Article XVI granted the Tsar a limited protectorate in times of civil unrest, but only over the populations of Moldavia and Wallachia.[14] The most liberal interpretation that the Treaty of Kutchuk-Kainardji could possibly bear was that it permitted the Russian government to make representations to the Porte on behalf of the rights of the Orthodox *clergy* in the Ottoman Empire.[15] It explicitly provided for a protectorate over Orthodox *churchgoers* only in a single congregation in Constantinople, and over a general Christian population only in the Danubian Principalities of Moldavia and Wallachia.[16] The sultan himself undertook to protect the rights of the Orthodox in Turkey in all other cases.

The consensus among historians of the event is that Nicholas and Nesselrode were simply unfamiliar with the details of the Treaty of Kutchuk-Kainardji, not that they put forth their demands disingenuously.[17] This suggests that had they taken the trouble to acquaint themselves with its particulars, the dispute with Turkey and France might well have come to an end with the settlement of the Holy Places question, and war might well have been avoided. Matters were only made worse by the roughness with which Menshikov handled his mission: the Tsar authorized him to intimidate the Sultan if efforts at persuasion failed. The negotiations took place against the backdrop of conspicuous preparations for war in Russia's southwestern provinces that only bolstered Turkish resolve to resist.[18] Fully expecting the Sultan to object to his demands on the ground that the French would not tolerate any diminution of their rights in the Holy Land,

Menshikov came prepared to offer Turkey defensive guarantees. Indeed, in March, when the Tsar's temper had cooled considerably and a negotiated settlement seemed once again possible, the French suddenly moved their fleet from Toulon to Salamis in a gesture seemingly calculated to offend Russia, prompting angry despatches from St. Petersburg instructing Menshikov to bring his mission to a close and to be peremptory with both the Turks and the French.[19]

Menshikov's prospects for success took a turn for the worse when British Ambassador Lord Stratford de Redcliffe returned to Constantinople on April 5, 1853. Redcliffe exercised an unusual influence over the Porte, and he did not hesitate to use it to thwart the Russian emissary. The British government had instructed him to safeguard the integrity and independence of the Ottoman Empire, to counsel prudence to the Sultan, and to urge forbearance on the other powers pressing demands. He proceeded by attempting to split the disposition of the Holy Shrines from the Tsar's demands for a protectorate, correctly noting that European statesmen considered the latter baseless and inappropriate. If he could succeed in separating the two issues, Redcliffe surmised, Russia would face the united opposition of the European powers in his quest for a protectorate, and would have to back down. To ensure that the Porte did not waver in the face of Russian intimidation, London authorized Redcliffe to request the Admiral of the British squadron at Malta to hold his fleet in readiness, and so to inform the Sultan.[20]

Events transpired more or less as Redcliffe expected. On April 22, the parties finally worked out an ingenious compromise on the disposition of the Holy Places, which permitted the Latins to hold the key to the church at Bethlehem and left the silver star in place while specifying that these conferred no new rights. The agreement permitted a Greek priest to continue to guard the door to the church, but did not empower him to obstruct other nations in their right to enter. It also specified the hours at which the various denominations could worship at the Tomb of the Blessed Virgin. It assigned to the Greeks the first hour and a half after sunrise, and to the Armenians and the Latins an hour and a half each after that; the interposition of the pacific Armenians prevented Orthodox and Catholic monks from coming to blows. The agreement finessed the question of precedence at the shrine by representing the arrangement purely as a matter of convenience.[21]

With the Holy Places issue thus settled to everyone's satisfaction, all that remained was to resolve the question of the Russian protectorate. Menshikov tried every conceivable device to wrest a recognition of a protectorate from the Porte – a treaty, a sened, a note – but he never backed away from the essence of the Russian claim, which the Sultan was not prepared to concede. The Porte's resolve to resist intensified when Redcliffe privately informed him on May 9 of his instructions, which led the Sultan to conclude that Turkey could count on British naval support to resist Russian encroachments. This sealed the fate of the Menshikov mission.

After submitting a final draft of a note recognizing a protectorate and receiving a polite but negative reply, Menshikov left Constantinople with a suitable display of indignation, taking the entire Russian mission with him.[22] On May 31, Count Nesselrode wrote a letter urging the Porte to accept the final note submitted by Prince Menshikov, and announcing that if he did not receive a satisfactory reply within eight days, Russian forces would cross the frontier to obtain "by force, but without war" what the Sultan would not yield of his own free will.[23] In the meantime, the British government had decided to give Redcliffe the authority to call up the fleet himself, and with the French ordered a powerful naval squadron to Besika Bay, near the mouth of the Dardanelles, further aggravating Nicholas and hardening his determination. The French and British squadrons arrived off the Turkish coast in mid-June.

On July 2, Russian forces crossed the Pruth and quickly occupied Moldavia and Wallachia. The following day, a manifesto was read in the churches of Russia declaring that "various arbitrary acts of the Porte" had infringed the rights and privileges of the Orthodox Church, which the throne of Russia was entitled by treaty to protect. "Having exhausted all persuasion, we have found it needful to advance our armies into the Danubian Principalities, in order to show the Ottoman Porte to what its obstinacy may lead. But even now we have not the intention to commence war. By the occupation of the Principalities we desire to have such a security as will insure us the restoration of our rights. It is not conquest that we seek; Russia needs it not; we seek satisfaction for a just right so clearly infringed."[24]

It seems that Nicholas hoped that an occupation of the Danubian Principalities would force the Sultan's hand without precipitating a war. Part of his grounds for optimism lay in the somewhat unusual relationship of the Principalities to both Russia and the Ottoman Empire. While Moldavia and Wallachia were among the Ottoman dominions of Europe, they more closely resembled tributary states than provinces. The sultan had limited authority over them. Each was governed by a prince called a hospodar, invested by the sultan; but by treaty, the sultan was precluded from exercising any significant degree of control over their internal affairs, and was even forbidden to deploy troops there. Russia had acquired a *de facto* protectorate over the Principalities, and was empowered by treaty to help suppress domestic disturbances by means of military occupation. By seizing them, Nicholas sought to capitalize on their ambiguous status, holding them as a pledge for concessions on the protectorate while minimizing the dangers of escalation.[25] No matter how Nicholas construed the matter, however, the occupation of the Principalities was in reality a *casus belli*. Turkey formally protested the occupation on July 14, but was at that time not in a position to resist, and took the counsel of Stratford de Redcliffe to await diplomatic developments.

Representatives of the other European powers – Austria, Prussia, France, and Britain – were hard at work in Vienna attempting to draft an agreement satisfactory to both sides. The result of this effort was the "Vienna note," a draft of a note to be addressed to Russia by the Porte. Count Nesselrode unconditionally accepted it almost immediately, on August 5. The four powers instructed their representatives in Constantinople to lobby the Porte to accept it as well, but the Sultan detected in its carefully guarded prose the very Russian protectorate that he could not accept, and over Redcliffe's objections (though some believe with his tacit approval), he proposed modifications to the note to make clear that the sultan himself was the ultimate guarantor of the Orthodox Church in his dominions. On August 19, Turkey submitted the proposed modifications, triggering objections from St. Petersburg – Count Nesselrode's infamous "violent interpretation of the Vienna note" – that tended to confirm the Sultan's fears and caused the four powers to reevaluate their support for the initiative.[26]

With the failure of the Vienna note, war increasingly began to seem unavoidable. Russia's actions had inflamed Turkish militancy to the point where it threatened the stability of the Ottoman regime, leaving the Porte little room for maneuver. At the same time, it became increasingly clear to the Sultan that he could count on British and French support in the event of a war with Russia; domestic and international considerations therefore reinforced each other and inclined the Porte toward a harder line.[27]

Against this backdrop, the Tsar and Nesselrode traveled to Olmütz in the last week of September to meet with Austrian Emperor Francis Joseph. The Tsar was very conciliatory toward England at Olmütz, and even proposed that the British fleet pass the Dardanelles to escape the October storms in Besika Bay. In view of the restrictions of the Straits Convention, this was a remarkably gracious offer. He also withdrew from the position that he would accept nothing but the original text of the Vienna note, and spoke for the first time of evacuating the

Principalities as soon as the Porte accepted his terms. He stood firm, however, on the maintenance of treaties and on a return to the religious status quo. He asked Austria to present Turkey with the original text of the Vienna note, to which he was willing to attach the following interpretation:

> The Cabinet of St. Petersburgh gives a new assurance that it will in no way exercise itself the protection of a Christian cult inside the Ottoman Empire, and that the duty of protecting this cult and maintaining its religious immunity has devolved on the sultan and that Russia only reserves to herself that of watching that the engagement contracted by the Ottoman Empire in the Treaty of Kainardji be strictly executed.[28]

Thus the Tsar attempted to assuage the Sultan's fears that the recognition of his right to protect the Orthodox in Ottoman dominions would lead to a change in his behavior. But no amount of semantic legerdemain could mask the fact that the Tsar was asking, in effect, for the Porte to recognize formally his sovereignty over Turkish subjects. While the Tsar may have appreciated the force of his distinction between *rights* and *duties*, and while he may well have believed his protestation that recognizing his rights did not increase his *powers*, his protagonists believed that his true goal was to increase those very powers.

The "Buol Project," as this initiative came to be called (named after the Austrian foreign minister who was instrumental in crafting it), represented the last, best hope to avoid war. The Tsar had gone as far as he could to assuage the Sultan's fears without losing face and abandoning his claims entirely. Historians disagree on why the initiative failed. One view is that the British government did not believe it; another is that Britain had already decided that Turkey would reject it (no doubt an accurate assessment, in view of the Porte's modifications to the Vienna note); a third is that Britain preferred war to a settlement at this point. Whatever the case may be, Britain's failure to support the initiative doomed it.[29] The British cabinet instead ordered Redcliffe to call up the squadron to Constantinople. Redcliffe received the order on October 4, but delayed acting on it until October 21, knowing it to be a clear violation of the Straits Convention of 1841 that could only inflame the situation.[30]

In early October, Turkey finally delivered an ultimatum giving Russia fifteen days to evacuate the Principalities. Russia did not comply and, on October 23, 1853, Turkey and Russia were at war.[31] With astoundingly poor timing, the British fleet entered the Dardanelles on the previous day; had Admiral Dundas waited one day longer, his movement would not have been a violation of the treaty of 1841. The Tsar interpreted this, too, as a hostile and offensive act.[32] But, on October 31, the Tsar declared that, notwithstanding the state of war between Russia and the Porte, he would refrain from taking the offensive, and merely continue to hold the Principalities as a pledge.[33]

The Turkish armies acquitted themselves well during the opening months of the war. Under the command of Omer Pasha, the Turks won a number of small engagements in Lesser Wallachia, pinning down a much larger Russian force. But Turkey was clearly incapable of dislodging the Russians from the Principalities, and the Tsar was not eager to give the other European powers any incentive to join in the fray by taking the offensive. Russia's one significant military accomplishment in 1853, however, proved to be enough of a spark to bring Britain into the war on the Turkish side. A squadron of Russian warships based in Sevastopol began patrolling the Turkish coast in November, and in one swift engagement caught and annihilated a smaller Turkish squadron in the port of Sinope. The attack was not without forewarning – the Russian ships had been hovering out of range of the shore batteries for days – nor was it unprovoked: the Turks fired the first shot. Moreover, it could hardly be denied that the action was perfectly legitimate given the fact that Russia and Turkey had been at war for over a month and Turkey had already fought the war aggressively. But, as Harold Temperley put it, "The news of Sinope unloosed a storm of extraordinary violence against Russia. The wave of emotion was resistless in England and took no account of the true facts."[34] Britons received news of the attack on Sinope in much the same way as Americans received news of the Japanese attack on Pearl Harbor in 1941 – with shock and anger, as though the attack were an act of treachery.[35]

In response to the news, on January 4, 1854, the British and French fleets entered the Black Sea. Napoleon III proposed giving Russia notice "that France and England were resolved to prevent the repetition of the affair of Sinope, and that every Russian ship thenceforward met in the Euxine [Black Sea] would be requested, and, if necessary, constrained, to return to Sebastopol; and that any act of aggression afterwards attempted against the Ottoman territory or flag would be repelled by force."[36] Napoleon's timing could not have been worse; winter was approaching, and the diplomats in Vienna were hopeful that the breathing space afforded by the inability to conduct large-scale military operations during bad weather would provide time enough to work out a negotiated settlement.

The British and French note reached St. Petersburg on January 12,

1854. Nesselrode's first reaction was muted by his understanding that Britain and France might have issued a similar warning to the Turks.[37] However, Brunnow sought clarification of this point from the British Prime Minister, Lord Aberdeen. Did the note mean, Brunnow asked, that the Russian coast and flag would receive the same protection against attack as would be accorded Turkey? When Aberdeen replied negatively, Brunnow requested his passport.[38] The French and British Ambassadors in St. Petersburg followed suit; on February 21, 1854, diplomatic relations between Russia and the Western Powers came to an end.[39]

The British and French note ruined any prospect of successful negotiations. Kinglake explains it thus: "It was one thing for the Western Powers to enforce the neutrality of the Black Sea, and another and a very different thing to announce to the sovereign of a haughty State that, even although he might be bent on no warlike errand, still, upon the very sea which washed his coast – upon the very sea which filled his harbours – he was forbidden to show his flag."[40] With diplomatic relations cut off and no further prospect of persuading Nicholas to quit the Danubian Principalities, Britain and France resorted to an ultimatum, giving Russia until April 30, 1854, to evacuate Moldavia and Wallachia.[41] Nesselrode declined to answer the French and British notes, and on March 27 Louis Napoleon informed his Senate and Legislative Assembly that France and Russia were at war. England followed suit on March 28.[42]

RUSSIAN MOTIVATIONS

From a Realist perspective, the Crimean war was anomalous in a number of ways. In the first place, Russia persisted in pursuing a line of policy that gave her no reasonable prospect of enlisting the support of any other Great Power, and risked provoking an overwhelmingly powerful coalition against her. Britain, France, Austria, and Prussia were united in their opposition to Nicholas's demands against the Porte and to his continued occupation of the Danubian Principalities, and yet the Tsar refused to yield or compromise. A simple balance of power calculus should have alerted him to the hopelessness of his obstinacy. Moreover, Austria – the Great Power best suited to exercise influence in St. Petersburg, and the power whose interests were most directly engaged by Russia's actions owing to the proximity of the conflict and the potentially explosive nature of nationalist or sectarian struggles in the region's multinational empires – confined herself to a mediating role and failed to take the lead in resisting Russia.[43] Britain and France – geographically the most remote of the Great Powers – were the most active in resisting Russian encroachments; and while British interest in maintaining the Ottoman Empire was fairly clear, there was no compelling interest requiring France to be in the forefront of the effort.[44] The war involved no hegemonic transitions, no core security interests, served only to disrupt the workings of a system that had effectively promoted order for almost half a century, and resulted in a settlement that only temporarily altered the regional status quo.

Despite these considerations, many of the most common interpretations of the origins of the Crimean war are Realist in nature, emphasizing power and interest as motivations. It is worth surveying a few of them briefly, if only to show how powerfully common understandings of events can be influenced by power political modes of analysis despite an almost total absence of supporting evidence.

Perhaps the most common interpretation of the event is that it was the result of Tsar Nicholas's attempt to fulfill the putative dream of every Russian monarch since Catherine the Great: to seize Constantinople and to secure control of the straits which had for so long confined the Russian navy to the Black Sea.[45] Some historians have been less specific about Nicholas's territorial aims, and have simply understood the war to be the result of Russian "expansionism" and "self-assertion."[46] Still others explain it in terms of the imperial rivalries of Britain and Russia, "in which the commercial and strategic potentialities of the Near East played a dominant role."[47]

Much is made in the historiography of the Crimean war of conversations between Tsar Nicholas and his representatives on the one hand, and British statesmen and diplomats on the other, concerning the ultimate fate of the Ottoman Empire. The Tsar's fears of the collapse of the Ottoman Empire, and his desire to have contingency plans in place so as to avoid a general war over the spoils, are well-documented and date as far back as 1833.[48] "The Tsar was undoubtedly much too pessimistic and despondent about the stability and vitality of the Turkish empire," writes G.H. Bolsover. "In 1844, for example, he is reported to have told [Prime Minister Sir Robert] Peel and Aberdeen [then Minister of Foreign Affairs] that there were two views about Turkey current in Russia. The first was that she was on the point of collapse and the second that she had collapsed already. 'The first view is held by Nesselrode,' the Tsar said, 'the second by myself.'"[49]

In January 1853, the Tsar had a frank exchange of views with the British Ambassador in St. Petersburg, Sir Hamilton Seymour. In those discussions, the Tsar disavowed any ambitions against the territory of the Ottoman Empire, but sought to reach an understanding with Britain in case the "sick man of Europe" should suddenly die. Nicholas proposed that in the event of the empire's collapse, the Danubian Principalities, Serbia, and Bulgaria would become independent principalities under Russian protection, and Britain would take control of Egypt and Crete. No Great Power would be permitted to take possession of Constantinople. Seymour responded that Britain had no territorial designs on the Ottoman Empire, and accepted the Tsar's like assurances; but he objected to the idea of planning for the anticipated demise of an old friend and ally. Nicholas acknowledged that as a general rule this was a prudent policy, but he took the occasion to warn Seymour frankly that he would not allow England to establish herself at Constantinople, forswearing at the same time any intention to take permanent possession of the city himself.[50]

At least one prominent historian of the event concluded that Britain and Russia had reached a secret agreement on the ultimate partition of the Ottoman Empire, and that an "untimely disruption" of that understanding "was the principal cause of the Crimean War." This is not at present a view given much credence by historians.[51] What does seem clear is that Nicholas was less than entirely forthcoming with Seymour as to what he had in mind. His private hand-written notes show that "his real views as to the ultimate partition, though less selfish than Seymour thought, were more ambitious than he actually admitted." He believed Constantinople should become a free port; that Moldavia and Wallachia should become "Russian;" and that it might be necessary to maintain a Russian garrison on the Bosporus, and an Austrian garrison on the Dardanelles, for some period of time, to keep the Mediterranean powers out of Constantinople.[52]

But the prospective fall of the Ottoman Empire was evidently a cause of dread for the Russian Tsar, not something he anticipated with relish, and the preservation of Turkey was near the top of the Tsar's foreign policy agenda throughout his reign, including the period immediately prior to the outbreak of the Crimean war.[53] In 1829, for example, while at war with the Porte, Nicholas had held back militarily precisely to prevent a collapse of the Ottoman Empire, even as Constantinople lay within his grasp.[54] In 1833 and 1840, Nicholas had actively helped to preserve Turkey, and in the Treaty of Unkiar-Skelessi of July 8, 1833, pledged his support for the peace and security of the Ottoman Empire.[55] Nesselrode even took the trouble to caution Prince Menshikov, on the eve of his infamous mission, that "the Ottoman Empire would dissolve at the first touch [of war] and that the Emperor does not wish to accelerate that catastrophe."[56]

First and foremost, then, Nicholas was a defender of the status quo in southeastern Europe. His marginal comments on Lord John Russell's reply to the Seymour message, penned in his own hand, clearly show that he preferred the continued security and independence of the Ottoman Empire to any scheme of territorial division.[57] Temperley writes:

> The efforts of Nicholas to arrive at a good understanding with England were inspired by a sincere and even noble emotion. It was unwise for an Emperor to try to negotiate with British diplomats or to believe that the word or the friendship of Queen Victoria was all-important. It was unwise to try to discuss potentialities with parliamentarians. But the suggestion that there was anything criminal in such an attempt is ridiculous. An explanation, which might have passed in the hour of war mania, cannot serve as a judgement of history. It is thus denounced by Prokesch-Osten: "If people want to make out that it is a crime on the Czar of Russia's part, that he proposed a peaceful and friendly negotiation about the eventuality of the fall of the Turkish Empire, it is a proof of their own stupidity."[58]

Nicholas was too devoted to the principle of legitimate monarchy and too fearful of revolts in multinational empires such as Turkey's (and his own) to look favorably upon the dissolution of the Ottoman Empire. Moreover, if Nicholas had been operating on the basis of expansionist designs in 1853, his timing could not possibly have been worse. In the first place, Russian power had reached its apogee in 1815; the middle of the century was no time to take on the challenge of expansion into politically explosive territory.[59] Prudence suggested that for encroachments against Turkey he should choose a time when Europe was distracted and might acquiesce; instead, he chose a time when the other European powers had nothing else to do but watch and resist Russian aggression.[60]

The common view that Nicholas harbored designs on Constantinople is similarly flawed. Kinglake pinpointed the heart of the matter:

> The sovereignty of European Turkey could scarcely be added to the possessions of the Czar without tending to dislocate the system of his empire; for plainly it would be difficult to sway the vast Northern territories of All the Russias by orders sent from the Bosphorus, and yet, by force of its mere place in the world, Constantinople seemed destined to be the capital of a great State. Therefore, in the event of its falling into the hands of the Romanoffs, it may be thought more likely that the imperial city would draw dominion to itself, and so become the metropolis of some new assemblage of territories, than that it would sink into the condition of a provincial seaport. The statesmen of St Petersburg have always understood the deep import of the

change which the throne of Constantine would bring with it; and it may be imagined that considerations founded on this aspect of the enticing conquest have mingled with those suggested by the physical difficulties of invasion, the obstinate valour of the Turks, and the hostility of the great powers of Europe. Still, the prize was so unspeakably alluring to an aristocracy fired with national ambition, and to a people glowing with piety, that apparently it was necessary for the Czar to seem as though he were always doing something for furthering a scheme of conquest thus endeared to the nation.[61]

This was an analysis that Metternich once said was held by "all thinking men" in St. Petersburg;[62] and it was primarily for this reason that Russian Tsars were fundamentally ambivalent about the city – "always threatening Constantinople and never taking it."[63]

But even if control of Constantinople had been psychologically irresistible, it would plainly have been more trouble to Nicholas than it was worth. Its importance to Russia lay simply in its command of the Bosporus, and thus of seaborne communications between the Black Sea and the Mediterranean. Economically, the Turkish straits were important because of Russia's burgeoning export trade in grain.[64] But Article XI of the Treaty of Kutchuk-Kainardji had opened the straits to unrestricted Russian commercial shipping before any other European power had secured a similar right.[65] This treaty right guaranteed freedom of commercial navigation more surely than even physical control of Constantinople could have done, given the likelihood that an occupation would have triggered a war that, at a minimum, would have resulted in a naval blockade, and that could well have resulted in Constantinople falling into a hostile power's hands. In such a case, the straits might have been closed to Russian commercial shipping altogether. Strategically, the straits were almost valueless to Russia. In the first place, she had no Mediterranean possessions requiring the protection of a navy. Second, even with Constantinople as a base, Russia could not hope to dominate the Mediterranean because of its distance from the main Mediterranean trade routes. Third, a fleet based in Constantinople could easily be bottled up either by a close blockade in Besika Bay, or by a more distant blockade in the vicinity of Crete. Russian interests were far better served by arrangements preventing other nations' warships from entering the Black Sea than by efforts to facilitate Russian sorties into the Mediterranean, and that purpose was much more efficiently accomplished by the Straits Convention of 1841 than it could possibly have been by an occupation of Constantinople. If any other proof were required that Nicholas harbored no designs on the city, it may be recalled that in 1830, a strong Russian fleet anchored in the Golden Horn and a sizeable Russian force landed on the Bosporus to protect it from Mehemet Ali of Egypt. The Tsar could easily have established a permanent presence in the region at that time; instead he withdrew his forces at the earliest opportunity.[66]

If traditional explanations of the Crimean war emphasizing Russian expansionism in its various forms cannot stand close scrutiny, to what motivations should we assign responsibility? The clearest understanding can be reached by treating the proximate causes first, and ultimate causes second.

The only person whose motivations really counted in the Russian case was Tsar Nicholas himself. He was an autocrat in the fullest sense of the word: he alone was the state. He was dependent politically upon no domestic constituency, and he did not make a practice of soliciting or relying upon the advice of others in making major decisions. Thus, for example, he consulted neither Nesselrode, his Vice-Chancellor and Foreign Minister, nor Dolgorukov, his War Minister, nor Count Orlov, Head of Internal Security, before he put his Fourth and Fifth Army Corps on a war footing near the Ottoman border. Nor did he consult his Foreign Minister about the Menshikov mission; indeed foreign diplomats found out about it before Nesselrode did. And when Nicholas informed Orlov that he had signed the orders to occupy the Danubian Principalities and Orlov proclaimed, "This is war," the Tsar merely responded by expressing disdainful surprise at the Count's pessimism.[67]

No account of Nicholas's motivations can be accurate without due regard for his personality and character.[68] He was in many ways an unusual man. By all accounts he was "honest, very limited in mind, but full of a sense of duty;[69] he was extremely emotional, insecure, given to fits of rage, and possessed a powerful sense of honor; he prided himself on his integrity, his truthfulness, and liked to style himself a "gentleman" (always using the English word); he had none of the cool, calm, calculating characteristics often associated in the popular mind with autocrats, and no sense of humor whatsoever. But perhaps most important for our purposes, Nicholas had a highly developed moral sensibility, a powerful sense of justice, a tendency to react violently to perceived injustices, and an inability to view situations touching his core values with objectivity or detachment. At the top of his list of core values was his faith. The Tsar "was fully Orthodox in that he was devoted to the Orthodox Church in the same complete and unquestioning manner in which he was devoted to his country or his regiment;" his religious convictions "were all-pervasive, affecting every phase of his life in an important manner."[70]

When the French attempted to alter the status quo in the Holy Land, they engaged Nicholas's sense of injustice directly. The Tsar interpreted France's assertion of the treaty of 1740 simply as a violation of his entitlements as protector of the Orthodox Church.[71] His reaction was so vehement and so indignant that he was completely unable to take the counsel of prudence and work quietly behind the scenes for an accommodation. This was most unfortunate, for the disposition of the Holy Places was not an intractable issue, as the April settlement of 1853 clearly showed; and the Tsar should have been able to recognize that France's claims had some merit, given that they were grounded in a valid and binding treaty. But Nicholas's belligerence delayed a settlement for so long that by the time a compromise was reached – three years after the matter arose – the shrines themselves had ceased being the issue.

It is not difficult to understand Nicholas's reaction to the French demand. The Holy Sites, by established usage, had come to occupy a place of importance in the Orthodox faith that had no correlate in Roman Catholicism. The heart of the matter was the importance of pilgrimage to the Orthodox faithful; "whilst the Greek pilgrim ships poured out upon the landing-place of Jaffa the multitudes of those who had survived the misery and the trials of the journey," Kinglake notes, "the closest likeness of a pilgrim which the Latin Church could supply was often a mere French tourist, with a journal and a theory, and a plan of writing a book."[72] During Christmas in 1831, a French monk in Jerusalem found only four Latin pilgrims out of four thousand, and was informed that, at Easter, one might find perhaps twenty out of ten thousand.[73] To all intents and purposes, most of the shrines in the Holy Land were Orthodox places of worship. The Tsar, as head of the Orthodox Church in Russia and spiritual superior to the patriarchs of the Ottoman Empire, understood France's claims on behalf of the Latins as a frontal assault on Orthodox rights, privileges, and practices long established and accepted by France and everyone else.

The Tsar's demands on the disposition of the Holy Places were actually quite moderate; he did not seek a withdrawal of the privileges granted the Latin Church, in part because he had no desire to exclude other Christians from the Holy Shrines. He sought only to protect Orthodox access and to prevent alteration of the shrines in ways that would offend the members of his church. But he was peremptory in delivering his demands.[74] The French, of course, were also less than fully cooperative and conciliatory. The result was that the Sultan was forced to make choices between the Greeks and the Latins under circumstances calling for careful, quiet diplomacy and compromise.

For technical legal reasons, the French claim had to be upheld; but, as Temperley notes, "The victory of the French in the battle of the Holy Places had wounded Nicholas too deeply for him to accept defeat."[75] Russian counter-pressure succeeded in wresting a temporary concession from the Porte: the Greek firman. But whatever minor satisfaction this gave the Tsar only aggravated his fury when the French refused to leave the issue benignly ambiguous and forced the Sultan to transfer the keys to the Church at Bethlehem to the Latins and place a French star on the Holy Grotto.

Keys, silver stars, hours of worship, and guardianships at shrines were quite trivial issues in and of themselves, and acceptable compromises were reached on all of them once serious conversations began. But France's demands raised larger questions about the relationship between foreign powers and the Porte's Christian subjects – questions that were better left alone. France, therefore, must be blamed for opening Pandora's Box.[76] For Nicholas believed that France's insistence on a strict interpretation of the Capitulations of 1740 derogated Russia's rights as protector of the Orthodox Church in Turkey.[77] Technically, as we have already seen, Nicholas misunderstood the nature of the treaty rights he sought to defend. Moreover, while the rest of Europe seems to have believed that a Russian protectorate over the Orthodox Church in Turkey would have had the effect of transferring sovereignty over large areas and sizeable populations from Constantinople to St. Petersburg, the Tsar seems to have understood his demands as moderate and fully consistent with the status quo.[78] He had been interfering in Turkish domestic affairs on behalf of the Orthodox Church for quite some time;[79] he had no intention of changing his behavior toward Turkey, and said as much at Olmütz. Anything else would have been flatly inconsistent with his oft-repeated desire to prevent the collapse of the Ottoman Empire as long as he possibly could. Believing that he possessed treaty rights giving him a protectorate over the Orthodox Church in Turkey, unable to understand how such a claim could be seen as dangerous or ungrounded, the Tsar could only interpret Turkey's resistance to the Menshikov mission as a deliberate attempt to infringe entitlements he already held. The Holy Places themselves soon became the minor point; the unexpected resistance encountered by Menshikov quickly established the protectorate as the major point. Once the Tsar's sense of injustice was thus fully engaged, France's success in wresting a treaty guarantee from the Turks, and Menshikov's failure to do so, reinforced his unbalanced and rather paranoid understanding of the situation.[80] Hence his rage when the Porte offered to issue a firman confirming *the*

Sultan's undertaking to protect the interests of the Orthodox Church. Since the interests of the Orthodox Church were ostensibly what the Tsar was seeking to secure, his rage could only have come from his conviction that the Sultan was, in essence, usurping his own position.[81]

The parties being thus engaged, the issue soon became intractable: "The Porte would promise anything except to sign a treaty or note which would allow Russia to make representations on behalf of the Greek Christians; Russia would be content with nothing less."[82] At every turn, Nicholas was denied – the Menshikov mission, the Vienna note, the Buol Project – and despite the obviousness of the gathering storm clouds and the strength of his opposition in Europe, he was unable to back down and prevent a needless catastrophe. All he had wanted from the start was an affirmation of entitlements he already believed he had; when the affirmation was not forthcoming, he was blinded by his pride and his unswerving belief in the justice of his cause, and was unable to prevent the consolidation of an irresistible coalition against him.[83]

Almost unbelievably, there are lengthy histories of the event that dismiss the religious issues in a few pages or less.[84] To do so is to ignore the fact that the substance of Russia's pre-war diplomacy overwhelmingly concerned the Holy Places issue and the question of the protectorate, to dismiss the public and private declarations of the Tsar virtually *in toto*, and to charge him with a dishonesty, wickedness, and lack of integrity flatly inconsistent with his own self-understanding and the understanding of his biographers. The Tsar made his views quite plain to Seymour in the very discussions some have seized upon to argue that what he truly sought was a partition of Turkey:

> [I]n that empire there are several millions of Christians whose interests I am called upon to watch over, while the right of doing so is secured to me by treaty. I may truly say that I make a moderate and sparing use of my right, and I will freely confess that it is one which is attended with obligations occasionally very inconvenient; but I cannot recede from the discharge of a distinct duty. Our religion, as established in this country, came to us from the East, and there are feelings as well as obligations which never must be lost sight of.[85]

Nicholas made a full and public confession of his motivation for occupying Moldavia and Wallachia by authorizing his military commander in the Principalities, Prince Gorshakov, to proclaim that "[o]n the day on which [the Tsar] obtains the reparation which is due to him, and the guarantees which he has a right to claim for the future, his troops shall return within the frontiers of Russia."[86] His sense of injustice was undoubtedly oversensitive, and his self-righteousness was undoubtedly somewhat misplaced; but there can be no mistaking the sincerity of either.[87]

Notwithstanding the passion of his sense of injustice, war might well have been averted in the absence of other factors. Each time the Tsar's temper seemed to cool to the point where rational deliberations on the issues in question seemed possible, a fresh affront would inflame it once again. The approach of the French and British fleets to Besika Bay, the allies' flagrant violations of the Straits Convention, and the French and British declaration prohibiting Russian ships from venturing out into the Black Sea were simply the most dramatic instances of these affronts.[88] In addition, there is strong evidence to suggest that the personal animosity the Tsar harbored toward Lord Stratford de Redcliffe blinded him to meaningful opportunities for constructive negotiations.[89] Not least importantly, the Tsar seems grossly to have miscalculated the likelihood that Britain would oppose his demands with force. Lord Aberdeen's appointment as prime minister on December 20, 1852 seemed to the Tsar to herald a radically pacific British foreign policy. Aberdeen's abhorrence of war was well-known, and the Tsar had come to believe that the Manchester School and the Society of Friends represented the dominant modes of thought in a liberal, free-trading, industrializing Britain. In November 1852, Aberdeen confessed to Baron Brunnow that he feared a French invasion of England. The Tsar's response, penned in the margins of Brunnow's dispatch, was that Aberdeen's confession "serves to show the cowardice of the government."[90] "To all who would listen, Lord Aberdeen used to say that he abhorred the very thought of war; and that he was sure it would not and could not occur. He caused men to believe that, except for weighty and solemn causes, no war would be undertaken with his concurrence. Relying on a Prime Minister's words, the Emperor Nicholas felt certain that Lord Aberdeen would not carry England into a war for the sake of a difference between the wording of a Note demanded by Prince Mentschikoff and the wording of a Note proposed by the Turks."[91] But these misperceptions, miscalculations, personal animosities, and oversensitivities would have been entirely innocuous in the absence of the Tsar's overwhelming perception of injustice. Without doubt they made war more likely by making its avoidance more difficult; but without the tangible, burning indignation of a pious and passionate tsar, there simply would have been no war at all.

ALLIED MOTIVATIONS

What of the allies' motivations? The evidence suggests that Turkey's motives for prosecuting the war were mixed, and that various constituencies in the Ottoman Empire understood the war in various ways. While the sultan was technically an autocrat, the Turkish regime during the nineteenth century was notoriously unstable and ignored groundswells of opinion at its peril. Thus, when the cry for war spread through the empire's mosques, the Porte found it very difficult to resist.

There is no doubt that public opinion in Turkey overwhelmingly wanted war primarily because of the perceived injustices committed by the Russian Tsar, first by attempting to wrest from the Sultan a right of protection over the Orthodox Church to which he was not considered entitled, and then by occupying sovereign Turkish territory to enforce his unjust claim. These would have been serious enough offenses, from the Turkish point of view, had they been committed by an Islamic prince; but the fact that they represented encroachments upon Islam by the infidel gave Turkish perceptions of injustice an unmistakable potency and vehemence.[92]

On September 23, 1853, the Sultan announced a special meeting of the *Meclis-i umumî*, a council composed of elders and clerics, in which the "Europeanized" ministers faced a "stinging attack" from the traditional ulema and *hocas* for their unpreparedness for war, and their reluctance to declare it, almost three months after the Russian occupation of Moldavia and Wallachia.[93] What is notable about the meeting is the clarity with which the regime's critics understood resisting the Tsar's encroachments to be a religious duty, and how poorly they understood the strategic situation.[94] The Sultan and his ministers, however – even those who were inclined toward war – understood the strategic situation very well. Partly on the counsel of Stratford de Redcliffe, the Sultan avoided committing himself to war when Russian troops first crossed the Pruth, preferring, if at all possible, to settle the matter diplomatically, since Russia was clearly the superior military power.[95] In any case, Russia had provided the necessary *casus belli*, and the Sultan could choose the time and circumstances under which to act.[96]

Preparations for war began almost immediately; in the empire's mosques the call went out to the faithful to steel themselves for battle, and within two weeks of the occupation of the Principalities, the price of arms in Turkish markets had skyrocketed as a result of the sudden increase in demand.[97] But the Sultan waited to deliver an ultimatum until diplomacy ceased to be a viable option, until Turkish forces were in condition to fight, and until he was absolutely certain that he would have the support of France and Britain if his military situation became untenable. In October, he finally gave in to the popular clamor.

The Porte's public stance on the war downplayed the religious conflict altogether; there was nothing of *jihad* in the Turkish declaration, and indeed, for the first time ever in a Moslem country, Christian troops fought under the banner of the Crescent. The ostensible aim of the war was to redeem Turkish territory from unlawful Russian occupation.[98] It is plausible to believe that the Sultan understood this as the redemption of an entitlement, but the evidence suggests that Turkish motivations were more complex. Foreign Minister Reshid Pasha explained Turkish war aims to Redcliffe and French Ambassador de la Cour in a note dated October 19: "The unique object of the Sublime Porte, the salutary aim that she entertains, is to come to the end of this war completely protected from any exterior anxiety, in order to busy herself solely with interior regulations to assure the well-being of the Empire by the perfecting of her progressive system of administration, by the just amelioration of the condition of all classes of her subjects, and by the development of her commerce and industry without any impediment ... "[99] The Turkish Ambassador to London, in a letter to his Minister for Foreign Affairs in November, likewise related his understanding of Turkish war aims to be "an end, once for all, to the encroachments of Russia and specially to any intervention on her part in the affairs of the Principalities."[100] Whatever injustice the Porte may have perceived as a result of the Russian occupation of the Principalities, it was evidently inextricably linked to a basic concern for security. The rather unusual semi-autonomous status of the Principalities, and the prior history of Russian intervention there, suggest that the regime's security motive may well have been more powerful than its perception of injustice. Given the diversity of factors, the differences between the popular and elite understandings of the war, and the insufficiency of the historical record for making a more precise determination in this case, it would seem prudent to make a conservative evaluation of the role played by the justice motive in Turkey's decision to declare war, and this is reflected in Table 2.1.[101]

Even more so than Turkey, British policy had both popular and elite components. The government itself was split between those, like Aberdeen, who sought to avoid war at almost any cost, and those, like Home Secretary Lord Palmerston and Lord John Russell, who relished the idea.[102] Ultimately, when the government made its fateful decision to issue an ultimatum and to declare war when the Tsar refused to evacuate the Principalities, it did so for a variety of reasons.

From the British perspective, the war was, at least in part, a war of containment.[103] Nicholas did not harbor the designs on the Ottoman Empire that some British statesmen feared, but many nonetheless sincerely believed that he did; Russell, for example, wrote to Clarendon in March 1853 warning that "the Emperor of Russia is clearly bent on accomplishing the destruction of Turkey, and *he must be resisted.*"[104] Given this fear, it was only natural for Britain to try to resist; for next to Austria, she had the most compelling interest in maintaining the Ottoman Empire.[105] Russian control of Constantinople was a particularly alarming prospect, not only because it could severely hamper British trade in the region, but also because it seemed to some likely to threaten Britain's sea lines of communication to the East. As Sidney Herbert, a younger member of the cabinet put it in a confidential assessment, "we are all agreed as to the objects in view. We must have a power at the Bosphorus to hold the keys of the Mediterranean from the East, which shall not be Russia, and we cannot allow Russia to encroach upon or undermine the power which is there necessary to us. We are not bound by treaty to interfere but we are bound by our own interest and by European interests, not to allow Turkey to be overborne. We are further bound in honour not to abandon Turkey in difficulties consequent on a course taken with our sanction and by our advice."[106]

Herbert's last point is worth highlighting, because it is not an appeal to the national interest. It is indeed true that Britain, through Redcliffe, had been closely advising the Porte on how to deal with Russia throughout, and that she felt certain obligations incident to that role. It is largely for this reason that Kinglake concluded that Aberdeen drifted into war despite his horror of it.[107] A sense of honor and obligation therefore reinforced considerations of power and interest when Britain finally chose war with the Tsar on Turkey's behalf. Some members of the cabinet, of course, probably saw in it more opportunity than obligation. Palmerston, for example, presented the cabinet on March 19, 1854, with a list of war aims that included, *inter alia,* the restoration of Poland as of 1772; the detachment of Finland from Russia and its union with Sweden and Norway; Austrian control of the Danubian Principalities, with the surrender of Lombardy and Venetia; and the transfer of Georgia and the Crimea to Turkey.[108] These were hardly consistent with Britain's stated motives, and, had they been accepted, would have dramatically altered the character of the war.

Curiously, it was Palmerston who was most inclined to take Nicholas's demands at face value: "the Emperor of Russia is ambitious and grasping," Palmerston wrote Clarendon in 1853, "but he is a Gentleman, and I should be slow to disbelieve [him] ... at all events we are right in accepting his assertions ... "[109]

Palmerston's understanding of the situation was in many respects unusual, as these remarks indicate. They clearly demonstrate that the cabinet did not share a single understanding of the situation, and operated on the basis of a variety of motivations. Aberdeen – the single most important player on the British side – evidently did not believe that Britain's vital interests were at stake, and conceived of his primary role as that of mediator, in view of what he called "the equivocal position of Great Britain in this contest."[110] One further thing is clear, however: the cabinet felt powerfully constrained by public opinion. Clarendon made the baldest confession: "Our pacific policy is at variance with public opinion so it cannot long be persisted in."[111] On October 8, 1853, Aberdeen himself privately confessed to the Austrian Ambassador that public feeling would not permit Britain to abandon Turkey.[112]

Public opinion in Britain was overwhelmingly against the Tsar because of the perceived injustice both of his demands and of his actions.[113] The allies of the Porte "must be prepared to meet armed injustice with the only argument to which it will yield," the *Morning Chronicle* proclaimed. "The supporters of the just rights of the Sultan reserve the appeal to force as a last resort, but, should all other expedients be exhausted, it is one the result of which they have no cause to fear."[114] Russia's occupation of the Principalities and subsequent intransigence were cause enough for British indignation; the final straw was the news of Sinope, which reached London on December 11.[115] Nesselrode's October 31 circular forswearing any intention to conduct offensive operations had been understood in Britain as the equivalent of a truce; the attack at Sinope was therefore perceived to be a breach of promise. This interpretation was unfair, since for more than a month fighting had been raging on the lower Danube and in Armenia. The Turks had even seized the Russian fort at St. Nicholas. It was unreasonable to expect the Tsar to sit with his hands tied under such circumstances. "But the people of England, not knowing all this at first, and hearing nothing of the Russian fleet until they heard of the ravage and slaughter of Sinope, imagined that the blow had come sudden as the knife of an assassin. They were too angry to be able to look upon the question in a spirit of cold justice."[116]

Both the Whigs and the Tories, reflecting the public mood, wanted

71

war.[117] Try as he might to avoid it, Aberdeen was in fact powerless to resist. If he resigned, Palmerston would undoubtedly have formed the next cabinet, dooming all hope of a peaceful resolution of the dispute. Aberdeen's overriding interest was to keep the cabinet together, but this alone would not enable him to avoid what he most feared.[118] That his hopes and fears were coloring his perceptions of events, inadvertently hastening the onset of hostilities, cannot be denied; almost unbelievably, Aberdeen expressed his hope that the instructions finally given to the admirals confining the Russian navy to port would not antagonize the Tsar or further endanger peace; a clearer mind would have recognized at once that they would have precisely the opposite effect.[119] It further cannot be denied that the British cabinet overhastily considered both the Buol Project and the proposed movement of the fleet through the Dardanelles, aggravating rather than ameliorating the situation.[120] British policy, too, was influenced by its share of misperceptions, miscalculations, motivated biases, and downright ignorance.

But it was not the British public alone whose sense of injustice had been triggered by the Tsar's actions, and it is important to recognize that even British statesmen who articulated eloquent rationales for resisting Russia in terms of the national interest betrayed their own senses of moral outrage at Russian policy. Malmesbury, for example, speaking with evident emotion, condemned the Tsar's demand for a protectorate of the Orthodox Church in Turkey by asking parliament what the British people would think of the justice of a foreign power demanding a treaty guaranteeing the privileges of Her Majesty's Roman Catholic subjects, despite the fact that those privileges had already been conferred by an act of Her own in 1829.[121] The reasons given in defense of the British declaration of war reflected the variety of concerns motivating the public and the government alike: the need to defend against injustice, to enforce the observance of treaties, and to maintain an empire whose independence was essential to the peace of Europe.[122]

French motivations may be dealt with fairly briefly, since there is little evidence to suggest that the policies of Napoleon III were a function of the justice motive. Historians disagree on the reasons prompting Napoleon to raise the question of the Holy Shrines in the first place, but the two most popular theories have nothing to do with any attempt to right a perceived wrong. One explanation is that Louis Napoleon raised it to secure the domestic political support of the Catholics, for whom Palestine had become an important issue with the rise of the Ultramontane party in the 1840s.[123] As John Curtiss puts it, "the French government chiefly wanted to placate the Catholic clergy in France" and "repeatedly told the Russian envoy at Paris that it did not regard the [Holy Places] question as important."[124] Equally plausible is the interpretation that Napoleon was attempting to find an issue that he could use to subvert the Holy Alliance. France felt isolated and denied its rightful place in Europe, largely because of Russian hostility.[125] Indeed, several months after the siege of Sevastopol began, French Foreign Minister Drouyn de Lhuys confided to a relative that France's sole interest in the event was to dislocate the continental alliance that had paralyzed France for nearly half a century.[126] Many historians have concluded that Napoleon III was operating largely on the basis of both motivations simultaneously.[127]

It is interesting to note that French public opinion appears not to have reacted to Russian actions in the same way as British public opinion. The French as a whole received news of the attack at Sinope, for example, with equanimity. To the extent that Russian actions triggered moral outrage of any kind in France – that is, hardly at all – it was the Emperor himself who felt it.[128] On the whole, it seems safest to conclude that French policy was motivated overwhelmingly by domestic political considerations, geopolitical considerations, or both.

CONCLUSIONS

The complexity and multiplicity of proximate causes, and the evident importance of catalytic factors in the frustration of a peaceful settlement of the disputes ultimately leading to war, make it very difficult to identify the ultimate causes of the Crimean war precisely. The grievances that unexpectedly led to war struck like a bolt from the blue; it would have been very difficult even for a fully informed observer in 1850 to identify in contemporary circumstances the conditions likely to lead to a war involving three Great Powers and resulting in the collapse of the Concert of Europe within three years. Indeed, it would probably have been very difficult to convince such an observer that a war was even possible.

Kinglake traced the ultimate cause of the war to autocratic personal government.[129] His argument is not without merit; Tsar Nicholas's idiosyncrasies, and his total free agency over the conduct of Russian affairs, certainly played an important role in the outbreak of war, as did the considerations that seemed to be driving French policy. Had these two great states been democracies, it is likely that the disputes over which the war was fought would never have gotten off the ground. Schroeder argues that the war was ultimately the result of conflict between Austrian interest in maintaining the Concert and Western (primarily British) interest in disrupting it.[130] Wetzel traces the ultimate causes of the war to the revolutions of 1848 and latent nationalist pressures on multinational empires.[131] Plausible arguments can be made for all of these points of view, and due regard for the irreducible element of mystery in the situation forbids overhasty endorsements or denunciations of any of them.

At least one other consideration seems to have been important as an ultimate cause of the war, however, and that is the anomalous political status of the Ottoman Empire. A Realist might, with considerable justification, note that a power vacuum existed in southeastern Europe and Asia Minor that attracted, and ultimately rendered inevitable, serious Great Power conflict. However, it would not be accurate to describe that power vacuum in terms of the financial, economic, and military weaknesses of the Ottoman Empire itself. Although indisputably weaker on all of these dimensions than other European powers, Turkey was nevertheless resilient enough to last another half century before finally succumbing to an overwhelming combination of internal and external pressures. Reports of the death of the Ottoman Empire had always been greatly exaggerated. The "vacuum" that invited Great Power conflict in the 1850s was of a different sort: it was the result of Turkey's policy of permitting forms of foreign penetration, through devices such as capitulations, that were *perceived* to be signs of weakness in Europe, but were in reality manifestations of basic cultural differences. Turkey was not a European power in either form or substance; its integration into the European states system was slow, piecemeal, and never complete.[132] Turks tolerated Christian pilgrims to the Holy Lands, and foreign protectorates over Christian churches, not, as Europeans often surmised, because Turkey was weak, but because of the centrality of holy sites and pilgrimages to the Islamic consciousness.[133] Likewise, the Porte was willing to tolerate shared or incomplete sovereignty over Christian populations and provinces not because it had no choice, as Europeans commonly assumed, but because the Turkish understanding of political community was not, in its essentials, European. Christians were out-groups that just so happened to live within the territorial boundaries of an Islamic state, and were simply ignored as far as possible; hence their relative independence from Turkish laws and customs. No European power would have tolerated such a state of affairs. From the perspective of a European state playing by European rules, Turkey could only be understood as sickly, fragile, timid, and second-rate. It was therefore treated accordingly.

74

None of this would have led to the Crimean war, of course, were it not for the fact that the hooks to which European powers attached their various claims in Turkey were identifiable communities with aspirations for more complete autonomy than even the Turks would allow. Religious irredentism in Russia and, to a much lesser extent, in France, combined synergistically with those aspirations to generate pressures that were neither entirely foreseeable nor capable of being peacefully contained. France's assertion of the Treaty of 1740 was an unlikely spark, but a fully sufficient one; the variety of unsatisfied claims inherent in the Ottoman Empire itself, and among the powers of Europe that failed to understand and respect the uniqueness of the Ottoman system, provided ample combustible material once the spark was applied. Those claims were claims of justice. To that extent, perceptions of injustice were both endemic to the situation, and ultimately responsible for the outbreak of war. Wetzel is correct to note the nationalist expressions these had been given in 1848; more important in this case were their religious manifestations. These unsatisfied claims contributed heavily to the farrago of circumstances that made the Crimean war possible, helped to trigger it, and ultimately made it impossible to avoid.

The justice motive, therefore, played a crucial role in the outbreak of the Crimean war. At the level of ultimate causes, it was responsible for the pressures within the Ottoman empire that set up the interventionist dynamic eventually leading to a collision between the Great Powers. As a proximate cause, it generated the grievance that drove Russia headlong into war. Without sincere and compelling perceptions of injustice, Russia would neither have dared nor desired to jeopardize the stability and independence of the Ottoman Empire or the smooth functioning of the Concert, both of which she considered vital to her national interest. Nor, presumably, would Russia have risked bringing against her an overwhelming combination of European powers at a time when she stood to gain nothing – and to lose so much – from a major war. And even though some in Britain and France may well have seen some advantages in a war with Russia (Napoleon and Palmerston are the most likely candidates), it is difficult to imagine that one could or would have been engineered in the absence of the existing dispute over the Russian protectorate. Realism, in short, cannot explain the Crimean war. The evidence would suggest that this is very largely a function of the fact that the central figure in the history of the event – Tsar Nicholas I – was not himself a "Realist."

3 THE FRANCO-PRUSSIAN WAR

Table 3.1. *The Franco-Prussian war*

Role of justice motive in conditioning conflict	Role of justice motive as proximate cause (by participant)	
Weak	France	Weak
	Prussia	Imperceptible

In the years between Crimea and the outbreak of World War I, the political face of Europe underwent enormous change. Italy unified in 1861, followed ten years later by Germany; Austria, France, and Russia suffered serious military reverses in 1866, 1870, and 1905, emerging from the period weaker than they had entered; only Britain among the Great Powers enjoyed a period of relative peace and prosperity, but that, too, proved to be the calm before the storm. Her misfortunes in southern Africa at the turn of the century heralded a period of graceful, but unmistakable, decline. Also during this period, for the very first time in the history of the nation-state system, two non-European countries – Japan and the United States – rose to Great Power status. No longer could high politics be considered coextensive with European politics, and no longer would imperial concerns exhaust the European powers' interests in the outside world. Britain was the first to come to terms with this change. After the Boer war, she was forced to conclude an alliance with Japan for the defense of her Far Eastern possessions, to appease the United States in Latin America, and to concede control of the Western Atlantic to the rapidly growing US Navy.

The Franco-Prussian war of 1870–1871, a brief but decisive encounter, ushered in this period of fundamental change in world politics. At one stroke, it transferred the military and political hegemony of Europe from France to Germany. Michael Howard notes that ten years before the war, Prussia "had been the least of the continent's major military powers. Within a month Prussia established a military pre-eminence and a political hegemony which made the unification of Germany under her leadership a matter of course, and which only an alliance embracing nearly every major power in the world was to wrest from her half a century later."[1] Indeed, in an important sense, it set the stage for that later encounter.[2] Although modern history has seen significantly more destructive wars, few have had such far-reaching consequences.

The Franco-Prussian war is a useful case study for two reasons. First, it starkly illustrates the power of Realism as a way of understanding international politics, for it was very clearly the product of Realist motivations. It therefore provides a sober reminder that, whatever Realism's weaknesses may be as a paradigm, it is not without historical foundation and should not lightly be dismissed. Second, it demonstrates the limitations – and helps us fix the boundaries – of the justice motive as an analytical concept. The *consequences* of the Franco-Prussian war, however, kindled grievances that powerfully engaged the justice motive and conditioned later, more destructive wars. A few words about those consequences will help set the stage for our discussions of the First and Second World Wars.

THE SETTING

G.P. Gooch writes, "The fundamental cause of the Franco-German war of 1870 ... was French fear of the increase in Prussian power since the Austrian war of 1866 and the determination to prevent its further growth."[3] Historians widely accept this view;[4] indeed, the case can be made that the Franco-Prussian war more perfectly reflects the dynamic Thucydides used to explain the outbreak of the Peloponnesian war than does the Peloponnesian war itself.

With the defeat of Austria in 1866, Prussia annexed Hanover, Hesse, Nassau, Frankfurt, Holstein, and parts of Schleswig, adding $4\frac{1}{2}$ million inhabitants to its 19 million, and 25,000 square miles of territory, for an increase of some 25 percent. In addition, under the terms of the Treaty of Prague, Austria consented to a new German constitution from which she would be excluded, and she permitted Prussia to form the North German Confederation, which was to include an independent Saxony. Prussia, in short, gained unchallenged ascendancy in Germany, radically and suddenly altering the Central European order that had seemed so safe to France for so long.[5] After 1866, the common wisdom in Europe held a war between France and Prussia to be inevitable. In his memoirs, the Prussian Chancellor, Otto von

Bismarck, recalled believing that a war with France would be necessary for Germany's further national development, since France was unlikely to permit further steps toward German unification, and since the South German states – especially Bavaria – needed a war with France to convince them of its merits.[6]

For his part, Napoleon III had no enthusiasm for a war with Prussia, because of his advancing age and deteriorating health, and because of his commitment to the "principle of nationalities," which – according to his understanding – sanctioned German unification.[7] Nevertheless, in the years following 1866, he sought territorial gains to offset Prussia's own precipitate growth. He justified his claims by arguing that France was entitled to some reward for her neutrality and mediation in the Austrian war, and that they were necessary to maintain the continental balance.

As the price of his consent to Prussia's annexations, Napoleon first insisted on a return to the frontier of 1814 and the transfer to France of the Grand Duchy of Luxembourg, for which he was willing to grant compensation to the King of Holland, the nominal owner.[8] Bismarck did not object to the restoration of the frontier of 1814, but he demurred on the fate of Luxembourg, expressing doubt that adequate compensation could be found for the King of Holland. Stalling for time, Bismarck asked the French Ambassador in Berlin, Count Vincent Benedetti, to keep the negotiations under wraps. It would require considerable time and delicacy to prepare King William for the French demands, Bismarck insisted, to avoid a strongly negative reaction.

Meanwhile, hard-liners in Napoleon's government prevailed upon him to present even more extreme demands, including the restoration of territory ceded by France in 1815 in addition to portions of Bavaria and Hesse on the left bank of the Rhine and the fortifications at Mainz. Napoleon further proposed that Limburg be separated from Germany, and that Prussia relinquish the right to garrison the fortress of Luxembourg. King William flatly refused these demands on the ground that he would not concede a single German village to France, and his refusal nearly precipitated a break in Franco-Prussian relations. Bismarck exploited the situation by leaking Napoleon's demands, thus arousing the indignation of the German people, and seized the opportunity to persuade the South German states to conclude offensive and defensive alliances. Hostilities with France henceforth would constitute a *casus foederus* giving Prussia control of all of Germany's military forces.

To defuse the situation, Napoleon backed away from his demands and fired his Minister for Foreign Affairs. But he tried yet a third time to secure Prussian concessions, once again in Luxembourg, and now also in the Saar. As a sweetener, Napoleon offered Prussia an alliance, the terms of which would have permitted France to annex Belgium. Napoleon quickly dropped the demand for the Saar in the face of Prussian resistance, and Bismarck persuaded him to agree to a clause whereby France would not object to a common parliament for the North German and South German confederations; but the Prussian Chancellor dragged his feet on the negotiations for so long that war broke out before the two countries could reach an agreement, at which point, to secure international sympathy for Prussia by demonstrating the aggressiveness of French policy, Bismarck published Napoleon's proposals in the *Times of London*.[9]

Gooch is certainly correct to note that Prussia's rapid growth unsettled France. Lynn Case's exhaustive study of French public opinion shows clearly that before and during the Austro-Prussian war, French public opinion had been strongly in favor of peace and against intervention; but between June and August 1866, it underwent a major reversal. The Treaty of Prague spawned considerable belligerence. Case maintains that this change, and the ensuing demand for territorial compensation, were primarily the results of an awakening to balance of power considerations.[10] But France was not of one mind, and it would be a mistake to ignore important divisions of opinion, especially within the French political establishment. These found expression in three schools of thought. One, represented by the Orleanist Adolphe Thiers, the republican Leon Gambetta, the generals, and most of the conservative party, strongly desired to keep Germany divided and advocated an activist policy designed to accomplish that objective. The Emperor himself represented a second school, which approved of German unification in principle, but was wary of the growth of Prussian power and prestige and sought offsetting territorial compensation. A third school, represented by Jules Simon and Jules Favre, favored a peaceful policy toward Germany.[11] Émile Ollivier was one of this last school's most eloquent spokesmen. While he shared the Emperor's commitment to the principle of nationalities, Ollivier did not believe that German unification was the logical conclusion of the principle, and denied that French prestige required territorial compensation.[12] "Have not the treaties of alliance brought about the military unification of Germany, and the renewal of the Zollverein its economic unity?" Ollivier asked in November 1869. "German Unity, as against us, is complete; that which remains to be completed, political union, concerns Prussia alone, to whom it will bring more embarrassment than strength. What interest have we in

79

preventing the democrats of Würtemberg and the Ultramontanes of Bavaria from annoying Bismarck in his parliaments, when, in the day of battle, all of Germany would be united against us?"[13] It is ironic that it was Ollivier's cabinet that led the nation into war; for Ollivier did not particularly fear German unification, had no taste for expansion, and attempted to pursue a pacific foreign policy once in power.[14]

While the French political establishment remained divided on the proper policy to pursue, it was widely recognized in the years following 1866 that Franco-German relations were in a tailspin. By 1870, conditions were ripe for an outbreak of hostilities. The question remains how much of a role the justice motive played in that process. From the Prussian perspective, Napoleon's demands on German territory on the west bank of the Rhine were certainly cause for alarm, and the King's outraged refusal to cede a single German village was a clear indication that Napoleon was perceived to be making claims to which he was not entitled.[15] But Napoleon did not press these claims particularly vigorously, and there is no evidence to suggest that Bismarck, who conducted every important transaction with France between the two wars, perceived them to be unjust. After all, it was Bismarck himself who had first raised France's hopes of territorial expansion. He was anxious to secure French acquiescence in Prussia's own gains in order to avoid a Franco-Russian push for a general congress to examine the question of territorial revisions in Europe. Russia had made no secret of its opposition to the terms of the Treaty of Prague, and Bismarck knew that the treaty could not survive a European congress intact. By buying off France and isolating Russia diplomatically, Bismarck calculated, he could avoid a congress and force acquiescence to the treaty. On his own initiative, he sought out Benedetti and raised the possibility of French territorial compensation, mentioning both Bavaria and Belgium as areas into which France might expand.[16] He could hardly have perceived France's repeated attempts to cash in on his offer as groundless, even if his overture had been a ruse. The most that can be said, therefore, is that, from the Prussian perspective, suspicions that France harbored unjust intentions toward German territory contributed to an atmosphere of mistrust. But those suspicions were the consequences, not the causes, of Bismarck's policy toward France.

Napoleon, for his part, seems genuinely to have perceived an injustice in Bismarck's persistent refusal to make good on his promise of territorial compensation. Bismarck had reneged on an explicit deal.[17] This, too, contributed to the atmosphere of hostility and suspicion between the two countries. But it is important to note that the swing in

French public opinion against the Treaty of Prague *predated* Napoleon's inability to secure his promised territorial gains, and that, in any event, Napoleon's reasons for seeking territorial gains were more complex and more profound than the simple fact that Bismarck had promised them. In the absence of more pressing considerations of power and interest, it is unlikely that France would have sought them at all. While Bismarck's false promises undoubtedly contributed to the deterioration in Franco-Prussian relations, therefore, there is little reason to suspect that they were the engine behind it.[18]

THE COMING OF THE WAR

The events immediately leading to the outbreak of war are well known and widely documented. French and German diplomatic archives have long been available to historians, and the fact that many thousands of books and articles have been written on the subject – hardly any of them in the past thirty years – is a strong indication that relatively little is left to be gleaned from the threshing-room floor.

In September 1868, a revolution in Spain forced Queen Isabella II to flee the country, leaving a vacant throne.[19] It proved extraordinarily difficult for Marshal Prim, President of the Spanish Council of Ministers and the Regency's *de facto* ruler, to find a candidate both willing and qualified to occupy it. Ferdinand of Saxe-Coburg-Gotha was everyone's favorite candidate, but he flatly refused the offer. Don Antonio de Orléans, duc de Montpensier, eagerly sought the crown, but was strongly opposed by Prim and the Progressist party, who were determined not to permit the return of Bourbon rule.[20] Searches in Portugal, Savoy, and Italy failed to produce a candidate, and Prim eventually came to rest his hopes on a Prussian prince, Leopold of Hohenzollern-Sigmaringen.[21] In certain respects, Leopold was an obvious candidate: he was old enough without being too old; he was Catholic but not ultramontane; his father, Prince Karl Anton von Hohenzollern-Sigmaringen, had presided over the Prussian Council of Ministers, and his brother was a constitutional monarch in Rumania, suggesting that Leopold could be expected to have acceptably moderate liberal sympathies; he was more closely related by blood to Napoleon III than to King William of Prussia, which seemed likely to mollify the French Emperor somewhat; and his wife was a Portuguese princess, holding out the prospect that some day, his heir might unite the Iberian peninsula.[22]

Prim's deputy, Eusebio Salazar y Mazarredo, formally broached the question of Leopold's candidacy with the Hohenzollern princes in

February 1870. Twice before, in April and September 1869, the Spanish had raised the possibility with Karl Anton informally, and twice before he had expressed his reservations. Spain had an unfortunate susceptibility to revolution, and the Sigmaringen Hohenzollerns – father, mother, and son alike – had no enthusiasm for such a dangerous and potentially humiliating post. They referred the matter to King William, who objected to the proposal on essentially similar grounds; but he would neither prohibit Leopold from accepting the candidacy, nor order him to do so.[23]

Bismarck, for his part, welcomed the change of government in Spain, and saw in it opportunities to promote Prussian interests. Historians disagree on whether Bismarck had a hand in engineering the candidacy, or whether he took up the cause only after Spain had made the offer; but in any case, he and Helmuth von Moltke, Chief of the Prussian General Staff, became two of the plan's strongest advocates.[24] On March 9, Bismarck wrote a memorandum to the King presenting a detailed argument in favor of the Hohenzollern candidacy. He contended that improved relations with Spain would be an important counterweight to France; that having a Prussian prince on the throne of Spain would decrease the dangers of war with France by forcing Napoleon to divert one or two army corps from the German frontier; that the candidacy would increase the prestige of the Hohenzollern dynasty, with beneficial domestic consequences; that it would open new opportunities for trade; and that a refusal would have severe negative consequences, such as angering the Spanish and forcing them to turn to a candidate more likely to have French support, or pushing Spain toward the republican option. The King's marginal comments throughout the document show that he did not find Bismarck's arguments particularly persuasive.[25] But Karl Anton did, and through the father, Bismarck managed to persuade the son that his candidacy would be a selfless and magnanimous gesture in the service of the Prussian national interest.[26]

The King disagreed, but would not stand in the way. "It is very painful to me to be unable to give my assent joyfully in so important a matter," William wrote Karl Anton. "We will leave everything in God's hands, and some day, even if long hence when I am no longer here to see it, time will show whether we have done *His Will*."[27] Leopold wrote Prim in June that he would indeed be a candidate for the Spanish throne.[28]

Salazar conducted his negotiations with Leopold in secret, and Bismarck and Prim hoped to present France with a *fait accompli* by having the Cortès vote on the candidacy before Napoleon had a chance to voice his objections. In case the Emperor's reaction were strongly negative, this would force him to choose between taking the election in stride or intervening directly in Spain's affairs in flagrant violation of the express will of the people. Prim and Bismarck calculated that Napoleon would be likely to choose the former of the two unpleasant alternatives. But Fate stepped in to frustrate the scheme. When Salazar returned to Madrid on June 28, he discovered that, because of a telegraphic error, the Cortès had adjourned for the summer.[29]

Before long, the secret was out. Nowhere did it cause greater consternation than in France.[30] Napoleon and his ministers decided to call Prussia to account for the scheme, rather than Spain. The duc de Gramont's July 6 declaration in the Corps Législatif caused a considerable sensation in Europe:

> [W]e do not believe that respect for the rights of a neighboring people obliges us to permit a foreign power, by placing one of its princes on the throne of Charles V, to disturb to our detriment the present equilibrium in Europe and to place the interests and the honor of France in peril. This eventuality, we firmly hope, will not be realized. To prevent it, we count upon both the wisdom of the German, and the friendship of the Spanish, people. But if it should be otherwise, strong in your support, gentlemen, and in that of the nation, we should know how to do our duty without hesitation and without weakness.[31]

The thinly veiled threat of war at the end of the declaration did not fail to make an impression.

France immediately embarked upon four separate diplomatic campaigns that clearly demonstrated its commitment to defeating the Hohenzollern candidacy. French envoys pressured Spain directly to withdraw the offer; approached the Hohenzollern-Sigmaringen princes to persuade them to renounce it; began negotiations with Prussia to secure King William's cooperation in bringing about a renunciation; and lobbied Britain, Russia, Austria, and Italy to support France's position.[32]

Bismarck attempted to maintain the fiction that Leopold's candidacy was a matter between Spain and the Hohenzollern family, and no concern of either Prussia or France. "Respecting the independence of Spain and not called upon to interfere in Spanish constitutional questions," Bismarck said, "we leave the latter to the Spaniards and those who wish to become such."[33] Napoleon, quite rightly, suspected the sincerity of Bismarck's disclaimer. And while King William may have believed the official line that he had been involved in the decision only in his capacity as head of the Hohenzollern family, and not as the king of Prussia, this was a distinction too fine to be persuasive in Paris.[34] With France insisting that Prussia rescind the candidacy, and Prussia disavowing any right or power to do so, the two Great Powers seemed destined for a confrontation.

The intensity of France's reaction came as a great surprise to Karl Anton, and reawakened his deep-seated uncertainties about the wisdom of his son's candidacy.[35] Leopold himself was traveling in the Alps in early July, and could not be reached for consultation. After considerable soul-searching, Karl Anton decided on his own authority to withdraw his son's name from consideration, on the ground that a minor family matter should not be the occasion for war.[36] To make his decision known to the Emperor, he addressed the following telegram to the Spanish Ambassador to Paris on July 10:

> I think it my duty to inform you, the representative of Spain in Paris, that I have just dispatched the following telegram to Marshal Prim at Madrid:
>
> In view of the complications which my son Leopold's candidature for the throne of Spain seems to meet with and the difficult situation created for the Spanish nation by recent events placing it in a dilemma in which it cannot be guided otherwise than by its own feeling of independence, and being convinced that in such circumstances its vote could not have the sincerity and spontaneity on which my son had counted in accepting the candidature, I withdraw it in his name.[37]

That very day, Napoleon had spoken with the emissary of the King of Italy and announced that there would be no war if the candidacy were renounced in any form.[38] Karl Anton's telegram should therefore have ended the matter. But it did not. Napoleon did not consider the renunciation entirely satisfactory. On July 12 he wrote the following to Gramont:

> Upon reflecting on our conversations to-day, and upon rereading the despatch from "Père Antoine," as Cassagnac calls him, I think that we must confine ourselves to making more emphatic the despatch which you were to send to Benedetti, bringing out the following facts: (1) We have had to do with Prussia, not with Spain; (2) Prince Antony's despatch addressed to Prim is an unofficial document so far as concerns us, which no one has been formally instructed to transmit to us; (3) Prince Leopold accepted the candidacy for the throne of Spain, and it is his father who renounces it; (4) Benedetti should insist therefore, as he has orders to do, upon a categorical response wherein the King should agree for the future not to allow Prince Leopold, who has made no promise[,] to follow his brother's example and set out for Spain some fine day; (5) So long as we have no official

communication from [King William at] Ems, we are not supposed to have had any reply to our just demands; (6) So long as we have no such reply, we shall continue our armaments; (7) it is impossible, therefore, to make any announcement to the Chambers until we are more fully informed.[39]

Gramont therefore instructed Benedetti to approach the King and wrest from him a statement associating himself with Leopold's withdrawal and undertaking not to permit the Prince to renew his candidacy in the future.[40]

Benedetti's mission to Ems was a failure. In retrospect, it was clear that by insisting on pressing the matter, Napoleon and his ministers had made a grave mistake. Persuading Karl Anton to renounce his son's candidacy had been a considerable diplomatic triumph – and very nearly the cause of Bismarck's resignation. But Benedetti's further demands amounted to a public humiliation of Prussia, and King William would not consider them. He had been unwilling either to command or to forbid the candidacy when it had been a private family matter; he was all the less willing to forbid it under pressure from France. He politely but firmly informed Benedetti on the morning of July 13 that he could not give any guarantees, but he insisted that he was satisfied with Karl Anton's renunciation and that he considered the matter closed.

Benedetti hoped that he might yet persuade the King to give him something more palatable to cable back to Paris during a scheduled audience on July 14. But in the meantime, word reached Ems that Gramont had suggested to Baron von Werther, the Prussian representative in Paris, that a private letter from the King to the Emperor associating himself with the withdrawal of the candidacy might satisfy French opinion. Heinrich Abeken, the Foreign Ministry official attending the King, described it as a demand for "a personal letter of apology from the King to the Emperor, to pacify the French nation." William was incensed. "Has anyone ever heard of such insolence?" he wrote to the Queen; "I am to appear before the world as a penitent sinner, for an affair which was originated, carried on, and directed, not by me but by Prim, and he is now left out of the question altogether." He found the demand "inconceivable" and "humiliating," and Werther's decision to transmit it "very difficult to explain."[41] He refused to acknowledge receipt of the message, and resolved not to see Benedetti again. He proclaimed that all further questions would have to be addressed to Bismarck.

Abeken described the morning's events at Ems to Bismarck in a telegram that afternoon, the final phrase of which indicated that the

King had given his permission for Bismarck to relay the information to the press. With a little judicious editing, Bismarck managed to alter the tone of Abeken's telegram dramatically and make it sound as though all relations with France had been terminated abruptly. A special evening edition of the *Norddeutsche Allgemeine Zeitung*, containing nothing but Bismarck's version of the telegram in extra-large type, hit the streets at 9 p.m.[42]

If there had been any hope of avoiding war, the "Ems Telegram" soon dashed it. "We can delude ourselves no longer," Ollivier told Gramont on hearing the news; "They propose to force us into war."[43] The Council of Ministers met during the afternoon of July 14. General Le Boeuf reported that his intelligence indicated Prussia had begun to arm, and he insisted that if the decision were to be for war, time was of the essence. After a prolonged debate, the Council finally authorized him to call out the reserves.[44] The Council briefly considered proposing a European congress to consider the whole matter of the Hohenzollern candidacy; but when news arrived that Bismarck had instructed Prussia's ambassadors to transmit the text of the Ems Telegram to the capitals of Europe, it was plain that they could no longer delay the inevitable. On the morning of July 15, the Council voted unanimously for war; a formal declaration left Paris on July 17, and reached Berlin on July 19.[45] Ollivier addressed the Chamber of Deputies and to, enthusiastic applause, defended the decision as necessary "to safeguard the interests, the security, and the honor of France."[46]

FRENCH AND PRUSSIAN GOALS

The Emperor and his ministers eventually chose war with Prussia for a complex variety of reasons, but fortunately, the richness of the historical record permits us to reconstruct their motivations with some accuracy. They may be divided into strategic considerations, domestic political interests, and normative motivations. Of these, the evidence suggests the first and second to have been the most significant; the justice motive was at most a minor contributing factor.

The strategic implications of the Hohenzollern candidacy were straightforward: a Prussian prince on the throne of Spain would have complicated France's defensive position considerably. Bismarck and Moltke had been correct to estimate that the Emperor would be forced to redeploy troops from the German to the Spanish frontier to guard against incursions from the south, and, in the event of conflict with Prussia, he would have faced the prospect of a two-front war. In addition, with one of its own on the throne of Spain, Prussia might gain control of the Strait of Gibraltar, threatening France's ability to move its fleet between the Mediterranean and the Atlantic.[47] Reinforcing these considerations were the worrisome trends in relative military capability. No future time was likely to find the French military in a better position vis-à-vis Prussia to force a renunciation of the candidacy. Despite Prussia's impressive victory over the supposedly superior forces of Austria in 1866, the French perception in 1870 was that France was still, for the time being at least, Prussia's military superior. For those who believed war with Prussia to be either inevitable or desirable on its own merits, no time seemed better than the present, since the Hohenzollern candidacy provided both the threat and the opportunity.[48]

Public opinion also played an important role in the French decision for war. Most observers have noted that war fever had engulfed France by the summer of 1870, and that the Emperor and his cabinet had difficulty resisting it. The Hohenzollern candidacy would have been unpopular enough in France under any circumstances; against the backdrop of four years of frustration with Bismarck's diplomatic trickery, it proved to be the final straw.[49] It would be a mistake to think that French policy was wholly determined by public opinion, however, or even that French public opinion was unanimous in its support for belligerence. Neither the July 6 declaration nor the demand for guarantees was the direct consequence of popular pressure (although Karl Anton's renunciation of his son's candidacy had been widely derided in the French press). But the publication of the Ems Telegram so inflamed French opinion that the cabinet could not have resisted the clamor for war even if it had wanted to.[50] The government was weak and vulnerable to public pressure; if it fell, it would surely be replaced by a more belligerent one, dashing any hope of a peaceful settlement. The Right seemed bent upon using the Hohenzollern candidacy as the occasion for humiliating Prussia or precipitating war and, to prevent that, Ollivier consciously sought refuge in the approbation of public opinion, only to be swept along by it.[51] "You see in what a situation a government can sometimes find itself," Napoleon lamented to his ministers; "even if we should have no avowable cause for war, we should still be obliged to decide for it in obedience to the will of the country."[52]

But neither strategic interests nor an appeal to the exigencies of domestic politics can fully describe the reality of France's inexorable drift toward war. For Ollivier, popular pressures provided not only a convenient apologia, they also provided a justification of his actions. "A war is not legitimate," Ollivier had written in 1863, "except when it is indispensable, when it is desired by a whole nation."[53] Despite his commitment to a peaceful foreign policy and an accommodation with Prussia, Ollivier could not, in good conscience, resist the popular call for war when it reached its crescendo. Nor was he insensitive to the offenses that the Emperor and the people of France felt Prussia had inflicted upon them. It is no accident that all of France's public statements referred in one breath to the importance of defending France's interest, honor, and dignity.[54]

Did France perceive Prussian injustices? The answer to this question depends upon the definition of the term. One might argue that two of France's complaints counted as perceptions of injustice. The first and more controversial would be the perception that Prussia had failed to treat France with the respect to which she was entitled. There can be no doubting the sincerity of this perception, which resonated through the government and public alike. Bismarck's duplicity on the matter of territorial compensation was the first offense. "Bismarck," Napoleon exclaimed after the Luxembourg affair, "has striven to dupe me; an Emperor of the French must not let himself be duped."[55] The Hohenzollern candidacy itself was not offensive to France, but the manner in which it was pursued – particularly the attempt at a *fait accompli* and Bismarck's transparent fiction that Prussia had nothing to do with it – amounted to "a serious affront."[56] Even Karl Anton's renunciation of his son's candidacy was offensive, because it strongly implied that France was infringing Spanish independence.[57] The Ems Telegram was the last in a long line of abuses. It badly insulted the Emperor's envoy, and by implication, the Emperor himself. European society in the nineteenth century placed a high value on the currency of decorum, and Prussia's offenses were too injurious to go unavenged – all the more so given the fact that the legitimacy of the empire relied heavily upon the dignity of the emperor. Prussia had violated an important system of rules, and the public clamor for war was at least in part a result of sensitivity to that violation.

I hesitate to admit this perception as evidence of the justice motive as I have defined it, however. In the first place, we might well ask whether an offended sense of dignity or honor is in all relevant respects fully equivalent to a perception of injustice. Here, I am using the term "justice" with reference to the satisfaction of claims to entitlements. While this definition will bear the inclusion of an offended sense of dignity and honor, so long as a particular code of international etiquette is taken to define entitlements, the norms of etiquette do not define material benefits, and there is reason to doubt whether violations of etiquette are phenomenologically equivalent to, say, violations of property rights or due process. Moreover, the offense taken at violations of international etiquette is closely related to other passions and attitudes that may be entirely independent of perceptions of injustice. These include patriotism, nationalism, and chauvinism. An article by M. Lavedan in the *Correspondant* that appeared immediately after the July 6 declaration provides a useful illustration:

> For too long a time our courtesy has been at the service of other people's aggrandizement: we are relieved to find that we have become Frenchmen once more! Like the Chamber, all patriotic hearts salute the declaration of the powers that be, rejoicing to recognize therein the old-time accent of the national pride![58]

A perception of injustice is not the same thing as an expression of national pride, and while perceived violations of dignity and honor may occupy the middle ground between the two on the spectrum of human experiences, the safest course methodologically is to restrict our operative concept to instances of perceived violations of tangible entitlements, thereby avoiding a debate about the perils of conceptual stretching.[59]

If we therefore set aside the popular perception that Prussia had not treated France with due respect, we are nevertheless left with one genuine French perception of injustice. Prussia's method of pursuing the Hohenzollern candidacy violated an international norm forbidding Great Powers from placing members of their reigning houses on a foreign throne without the prior consent of all the other Great Powers. The principle was first recognized in 1815, and reaffirmed in 1830 (Greece), 1831 (Belgium), 1848 (Spain), 1859 (Tuscany), and 1862 (Greece).[60] "Wherein does one offend or humiliate a sovereign," Ollivier asked, in reference to King William of Prussia, "by asking him to submit to a general rule of international law to which everybody before him has submitted, and which he himself helped to establish?"[61] Napoleon, in essence, had been entitled to a veto over the Hohenzollern candidacy, and Prussia had attempted to push the candidacy through without giving him a chance to exercise it. This was no doubt deliberate; had he been given the chance to exercise his veto, he clearly would have done so.

It is largely on this ground that France rested its appeal to the justice of its complaint. Reason of state, and Prussia's apparent bad faith, would have been fully adequate justifications for objecting to the Hohenzollern candidacy; the additional unnecessary appeal to the violation of France's entitlements suggests that the perception of injustice was a sincere one. Ollivier expressed his moral outrage more clearly than anyone else. Given his unquestioned reputation for integrity and a strong sense of honor, it is difficult to discredit his testimony when he insists that he felt Prussia had treated France unjustly.[62]

This does not, of course, absolve Ollivier and his cabinet – or even more importantly, the Emperor, who bore ultimate responsibility for French policy – from all censure and blame. Both the July 6 declaration and the demand for guarantees, for example, were, if not exactly reckless, at least imprudent. Nor does it imply that this perception of injustice was a more powerful determinant of French policy than strategic and political concerns. There is little reason to suppose that it was. But this perception was at least a reinforcing proximate cause of the French decision to go to war, and by shedding light on the intensity of French passions, it helps explain how France could enthusiastically embark upon a disastrous campaign ill-prepared, overconfident, and without allies.[63] A belief in the justice of one's cause can powerfully distort one's perceptions of reality.

What of Prussian motivations? The only Prussian perception of injustice that can be identified from the available evidence is of the kind bracketed off above – namely, an offended sense of dignity and honor. Gramont's declaration of July 6 was widely interpreted in Prussia as an insult and provocation, because it called Prussia to account for the Hohenzollern candidacy and strongly implied ill intent.[64] The King also found France's demands profoundly offensive, particularly the call for what he interpreted to be a letter of apology. But since these perceptions are not for present purposes being counted as evidence of an inflamed sense of justice – and since, in any case, they must be understood in light of the fact that Bismarck was doing his best to engineer a war deliberately by inflaming these perceptions – they must be discounted.[65]

Since Bismarck sought to engineer the war, his motivations must largely be understood as the proximate causes of Prussia's participation in the war. In his memoirs, Bismarck claimed that he became convinced after Sadowa that war with France was inevitable.[66] He recalled that in the fall of 1869 he provided the following analysis to Richard von Friesen, Saxon Minister of State:

> The Emperor Napoleon is becoming more and more insecure in his position at home; he has lost his power of clear decision and is making all kinds of mistakes in his domestic policy. Disaffection is spreading among the French people and the influence of his opponents growing more dangerous to him day by day. Soon he will have nothing left but to distract the attention of a nation from its internal affairs by a foreign war and to try by a victorious campaign to satisfy the vanity of the French who have not yet been able to forget his

90

inglorious and weak attitude in 1866. Thereby he can consolidate anew his own position and that of his dynasty. For the North German Confederation, too, a war with France is not only unavoidable but also needed, for, so long as the present unstable situation continues in France, a viable and secure development of our own affairs is unthinkable.[67]

To the Russian Minister in Berlin, Pavel Petrovich Oubril, Bismarck said in 1869 that he intended to "provoke France" to attack Germany for the purpose of arousing German national feeling. "Nothing would be easier," Bismarck said in his report of the conversation. "Troop concentrations, national manifestations in Germany and Italy, [incidents connected with] our relations with Belgium, even Spain, would offer us opportunity for diversions which might bring about our entrance into the fray without giving it the appearance of an aggressive war cabinet."[68]

There is considerable debate on the question of whether Bismarck expected the Hohenzollern candidacy to provide the appropriate spark. He did not create the candidacy, and appears only to have actively promoted it after February 1870.[69] Some historians believe that Bismarck thought Napoleon would give way because of his age, his lack of desire for conflict, and the poor preparations of the French military; others believe Bismarck was either willing to run the risk of war over the candidacy, or that he actively courted it.[70] Whatever the case may be, by July, Bismarck seems to have decided to provoke a war, and may even have resolved to resign should he fail to do so.[71] He did not fail, and he boasted of the accomplishment the rest of his life. Bismarck's reasons for wanting to provoke a war with France were complex; in his memoirs, he described them in terms of honor, prestige, and the cause of German unification.[72] He did not refer to the perceived demands of justice, and there is no evidence of any in his machinations.

Apart from Bismarck, the only significant player on the Prussian side was King William himself. The King was strongly inclined toward peace; he had no interest in the Hohenzollern candidacy; he was delighted when it fell through; and he had no intention of provoking France.[73] Nor did he particularly approve of Bismarck's behavior during the whole affair. When he saw a copy of the Ems Telegram as it appeared in the *Norddeutsche Allgemeine Zeitung*, he proclaimed, visibly anguished, "That is war."[74] But he did not disavow his Chancellor, nor run the risk of losing him. In his own unwitting way, the King, too, had been a pawn in Bismarck's game.

RETROSPECT AND PROSPECT

"From what cause did the war arise?" Ollivier asked in his memoir; "From the Hohenzollern candidacy in the first place, and then from Bismarck's disclosure of the King's refusal to receive our Ambassador. No Hohenzollern candidacy, no war. Even after the Hohenzollern candidacy, no disclosure of the King's refusal, no war."[75] Perhaps; but Ollivier ignores the fact that the Hohenzollern candidacy itself constituted a threat to the peace only because of more basic and more ominous dynamics in the Franco-Prussian relationship. He also ignores the fact that it is very difficult to avoid a war that powerful figures and forces on both sides are doing their best to precipitate. Lord accuses both governments of "criminally playing with fire;"[76] but this is to misunderstand the situation. Bismarck was not merely playing with fire; he was actively engaged in arson.

If one were seeking the single best theoretical perspective from which to explain the outbreak of the Franco-Prussian war, one would have to look closely at power transition theory.[77] There was in France's policy an unmistakable drive to prevent Prussia from threatening France's position as the continent's dominant military power, and there was in Bismarck's policy an equally unmistakable impulse to do exactly that. The justice motive played some role both in setting the stage for war and in shaping French behavior immediately before it; but it would appear to have been ancillary to more powerful strategic and political forces.

Victorious on the battlefield, Prussia was able to dictate most of the terms of the peace settlement.[78] The crucial consequence of the war, for present purposes, was the transfer of Alsace and parts of Lorraine from France to Germany. Bismarck had insisted that, since France had attacked Prussia, she must be chastised "for her arrogance and her eternal love of aggression threatening peace, and must be made incapable of resisting us, if permanent peace is to be obtained."[79] This was not the first time a victor had attempted to prevent a future war by imposing a harsh peace, nor would it be the last; and there was rather more wishful thinking than historical wisdom in the proposition, for the loss of Alsace-Lorraine would do more than anything else to ensure that France and Germany would be completely unable to live in peace.

Bismarck, of course, cannot have believed that the peace settlement was *just*, because he himself had been the aggressor, in the sense that he had engineered the French declaration of war. Nor could he find an easy moral justification for the annexations in his vision of a unified

Germany. The creation of a German nation state was hardly consistent with the annexation of territory whose population did not conceive of itself as German.[80] Of course, the territories ceded by France in the Treaty of Frankfurt had, at various times long past, been parts of Germanic kingdoms. It was not difficult, therefore, for many Germans to justify the annexations in irredentist terms. Bismarck does not appear to have done so, however. His motivations in securing the annexations were primarily strategic and political. Possession of the territories, he believed, would facilitate the defense of the new German Reich and would feed the nationalist sentiment upon which its success ultimately depended.[81]

Others in Prussia reconciled themselves to the annexations by appealing to a variety of considerations. The Crown Prince, for example, expressed the belief that it was "a simple impossibility" not to keep Alsace and Lorraine because of German public opinion, military necessity, and the fact that Prussia had been the aggrieved party.[82] One of the most influential apologists for the annexation was the militant nationalist, Heinrich von Treitschke, whose views received a wide audience. Treitschke brewed a confused but heady mixture of irredentism, right of conquest, chauvinistic nationalism, and xenophobia:

> The sense of justice to Germany demands the lessening of France. Every intelligent man sees that that military nation cannot be forgiven, even for the economic sacrifices of the war, on the payment of the heaviest indemnity in money. Why was it that, before the declaration of the war, the anxious cry rang through Alsace and Lorraine, "The dice are to be thrown to settle the destiny of our provinces," before a single German newspaper had demanded the restitution of the plunder? Because the awakened conscience of the people felt what penalty would have to be paid in the interests of justice by the disturber of the peace of nations ...
>
> In view of our obligation to secure the peace of the world, who will venture to object that the people of Alsace and Lorraine do not want to belong to us? The doctrine of the right of all the branches of the German race to decide on their own destinies, the plausible solution of demagogues without a fatherland, shiver to pieces in presence of the sacred necessity of these great days. These territories are ours by the right of the sword, and we shall dispose of them in virtue of a higher right – the right of the German nation which will not permit its lost children to remain strangers to the German empire. We Germans, who know Germany and France, know better than these unfortunates themselves what is good for the people of Alsace, who have remained under the misleading influence of their French connection outside the sympathies of the new Germany. Against their will we

shall restore them to their true selves ... Are we to believe that [a] rich millennium of German history has been utterly destroyed by two centuries of French dominion?[83]

For their part, the inhabitants of Alsace and Lorraine had no interest in becoming Germans. In the Assemblée Nationale on February 17, 1871, the deputies from Bas-Rhin, Haut-Rhin, la Moselle, and la Meurthe read an impassioned declaration on the non-alienation of Alsace and Lorraine, in which they proclaimed that France had as little right to forsake the territories as Germany had to demand them.[84] Here was the ultimate expression, as against Treitschke, of the doctrine of self-determination of peoples. These two conceptions of justice were, quite simply, opposite and irreconcilable.

France, of course, could have mounted a defense of its historical claim to Alsace-Lorraine fully the equal of Germany's; but, in 1871, the realities of the situation did not permit much in the way of philosophical debate. With evident emotion, Adolphe Thiers, the head of the new government charged with negotiating the terms of the peace, chastised the representatives of Alsace and Lorraine. "Have the courage of your convictions," he cried. "Either war or peace. This is serious. There's no room for childishness when it's a matter either of the fate of two very important provinces or the fate of the country as a whole."[85] The provinces would be sacrificed for the sake of peace, but the wound left in the French psyche would not heal. Michael Howard writes:

> [T]he cession of Alsace-Lorraine was a sacrifice to which France was never to reconcile herself. A century earlier the transfer of such provinces to the sovereignty of a victorious prince had been commonplace. A century later it would have been completed by the brutal surgery of transfer of populations. To the nineteenth century, with its growing belief in national self-determination and plebiscitary voting, the process, carried out in defiance of the wishes of the populations, seemed an open flouting of that public law on whose development Europe was beginning to pride itself.[86]

Ollivier loudly proclaimed France's "incontestable right to reconquer our dear Alsace, brutally wrested from us by conquest, and annexed to the foreigner without her consent."[87] It would be nearly half a century before she had an opportunity to exercise that right, in the largest armed struggle the world had yet seen; and the clash of claims over Alsace and Lorraine would play no small role in bringing that struggle about.

4 WORLD WAR I

Table 4.1. *World War I*

Role of justice motive in conditioning conflict	Role of justice motive as proximate cause (by participant)	
Very strong	Austria-Hungary	Very weak
	Serbia	Very weak
	Russia	Moderate
	Germany	Moderate
	France	Very weak
	Britain	Very strong

General wars involving all or most of the Great Powers are clearly the most important of all wars to understand, both because of their raw cataclysmic destructiveness and their profound social, political, and economic implications. Not surprisingly, more effort has been spent attempting to understand the First and Second World Wars than any other political events in recent times.

If the justice motive has been overlooked by political scientists in the study of the origins of these wars, it has most certainly not escaped the notice of historians. It is interesting to note, however, that the justice motive seems to have played a more important role in *conditioning* than in *triggering* conflict in both cases. Mainstream Realist motivations of self-preservation and self-aggrandizement undoubtedly played an important role in each; but a proper appreciation of the roles played by normative considerations is essential both for an accurate understanding of the unfolding of events, and for insight into the poignancy of Realist concerns. That is to say, one cannot fully understand *why* Realist motivations were relevant and operative – and why the patterns of enmity took the configurations they did – without appreciating the *moral* force of more basic underlying concerns. The justice motive may not have been a sufficient condition for the outbreak of the two world wars, but a strong case can be made that it was a necessary condition for both.

In 1898, Bismarck told the German shipping magnate Albert Ballin, "I shall not see the World War, but you will; and it will start in the Near East."[1] In February 1913, German Chancellor Theobald von Bethmann Hollweg did Bismarck one better. In a letter to the Austrian Foreign Minister, he accurately predicted the very chain of events that would lead to the conflagration a year later: Austria-Hungary would move against Serbia; Russia would come to Serbia's aid against Austria; Germany would rush to support her ally Austria; France would support Russia; and a general war would then engulf Europe.[2] Bethmann Hollweg was expressing his fears, not his expectations; but the nature of the powder keg on which Europe sat was a mystery to no one.[3]

Given the complexity of the international situation prior to 1914, it is particularly important to begin our analysis of events by recalling the distinction between *motivations* (spurs to action – grievances, wants, desires) and other circumstantial factors – beliefs, attitudes, institutional constraints – that affect *calculations* and that may correctly, in their own way, be thought of as "causes" (or, better, catalysts) of the war. There is no doubt that crisis management was complicated in July 1914 by such factors as the rigidity of war plans, the inflexibility of mobilization schedules, and the crisis instability caused by the "cult of the offensive."[4] There can be no question that the main actors involved, particularly in Germany, grossly misperceived events and miscalculated in crucial ways.[5] Some of the key players, such as Kaiser William II, appear to have performed poorly in the crisis partly as the result of mental instability; others, such as Bethmann Hollweg, because of a more pedestrian incompetence.[6] Matters were only made worse by the pervasive attitude that a European war was inevitable, which, as we shall later see, diminished key players' risk aversion and all but made war unavoidable once events began to take on a momentum of their own.[7] However important these circumstantial factors may have been to the outbreak of war, they should not be permitted to obscure the facts that in the absence of specific *motives* to action, *constraints* on action must be entirely innocuous, and that motivations can influence the nature of the constraints under which decision-makers operate, and the degree of their importance.

One last caveat is in order before I proceed to examine the motivations that conditioned the conflict: namely, that I am not here concerned with the question of war guilt. Many of those who have written on World War I have had as their primary concern either the

96

condemnation or exoneration of the Central Powers. Of course, whether one lays the blame for the war at the feet of Germany and Austria, or with Britain, France, and Russia, will depend in important respects upon what one believes about their aims and intentions prior to the outbreak of war. Thus the question of war guilt cannot be answered without consideration of motivational issues. But the opposite is not the case; here I am not concerned with passing judgment on the motivations that led to conflict, only with elucidating them.[8]

It is not common for students of World War I to distinguish motivations from circumstantial factors when attempting to explain its ultimate causes. Thus, for example, of Sidney Bradshaw Fay's five "underlying causes of the war" (the system of secret alliances, militarism, nationalism, economic imperialism, and the newspaper press), only two – nationalism and economic imperialism – can straightforwardly be analyzed in motivational terms.[9] Fay's list is both eclectic and somewhat arbitrary, attributes shared with most others'. But a broad survey of writings on the ultimate causes of the war shows that three motivational issues repeatedly stand out: Germany's drive for world power and the reactions it elicited in the other capitals of Europe; France's desire to recover her lost provinces of Alsace and Lorraine; and the aspirations of the Slav populations of the Balkans for self-determination. Together, these three factors both created the pressures that led to war, and contributed heavily to the circumstances that made it virtually impossible to avoid. To what extent are these representative of the justice motive, and how important was each in conditioning the conflict?

THE RISE OF GERMANY

In his Inaugural Lecture at Freiburg University in May 1895, Max Weber proclaimed, "We must understand that the unification of Germany was a youthful folly, which the nation committed in its declining days and which would have been better dispensed with because of its expense, if it should be the conclusion and not the starting point for a German *Weltmachpolitik*."[10] Germany's impressive economic growth in the years since unification had certainly placed it among the first tier of world powers; it was only natural that she would seek to play a role on the world stage commensurate with her new status.[11] It was also only natural for the other Great Powers to view Germany's aspirations with apprehension and suspicion. That suspicion was not entirely unfounded; in 1892, the Kaiser privately expressed to his friend and advisor Count Eulenburg that the "fundamental principle" of his policy would be "a sort of Napoleonic supremacy ... in the peaceful sense."[12]

Germany's quest for world power took a variety of forms and had a variety of causes. A common strain of German nationalism was Social Darwinist in nature. This view held that Germany faced a choice between growing and dying. As Hans Delbrück wrote in the November 26, 1899 edition of *Die Preussischen Jahrbücher*, "We want to be a world power and pursue colonial policy in the grand manner. That is certain. Here there can be no step backward. The entire future of our people among the great nations depends on it."[13] This conviction fed the belief in the inevitability of war, and counted among its proponents many prominent friends and associates of the German leadership, such as Kurt Riezler, an influential advisor to Bethmann Hollweg, who subscribed to the general thesis that world domination was the supreme aim of all nations.[14]

Closely associated with Social Darwinism in pre-war Germany was militant racism. In foreign affairs, this was primarily directed against the Slavs. The Kaiser himself was a well-known Slavophobe;[15] so was Chief of the General Staff Helmuth von Moltke, nephew of the architect of Germany's victory over France in 1871.[16] Racial hatreds had at least some effect on German policy and contributed something to the outbreak of war, if only because they contributed to the strength and vehemence of Germany's support for Austria's hard-line policy against the Serbs in 1914.[17] Organizations such as the Pan-German League, which agitated for an activist, expansionist foreign policy grounded in the doctrine of racial supremacy, perpetuated and institutionalized these attitudes.[18] Social Darwinism and Pan-Germanism did not influence all of the architects of German policy, however. Indeed, for the most part, the German élite derided the Pan-German League. Key officials attached little importance to the organization or to its work, and dismissed it as a relatively minor factor in a rising nationalist tide.[19] Many prominent Germans advocated keeping to the course charted by Bismarck, who had no interest in imperialist ventures and sought to cultivate self-sufficiency by concentrating on the orderly consolidation and development of the German homeland.[20]

Germany's *Weltpolitik* began with Bülow's arrival at the Foreign Office, Admiral Tirpitz's naval program, and the seizure of Kiaochow in 1897.[21] For Bülow, the goal of *Weltpolitik* was the peaceful development of industry, trade, and shipping through the expansion of Germany's activities and possessions overseas. Its success depended upon Germany's position as a European Great Power, not vice versa; in no way did he conceive it as an abandonment of Germany's continental power base.[22] Since Germany's welfare did not crucially depend upon overseas trade and a captive imperial market, *Weltpolitik* under Bülow "remained a policy of limited risks and limited aims," always ambiguously formulated, never consistently pursued.[23]

Perhaps the most ominous feature of *Weltpolitik*, at least as far as Germany's imperial rivals were concerned, was her precipitate naval build-up.[24] The German High Seas Fleet was the creation of Grand Admiral Alfred von Tirpitz, strongly supported by the Kaiser. Tirpitz had been heavily influenced by Alfred Thayer Mahan's *The Influence of Sea Power on History*, an elaborate economic argument for a national merchant marine and a navy to protect it. Tirpitz wrote that Germany had a vital interest in a seagoing fleet to protect her commercial and colonial interests, and insisted that England, the world's foremost commercial and naval power, was thus her natural enemy.[25] Bülow never quite understood the connection between Tirpitz's logic and his policies; if Germany truly needed a fleet to protect her commerce and colonial interests, Bülow correctly surmised, then what she needed was a fleet of fast, long-range cruisers, not heavy, short-range battle-ships.[26] Tirpitz rationalized his Dreadnoughts by means of a dubious theory whereby a sufficiently powerful naval force would tie up a much larger British fleet, weaken British control of the sea lanes, and jeopardize her naval superiority in the event of war.[27] But the war itself would demonstrate Bülow's wisdom and Tirpitz's folly: while German cruisers enjoyed considerable success on the open seas, the Royal Navy effectively bottled up the prized High Seas Fleet for most of the conflict. It is difficult not to agree with David Kaiser that, for Tirpitz, and perhaps for the Kaiser as well, the navy was actually an end in itself, not a means.[28]

Germany's naval build-up, coupled with her increasingly assertive behavior on the continent and overseas, succeeded in arousing British suspicions.[29] It became increasingly difficult to reconcile Germany's pacific rhetoric with her outward behavior. In 1907, Assistant Under-Secretary of State Sir Eyre Crowe wrote that Germany was either actively seeking hegemony in Europe and the world, or that her policy was the product of vague and confused statesmanship.[30] At times, Foreign Secretary Sir Edward Grey seemed inclined toward the former view; in 1908, he wrote the British Ambassador to France that Germany "has reached that dangerous point of strength which makes her itch to dominate."[31] But, at other times, Grey shared the view expressed by Prime Minister Asquith, that Germany's *Weltpolitik* was exactly what Bülow insisted it was – an attempt merely to claim for Germany the advantages enjoyed by the other Great Powers.[32] As such, it was not considered unwarranted, and British policy was to accept an expansion of German power and influence in the world provided it neither directly threatened British vital interests nor threatened to destroy the European equilibrium.[33] Thus, in the middle of the Agadir crisis of 1911, Grey made the following remarkable confession to Sir Francis Bertie: "If one looks at the map of Africa and considers the large amount coloured British and coloured French, much larger each of them than all that Germany has, it is obvious that neither France nor we can put more of our own colour on the map without Germany getting some substantial addition to her sphere."[34] In 1913, Grey thought it desirable that Germany assume control of some of Portugal's colonies, and that same year Grey and the German Ambassador to London, Prince Karl Lichnowsky, initialled an agreement amicably adjusting their spheres of interest in Africa.[35]

The one claim that an expanding Germany advanced as a claim of entitlement, therefore, even her "natural enemy" was inclined to accept and accommodate, demonstrating that German expansion *per se* was not an intractable problem. But the high-handed style of German foreign policy, the Kaiser's penchant for bluster, and Germany's undeniable economic and military ascendance, were quite naturally cause for alarm in the other capitals of Europe and helped bring about the Anglo-French *entente* of 1904, and the Anglo-Russian *entente* of 1907, which were interpreted in Germany as evidence of hostile intent. Thus, ironically, the most significant effect of Germany's rise was the fear of "encirclement" it caused in Germany itself.[36] During Lloyd George's visit to Berlin in 1908, Bethmann Hollweg bitterly complained about the iron ring being drawn around Germany.[37] Field Marshal Count Alfred von Schlieffen, in a 1909 article entitled, "Der Krieg in der Gegenwart," wrote that Germany was surrounded by implacable enemies – Britain envious of her economic achievements, France thirsting to redeem Alsace-Lorraine, Slav Russia resentful of the Teutons, treacherous Italy eager to lunge at Austria-Hungary – who awaited only a propitious occasion to strike. "An endeavour is afoot to bring all these Powers together for a concentrated attack on the Central Powers," Schlieffen wrote. "At the given moment, the drawbridges are to be let down, the doors are to be opened and the million-strong armies let loose, ravaging and destroying, across the Vosges, the Meuse, the Niemen, the Bug and even the Isonzo and the Tyrolean Alps. The Danger seems gigantic." Both the Kaiser and Moltke read the piece with admiration.[38] When Lord Haldane informed Lichnowsky on December 3, 1912, that England was inclined to be pacific but that she could hardly stand aside in a general

European war which might be triggered by an Austrian move against Serbia, the Kaiser commented that this was a "welcome clarification on which we must found our policy. We must make military agreements with Bulgaria and Turkey, Roumania and Japan. Any available Power is good enough to help us. For Germany it is a question of life or death."[39]

To what extent, then, was Germany's rise to world power status a contributing factor to the outbreak of World War I, and to what degree was the justice motive operative in it? Without doubt it was a source of unease, and the armaments race associated with it was a cause of considerable fear.[40] The other Powers' apprehensions of German growth stimulated balancing behavior and facilitated the consolidation of the Triple Entente; this in turn confirmed German fears of encirclement, reinforced the conviction that Germany would one day face a fight for her very survival, led German statesmen to toy with the idea of preventive war, and markedly diminished their risk-aversion in the July crisis itself.[41] We see here Realist psychology at work. But there is some ambiguity about whether the motivations behind Germany's *weltpolitik* can be fully described in the language of Realism. To the extent that German policy was motivated by a sincere desire merely to enjoy the entitlements appertaining to Great Power status, it was the product of the justice motive; to the extent that it was the product of economic drives, Social Darwinism, Pan-Germanism, racism, or any other of the handful of unsavory creeds in general currency in the late nineteenth and early twentieth centuries, it was not. It is difficult to disentangle the strengths of the various contributing motivations, and therefore it seems prudent to assume for present purposes that considerations of justice played a minimal role.

It is important to note, however, that *Weltpolitik* and the other Powers' reactions to it did not establish sufficient conditions for the outbreak of war. *Weltpolitik* was not a program of conquest and domination. As Bethmann Hollweg proclaimed in his own post-war apology, "The supposition that Germany let loose war out of mere lust of world power is so silly that a historian would only take it seriously in the entire absence of any other explanations at all."[42] German policy was certainly expansionist, but not hegemonic. Before 1914, German imperialism was minor compared to Britain's and France's, and was clearly more aggressive in style than in substance.[43] The Kaiser and his post-Bismarck chancellors all talked a good game, but their weaknesses and timidity were widely acknowledged. By 1914, Europe had quite successfully adjusted itself to a larger German role. Three facts in particular strongly suggest that *Weltpolitik* and the Great Powers'

101

reactions to it played at most a subsidiary role in conditioning the conflict: first, Germany and her "natural enemy" enjoyed a considerable period of détente before the outbreak of war; second, Britain was slow and reluctant to intervene once war broke out; and third, the issues that provided the spark which set Europe aflame had nothing to do with German expansion. This was not a war either for domination or containment. Indeed, Germany's *weltpolitische angst*, her fears of encirclement, her flirtation with preventive war, and her desperate gamble in support of Austria in 1914 – all of which undoubtedly played a key role in the outbreak of the war – cannot be understood simply in terms of Germany's precipitate rise and the motivations underlying *Weltpolitik*. Other, more important factors were at work.

ALSACE-LORRAINE

The French desire to recover the provinces of Alsace and Lorraine annexed by Germany at the conclusion of the Franco-Prussian war is considered by many historians to have been one of the major underlying causes of the First World War.[44] The primary rationale for the annexation had originally been strategic, but the official German line in the decades after 1870 held that the territories belonged to Germany by right. German writers advanced a variety of arguments to defend that claim, appealing variously to common kinship, common language, common race, and historical possession. Each such attempt elicited an outpouring of passionate, often vituperative condemnation in France.[45] Every German attempt to reconcile Alsace and Lorraine to its destiny within the *Reich*, therefore, constituted a reopening of the wound that the annexation had left in the French national soul. The price Germany paid for Alsace-Lorraine was the unrelenting hostility of France, recognition of which prompted Sidney Fay to conclude that the annexation "was worse than a crime, it was a blunder."[46]

The nineteenth century had shown that European states were clearly capable of forgiving and forgetting. A short six years passed between Sadowa and the formation of the Three Emperors' League. Another six separated Fashoda and the *Entente Cordiale*. But the issue between France and Germany was altogether different. As Raymond Poincaré put it, France "could forget Sedan, she could forget a military disaster; she could not forget the wrong done to the liberty of her nationals."[47] As far as France was concerned, the German possession of Alsace and Lorraine was the determining factor in her relations with Berlin, and every German overture to improve those relations ran into the same insuperable obstacle.[48] The best that could be arranged between the two countries was a cold, civil politeness. As the French envoy to Berlin put it in 1884,

> I have never said a word to the German Chancellor which could encourage him in any illusions as to us ... To work for peace for the present and to reserve the future, such is the program I have always had before my eyes ... At the beginning of our discussions I specified with Count Hatzfeldt and with the Chancellor himself that neither Alsace nor Lorraine should ever be a question between us, that here was a domain reserved on both sides where we ought to be forbidden to penetrate, because we could never meet in good agreement on it. I shall never speak of Alsace, I have said; and on your part, if you sincerely desire an understanding with us on various points, avoid drawing the sword over our wound, because the French nation will not remain in control of its feelings.[49]

More than once in the decades after 1870, the Alsace-Lorraine question threatened to develop into war. French moves to increase the size of the army triggered the War Crisis of 1875, for example, because Germany thought they heralded a war of revenge.[50] The Boulanger affair in the late 1880s led directly to an expansion of the German army and talk of preventive war against French *revanchisme*.[51] Germany always held out the hope that the passage of time would heal the French wound, but this hope was constantly rebuffed. In 1913, for example, the German Ambassador, Baron von Schoen, spoke to the French Premier, M. Barthou, about the desirability of reducing popular tensions on both sides of the border. "Return Alsace-Lorraine to us," Barthou shot back, "and we shall then be the best friends in the world," whereupon Schoen "promptly dropped the subject."[52] In 1914, J.J. Ruedorffer concluded, "Formally, this question is settled. France finally renounced the two provinces in the Peace of Frankfort. Nevertheless, this dead question, which not once since the peace of Frankfort has been the object of any conversations or negotiations whatever between German and French statesmen, indirectly dominates the central problem of French policy – the relations with Germany – and through this the whole policy of France. France has thus far not forgotten, and will not forget so long as it exists."[53] The Kaiser himself declared to the King of Belgium that war with France was inevitable because she was obstinately bent on recovering the provinces and was simply unwilling to come to an understanding with Germany. Moltke agreed.[54]

There is no evidence to suggest, however, that at any time between 1870 and 1914, the French actively sought a war to recover the provinces. If they had been so inclined, a simple balance-of-power calculation would have forced upon them the obvious conclusion that war with Germany was hopeless. Moreover, although *revanche* was extremely popular, few in France relished the prospect of the cost in blood and tears that would have to be paid to recover the provinces in the context of a wider European war. But although France did not seek war, she was prepared to accept it if it came, and knew what she wanted from it. As Poincaré put it, "Interest, as much as reason, required us to work for the maintenance of peace. But we told ourselves that, if it ever happened that we were troubled by Germany, we would then have a great duty to discharge, that at any cost we would press war unto victory and victory unto the liberation of the annexed provinces. In these sentiments, which were those of the immense majority of the French, there was nothing incompatible."[55] The more astute Germans – including the Ambassador to Paris, Baron von Schoen – understood this. In February 1914, Schoen reported that "The wound of 1871 burns in every French heart; but nobody is inclined to risk his bones or those of his sons for Alsace-Lorraine – unless a constellation appears to open up a good chance of success. That however becomes ever more improbable. The hope of reaching the goal by Russia's aid has vanished long ago ... The idea is steadily growing that France's salvation is to be sought in better relations with Germany."[56] But, in general, German leaders tended to take France's cries of *revanche* quite literally – or, at any rate, were inclined not to risk taking them too lightly – and conducted foreign policy accordingly.[57] In such an atmosphere, true détente was impossible. Both sides felt obliged to strengthen their militaries, and constantly eyed each other with suspicion. After Agadir, cries for *revanche* grew louder and Franco-German hostility began to rise.[58] Works such as Maringer's *Force au Droit: Le Problème d'Alsace-Lorraine* – a call to arms – sold widely and exacerbated German fears.[59]

Of course, the Alsace-Lorraine question was not the immediate cause of World War I. But it nevertheless played a key role in setting the stage for the rapid escalation of a wholly unrelated conflict in the Balkans to a general European conflagration, in the first place by contributing to the conclusion of the Franco-Russian alliance.[60] General Nikolai Nikolayevich Obruchev, Chief of the Russian General Staff, met his French counterpart, General Raoul le Mouton de Bois-deffre, at Dordogne in July 1891, to explore the bases of a possible military accord. When the discussion turned to the objectives each of the states would pursue in the event of a European war, Obruchev noted Russia's interest in Galicia and in securing a favorable arrangement governing access to the Turkish straits. He then inquired what

France's aims might be. Boisdeffre answered without any hesitation, "the recovery of Alsace and Lorraine."[61] "From the start of the Dual Alliance," writes Christopher Andrew, "France had made very clear to her ally the importance she attached to the return of the lost provinces. Although the terms of the military convention of 1893–1894 appeared to commit France to general mobilization even in the event of Austria's involvement in a Balkan war which did not directly threaten Russia, President Faure warned the Russian Government in 1895 that France would support Russia in a Balkan war only if such a war offered her the opportunity to recover Alsace-Lorraine: *'ce jour-là tout est possible.'*"[62]

The Alsace-Lorraine question also had an interesting and important effect on German military planning, which would prove to be such an obstacle to successful crisis management in the summer of 1914. Until 1888, the German plan for a two-front war called for offensive operations in the east and defensive operations in the west, where the terrain was considered better suited for defense, and where French actions might easily be anticipated owing to their desire to retake the annexed provinces. The elder Moltke was willing if necessary to retreat all the way to the Rhine in order to concentrate most of his forces against Russia. Schlieffen, his successor, also anticipated a French thrust into Alsace and Lorraine; but he thought Moltke's plan ill-conceived. Schlieffen believed that a two-front war was more likely to break out in the west than in the east, given the intractability of French irredentism and the significantly greater hostility of Franco-German than Russo-German relations. Moreover, France could bring forces to the battlefield more quickly than could Russia. He therefore sought to capitalize on the predictability of French irredentism. The Schlieffen plan called for the bulk of the German army to be thrown against France in a quick, decisive blow while smaller screening forces in the east held the slower-mobilizing and slower-moving Russian forces at bay. The victorious veterans of the western campaign would then shift east to meet them. He deliberately left the Alsace-Lorraine flank thinly protected, calculating that French enthusiasm for liberating the lost provinces would tempt them into a "sack" between Metz and the Vosges while the heavy German right would swing around through Belgium to crush them from the rear.[63] Events in 1914 did not unfold as Schlieffen expected; the immediate threat of war came from Russia, not from France. Germany was left saddled with an inflexible and highly destabilizing operational plan that all but guaranteed a westward escalation of the Balkan conflict once Russia became involved.[64] Thus did the annexation of Alsace-Lorraine come back to haunt Germany. "For the sake of this military advantage," wrote Karl Kautsky shortly after the war, with evident irony, "Germany had immeasurably impaired her international political position, had raised an eternal feud between herself and France, driven the latter into the arms of Russia, roused the armament rivalry and the constant danger of war in Europe, and laid the seeds of the unfavourable position in which the German Empire entered the war in 1914."[65]

SERBIAN NATIONALISM

Without doubt, the most important motivation conditioning the outbreak of World War I was the Serbian drive for self-determination and the intractable conflict it generated with Austria-Hungary.[66] The essence of the problem was an almost total lack of fit in the Balkans between ethnic groups and borders. The principle of nationalities, which held that individual peoples were entitled to control their own affairs and destinies, was strongly rooted in the attitudes of the former European subjects of the Ottoman Empire, and served as a constant source of conflict because of the multiplicity of ethnic groups in the region and a tangled web of overlapping territorial claims. In particular, it constituted a serious threat to the legitimacy and authority of Austria-Hungary, a multicultural polity founded on the conflicting principle of historical dynastic right.

The nationalities problem in Austria-Hungary had always posed a threat to the unity and stability of the Empire. Since the formation of the Dual Monarchy and Turkey's European decline, however, the situation had become acute. The Magyars enjoyed a privileged position in the Austro-Hungarian Empire, and they exploited it by ruthlessly suppressing the Slavs and stubbornly resisting any move toward federalism or trialism that would dilute their influence. Thus they unwittingly encouraged Austria's Slav populations to look to Serbia for their eventual redemption.

Serbia counted among its ethnic kin the Serbs of Bosnia-Herzegovina, Dalmatia, and Hungary, and – somewhat ironically, in view of the recent violent dissolution of Yugoslavia – the Croats of Croatia, and the Slovenes. The principle of self-determination of peoples, therefore, could not be furthered without the dissolution of the Austro-Hungarian Empire. In its Pan-Serb form, self-determination would have detached vast areas in the south from the Hapsburg Monarchy; in its broader Pan-Slav form, it would have reduced the Monarchy to a second-tier power confined to the Danube basin.[67]

Serbia had been the leading Balkan power in the late Middle Ages under the Nemania dynasty, in the reign of Dušan the Great (1331–1355). The Turks defeated Serbia at the battle of Kosovo on June 15, 1389, and occupied Serb territory in 1459, ruthlessly suppressing the native inhabitants, who succeeded in retaining only limited village autonomy. But the worst repression did not succeed in stamping out the flames of Serbian nationalism, kept alive largely by the national Orthodox Church. For much of their time under Ottoman rule, Serbs pinned their hopes for redemption on Catholic Austria, the only power then capable of playing the role; but religious ties, and Russia's frequent wars with the Turks, ultimately persuaded the Serbs to look to St. Petersburg for protection and liberation and, by the nineteenth century, Russia had become the acknowledged champion both of Slavism and Orthodoxy in Serbia.[68]

Although Russia came to be regarded as Serbia's patron and protector, proximity made Austria her virtual lord and master once Turkish rule had effectively come to an end and Serbia had gained nominal independence.[69] From the Treaty of Berlin in 1878 until the assassination of King Alexander Obrenović in 1903, Austria kept Serbia in a condition of tutelage through her influence over the sovereign. But the coronation of Peter Karageorgević on June 15, 1903, heralded an ominous change. Peter was a man of remarkable gifts and wide-ranging interests; among other things, he translated John Stuart Mill's *On Liberty* into his native tongue. At once relations with Austria began to deteriorate. Albertini writes, "Around him revolved the hopes of the Jugoslav youth who regarded him as predestined to make Serbia a Piedmont which would rally round itself all the Southern Slavs of Austria-Hungary. When, in June 1903, Peter passed through Vienna on his way to Belgrade, he was greeted at the station by the University Students' Organizations of the Jugoslav subjects of the Emperor Francis Joseph with the cry: 'Long live the King of Croatia.'"[70]

Control of the government passed into the hands of the Radical Party, which was openly pro-Russian and anti-Austrian. The central pillar of the Radical platform was the concept of a Greater Serbian fatherland. The most powerful figure in Serbian politics was Nikola Pašić, who became Minister of Foreign Affairs on February 9, 1904, and served as Prime Minister on four separate occasions before the outbreak of war. Pašić's general policy was to ease Serbia out of the Austrian orbit and make it, as he said in 1905, "the Piedmont of Serbism."[71]

With the handwriting on the wall, Austria sought to shore up her southern flank and build ramparts against further Serbian growth. In 1908, Foreign Minister Count Aehrenthal moved to annex Bosnia and

Herzegovina, which had been under Austrian protection since the Treaty of Berlin, triggering a major diplomatic crisis. Aehrenthal saw the annexation as part of a larger scheme to secure safe frontiers. "Such safe frontiers we shall not obtain," he wrote in a private memorandum, "unless we decide to grip the evil by the root and to make an end of Great-Serbian dreams."[72] To make the annexation more palatable to European opinion, Austria at the same time evacuated its troops from the Sanjak of Novibazar, a narrow strip of land separating Serbia and Montenegro; but this concession failed to prevent an explosion of Serbian outrage.

The ties between Serbia and Bosnia-Herzegovina were strong and direct. The earliest known Serbian document, the letter of Ban Kulin, had been written in Bosnia. Vuk Karadžić and the Croats adopted as their literary language the dialect in which the letter had been written. Many of the most prominent Serbian nationalists were Bosnian in origin. And Bosnia had best preserved some of Serbia's national traditions during Turkish rule. "For the Serbs," writes Albertini, "Bosnia-Herzegovina was what the Moscow region is for Russia, the region in which their national feeling was centred. In 1870 Kallay had written, 'It is the sensitive spot of all political minded Serbs, the centre round which revolve their aspirations and their hopes.'" Serbians therefore reacted to the Austrian annexation much the same way the French reacted to the German annexation of Alsace-Lorraine.[73] Momčilo Ninčić, at one time Minister of Foreign Affairs, wrote that "there was a feeling that irreparable harm had been done, that we were on the eve of national disaster, and that Austria-Hungary, the implacable enemy of Serbia and the Serb race, was preparing to destroy every symptom of resistance in a people who wanted to live independent and free." Many in Serbia, including Ninčić, believed that the annexation was only a prelude to a decisive move against Serbia itself.[74]

In response to the annexation, Serbia mobilized 120,000 troops. Pašić himself spoke of war.[75] The Austrian Minister in Belgrade reported to Vienna that "Serbia was like a madhouse and that every Serb wished to die for his country."[76] Serbian nationalists founded the *Narodna Odbrana* (National Defense), "a society for the protection and further-ance of national interests in the annexed provinces."[77] Originally organized for special operations behind enemy lines in the event of war with Austria-Hungary, the *Narodna Odbrana* transformed itself into a "cultural society" after circumstances forced Serbia to acquiesce in the annexation and to promise an end to anti-Austrian agitation.[78] She did so only under pressure from Russia, who was too weak from the disastrous Japanese campaign and the 1905 revolution to offer any support, and only after it became clear that the other capitals of Europe were unwilling to risk a general conflict over the issue. But her submission was only a temporary one. On the eve of Serbia's capitulation, Foreign Minister Milovanović made the following remarks to some of his friends in a Belgrade café:

> Our situation is very difficult. We must give way. Europe demands peace. The justice of our claims is recognized, yet nobody will help us to attain them. But Europe too is in a bad way. Violence will receive its penalty. Europe will not remain long as it is to-day. In my journey around the capitals I have seen how much is rotten. How the *débâcle* will occur nobody knows. Perhaps a social revolution – in Russia first. I may be wrong. But of one thing I am sure. Bosnia and Herzegovina will not remain long in the possession of Austria. It may be two, three, or several years. But I stake my head that by 1920 Bosnia will be free.[79]

Irredentist agitation grew much stronger after the annexation, and the ultra-secret *Uyedinyenye Ili Smrt* (Union or Death), better known colloquially as the "Black Hand," took up the militant pursuit of Serbian self-determination. Article One of the organization's statutes proclaimed, "This organization has been created with the object of realizing the national ideal: the union of all Serbs." In Bosnia, the Black Hand flourished. It never found itself in need of willing, even fanatical members. The organization started on excellent terms with the Serbian government; but the harmony broke down rather quickly when the Serbian military, many of whose leaders were members, broke with the politicians on tactical issues.[80]

In the years following the Austrian annexation, the Serbian government tried repeatedly to improve relations with her more powerful neighbor. In August 1909, for example, Milovanović traveled to Vienna in search of a détente; but, in the course of his overture, he gave notice that Serbia might at some point occupy the Sanjak, contiguous territory both ethnically and religiously.[81] From the Austrian perspective, this would have been a disaster, bringing Serbia and Montenegro into direct contact and making possible a united Slav state with access to the sea. Such a state might prove irresistibly attractive to Austria's Southern Slav populations.[82] If this was Serbia's idea of a détente, Vienna saw little hope for a *modus vivendi*. Decisive action seemed increasingly necessary to deal with the Greater Serbian threat. In July 1909, Austrian Chief of General Staff Conrad von Hötzendorf openly advocated absorbing Serbia to forestall the future danger.[83]

In the Balkan wars of 1912–1913, some of Austria's gravest fears were nearly realized. Serbia's remarkable military successes stimulated wild enthusiasm both within Serbia and among the Slavs of the Dual

Monarchy. She emerged with nearly double the territory and a population almost half again as large as when she entered.[84] Serbia occupied the Sanjak, and sought recognition for her claim to an Adriatic port, which she considered essential to her economic independence.[85] Berchtold ingeniously argued against it on the ground that, since the territory in question was Albanian, granting Serbia access to the sea would violate the very principle of ethnic autonomy proclaimed by the Serbs themselves.[86] Austria reaped the fruit of her intransigence when an international compromise worked out in December 1912 called for the creation of an independent and neutral Albanian state.

Thwarted in her quest for a port, Serbia had to console herself with promises of free access to the sea through foreign territory. Most disappointing of all throughout the affair was Russia's lukewarm support. Although the Tsar's Ambassador in Belgrade, the enthusiastic Slavophile N.H. de Hartwig, had actively worked to incite Pan-Serbism during the Balkan wars, Foreign Minister S.D. Sazonov attempted to exert a moderating influence on Serbian policy. He wired Belgrade, "Neither we nor our friends can allow the Servian Government to decide whether there shall be a European war. We believe that the best way to avoid complications is a prompt declaration that Servia will bow to the advice of the Entente Powers in regard to access to the sea. In this way she would avert the danger of an Austrian ultimatum."[87] But Sazonov bought Serbian moderation at the price of exorbitant assurances that Russia would actively help Serbia realize her national goals when the time was ripe. This was a moral commitment that Serbia did not hesitate to invoke in 1914.[88]

The most ominous result of the Balkan wars was a dramatic rise in Austrian fatalism. Instead of taking comfort in the effectiveness of international cooperation in holding Serbia in check, Vienna began to wonder how long it could count on the uncertain processes of Great Power diplomacy to contain an increasingly powerful idea. As Berchtold wrote to Berlin, "The essence of the antagonism between us and Servia is that Servian policy, since the Radical party took office (and under foreign influence adopted the Great Servian idea as its governing political principle), aims at the union of all Serbs in the Serb state and therewith the separation of Austrian territories peopled by Serbs. This antagonism is permanent, for the realisation of the Great Servian idea, which would procure the coveted access to the sea, is no longer the programme of a party but the ideal of the whole people."[89]

Berchtold's apprehensions were perfectly reasonable. Colonel Dragutin Dimitrević, one of the leaders of the Black Hand, had written in 1912, "The war between Serbia and Austria ... is inevitable. If Serbia wants to live in honour, she can only do this by war. This war is determined by our obligation to our traditions and the world of culture. This war derives from the duty of our race which will not permit itself to be assimilated. This war must bring about the eternal freedom of Serbia, of the South Slavs, of the Balkan peoples. Our whole race must stand together to halt the onslaught of these aliens from the north."[90] Pašić himself told the Greek representative to the Bucharest Peace Conference in 1913, "The first round is won; now we must prepare the second against Austria."[91] Many in Vienna preferred to fight the inevitable war sooner rather than later, and were prepared to run the risk of a general European war in order to deal decisively with the Serbian problem once and for all. Conrad, for example, is said to have proposed a war with Serbia twenty-five times between January 1, 1913, and June 1, 1914.[92]

The Austro-Serbian conflict might well have run its course without disturbing the peace of Europe were it not for the fact that there were limits to the other Powers' willingness and ability to stand aside. During his visit to Potsdam in November 1910, the Tsar expressed his desire to maintain peace in the Balkans and to help localize any conflict that might break out, but he noted that Russia's historic mission was to liberate the Christian peoples of the Balkans and that he could not be expected to ignore it.[93] A popular view in Russia was that expressed by V.A. Maklakov in 1908: the future unification of all Serbs "must come naturally," although its attainment "will cost much blood and tears."[94] The combination of Russia's strategic interests in the Balkans and her moral bond to Serbia would prove irresistible in 1914, and despite the Tsar's sincere and passionate desire to avoid a general European war, he would be unable to stand aside and watch Austrian troops shell Belgrade.

For its part, Germany could not stand aside and watch Russia crush Austria, her only remaining ally. On November 28, 1912, the German Foreign Secretary spoke to the issue in the Reichstag. "It has often been said that Germany does not need to fight for the Albanian or Adriatic interests of Austria or for the harbour of Durazzo," said Gottlieb von Jagow. "But that is not the point ... If Austria, whatever the reason, is forced to fight for her position as a Great Power, we must stand at her side in order that we do not afterwards have to fight alone."[95]

Two clashing conceptions of justice, therefore, which threatened the very existence of a waning European Great Power, generated a conflict that would ultimately touch off a war between the continent's two military blocs. As *Matin* put it on July 26, 1914, "Russia cannot allow Austria to achieve the ruin of the Slavic nations of which she has declared herself the protector ... The day that Russia enters on the scene, the clauses of the Triple Alliance will come into play, Germany will have to come to the aid of her ally, and then it will be the turn of France to fulfill her engagements."[96] Thus the Serb dream of self-determination and the danger it posed to the existence of Austria-Hungary connected up the various other components that together constituted the fuse, the detonator, and the powder keg on which the entire continent sat in 1914.

SARAJEVO AND AFTER

The event that ignited the powder keg was the assassination of Austrian Archduke Francis Ferdinand in Sarajevo on June 28, 1914. The man who pulled the trigger, Gavrilo Princip, proudly declared at his trial, "I killed him, and I am not sorry, for he was an enemy of the Slavs."[97] In this statement can be found both considerable irony and the key to the intractability of the nationalities problem. The Archduke was a well-known opponent of Austro-Hungarian dualism who favored a federal system that would have enhanced the power, influence, and welfare of the Empire's downtrodden and dispossessed, including the Slavs; but he was considered an *enemy* of the Slavs because he sought a solution to the South Slav problem *within* the Dual Monarchy.[98]

There was no hard evidence at the time that the Serbian government was involved in the plot on the Archduke's life, or even that it had been aware of it.[99] But the attack was the work of the Black Hand, and the threads of the conspiracy could be traced to Belgrade. Both the government and public opinion in Vienna held Serbia morally if not materially responsible for the crime, because Serbia was the source of much of the nationalist propaganda that incited violence in Austrian territory.[100] Austria had had enough. She decided to end Greater Serbian agitation once and for all. It was upon this motivation that Austria-Hungary acted when it took the fateful decision to deliver an ultimatum to Serbia on July 23 and to declare war five days later.[101]

There are certain situations in which it can be easily imagined that the justice motive is present and active, but that, for a variety of reasons, one cannot gauge its contribution to the unfolding of events. Austria's reaction to Sarajevo provides a case in point. The language in which the subject was treated in both public and official circles – it was held to be a *crime* or an *outrage* for which Serbia was *responsible* and had to be *punished* – is the language of moral indignation and a thirst for justice. But it is so unmistakably clear that Austrians perceived Pan-

Serbism and Pan-Slavism to be a threat to the very survival and integrity of Austria-Hungary as a state that it is difficult to resist the conclusion that the self-preservation motive would have been fully sufficient in and of itself, irrespective of whatever reinforcement the justice motive may have supplied, to determine Austria's course of action. The situation is similar with both Serbia and France. With respect to these three players, although we can take note of the evidence concerning the presence and operation of the justice motive, we are forced to discount its role so as not to risk overstating the case. The matter is somewhat different for Germany, Russia, and Britain, where the available evidence renders possible rough discriminations between the roles of various motivations.

Count Hoyos traveled to Potsdam and, on July 5, succeeded in securing Germany's unconditional support for action against Serbia. The Austro-Hungarian Council of Ministers met on July 7 to consider its options. Berchtold argued for prompt decisive action. Austria's situation would only deteriorate, Berchtold maintained, because a failure to act decisively would be interpreted as evidence of weakness by the Southern Slavs and by Romanians within the Monarchy, aggravating the nationalities problem even further. Moreover, he was not convinced that Russia was yet in a position to intervene. The Hungarian Premier, Count Tisza, objected to the idea of a surprise attack because of the international hostility it would arouse, and advocated presenting Serbia with exacting demands that she could nonetheless accept. If Serbia complied, Austria would win a stunning diplomatic victory and deal a severe blow to Serbian prestige; if it came to war, Austria could so reduce Serbia in size that she would no longer pose a serious threat. This Russia might permit, although Tisza was convinced that under no circumstances would the Tsar tolerate the complete annihilation of Serbia. In any case, Tisza argued, annexing Serbian territory would only exacerbate the nationalities problem within the Dual Monarchy itself. The Council essentially followed Tisza's advice and agreed to present Serbia with stiff demands; all but Tisza hoped and expected that they would ultimately lead to war.[102]

Throughout Austria's deliberations, self-preservation was the dominant theme. Assured of German support, satisfied that Russian intervention might somehow be forestalled, convinced that a showdown with Serbia was inevitable in any case, and persuaded that the present time was favorable, Austria's leaders chose a course of action that all but committed them to war.[103] To the outside world, Austria-Hungary justified the ultimatum by appeal to the Serbian threat. "If the struggle with Servia is forced upon us," stated the dossier distributed to the capitals of Europe, "it will not be for territorial gain but simply a means of self-defence and self-preservation." Austria justified the action to Russia by appeal to the necessity of defending her existence as a Great Power, and hence the very existence of the European equilibrium.[104] The *injustice* either of the assassination or of Pan-Serb claims did not figure heavily in Austria-Hungary's internal deliberations, or in her diplomatic representations.

Whether Serbia's response to Austria's ultimatum and subsequent declaration of war were motivated by considerations of justice cannot be determined, simply because of a lack of evidence. The most straight-forward explanation of Serbia's behavior is that the country was fighting for its life. Few would question that the Austrian ultimatum was perceived to be *unjust*, since it made claims on Serbia that were inconsistent with her sovereign rights and which Austria could not justify by appeal to her own. Anticipating the *démarche*, Pašić tele-graphed Serbia's missions abroad on July 19 with the message, "We can never comply with demands which may be directed against the dignity of Serbia, and which would be inacceptable [*sic*] to any country which respects and maintains its independence" – clearly indicating that the prospect filled him with at least some measure of moral outrage.[105] But when the ultimatum came, it fooled no one in the Serbian government: it meant war.[106] Serbia ordered general mobili-zation and moved the seat of government from Belgrade to Niš *before* replying.[107] With the survival of the nation in peril, the relevant actors did not take the trouble to document their subjective reactions to the *démarche* or to reflect on the grounds of their response.

Nevertheless, Serbia made an extraordinary effort to accommodate Austria-Hungary, conceding most points completely, accepting several with relatively minor modifications, and rejecting only one outright: the demand to allow Austrian officials to participate in a judicial enquiry into the conspiracy on Serbian territory. The response was so unexpectedly conciliatory that many in Europe believed that although it fell short of the unconditional acceptance that Austria demanded, it undercut any justification for war.[108] Austria was not satisfied, however, and immediately broke off relations.

Faced with a direct threat to the country's very existence, Pašić sought support from Russia. The self-preservation motive may be sufficient to explain his actions, but Serbia's approach to St. Petersburg is instructive because it was based upon a direct appeal to the justice of Serbia's cause and Russia's moral obligation to come to Serbia's aid.[109] Belgrade must have believed, therefore, that *moral* appeals would be more efficacious than an appeal to Russian self-interest.

Russia responded to Serbia's appeals for support, though her reasons for doing so are somewhat difficult to disentangle. The available documentary record makes it abundantly clear that Russia was determined not to permit the destruction of Serbia, but it offers very few clues as to *why*.[110] Most observers believe that Russia responded both on the basis of her attachments and obligations to Serbia, and in furtherance of her own national interests.[111] The available evidence suggests that this conclusion is sound, but it is difficult to know which motivation was the more important on balance. That Russia's narrow self-interests were engaged can hardly be disputed. Her influence in the Balkans was a source of prestige in its own right, and therefore an emblem of her status as a Great Power; but not less importantly, it provided protection against other Powers' encroachments on the Turkish straits. At the same time, she had obligations, as the ancient patron and protector of the Slavs and Orthodox, not to desert her clients when they were threatened with domination or conquest by a foreign Power. As I have already noted, when her own state of weakness had forced her to accept the Austrian annexation of Bosnia and Herzegovina in 1908 and to compel Serbia to acquiesce, she only succeeded in salvaging her position in the eyes of the Serbs by re-affirming her commitment to their cause, thereby accepting the obligations on the basis of which Serbia made its appeal for support in 1914.

Occasionally, Russia's interests and obligations in the region had conflicted, for example, during the First Balkan War, when Serbia and Bulgaria, fighting together to redeem their brethren under Ottoman rule, threatened to so weaken Turkey that she would be unable to maintain control of the straits, possibly triggering a wider European war. But while a Turkish victory would have been less of a threat to the general peace and to Russia's interest in preserving Turkish control of the straits, Russian public opinion would have forced the Tsar to come to the rescue of the Slav states if the tide of battle turned against them. Fortunately, Serbia and Bulgaria did well, but not *too* well, and the Tsar did not have to make an awkward choice between his interests and his obligations.[112]

In 1914, Russian interests and obligations were approximately – but not entirely – coincident, and different personalities appear to have ascribed different weights to each. Foreign Minister S.D. Sazonov was undoubtedly one of the more important players. His contemporaries thought of him as a realist, an evaluation based very largely on statements such as those he made to the German Ambassador to Russia, Count Pourtalès, on July 24: "First Serbia would be gobbled up, then will come Bulgaria's turn; and then we shall have [Austria] on the Black Sea."[113] That same day he had a conversation with the Austrian Ambassador, Count Szápáry, who reported to Berchtold that Sazonov "never once mentioned Russia, Slavdom, orthodoxy; but he was continually referring to England, France, Europe and the impression, which our step would make in these parts of the world and else-where."[114] But statements such as these do not constitute denials of the importance of considerations of justice, nor are they unambiguous testimony to an overriding concern with Russian national interests. Indeed, it seems odd that "he never once mentioned Russia" to Szápáry if he considered Russian interests decisive. On occasion, when Sazonov *did* mention Russia, he would justify his support of Serbia in terms of Russia's "historic mission."[115] Moreover, he displayed his sensitivity to normative concerns in other, sometimes very subtle ways: for example, when he complained bitterly to Pourtalès on July 25 that "Austria could not be both accuser and judge in her own case;"[116] when he criticized Austria on moral grounds for not extending the time limit of her ultimatum;[117] and when he advised Serbia not to resist Austrian military action and to put her faith in the other Powers' sense of justice.[118] Sazonov, in short, was fully capable of reacting to events on both prudential and moral grounds, and when his sense of justice and his concern with national interests were both engaged, he sought guidance from each. Thus, in his memoirs, he objected that the Central Powers were attempting to dominate the Balkan States "without regard to the rights of those states, or the vital interests of Russia," suggesting that he deemed both considerations weighty.[119]

For his part, the Tsar left little testimony about his own motivations. Like Sazonov, he expressed concern for the fragile balance of power in the Balkans and Russia's interest in maintaining it.[120] At the same time, he was a devout and somewhat romantic figure who took his obli-gations as defender of the Orthodox and Slav causes very seriously. He was also extremely eager to preserve the peace.[121] Sazonov's memo-randum of the day for July 30 noted the Tsar's "firm desire to avoid war at all costs, the horrors of which filled him with repulsion."[122] His fear of war helps explain his unwillingness to consent to the military's demands for an early and complete mobilization, and his desperate last-minute appeals to the Kaiser to restrain his Austrian ally.[123] But in the end, the Tsar opted to stand up for Serbia, even at the risk of a general European conflict.

The Tsar's weakness and indecision left him vulnerable to argument and pressure. Some of his advisors, such as Minister of Agriculture A.V. Krivoshein, urged him to act on the basis of Russia's "vital

interests," while others, such as the Chairman of the Council of Ministers, I.L. Goremykin, appealed primarily to Russia's "duty" to Serbia.[124]
He was powerfully affected by public opinion as well. While the
Petersburgsky Kuryer trumpeted Russia's vital interest to defend the
Slav nations on the grounds that they blocked Austria's move toward
the straits, the main current of Russian thought was reflected in
journals such as *Novoye Vremya*, the most authoritative and most
influential newspaper in Russia, which strongly supported Slav
nationalism.[125] News of the bombardment of Belgrade generated
"intense" excitement in St. Petersburg and an outpouring of support
for the Serbian cause, because it touched a deeply rooted nerve.[126] In
the face of a two-front assault from those immediately around him and
from the public at large, the Tsar's resistance to war eventually wore
down. As France's Acting Foreign Minister put it, "Russian opinion
makes it clear that it is both politically and morally impossible for
Russia to allow Serbia to be crushed."[127] The world might well have
avoided a catastrophe if Germany and Austria had understood this; for
they calculated that Russia was not yet strong enough to stand up to
the Triple Alliance and would not risk a European war over Serbia.[128]
While it is true that they appreciated Russia's interest in the region,
they calculated that Russia had an even greater interest in avoiding a
major war. This calculation was probably correct as far as it went. But
what they failed to appreciate was that they had run up against
Russia's interests *and her obligations*, the combination of which was
simply irresistible.[129]

Germany's motivations in the period leading up to the outbreak of
war have been the subject of considerable debate, and are in many
respects the most difficult to fathom. One source of puzzlement is the
fact that German policy in the Balkans had previously been quite
cautious and restrained. On November 9, 1912, for example, William
informed his Foreign Office that under no circumstances would he
fight against France and Russia for the sake of Albania and Durazzo;
and, in March 1914, he annotated a report from his Minister in Belgrade expressing his view that the union of Serbia and Montenegro "is
definitely not to be prevented, and if Vienna were to attempt this, it
will be creating a great stupidity and conjuring up the danger of a war
with the Slavs, which would leave us quite cold."[130]

William's reaction to the assassination of Francis Ferdinand,
however, was profound. To Bethmann Hollweg he remarked, "The
cowardly and execrable crime to which his Imperial Highness the Heir
Apparent, my dear friend, and his consort have fallen victims, moves
me to the depths of my soul."[131] It appears to have confirmed him in

117

the belief that Austria had to deal with Serbia decisively once and for all, a conclusion toward which he and other prominent Germans had been drifting for some time.[132]

It is possible to discern three motivations behind the Kaiser's unqualified support for an Austrian move against Serbia: the desire to punish Serbia for her role in the assassination;[133] the urge to strike a blow at Slavdom;[134] and the impulse to secure his ally's power and prestige.[135] The first is unambiguously a manifestation of the justice motive, and the second can be so construed if one interprets doctrines of racial superiority as defining proper distributions of power and authority. The third, of course, served an important German interest, since the other European powers were either actively allied against the *Reich* or on cordial terms with those who were. But the Austrian alliance also placed upon Germany certain duties and obligations that in their own right exercised some influence on German policy. As Moltke wrote to Bethmann Hollweg on July 29, "Germany does not want to bring about this frightful war. But the German Government knows that it would be violating in ominous fashion the deep-rooted feelings of fidelity which are among the most beautiful traits of German character and would be setting itself against all the sentiments of the nation, if it did not come to the assistance of its ally at a moment which was to be decisive of the latter's existence."[136]

German support for Austria-Hungary, therefore, was evidently the product of both normative and prudential considerations. The key question is, how important was each? The overall tenor of the available evidence suggests that the justice motive was at its strongest immediately after Sarajevo and in the early part of July, when moral indignation against Serbia was at its peak. The dominant theme running through this period was the insistence that Austria was an aggrieved party, and that she was entitled to deal with Serbia accordingly.[137] As the crisis developed, however, and as the situation began to look increasingly threatening, German statesmen became increasingly preoccupied with the danger of war and the normative issues began to fade into the background. Normative considerations significantly influenced the course of German policy in the summer of 1914, but basic considerations of power and interest came to the fore in an ultimately futile attempt at crisis management.[138] On balance, therefore, the justice motive appears to have played only a moderate role in determining German behavior during the crisis itself.

It is important to emphasize that German policy was powerfully shaped by misperceptions, miscalculations, misjudgments, fears and anxieties. When the edifice of Germany's policy finally crumbled in ruins around its architects, they invoked the old paranoid fears of encirclement to explain their inability to avoid catastrophe.[139] Whether or not they sincerely believed the encirclement myth, it was clear to all by early August that Germany had somehow managed to find herself forced to choose between leaving her only ally in the lurch and carrying out the Schlieffen Plan, taking her chances in a European war. What had started out being at least partly (and perhaps largely) a question of justice evolved into a question of survival.[140]

Although France had no active quarrel with Germany in the summer of 1914, circumstances dragged the two nations into war: Germany's commitment to Austria; Russia's commitment to Serbia; France's commitment to Russia; and Germany's commitment to the Schlieffen Plan. Events transpired so quickly and constituted such a grave danger that French statesmen had little room for maneuver and could not even afford the time to reflect on the motivations that drove their actions. French policy was reactive and instinctive. It was, if anything, over-determined, and can easily be explained by a simple appeal to the requirements of self-defense. The justice motive may well have been present and active, but, as in the Serbian case, its presence is not required to make sense of events. We must therefore discount its role.

French policy, as Poincaré put it, was determined by two dichotomies: the desire to prevent a conflict but to be prepared if one broke out; and the need to preserve the alliance with Russia while at the same time moderating her behavior.[141] No stable equilibrium existed as between these various goals, and the requirements of national security forced France to opt for preparing over preventing, and preserving over moderating. Thus, on July 30, Paléologue communicated to the Russian government France's determination to meet the obligations of the alliance, bolstering the Tsar's confidence in his decision to stand up to Austria, and undercutting a crucial calculation on which Germany's attempts at crisis management had been based: namely, that Russia would back down.[142] To avoid being caught off guard militarily, the French armed forces closely monitored and kept pace with German military preparations, generating considerable escalatory pressure in an already unstable crisis situation.[143] Throughout the day on July 31, General Joffre received alarming reports of German military preparations.[144] At 8 a.m. on August 1, he addressed a note to the Minister of War demanding an immediate mobilization, on the ground that Germany stood to gain a considerable advantage if France delayed. The cabinet granted his demand without protest or discussion and, before dinner time, France and Germany had begun to mobilize.[145]

Would considerations of justice have brought France into war under less crisis-unstable conditions? The argument can be made. Poincaré insisted after the war that he and Viviani were of one mind on France's intention to honor the Franco-Russian alliance if the need arose, suggesting that they held the fulfillment of obligations to be a consideration of some weight.[146] Considerations of justice also appear to have inflamed the public mind, presumably generating pressures for war. Recalling his journey from Dunkerque to Paris on July 29, for example, Poincaré gave witness to the outpouring of popular moral outrage at the wrong done to Serbia, which he interpreted as an empathetic response to violence against the right of peoples.[147] On July 31, Bethmann Hollweg instructed Schoen to ask Viviani whether France would remain neutral in the case of war with Russia, evidently not expecting a positive reply, but further instructing, if one were forthcoming, to demand that France turn over the fortresses of Toul and Verdun as a pledge.[148] It is difficult to fathom the state of mind of a man who could suppose that such a request could actually be accepted, and one can only suppose that an outraged reaction to the injustice of the demand would have immediately wrecked any prospect of compliance and may well have hastened war.[149]

It is interesting to note the contrasting terms in which Poincaré and Viviani represented the situation to Parliament on August 4, after war had broken out. While Poincaré's very first complaint was that the German violation of French territory was "an insolent defiance of the law of nations," he spoke predominantly of honor and security. But he did not fail to mention that "For more than forty years the French, in sincere love of peace, have buried at the bottom of their heart the desire for legitimate reparation." Viviani's speech in the Chamber of Deputies was a moral frontal assault, emphasizing the "hateful injustice" of the German attack.[150] Questions of justice, therefore, were evidently on their minds.

It would be surprising to find otherwise. *Matin* offered this analysis on August 1:

> We well know that never has war offered itself under aspects more favorable to us. When Austria has thrown her best troops against the Near East, when Russia has just built up her army anew, when the three-years term of service has just come into full force in France, when Germany will have to bear almost alone the brunt of the attack from the *Entente* armies and navies, in truth if we are inclined to war, if we were not deeply attracted to the cause of civilization and peace, would we not feel the strong temptation of war? Nevertheless it is not for this war that we shall be held responsible by posterity. If it comes, we shall meet it with high hopes. We are convinced that it will bring us the reparations which are our due.[151]

G.P. Gooch writes that France "had no desire for war, and took no steps to precipitate it. Nor, on the other hand, did she seriously endeavour to keep the sword of her ally in its scabbard. She had never abandoned the hope of recovering the Rhine provinces and, for that reason, could not be included among the 'satiated Powers' who at any given moment are the most effective champions of peace."[152] If the justice motive is not needed to explain the French action in 1914, therefore, it certainly cannot be said to have had a calming influence, either. Quite the reverse, if the chant to which French soldiers marched through the streets of Paris on the way to the front is any indication:

> C'est l'Alsace et la Lorraine,
> C'est l'Alsace qu'il nous faut,
> Oh, Oh, Oh, OH![153]

What can be said of British motivations? The evidence strongly suggests that the justice motive – triggered by the German violation of Belgian neutrality – was primarily responsible for Britain's entry into the war on the side of France and Russia in early August 1914. This does not mean that if Britain had initially decided to sit on the sidelines, she would not later have joined the fray if her interests so dictated; but it does mean that her actual entry into war at *this* particular time was more strongly influenced by normative than by prudential considerations. As the Prime Minister put it, "It is useless to speculate upon what might have happened had Germany avoided the fatal blunder of the Belgian violation. But it is certain that the British nation could not then have gone into war with a united front."[154]

There were those in Britain, of course, who believed that British interests required supporting France against Germany, and this group included the single most important figure in the episode, Foreign Secretary Sir Edward Grey, a champion of balance-of-power policies.[155] In 1906, at the time of the conference of Algeciras, Grey wrote an internal memorandum analyzing Britain's geopolitical goals, which stated, "I think we ought in our own minds to face the question now, whether we can keep out of war if war breaks out between France and Germany. The more I review the situation the more it appears to me that we cannot, without losing our good name and our friends and wrecking our policy and position in the world."[156] In the summer of 1914, Grey believed that British interests demanded supporting France against Germany. He agreed emphatically with Sir Eyre Crowe, who surmised that "Should the war come, and England stands aside, one of two things must happen: (a) Either Germany and Austria win, crush

France, and humiliate Russia. With the French fleet gone, Germany in occupation of the Channel, with the willing or unwilling co-operation of Holland and Belgium, what will be the position of a friendless England? (b) Or France and Russia win. What would then be their attitude towards England? What about England and the Mediterranean?"[157]

Grey was acutely aware, however, that Parliament, the Cabinet, and the country at large strongly opposed intervention.[158] The question of Irish Home Rule and the threat it posed of civil unrest consumed the country, and the prevailing attitude – even in the Cabinet – was that Britain should not become involved in a European war unless she herself were attacked.[159] The Cabinet strongly opposed even a precautionary mobilization.[160] While the *Times* advocated intervention on the basis of the "law of self-preservation," the Liberal press and the business community lobbied heavily against it.[161] The strength of opposition to war all but paralyzed the government, and Grey was completely unable to respond to France's requests for assurances. "The country in general," wrote Grey, "wanted peace."[162]

Ambassador Paul Cambon cabled Viviani on July 31 with the following concise analysis:

> Public opinion in Britain and the present mood of parliament would not allow the Government to commit Britain formally at present. It is thought that the coming conflict will plunge the finances of Europe into trouble, that Britain was facing an economic and financial crisis without precedent and that British neutrality might be the only way of averting the complete collapse of European credit. Cabinet could not commit Parliament without consulting it beforehand; the question of Belgian neutrality could become an important factor and it is probably that point which Parliament will raise first with the Cabinet. Finally, one wants to wait for further developments, since the disagreement between Russia, Austria and Germany is on a question in which Britain is not the least bit interested.[163]

Cambon's words were prophetic. The issue of Belgian neutrality would prove to be the decisive factor.

Britain had guaranteed Belgian neutrality in the treaty of 1839, but there has always been some question of whether the British government felt obliged to defend it in 1914. Michael Ekstein and Zara Steiner, for example, suggest that on July 29, the British Cabinet decided that the obligations of the 1839 treaty fell collectively on the five signatory powers – Britain, France, Prussia, Russia, and Austria – and that "the matter if it arises will be rather one of policy than of legal obligation."[164] This contradicts Grey's recollection that the obligation to defend *Luxembourg's* neutrality was collective, while the obligation to defend *Belgium's* neutrality fell on each of the signatory powers individually.[165] It seems that the Cabinet's precise view of the nature of the obligation was more subtle than either Ekstein and Steiner or Grey suggest. The treaty itself was ambiguous; it merely placed Belgium under "the guarantee" of the signatories.[166] Thus Asquith wrote the King, "It is a doubtful point how far a single guaranteeing state is bound under the Treaty of 1839 to maintain Belgian neutrality if the remainders abstain or refuse" – where by "doubtful" he evidently meant "debatable."[167] The Cabinet asked the Foreign Office to prepare background materials to provide guidance, dealing particularly with how Gladstone's government had interpreted the treaty in 1870, when Belgium seemed threatened by the looming war between France and Prussia.[168] These background materials included excerpts from diplomatic correspondence and selections from *Hansard*. Gladstone's view was that the obligations of the treaty of 1839 fell on the signatories *individually*, rather than *collectively*, because he acknowledged that Britain was obliged to defend Belgian neutrality even though France or Prussia might violate it. Gladstone's opinion, however, was that this obligation, though real, was merely one weighty factor to be considered among others when attempting to decide whether or not to go to war.[169] This, then, seems to be what Asquith meant when he wrote the King saying, "the matter if it arises will be rather one of policy than of legal obligation."[170]

There can be no doubt that the British considered this obligation very weighty indeed. When news reached London on July 31 that Russia had ordered general mobilization, Grey promptly asked both Germany and France whether they would respect Belgian neutrality. France replied in the affirmative, but Germany refused to commit herself, and Grey informed Lichnowsky in no uncertain terms that it would be very difficult to restrain public opinion if one of the belligerents violated the neutrality of Belgium.[171] When German forces entered Belgian territory on August 3, Britain demanded that they withdraw, and declared war on August 4 when they failed to do so.

The crucial fact to bear in mind is that British interests had not changed between July 31 and August 4, while opinion in the government, in Parliament, and in the country as a whole underwent a massive, rapid shift in the direction of intervention, accompanied by an impassioned, almost shrill vilification of Germany. Those who had not previously been impressed by appeals to the national interest were suddenly enthusiastically in favor of war. War between France and Germany was widely thought to be imminent in any case; the prospect had not roused the people. The defense of France was known to be considerably more important to Britain than the defense of Belgium, and so one can hardly imagine that the British *interest* in defending Belgium provided the necessary movement. What had roused the people was the unprovoked violation of Belgian neutrality. This was perceived to be an injustice that warranted condemnation as a crime. As Lichnowsky reported to Berlin on August 4, "The news that reached here yesterday about the invasion of Belgium by German troops brought about a complete reversal of public opinion, to our disadvantage."[172] In the House of Commons, Asquith declared, "If I am asked what we are fighting for, I can reply in two sentences. In the first place we are fighting to fulfill a solemn international obligation ... secondly we are fighting to vindicate the principle that small nationalities are not to be crushed, in defiance of international good faith, by the arbitrary will of a strong and overmastering Power."[173] Even those who felt that Britain's national interests warranted intervention often spoke of defending Belgium's neutrality as a moral obligation.[174]

German statesmen appear not to have appreciated this and thus to have misjudged British intentions accordingly, just as they misinterpreted the strength and nature of Russia's commitment to Serbia.[175] Before he left Germany, British Ambassador Sir Edward Goschen paid a last visit to the Chancellor, who harangued him for twenty minutes on the issue. Goschen reported that Bethmann Hollweg complained that "The step taken by His Majesty's Government was terrible to a degree, just for the word 'neutrality,' a word which in war time has so often been disregarded – just for a scrap of paper, Great Britain was going to make war on a kindred nation who desired nothing better than to be friends with her." Goschen's reply, as he reported it, was as follows: "I would wish him to understand that it was, so to speak, a matter of 'life and death' for the honour of Great Britain that she should keep her solemn engagement to defend Belgium's neutrality if attacked." When Bethmann Hollweg asked if the British government had considered the price, Goschen replied that "fear of consequences could hardly be regarded as an excuse for breaking solemn engagements."[176]

It is worth noting that various other aspects of British policy were influenced at least in part by explicitly moral considerations. The government rejected Germany's bid for British neutrality on July 29, for example, on both moral and prudential grounds. Bethmann Hollweg attempted to persuade Goschen that even if victorious in a war with France, Germany would seek no territorial acquisitions at her expense in Europe, though perhaps she might seek them in France's colonies. Grey replied that he could not entertain the request for neutrality for a moment. "From the material point of view such a proposal is unacceptable, for France could be so crushed as to lose her position as a Great Power and become subordinate to German policy without further territory in Europe being taken from her. But apart from that, for us to make this bargain with Germany at the expense of France would be a disgrace from which the good name of this country would never recover."[177] And although resistance to the idea of war prevented the British government from committing itself in response to French appeals for assistance as the crisis approached its climax, it is interesting to note that the suggestion that the Royal Navy undertake to prevent German ships from sailing down the Channel and shelling the French coast actually came from the *anti*-war faction in the Cabinet, and was grounded in the moral obligation Britain had assumed in 1912 when, as a result of Anglo-French naval talks, the French fleet had been redeployed to the Mediterranean and Britain had tacitly undertaken to guard her northern coasts.[178]

One can only wonder what Britain would have done if Germany had respected Belgium's neutrality. Grey doubted that he could have brought a united country into war, and claims that he was prepared to resign if he could not.[179] One thing seems certain: the question of whether Britain had a *moral* obligation to come to the aid of France would have become acute. Sir Eyre Crowe eloquently expressed his opinion of the matter on July 31:

> The argument that there is no written bond binding us to France is strictly correct. There is no contractual obligation. But the Entente has been made, strengthened, put to the test and celebrated in a manner justifying the belief that a moral bond was being forged ... The question at issue is not whether we are capable of taking part in a war, but whether we should go into the present war. That is a question firstly of right or wrong, and secondly of political expediency.
>
> If the question were argued on this basis, I feel confident that our duty and our interest will be seen to lie in standing by France in her hour of need. France has not sought the quarrel. It has been forced upon her.[180]

CONCLUSIONS

We normally think of World War I as the product of such things as Great Power rivalries, imperial ambitions, arms races, brinkmanship, and secret treaties, and we are accustomed when analyzing it to employ the vocabulary of power, hegemony, balances, and *raison d'état.* These terms and concepts have their place in any full explanation of the outbreak of the war, but their own hegemony often leads us to miss out on the crucial roles other terms and concepts played in conditioning the conflict, triggering it, and in determining the ways in which it spread. These include duty, obligation, self-determination, legitimacy, honor, justice, and right. We often forget that statesmen are not automata, but flesh and blood human beings whose minds operate – most of the time – within the full domain of normal human experience.

Through their actions, the players involved certainly demonstrated *their* belief that moral considerations mattered. For example, Serbia was convinced that a conciliatory reply to the Austrian ultimatum would redound to her advantage by putting Vienna in the wrong; but if moral sympathy has no bearing on state action, this would have been a futile gesture.[181] Germany believed that by pinning the blame for war on Russia, she could minimize the risk of British and French involvement; but if the question of who was in the wrong did not matter, this was nothing but wasted effort.[182] France thought it critical that Germany be the first to declare war even after both countries had mobilized, so as not to jeopardize the attempt to bring Britain in on its side; but if Britain were going to decide solely on the basis of her interests, this could not possibly have mattered.[183]

World War I clearly demonstrates the importance of classical Realist motivations such as self-preservation and self-aggrandizement; but it also shows how normative considerations can create a situation where self-preservation becomes relevant, where commitments become more rigid than mere interest would dictate, and where calculations based on interests are miscalculations with devastating consequences. Perceptions of injustice fueled Franco-German hostility, contributed strongly to the conclusion of the Franco-Russian alliance, shaped Germany's destabilizing military plans, threatened the survival of Austria-Hungary as a Great Power, reinforced and ultimately rendered acute Germany's fears of encirclement and isolation, helped bring Russia to Serbia's aid, and precipitated British entry into the war. Insensitivity to the importance of the justice motive also led German policy-makers to make the fatal miscalculation that an Austro-Serbian war could be localized. There is no question that World War I was a war in which power and self-preservation were at stake; but they came to be at stake precisely because of the power of the justice motive.

5 WORLD WAR II

Table 5.1. *World War II (Europe)*

Role of justice motive in conditioning conflict	Role of justice motive as proximate cause (by participant)	
Moderate	Germany	Imperceptible
	Poland	Imperceptible
	France	Very weak
	Britain	Strong

Germany emerged from World War I beaten, humiliated, and dismembered.[1] The terms of a peace she had no choice but to sign stripped her of her monarch, her fleet, and her air force; severely limited the size and composition of her army; demilitarized the Rhineland (sovereign German territory); blamed her for causing the war; saddled her with a crushing burden of reparations to atone for her crime; restored Alsace and Lorraine to France; transferred Eupen and Malmédy to Belgium; put the Saar under the temporary administration of the newly created League of Nations; gave France control of the Saar's mines to compensate for the destruction wrought by German armies; enlarged Austria at Germany's expense and prohibited the union of the two countries without the unanimous consent of the League Council; ordained a plebiscite that gave Denmark part of Schleswig; transferred Posen and part of West Prussia to Poland to give her access to the sea; made Danzig a free city whose foreign affairs would be directed by Warsaw; gave Memel and its hinterland to Lithuania; and mandated plebiscites to determine the fate of Marienwerder, Allenstein, and Upper Silesia. All told, the territorial clauses of the Treaty of Versailles reduced the size of Germany by 25,000 square miles and almost seven million inhabitants.[2]

The fact that the Treaty of Versailles was a dictated peace caused great resentment in Germany. Since the outbreak of war in 1914 the

127

German government had repeatedly told the German people that victory was just around the corner – which, when the Bolshevik revolution knocked Russia out of the war in 1917, it practically was. The military defeat on the Western front just one year later came as a complete shock. The initiative for ending the war came from the German high command, who saw the handwriting on the wall. Hundreds of thousands of fresh American troops began pouring into Europe in 1917, and when the Reichswehr's desperate all-or-nothing offensive in the summer of 1918 failed to break through the Allied lines, they realized all hope of victory was lost. But the view quickly spread in Germany that the army had been "stabbed in the back" by its own war-weary people, especially the civilians in Berlin, who could not muster the nerve and will at the eleventh hour to push the war to a successful conclusion.[3] To have the Allies dictate a punitive peace predicated on an assignment of "war guilt" that virtually no one in Germany accepted as valid was the crowning injustice, aggravated by the manner in which the peace was concluded. At the ceremony of signature at Versailles, the Allied representatives refused to allow the two German delegates to sit at the table, and had them ushered in and out of the hall like criminals escorted to and from the dock. As E.H. Carr has written, these "unnecessary humiliations" were the fully understandable consequences of the intense bitterness of feeling left over from the war; but they had "far-reaching psychological consequences, both in Germany and elsewhere. They fixed in the consciousness of the German people the conception of a 'dictated peace'; and they helped to create the belief, which became universal in Germany and was tacitly accepted by a large body of opinion in other countries, that the signature extorted from Germany in these conditions was not morally binding on her."[4]

A.J.P. Taylor has written that "Germany fought specifically in the second war to reverse the verdict of the first and to destroy the settlement which followed it . . . The first war explains the second and, in fact, caused it, in so far as one event causes another."[5] Just how far this assertion is true is one of the major questions examined here. What cannot be denied is that the settlement left Germany fundamentally aggrieved. What it did not do was reduce Germany to a position of such helpless weakness that she would be forced to accept her fate. Though beaten, she was not destroyed. In territory, population, and industry, she remained a Great Power. And a dissatisfied Great Power cannot long be expected to endure what it conceives to be gross injustices and humiliations. Moreover, the fact that the victors themselves came to recognize the peace as unjust and humiliating meant that some revision of the post-war status quo in Germany's favor was inevitable. What no one expected after "the war to end all wars," however, was another general war a scant twenty-one years later.

THE ROLE OF ADOLF HITLER

Most historians believe that World War II was Adolf Hitler's war, in both conception and execution, and they emphasize the importance of his uniqueness as a determinant of the course of events leading up to its outbreak. It was this contention that A.J.P. Taylor challenged in his controversial work, *The Origins of the Second World War*, a book that has been greatly misunderstood. Taylor did not believe that Hitler was "just another politician," or that the Nazis were "just another political party." He recognized quite clearly Hitler's unusual capacity for wickedness and the peculiar barbarism of National Socialism, neither of which he had any intention of whitewashing. His true iconoclasm lay in his assertion that "in one sphere alone" Hitler was entirely conventional:

> His foreign policy was that of his predecessors, of the professional diplomats at the foreign ministry and, indeed, of virtually all Germans. Hitler, too, wanted to free Germany from the restrictions of the peace treaty; to restore a great German army; and then to make Germany the greatest power in Europe from her natural weight. There were occasional differences in emphasis. Perhaps Hitler would have concentrated less on Austria and Czechoslovakia if he had not been born a subject of the Hapsburg Monarchy; perhaps his Austrian origin made him less hostile originally to the Poles. But the general pattern was unchanged.[6]

If Taylor is correct, it is conceivable that another German leader, or another German government, would have led the country into another European war, in which case a Gustav Stresemann or a Heinrich Brüning might occupy today the place of Hitler in history's diablerie.[7]

No interpretation of World War II can proceed without taking a stand on this important question. This analysis will proceed on the understanding that World War II *was* Hitler's war. While Taylor is correct to note that Hitler shared with the rest of Germany a profound dissatisfaction with the Treaty of Versailles, it is difficult to imagine that war would have broken out in 1939 if Stresemann or Brüning had been in charge. Such is the common wisdom that Taylor attacks; but often the common wisdom is no less wise for being common.

Hitler was clearly different.[8] He was a man with a clear vision of his

129

objectives, a vision that few in Germany shared, and certainly not the prominent figures of the Weimar Republic. For the most part he pursued his vision with a single-minded determination throughout his political career. But he was enough of a tactician to know when to advance and when to retreat, when to brandish the sword and when to proffer the olive branch. He combined tactical flexibility with strategic coherence.[9] It is difficult to imagine that Hitler could have achieved his goals without war. He was aware of that risk and accepted it. He may even have relished it. He certainly did not shy away from it.[10]

Hitler might not have succeeded in precipitating war if he had not enjoyed such unfettered control of German policy.[11] His bold foreign policy gambles – the remilitarization of the Rhineland in 1936, *Anschluss* with Austria, Munich, and the destruction of Czechoslovakia – were consistently opposed by his generals and greeted with apprehension by the German people.[12] Three times as war approached, the German military attempted to warn the British so that they might forestall it by diplomatic means. In August 1938, the moderates in the German General Staff arranged to dispatch Edwald von Kleist-Schmenzin to London, where he told Sir Robert Vansittart, chief diplomatic advisor to Foreign Secretary Lord Halifax, that Hitler was bent on war and that Britain alone could stop him.[13] In May 1939, Fabian von Schlabrendorff visited England under arrangements made by Admiral Canaris, head of German military intelligence, to warn Winston Churchill and Lord Lloyd that Hitler had decided to attack Poland and would soon strike a deal with the Soviet Union. He thought there was a "slim chance" that Britain could prevent such a move by trying to convince Hitler that an attack on Poland would mean full-scale war. Lieutenant-Colonel Gerhard von Schwerin, head of the English section of the Intelligence Department of the Ministry of War, followed Schlabrendorff in June, bearing the same message.[14] When Hitler finally unleashed his forces on Poland on the morning of September 1, 1939, there was no celebration in the streets of Berlin, only the stony silence of fear and uncertainty. Hitler was popular, but war was not. A leader who took the counsel of others or who paid heed to public opinion would not have conducted policy in quite the same way.

If we begin with the assumption, then, that World War II was fundamentally Hitler's war, we need to ask four questions to assess the relative contribution of the justice motive in conditioning the conflict:

1. To what extent did Hitler's aims reflect a particular vision of justice?
2. What role did the justice motive play in Hitler's rise to power?

130

3. How important were considerations of justice in solidifying Hitler's domestic support and securing his grip on power?

4. What role did the justice motive play in preventing other Powers, notably France and Britain, from resisting Hitler in a timely and effective way?

With respect to the proximate causes of the war, we need to ask two further questions:

1. What role did the justice motive play in Hitler's calculations between March and September 1939?

2. How far can the justice motive explain the Polish, French, and British responses to Hitler's September offensive?

None of these questions has a simple answer, and perhaps more than for any of the other wars examined here, there is ample room for reasonable debate. The evaluations given in Table 5.1 are meant to be appropriately conservative.[15]

HITLER'S AIMS

Of Hitler's objectives, A.J.P. Taylor wrote: "Whatever his long-term plans (and it is doubtful whether he had any), the mainspring of his immediate policy had been 'the destruction of Versailles.' This was the theme of *Mein Kampf* and of every speech which he made on foreign affairs. It was a policy which won the unanimous support of the German people."[16] Hitler himself said as much in 1941: "My programme was to abolish the Treaty of Versailles. It is nonsense for the rest of the world to pretend today that I did not reveal this programme until 1933, or 1935, or 1937 ... No human being has declared or recorded what he wanted more often than I."[17]

There is no doubt that the mass of German people believed the Treaty of Versailles to be fundamentally unjust, because of a specious assignment of guilt, an undeserved punishment, and the manifest injustice of the procedure by which it was concluded. Germany had agreed to an armistice in 1918 on condition that the peace itself be negotiated on the basis of President Wilson's Fourteen Points.[18] To this the Allies agreed, but insisted that Germany lay down her arms before negotiations began. Relying upon the Allies' good faith, Germany complied; further resistance was thenceforth impossible, and Germany found herself forced to accept a *diktat* at gunpoint. The peace itself seemed a mockery of Wilson's Fourteen Points. Wilson had proclaimed the principle of open diplomacy, but the peace was dictated; Wilson exalted the principle of self-determination, but Versailles forcibly alienated millions of ethnic Germans from the *Reich*; Wilson

131

insisted upon the fair arbitration of colonial questions, but the Treaty summarily confiscated Germany's overseas possessions.[19] Was it any wonder that Germany felt herself the victim of an enormous swindle?

Hitler's hatred of Versailles was as intense as that of any other German, perhaps more so. But, curiously, there is little evidence that the *injustice* of the peace inflamed him. According to his account in *Mein Kampf*, what he felt most acutely was anger toward those in Germany who had agreed to it.[20] Other Nazis, particularly former Army and *Freikorps* officers such as Ernst Röhm, commander of the SA, directed their hatred toward France, the primary architect of the loathsome peace; but for Hitler, the real enemy was the Republic.[21] "I do not believe for a moment that France's intentions with respect to us can ever change," Hitler wrote, "because they have their deepest motive nowhere but in the French nation's sense of self-preservation. Were I a Frenchman myself, and were France's greatness as dear to me as is Germany's sacred, then I could and would not act otherwise than Clemenceau himself did in the end."[22] Hitler thought Versailles a "disgrace" and a "shame," but not "unjust" in the sense of "unfair." This was not a word that was in his vocabulary. The real criminals were those in Germany who brought the war to an end; Germany's enemies only did what might have been expected. Hitler did not even think that the Treaty of Versailles was *undeserved*. Quite the contrary, he thought it merely the outward symptom of internal decay.[23] "The Treaty of Versailles in itself," he proclaimed in 1932, "is only the consequence of our own slow inner confusion and aberration of mind."[24]

While others railed against the injustice of Versailles, Hitler tried to sell his own vision of the world and Germany's place within it. He peddled an amalgam of anti-Semitism, anti-Bolshevism, Pan-Germanism, Social Darwinism, and nihilism. He was an admirer of Houston Chamberlain, whose influence on the Kaiser I noted in the previous chapter.[25] He fancied himself an apostle of Goethe, Herder, Wagner, Spengler, and Nietzsche;[26] in reality, he was probably most heavily influenced by two relatively unknown anti-Semitic pamphleteers in Vienna named Guido von List and Lanz von Liebenfels.[27] No subject could cause Hitler to spew forth as much venom as "the Jewish question." Hitler blamed the Jews for Germany's stab in the back. He blamed them for polluting Germany's racial purity and sapping Germany's national will and vigor. He blamed them for bringing the scourge of Bolshevism into the world. He blamed them for turning Britain – whom, in contrast to Tirpitz, he often called "our natural ally" – against Germany. No charge was too ludicrous to be leveled against the Jews. Solving the Jewish question was something never very far from Hitler's mind; it was simply the flip side of his "positive" program: *"What we have to fight for is the security of the existence and the increase of our race and our people, the nourishment of its children and the preservation of the purity of the blood, the freedom and independence of the fatherland in order to enable our people to mature for the fulfillment of the mission which the Creator of the universe has allotted to them."*[28] This required bringing all Germans within an economically self-sufficient *Reich*. His insistence on autarky is curious but conspicuous. He took no comfort from Germany's capacity to trade for the food she could not herself produce. Perhaps he took Malthus and Darwin too literally, or too seriously; but he constantly fretted about Germany's population density and the need for *lebensraum*.[29] He rarely expressed interest in the return of Germany's lost colonies;[30] instead, he set his eyes on the vast expanse of arable land to the east inhabited by what he considered to be inferior races.[31] What Hitler sought, therefore – at least in the first instance – was an economically self-sufficient Greater Germany uniting all ethnic Germans within a single polity extending from the Rhine to the Ukraine. In this vast expanse, inferior races would be eliminated or reduced to positions of servitude, as expedience might require.[32] Once in power, he set about turning his vision into reality, and set target dates for its implementation.[33]

This was Hitler's conception of the natural order of things. The question arises: does this qualify as a conception of justice? Some considerations suggest an affirmative answer. For example, Hitler often spoke of his design in the language of justice. In *Mein Kampf*, he stated flatly that "we National Socialists must cling unflinchingly to our foreign-policy aims, that is to guarantee the *German nation the soil and territory to which it is entitled on this earth.*"[34] The idea that one group or class of individuals is entitled to or somehow deserving of a superior existence is nothing new to philosophy. Plato, for example, had insisted that the best should lead, and the least should follow. Aristotle graded human beings on a moral-ontological scale which, among other things, classified women as defective males and placed them in a position of subjection. No Greek thinker ever thought of a Greek as being on a plane with – let alone inferior to – a barbarian, and few had any moral misgivings about the institution of slavery. Nazis could take solace even from Enlightenment figures: the egalitarianism of John Locke, for example, extended only as far as non-Catholic propertied white males. Distinctions between superior and inferior groups, and discriminations in moral entitlements, are much more common than is radical egalitarianism in the history of moral and political thought. And, more often than not, the authors of such distinctions invariably placed themselves, and the groups to which they belonged, in the superior position. To that extent, Hitler's conception of the natural order was rather prosaic: Germans were a superior people, *ergo* they were entitled to a superior existence.

Without doubt many Nazis and their supporters thought in these terms, and for those that did, what they believed to be the natural order they also thought a *just* order. But it is doubtful whether characterizing Nazi ideology as a conception of justice provides the most faithful rendition of Hitler's own thought. In the first place, it ignores the palpable fact of what Hitler's foremost biographer calls his "moral and intellectual cretinism."[35] Adolf Hitler's moral development was at the very least incomplete; here was a man who did *not* operate within the full domain of human experience. Secondly, characterizing Hitler's vision of the world as a conception of justice ignores the very powerful Nietzschean current running through it which vehemently denied the relevance of morality in human affairs. Thus, for example, Hitler dismissed a return to the boundaries of 1914 as a false goal for Germany, because boundaries are arbitrary: one is not *morally entitled* to them, one simply takes them if one can. "The reality of a nation having managed a disproportionate acquisition of territory is no superior obligation for its eternal recognition," Hitler wrote; "It proves at most the might of the conqueror and the weakness of the victim. And, moreover, this might alone makes right."[36] For Hitler, neither Versailles nor the borders it established were *unjust* – they were merely *unacceptable*.

The Nietzschean rejection of morality meant that the superiority and inferiority of peoples was not for Hitler a normative question, but a mere matter of fact. In foreign policy, as with every other aspect of Hitler's program, this had a simplifying effect:

> The most essential maxim and guiding principle which must always shine before us ... is that foreign policy, too, is only a means to an end, but the end must be exclusively the advancement of our own nationality. No consideration of foreign policy can be guided by any point of view but this: *Does it benefit our nation now or in the future, or will it be harmful to it?*
> *This is the sole preconceived opinion permitted in dealing with this question. Partisan, religious, humanitarian, and all other points of view in general are completely beside the point.*[37]

In other words, for Hitler, politics reduced to power – "first his own power in Germany, and then the expansion of German power in

Europe. The rest," writes Bullock, "was window-dressing."[38] Adolf Hitler was the Realist *par excellence.*

HITLER'S RISE TO POWER

If Hitler's aims cannot be described in the language of justice, one can nevertheless easily observe the justice motive at work in Hitler's rise to power – not his own justice motive, but that of the German people, which he consciously and effectively manipulated to his own ends.[39]

The National Socialist German Workers' Party proclaimed a twenty-five-plank program on February 24, 1920. The first three planks were as follows:

1. We demand the union of all Germans in a Greater Germany on the basis of the right of national self-determination.
2. We demand equality of rights for the German people in its dealings with other nations, and the revocation of the peace treaties of Versailles and Saint-Germain.
3. We demand land and territories (colonies) to feed our people and to settle our surplus population.[40]

The order in which these appear is quite revealing. The first two planks were designed to play on the widely accepted view both in Germany and in the liberal democracies that Versailles was fundamentally unjust. Both planks were entirely cynical. Hitler undoubtedly sought the union of all Germans in a Greater Germany, but certainly not on the basis of the right of self-determination of peoples, which is a general, abstract formula that would have obliged him to respect the equivalent right of those he intended to displace or subjugate. For this reason he did not seek an *equality* of rights for the German people in its dealings with other nations, but a superiority. Both planks flatly contradicted the third, a demand for *lebensraum* but, by preceding it, and by sounding so eminently reasonable, they masked both its centrality and its radicalism.[41]

In the early years, Hitler frequently spoke at Nazi meetings on such topics as Versailles, the loss of Upper Silesia, and the French occupation of the Ruhr. These meetings were among the best-attended.[42] Hitler's assault on the peace won for National Socialism generally – and for Adolf Hitler personally – many new disciples, including Hermann Göring, who leapt on the band wagon precisely because he believed that he had found in Hitler the man who would smash the Treaty of Versailles.[43] Whereas Hitler's other speeches, including his frequent polemics against the Jews, usually attracted a smaller crowd and were received with puzzlement, indifference, or scorn (Hitler was widely regarded as a lunatic by the local Bavarian establishment), his foreign-policy views struck a powerful chord in the German national consciousness. One commentator maintains that the perceived injustices of the treaties of Versailles and Saint-Germain explain "to a great extent" Hitler's success as a demagogue, "who, as the mouthpiece of a Germany determined to avenge her defeat, claimed to lead the fight for the liberation of the German people ... All the arguments tirelessly and methodically used to build a case against the great injustice of Versailles were used and amplified in Hitler's speeches." Hitler wielded them "with passionate violence, and repeated them unceasingly."[44] That these speeches reflected "superficial arguments" and not Hitler's "fundamental reasons" for abhorring the peace was entirely immaterial; Hitler was nothing if not a salesman.[45]

Germany was a house divided ideologically, economically, socially, and politically, but Germans were of one opinion in foreign affairs: the Treaty of Versailles had to be radically changed or overthrown.[46] The problem was that Hitler was not the only one hawking revisionism in the 1920s, and few of the others came in such an unattractive package.[47] Hitler's views on foreign affairs had undoubted appeal but, initially, they were not enough to compensate for his drawbacks. Those on the Right who liked the revisionism of National Socialism were repelled by its anti-capitalism; those on the Left who were attracted by its anti-capitalism were repelled by its nationalism.[48] Its only solid constituency in the early years were those at the fringes of society who found perverse sublimation in its militancy and fanaticism.

Only by abandoning anti-capitalism would Hitler ultimately attract enough support to become a factor on the national stage. But foreign policy provided Hitler with his first big break. In 1929, negotiations opened for a final settlement of the reparations question, resulting in the adoption of the Young Plan the following year (March 13, 1930). Hitler teamed up with Alfred Hugenburg, leader of the German National Party, to campaign for a plebiscite denouncing the new settlement and the thesis of German war guilt which served as the legal basis of the Allies' claims. In September 1922, the two published the draft of a "Law against the Enslavement of the German People," which repudiated the war-guilt thesis, demanded an end to reparations, and threatened the Chancellor, the Cabinet, and their representatives with charges of high treason if they committed Germany to further reparations. The bill itself was easily defeated, but it catapulted Hitler into the public spotlight. He so impressed big business with his skills as an agitator that funds normally channeled to main-stream conservative parties began to flow into National Socialist coffers.[49]

After the elections of September 1930, Hitler and the Nazis could no longer be ignored. Nazi representation in the Reichstag skyrocketed from twelve seats to 107, their 18.3 percent of the popular vote second only to the Socialists' 24.5 percent. In July 1932, the Nazis became the largest party, with 37.3 percent of the vote.[50] It was plain that no stable coalition could exclude the Nazis, and from that point forward, Hitler employed the entirely conventional methods of the back-room power broker to maneuver himself into the Chancellery. There was therefore nothing unconstitutional about his rise to power, although consti-tutionality did not long survive it.

What accounts for Hitler's remarkable electoral success? One common explanation is that Hitler rose to power on the crest of an economic wave of discontent. During the relatively prosperous years of the 1920s, the Nazis could make little headway because they offered nothing to the discontented that more respectable parties could not provide more effectively. But the Great Depression changed every-thing. Circumstances forced the hungry, the unemployed, and the dispossessed to look to radical groups for radical solutions when the politics of centrism and moderation failed catastrophically. According to this view, the injustice of Versailles had burned itself out as a political issue and contributed little or nothing to Hitler's rise.

There is both truth and error in this explanation. It is clearly too simple to explain the growth of Nazism in purely economic terms, not only because there was an unmistakable groundswell of support for Nazism prior to the Depression, but also because no other country experiencing a similar level of economic distress – France, Britain, the United States – experienced a similar turn toward radicalism.[51] Some-thing unique about the German case, something more than mere economics, made the people turn to Hitler. But the Depression did serve as a floodgate; it provided the opportunity Hitler needed to make his move. The German people did not simply turn toward Hitler; Hitler seduced them. How did he do so?

Quite simply, the Nazis advertised themselves to different audi-ences in different ways and in different places. Nazism was not simply a middle-class phenomenon, as the popular myth has it; people of all classes supported the Nazis in the early 1930s. In the countryside, Hitler's main message was debt relief; in the cities, anti-Bolshevism. Over everything was a heavy gloss of war guilt and Versailles, which Hitler knew would have universal appeal.[52] He offered the German

137

people little in the way of a concrete program, but a wealth of scapegoats:

> In 1930 the mood of a large section of the German nation was one of resentment. Hitler, with an almost inexhaustible fund of resentment in his own character to draw from, offered them a series of objects on which to lavish all the blame for their misfortunes. It was the Allies, especially the French, who were to blame; the Republic, with its corrupt and self-seeking politicians; the money barons, the bosses of big business, the speculators and the monopolists; the Reds and the Marxists, who fostered class hatred and kept the nation divided; above all, the Jews, who fattened and grew rich on the degradation and weakness of the German people.[53]

What provided Hitler with his opportunity, and distinguished the German case from that of France, Britain, and the United States, was not that the existing political establishment had failed to prevent economic catastrophe, but that the existing political establishment had never attained popular legitimacy. Weimar was unstable and vulnerable because it had won the loyalty of virtually no one. And this was the direct result of deeply rooted resentment against the peace – simple moral outrage, not resentment against its economic effects (Germany was a net gainer from the financial transactions of the 1920s: she borrowed, and failed to pay back, far more than she paid in reparations).[54] Thus Alan Bullock assigns "the heaviest responsibility of all" for Hitler's rise to power to the German Right, because they failed to come to the defense of the Republic at the crucial moment. The old ruling class had been remarkably well-treated by Weimar: army leaders maintained their independence; industrialists and landowners made a fortune out of the weakness and pliability of the central government, which left their wealth and estates untouched and permitted most of them to retain positions of power and influence. But, as Bullock remarks, "this won neither their gratitude nor their loyalty." As a class, they refused to acknowledge the verdict of Versailles, despised the regime that had accepted it, and came to see in Hitler a man who could help them reverse it.[55]

Hitler's rise to power and the collapse of Weimar were complex phenomena; the role of Versailles should be neither overemphasized nor underemphasized. Its psychological effects were more important than its material effects, and only under the extreme pressures of the Depression could Hitler use it to his advantage, because only under those conditions could his manifest extremism appear attractive. Without the dislocation of the Depression, it is doubtful that Hitler would have become chancellor. But the deeply rooted perception of the injustice of the peace nevertheless played a crucial role in three respects: first, it provided Hitler and the National Socialists with the one respectable issue that would allow them to grow from a fringe group to a mass movement; second, it provided Hitler with the occasion to break onto the national political scene; and third – but not least importantly – it so enfeebled the Weimar Republic that it would prove unable to resist Hitler when circumstances offered him the opportunity to destroy it.[56]

PUBLIC SUPPORT FOR HITLER'S PROGRAM

Once in power, Hitler set about to destroy the Versailles system, and, in so doing, solidified his political position so completely that by September 1, 1939, without any meaningful opposition, he was able to take his army and his country into a war that neither desired.[57] One source of Hitler's undoubted popularity was Germany's impressive economic recovery – largely fueled by a massive rearmament program – but the pivotal events that provided Hitler with the opportunity to arrogate greater and greater powers and to transform Germany into a one-party state were his unilateral moves to break the shackles of Versailles.[58]

The first of these was Hitler's announcement on October 14, 1933, that Germany would withdraw from the League of Nations and disarmament negotiations, owing to its unequal treatment and consequent humiliation. Affecting sorrow rather than anger, he declared that Germany's self-respect permitted no other course. He evidently thought this something of a gamble, because he gave orders to the Armed Forces in case the League responded with sanctions. But Hitler had correctly gauged the state of mind of the other Powers – "their embarrassment in face of a case which they felt was not without justice; the divided public opinion of Great Britain and France; the eagerness to be reassured and to patch up a compromise, all those elements on which Hitler was to play with such skill time and again." Most cleverly of all, he announced at the same time that he would submit his decision to a plebiscite – ingeniously scheduled to take place on November 12, one day after the anniversary of the hated armistice. "This was to invoke the sanctions of democracy against the democratic nations. All the long-pent-up resentment of the German people against the loss of the war and the Treaty of Versailles was expressed in the vote: 95 percent approved of Hitler's policy."[59] The mandate was so overwhelming that he was able, within a few weeks, to pass a law that unified the party and state.[60]

More dramatic was Hitler's precipitate remilitarization of the Rhineland in March 1936, which he justified in a speech to the Reichstag by appealing to Germany's sovereign right to equality with other Powers.[61] Hitler was extremely nervous during the Rhineland operation; he told his interpreter that they were the most nerve-wracking forty-eight hours of his life, and that if the French had responded militarily, German forces would have had to withdraw "with our tails between our legs, for the military resources at our disposal would have been wholly inadequate for even a modest resistance."[62] But France did not respond, and Hitler capitalized on his coup by dissolving the Reichstag and submitting his policy to a plebiscite. The response was overwhelming: 98.8 percent of the electorate approved it, prompting one of his biographers to remark that "No head of state in the world enjoyed such popularity."[63]

Impressed by France's inaction, Hitler felt secure enough on January 30, 1937, in a speech to the Reichstag, to announce the formal withdrawal of Germany's signature from the clauses of the Treaty of Versailles that denied her equality of rights and assigned her responsibility for the war.[64] In fact, by this point the Treaty had already been dead for some time, killed by the remilitarization of the Rhineland, Germany's decision to rearm, and Hitler's 1936 naval agreement with Britain.[65] The next step in the piecemeal dismantling of the peace was the consummation of the forbidden *Anschluss* with Austria in March 1938, which Hitler justified by appeal to the right of self-determination and Wilson's Fourteen Points, dismissing British and French objections by characterizing the union of the two states as "an internal affair of the German people."[66]

Hitler used the very same argument to bring pressure to bear on Czechoslovakia to cede the largely German-speaking Sudetenland to the rapidly growing *Reich*.[67] This was something of a new departure for Hitler. At least in the Austrian case, Hitler's move had been popular in the target state.[68] But the idea of transferring the Sudetenland to Germany was not popular in Czechoslovakia, nor in France, who by treaty engagement was committed to come to her defense. Hitler, undeterred, mobilized the tried-and-true appeal to self-determination.[69] It worked.[70] By the terms of the Munich agreement of September 29, 1938, Hitler secured French and British complicity in the dismemberment of Czechoslovakia.[71] Few Germans at the time were willing to fight a major war over the Sudetenland.[72] But Hitler's remarkable success only increased his domestic popularity and his mystique.

As George Kennan observed, Hitler's revisionism completely unified

Germany. "What Bonaparte and Napoleon III left undone in this direction, Versailles completed, and Hitler is now stamping out the last vestiges of particularism and class differences."[73] With a united country behind him, Hitler no longer felt any compunction to confine expansion to territories which he could plausibly argue belonged within the boundaries of the *Reich* by virtue of the principle of self-determination. On March 15, 1939, German troops marched into Prague.[74] Hitler had gone too far; Britain and France resolved to prevent any further expansion. If, as Hitler had remarked in 1941, no human being had declared or recorded what he wanted more often than he, what had taken them so long, and why had they not offered resistance when the circumstances were more favorable?

THE LULLING EFFECT OF THE SENSE OF JUSTICE

It was not the intention of the victors at Versailles to inflict on Germany an unjust peace. Quite the opposite. France pushed for harsh terms in part because the requirements of retributive justice seemed to demand them, but also (here making the same mistake Bismarck had made in 1871) to ensure that Germany would be incapable of attacking her again. Britain favored a milder peace, more wisely contending that a better way of preventing aggression is to remove the causes of dissatisfaction.[75] On March 26, 1919, in a note to Clemenceau, David Lloyd George argued that peace would "depend upon there being no causes of exasperation constantly stirring up the spirit of patriotism, of justice or of fair play," and he foresaw the great instability of a situation in which a proud and once-powerful Germany was surrounded by smaller states containing large numbers of ethnic Germans clamoring to be reunited with their homeland.[76] But France got its way. For the first time between the wars – but not for the last – the more perspicacious of the two Powers deferred to the less.[77]

John Maynard Keynes's *The Economic Consequences of the Peace* was the most forthright and most influential assault on Versailles from within the Allied camp. Today, Keynes's book is remembered primarily for its argument that a crushing burden of reparations would destroy the German economy, with adverse effects on the world economy as a whole. But Keynes's attack was as much a moral onslaught as an economic one, condemning the peace for its injustice and inhumanity at least as much as for its economic irrationality.[78] Some critics of the treaty primarily attacked its assignment of war guilt, others the forced alienation of millions of ethnic Germans. More of these critics could be found in Britain than France, and it was largely to

British sensibilities that Hitler directed his arguments between 1933 and 1939.[79]

France, of course, was the Power most clearly in a position to check Hitler's revisionism. For most of the interwar period, her army was the largest and best-equipped in Europe and, generally speaking, the French had fewer illusions about Hitler's intentions than did the British.[80] But a combination of war-weariness, economic upheaval, political polarization, a rigidly defensive military posture, and an ineffable but unmistakable national *malaise* combined to produce in France a powerful psychological dependence upon British support.[81] Paris would make no move without London by its side – another example of the more perspicacious of the two Powers relinquishing the initiative to the less.[82]

The first test of French resolve to resist Hitler came in 1936, when German troops marched into the demilitarized Rhineland, in flagrant violation of both the Treaty of Versailles and the Pact of Locarno.[83] Hitler's move was shocking to France not merely because it heralded a bold policy of revision, but also because it brought German forces once again into direct contact with French troops. But France had no will to resist. With elections two months away, the government's reaction would be governed by public opinion, the opinion of the General Staff, and the attitude of the British.[84] Among the public as a whole, the dominant passion was fear of war. This was entirely understandable for a country that had lost in battle one in every ten adult males just a generation before.[85] The French military, over-learning the lessons of 1914, had been reorganized on a purely defensive basis, lacked a plan for dealing with such a contingency, and could not bring itself to prepare one despite an abundance of forewarning from French intelligence and diplomatic personnel.[86] Their fear was quite simple: France could only resist the German move by means of a total mobilization, which could precipitate a protracted war with Germany. Given her inferior resources, France could not hope to win such a war without allies. That meant British support.[87] The British view was well-known in France: Germany's desire "to revise the treaties in order to correct injustices therein" was thought to have some merit. British support would not be forthcoming.[88]

So France acquiesced in the remilitarization of the Rhineland. But she could not remain indifferent to it; nor could she ignore the accelerated pace of German rearmament. Even the 1936–1937 Popular Front government of Léon Blum, which pursued an ambitious, divisive, and expensive program of social reform, managed to boost military spending dramatically.[89] But though France began to *prepare* for the worst, she was unable and unwilling to act decisively to *prevent* it. From *Anschluss* through Munich, France was committed to a policy of preserving peace at almost any price.[90]

In many respects, Munich was a repetition of the Rhineland, replete with the same ironies. On both occasions, France sacrificed a pillar of its security – Locarno in 1936, a militarily viable Czechoslovakia in 1938 – on the altar of Peace, weakening her position for a fight she was inadvertently making more and more likely, not because she harbored any illusions about Hitler, but because of her psychological dependence upon Britain, who did. Her own sense of impotence was completely paralyzing; she could see the impending collision clearly enough, but was helpless to avoid it.[91]

None of this should be taken to suggest that France as a whole was blind to the injustices of Versailles, or that France entirely dismissed German claims to self-determination. Professor Joseph Barthélemy, for example, in a widely-read article in *Le Temps* (April 12, 1938), questioned France's obligation to come to the defense of Czechoslovakia in the face of Hitler's demands on the Sudetenland. "Is it necessary," he asked, "that three million Frenchmen, all the youth of our universities, of our schools, our countryside and our factories should be sacrificed in order to maintain three million Germans under Czech sovereignty?"[92] But even here it is difficult to disentangle sympathy for the merits of Hitler's claims from aversion to the horrors of war. The uproar Barthélemy triggered reflected both a sincere concern for France's obligation to Czechoslovakia and well-founded skepticism about Hitler's motives. And yet the dominant French reaction to Munich was one of delirious joy, simply because peace had been preserved. The realization that France had sold out her ally was a source of some contrition, but the guilt could not compete with the manifest sense of relief.[93]

France did not fail to resist Hitler in a timely and effective way because she was seduced by his invocation of justice; she did so because of her aversion to war. But France had abdicated to Britain her natural role as the primary guarantor of the European order, and dutifully followed where England led. The crucial decisions were made in London, not Paris. To understand why Hitler was not resisted until he unleashed war on Poland, it is therefore necessary to examine the mainsprings of British policy. And here the justice motive was powerfully at work.

From the beginning, the British as a whole were sympathetic to the German demand for revision of the Treaty of Versailles. "Whether or not it was too hard on the Germans," writes Antony Lentin, "it was demonstrably too hard for much of British opinion."

From the outset, liberal England had no heart for it. In the years that followed, Versailles returned like a recurrent nightmare to plague its inventors. It is no use for Mr Correlli Barnett, in the *Collapse of British Power*, to castigate their lack of hard-headed realism. Such, for good and ill, is what the Protestant conscience and the public-school ethic had made them; and it would have been the mark of a true *Realpolitik* to take account of it. Given that the Treaty was not ultimately self-enforcing, what chance did it stand of durability if the victors themselves could not stomach it?[94]

As early as 1919, Lord Curzon refused to commit Britain to defending the settlement in all its particulars for all time; henceforward, British statesmen would acknowledge the need to "redress legitimate grievances."[95] Thus began the policy of appeasement.[96]

"Redressing legitimate grievances" was an easy policy to follow, because more often than not it was a policy of *in*action, rather than action. All that it required was acquiescence in Hitler's various coups. Appeasement did not mean that Hitler was popular, or that his ostentatious unilateralism was a matter of indifference. The remilitarization of the Rhineland, for example, came as a serious shock to British opinion. But it did not come as a shock because it was thought to be *unjustified*; it came as a shock because it signaled the end of Locarno.[97] The moral case was generally conceded. On this point, the typical British reaction was that of Lord Lothian, who dismissed the matter by remarking, "The Germans, after all, are only going into their own back garden."[98] No one saw in it cause for invoking the collective security provisions of the League of Nations. The *Times of London* drew a sharp distinction between "the march of detachments of German troops, sent to reoccupy territory indisputably under German sovereignty, and an act which carries fire and sword into a neighbour's territory."[99]

The British reaction to *Anschluss* followed essentially the same pattern. What the Prime Minister and the country deplored were Hitler's *methods* – brash demands, saber-rattling, a flamboyant display of military force – not his *intentions*.[100] The German absorption of Austria was even an occasion for a certain amount of autoflagellation: in a letter to the *Times*, Lord Lothian blamed the League Powers' denial of Germany's legitimate aspirations for "[driving] them to accept a totalitarian régime as the one method by which they could recover their unity and their natural rights."[101] Nazism, in other words, was our own fault.

But *Anschluss* – and the breakneck pace of German rearmament – began to stir British doubts and fears. Sir Archibald Sinclair – who offered no objection to the remilitarization of the Rhineland – provides a notable illustration. "If we cannot rally against aggression all the forces of the potential victims," he admonished the House of Commons, "they will be sacrificed one by one, till it comes to our turn. Other nations may then shrug their shoulders and say: 'Our national interests are not directly threatened.' And we are left friendless and alone."[102] Others who sounded an early warning included Winston Churchill – whom Prime Minister Neville Chamberlain scrupulously excluded from the cabinet – and Duff Cooper, First Lord of the Admiralty. But these, for the moment, were voices in the wilderness.

The British policy of "redressing legitimate grievances" survived an even greater shock than *Anschluss*: the dismemberment of Czechoslovakia and the annexation of the Sudetenland. Hitler once again made his pitch in terms of self-determination, and once again persuaded the British.[103] Three crucial figures – Chamberlain, Ambassador Henderson in Berlin, and Ambassador Newton in Prague – all maintained that the Sudeten claims were well-founded morally.[104] The Cabinet, by and large, agreed.[105] Lord Runciman, dispatched to Czechoslovakia on a fact-finding mission in the summer of 1938, returned a convert to the Sudeten cause.[106]

At Berchtesgaden on September 15, 1938, Hitler succeeded in convincing Chamberlain of his resolve. The Prime Minister returned persuaded that Britain and France faced a stark choice between permitting the Sudetenland to join the *Reich* peacefully, and watching Hitler take it by force. Back in London on September 18 to confer with Daladier, Chamberlain framed the Sudeten question principally as one of "whether or not to accept the principle of self-determination."[107] Noting that France, unlike Britain, had treaty obligations to Czechoslovakia, Chamberlain asked Daladier whether France "felt it necessary to resist what, after his conversation with Herr Hitler, he could only describe as the sole condition on which peaceful negotiations could proceed."[108] Daladier expressed well-founded concern about the slippery slope and Germany's "ultimate aims," and he insisted that France's obligations could not be ignored.[109] But Chamberlain would not be persuaded to abandon his conviction that at the present moment, they faced a choice between accepting the principle of self-determination and war. There was no question which choice he considered preferable.[110]

Chamberlain's biographers have attempted to cast his policy at this point in a favorable light. Keith Feiling, for example, portrays Chamberlain as a textbook realist, a follower of Canning's maxim that one should never issue a threat without the capability of carrying it out. Britain's unpreparedness so constrained her options that

145

Chamberlain's "first motive" under the circumstances simply had to be to avoid war, even at the cost of major concessions. Prudence, in short, guided Chamberlain at this moment of trial.[111] But Chamberlain was less of a realist and more of a moralist than this portrayal suggests. Why should he go to war, he wondered in the fall of 1938, over "a quarrel in a far-away country between people of whom we know nothing," in the absence of any treaty obligations, in order to prevent three million ethnic Germans from realizing their legitimate aspirations?[112]

Feiling also insists that Chamberlain harbored few illusions about the Nazis, quoting, for example, his letter to Mrs. Morton Prince of January 16, 1938, in which he proclaimed, "They pay no heed to reason, but there is one argument to which they will always give attention, and that is force."[113] Since Britain was in no position to resort to force, she had no choice but to bide her time until she was strong enough to take a harder line. But it is difficult to concur with this assessment, because Chamberlain's credulity is a matter of public record. He mistook Hitler's readiness at Munich to sign a declaration forswearing the use of force in Anglo-German relations as an assurance of "peace for our time;" in reality, it was an empty gesture to which Hitler had given scarcely a moment's thought. When Hitler told him at Munich that he would abide by the results of plebiscites determining the final frontier with a diminished Czechoslovakia, and participate in an international guarantee of the remainder, Chamberlain told the House of Commons, "I have no hesitation in saying, after the personal contact I had established with Herr Hitler, that I believe he means what he says when he states that."[114] And in a radio broadcast to the nation on September 27, Chamberlain declared, "If I were convinced that any nation had made up its mind to dominate the world by fear of its force, I should feel that it must be resisted. Under such a domination life for people who believe in liberty would not be worth living."[115] Clearly Chamberlain did not believe Hitler intended any such thing.

Chamberlain badly misjudged both Hitler's intentions and his sincerity. That he did so was very largely the result of Hitler's success in appealing to the British Prime Minister's own keen sense of justice. By combining those appeals with limited demands, threats of war, and professions of peaceful intent, Hitler was able to reap a handsome dividend from appeasement.[116] It is difficult to imagine that Chamberlain would have been so pliant and accommodating if Hitler's demands had been put forward in amoral terms. Indeed, Chamberlain's illusions – and those of the nation as a whole – lasted only as long as Hitler rested his case on the principle of self-determination and the injustice of Versailles. On the fateful moment when he made the mistake of violating the very principles of justice which had served him so well, he turned the entire British nation against him.

It would be a mistake to insist that the justice motive was the sole or overwhelming determinant of British policy.[117] Like France, Britain had a strong desire to preserve the peace, and also like France, she underestimated the strength of her position. But unlike France, Britain was lulled into a false confidence in appeasement by her own strong conviction that Germany had suffered grave injustices at the hands of the Allies, and that Germany's drive to correct them reflected legiti- mate – and satisfiable – grievances.[118] With France following Britain's lead, it can fairly be said that the British sense of justice unwittingly played a pivotal role in Hitler's program of revision and expansion.

THE APPROACH TO WAR

The British saw Munich as a triumph of morality, not a surren- der to force. But the occupation of Prague triggered "an underground explosion of public opinion such as the historian cannot trace in precise terms."[119] For the first time, Hitler had extended his control to non-Germans; no longer could he pretend that he was merely correc- ting the injustices of Versailles. For Chamberlain, the Cabinet, and the British people as a whole, the veil was finally lifted.[120]

It was now apparent that appeasement was no longer a viable policy.[121] But neither France nor Britain immediately declared war, in spite of their guarantees to Czechoslovakia. Chamberlain deftly dodged his responsibility by using the Slovak declaration of indepen- dence – engineered by Hitler – as an excuse not to discharge it: "The effect of this declaration put an end by internal disruption to the State whose frontiers we had proposed to guarantee ... His Majesty's Government cannot accordingly hold themselves any longer bound by this obligation."[122] France put on a better show: "The Governments, who gave their assent to a compromise intended to assure the survival of Czechoslovakia, cannot today watch in silence the dismemberment of the Czech people and the annexation of their territory without being accused in retrospect of complaisance and moral complicity," declared the official French response. "The enforced submission of the Prague Government, brutally imposed by German pressure, cannot be invoked to absolve Great Britain and France from their moral obli- gation in the eyes of their own people and of those of other States as well as of the Czechoslovak nation." Then came out the heavy

147

artillery: "They owe it to international opinion, as well as to themselves, to register a formal protest against this act of force by which Germany, in contempt of the rights of a nation, has destroyed the contractual basis of the first attempt at an understanding between the four great European Powers."[123]

But though neither France nor Britain took immediate decisive action to redress what they clearly perceived to be a gross injustice, both countries threw their military preparations into high gear. After March 15, war with Germany began to seem increasingly likely, perhaps even inevitable. Chamberlain and Daladier finally decided to draw the line: on March 31, in the House of Commons, Chamberlain committed Britain to defend the independence of Poland.[124] Daladier issued a parallel guarantee on April 13.[125] Hitler, it seems, was unimpressed. As the summer wore on, he turned up the pressure on Poland, demanding the return of Danzig to the *Reich* and a German right-of-way to East Prussia across the Polish corridor. This time, his appeals to self-determination went unheeded. On the morning of September 1, Germans in Polish uniforms staged a series of border attacks that Hitler used as an excuse to unleash his forces.[126] Two days later, Britain and France were at war with Germany.[127]

Hitler's motivations for attacking Poland are not in the least bit mysterious; they were laid out quite clearly in *Mein Kampf*. Poland merely signaled a change in the means by which Hitler pursued his larger aims. On April 3, Hitler told his generals that the situation on Germany's eastern frontier had become intolerable, and that all political possibilities of peaceful settlement had been exhausted, proclaiming, "I have decided upon a solution by force." He scheduled the attack on Poland for September 1.[128] In a conference held in the Führer's study in the Reich Chancellery on May 23, Hitler described Danzig as an incidental objective; his primary goal was *lebensraum*. To secure it, Hitler had determined *"To attack Poland at the first suitable opportunity."*[129]

We have already decided that Hitler's aims should not be understood as reflecting the perceived demands of justice.[130] Since Hitler had unfettered control of German policy, and since neither the German military nor the German people were enthusiastic about war with Poland, we can safely conclude that Hitler's personal motivations were the only ones that mattered. It is interesting to speculate, however, whether Hitler would have encountered greater internal resistance – or whether he himself would have been less bold – had events since 1936 not impressed him with the weakness and passivity of the Western Powers. He simply did not believe that France and

Britain would honor their guarantees to Poland.[131] Deterrence may have broken down in September 1939 in part because Britain's sense of justice helped destroy her reputation for firmness.

No appeal to the justice motive is necessary to explain Polish policy either before or after Hitler's attack, because of the fully compelling exigencies of self-preservation. The French Ambassador in Warsaw reported shortly after the German occupation of Prague that the Poles "have lost any illusions they may have had about Herr Hitler, and know that sooner or later they will have to defend their independence against the great adversary, which Germany has once more become for them."[132] At the same time, the Poles believed that Hitler could be deterred, since they had become convinced that he only moved when he was sure of meeting no resistance.[133] Throughout the summer of 1939, therefore, the Poles pursued an uncompromising and haughty policy toward Germany. They had recently observed what happens to countries that make territorial concessions to the Nazis; they also knew that satisfying Hitler's demands on Danzig would give Germany an economic stranglehold over Poland.[134]

Hitler's demands may or may not have been perceived in Polish circles as unjust. The concessions Hitler demanded most certainly would have constituted derogations of Poland's sovereign rights. But there is no evidence that Prime Minister Pilsudski, Foreign Minister Beck, or the Polish people as a whole understood Germany's demands as claims growing out of an aggrieved sense of justice, and consequently they did not believe that those claims represented the true stakes at hand. In August, Polish newspapers openly portrayed those claims as a pretext for establishing hegemony in the east.[135] Given this understanding, there was no point in complaining that Poland's *rights* were threatened when Poland's *existence* seemed to be in danger. No doubt the Poles were aware that it would have been ironic – and in appalling taste – to complain of the *injustice* of Germany's demands when Poland had quite happily helped herself to the rich industrial area of Teschen during the international dismemberment of Czechoslovakia just the previous year.

France's aversion to war had not abated by September 1939. No one was under its influence more completely than the Foreign Minister, Georges Bonnet, who desperately tried to restrain Poland from taking any action that could be construed as provocative or used as a justification for a German move.[136] The French and British Ambassadors in Berlin even discussed the possibility of settling the Polish–German dispute through an exchange of populations.[137] But Daladier and Bonnet ultimately stood by their guarantee to Poland, indicating that at last some force, or some combination of forces, proved even more powerful than their fear of war.

Judging from the terms in which French officials justified their decision, the French obligation to Poland played some role in that combination of forces. As Daladier declared in the Chamber of Deputies on September 2, "Poland has been the object of the most unjust and brutal aggression. The nations who have guaranteed her independence are bound to intervene in her defence."[138] Bonnet justified the French declaration of war in a circular to the diplomats accredited to Paris by appealing to the obligations she undertook to defend Polish independence.[139] But France had successfully avoided discharging her moral obligations before; it is difficult to imagine why they would serve as springs to action on this particular occasion. Indeed, French officials made it quite clear that there was much more to it than this. In the very same speech in which he invoked France's moral responsibility to Poland, Daladier appealed to France's vital interests. In fact, he drew a link between the two: "For a France that should allow this aggression to be carried out would very soon find itself a scorned, an isolated, a discredited France, without allies and without support, and, doubtless, would soon herself be exposed to a formidable attack."[140] Hitler's behavior since Munich had simply cut the ground from underneath French hopes that Germany would at some point become a satiated power; she seemed increasingly a threat to France herself.[141] It was the growth of this perception that accounts for the French decision to draw the line in March, and to act on that decision in September. Although the justice motive was evident, it seems clearly to have played a subsidiary role.

There were those in Britain who had reached the same conclusion and advocated resisting Hitler on essentially the same ground. Foreign Secretary Lord Halifax, for example, became convinced after Prague that the German government "were seeking to establish a position in which they could by force dominate Europe and, if possible, the world."[142] Chamberlain at times expressed a similar understanding, declaring on March 27 "that our object [is] to check and defeat Germany's attempt at world domination."[143] But this is not a sufficient explanation of Britain's behavior. The decision to guarantee Poland's independence, for example, was taken despite a warning by the British Chiefs of Staff that, by encouraging Polish intransigence, it might inadvertently trigger a war before Britain was ready to fight.[144] The Cabinet decided to approve a guarantee notwithstanding, prompting the Marquess of Zetland, Secretary of State for India, to remark, "We separated with a feeling almost of relief with the knowledge that a definite decision had been taken, even though we realised that we were burning our boats and that we might be committed to war over a principle which we have all come to think transcends even the vital material interests of this country."[145] By viewing the guarantee as a matter of principle transcending vital material interests, the government was clearly acting on the basis of a normative motivation.

Fidelity to its principles prompted the government to issue a rather puzzling guarantee – one that would have made no sense at all if Britain had been primarily concerned with calling a halt to the growth of Germany. Britain guaranteed Poland's *independence,* not her *territorial integrity.* She did so precisely to leave the door open for frontier adjustments.[146] This was because Hitler's specific claims were thought to have some merit – "The British public, rightly or wrongly, had always regarded the Versailles solution in regard to Danzig and Poland's access to the sea as particularly unfortunate and unjust."[147] Hitler might well have won concessions on these points if he had taken up the issue prior to marching into Prague. He may even have won them merely by being more patient. The British were always trying to do the right thing, and the people of Danzig had their sympathy and understanding.

Hitler expected Britain to renege on her guarantee. He badly miscalculated. He simply failed to take into account the strength of the very sense of justice which he had exploited so effectively up until this point.

Consider the terms in which the British people and their leaders reacted to Hitler's invasion. Chamberlain's very first remark to the Cabinet on September 1 was simply that "there should be no possible question now where our duty lay."[148] The Polish Ambassador, Count Edward Raczynski, informed Halifax that the Polish Government considered the German invasion "to be a case of aggression under Article 1 of the Anglo-Polish Treaty of Mutual Assistance," to which Halifax replied, "I have very little doubt of it." Sir John Simon – whom many considered "the epitome of appeasement" – met Raczynski in the corridor shortly after his meeting with Halifax, took him by the hand, and "said something to the effect that 'We can shake hands now – we are all in the same boat ... Britain is not in the habit of deserting her friends.'"[149]

In Parliament, the dominant themes were the necessity of faithfully discharging Britain's obligation to Poland, and the need to stamp out the injustices of Nazism. Arthur Greenwood delivered a passionate call to arms to fight a system inimical to liberty.[150] Winston Churchill rather extravagantly declared:

151

This is not a question of fighting for Danzig or fighting for Poland. We are fighting to save the whole world from the pestilence of Nazi tyranny and in defence of all that is most sacred to man. This is not war for domination or imperial aggrandizement or material gain; no war to shut any country out of its sunlight and means of progress. It is a war, viewed in its inherent quality, to establish, on impregnable rocks, the rights of the individual, and it is a war to establish and revive the stature of man.[151]

These noble sentiments could be dismissed as mere rhetorical flourishes had they not resonated so deeply in the British psyche. "Certainly this nation has never in its history been so unanimous in support of any decision taken by its leaders as it is now, on the eve of entering upon the war that must be waged," proclaimed the *Times of London*. "In coming to the help of Poland we have no material interest of our own to maintain. None the less we shall be fighting for that which is vital to our life, and to the life of all civilized peoples."[152]

Britain did, of course, have material interests to maintain, and it was preposterous to suggest otherwise. Britain could not afford to ignore the very palpable danger of a unified, mobilized, militaristic Germany growing in territory and resources at an almost exponential rate. Yet, remarkably, prudential considerations did not figure in the British decision-making process on the eve of war. It is striking to note that in the minutes of the cabinet meetings between the first and third of September, there is no statement of the inevitability or desirability of war from the perspective of British national interests, and no statement of the danger of an enlarged Germany. The Cabinet seriously considered a peace conference to settle the disputes between Germany and Poland, with the aim of achieving a better fit between borders and ethnic groups, indicating that the government did not regard the German attack on Poland a *sufficient* reason to declare war on Hitler. Various members of the Cabinet referred repeatedly to the public's moral outrage at Germany, however, and to the pressures of public opinion. The entire discussion, in short, was guided by moral rather than prudential considerations.[153] Hitler had engaged and offended Britain's moral sense. This was the source of Britain's unanimity in entering the war;[154] this was what gave the British war effort the complexion of a crusade; this would be the reason why, in contrast to 1918, the Allies would insist on nothing less than the unconditional surrender and total destruction of Nazi Germany.

It would be a mistake, however, to suggest that Britain relished the prospect of war. Most were sincerely repelled by it. Among the most strongly repelled was the Prime Minister himself.[155] In announcing to the House on September 3 that Britain and Germany were at war, Chamberlain freely confessed, "Everything that I have worked for, everything that I have hoped for, everything that I have believed in during my public life, has crashed into ruins."[156] He echoed this sentiment in his broadcast to the nation that evening:

> You can imagine what a bitter blow it is to me that all my long struggle to win peace has failed. Yet I cannot believe that there is anything more, or anything different, that I could have done, and that would have been more successful ... We have a clear conscience, we have done all that any country could do to establish peace, but a situation in which no word given by Germany's ruler could be trusted, and no people or country could feel themselves safe, had become intolerable ... Now may God bless you all and may He defend the right. For it is evil things that we shall be fighting against, brute force, bad faith, injustice, oppression, and persecution. And against them I am certain that right will prevail.[157]

It is testimony to the strength of Chamberlain's moral commitments that he thus overcame his visceral aversion to war.

CONCLUSIONS

It is extremely difficult to reduce the foregoing discussion to a neat evaluation of the role of the justice motive in setting the stage for World War II, and of its contribution to its outbreak in September 1939. The story is both complex and inherently controversial. A conservative assessment requires that we resist the temptation to describe Hitler's own aims as reflecting a conception of justice; that we guard against overestimating the role of resentment against Versailles in Hitler's rise to power; and that we emphasize his personal role in directing events from 1933 to 1939. We must give due consideration to the undoubtedly important contribution of economic considerations to the development of National Socialism, and to the power of motivations such as war-aversion in preventing France and Britain from checking the growth of Germany in a timely and effective way. But no interpretation of the events of the interwar period could possibly be complete or accurate if it neglected the important role of the justice motive in crucial respects and at crucial junctures. Without it, one simply cannot explain the fragility of Versailles; the instability of the Weimar Republic; the transformation of Hitler's National Socialists from a minor group on the extreme fringe of German society to a truly popular mass movement; the ease with which Hitler built a single-party dictatorship; the policy of appeasement and its remarkable

153

longevity; and Britain's failure for so long to see Hitler and Nazism for what they truly were. Somehow, these disparate considerations must be reduced to a single evaluation in the first column of Table 5.1. Since the justice motive clearly played more than a weak role in conditioning the conflict, a rating of "moderate" seems the most reasonable conservative evaluation possible.

The evaluations given in column two are more straightforward. The assessment of the role of the justice motive in British decision-making – "strong" – reflects the preoccupation of the British public and British decision-makers with considerations of justice, but acknowledges the concern of players such as Halifax who saw in Nazi Germany a direct threat to British national interests. An assignment proportionate to the tenor of the publicly articulated British self-understanding would be different – "very strong" – but prudence requires error on the side of caution.

It nevertheless seems surprising, from a Realist perspective, that *realpolitik* did not play a more important role in the genesis of either of this century's cataclysmic general wars. In both cases, considerations of justice played crucial roles in setting up and maintaining the dynamics and pressures that provided the occasions or opportunities for the high politics of bluff and bluster, threat and counterthreat, thrust and parry. The stories of these two wars do not demonstrate the falsity of the Realist account of motivation; but they clearly demonstrate its incompleteness.

6 THE FALKLANDS/MALVINAS WAR

Table 6.1. *The Falklands/Malvinas war*

Role of justice motive in conditioning conflict	Role of justice motive as proximate cause (by participant)	
Conclusive	Argentina	Very strong
	Britain	Very strong

In the early morning hours of April 2, 1982, Argentine forces stormed ashore on East Falkland and quickly overwhelmed the forty-two-man garrison of Royal Marines at Port Stanley. The invaders raised the Argentine flag, expelled British Governor Rex Hunt, and proclaimed the successful "recovery" of the islands after 150 years of British occupation.

In Buenos Aires, the response was euphoric. Argentine citizens of all ages and political persuasions flooded the streets, cheering, waving flags, embracing, and crying with joy. In London, there was shock and outrage. Prime Minister Margaret Thatcher immediately ordered a naval task force to the South Atlantic. But as it steamed slowly and inexorably towards its destination, diplomacy swung into high gear in an attempt to negotiate a peaceful resolution of the dispute. US Secretary of State Alexander Haig spent most of the month of April shuttling back and forth between the two capitals striving to hammer out an agreement. When he failed, President Belaúnde Terry of Peru took up the challenge. His effort also came to naught. At the United Nations, Secretary General Javier Pérez de Cuellar worked around the clock with the British and Argentine delegations. He, too, came up empty handed.

On May 21, British forces landed, and the fighting began in earnest. It was over fairly quickly. On June 14, Britain accepted the surrender of the Argentine garrison, thus bringing to an end a relatively small, relatively bloodless colonial conflict that seemed strangely out of place in the modern world.[1]

The Falklands/Malvinas war has attracted considerable interest in part because it is such a clear example of the consequences of misperceptions and misjudgments at the highest levels of government. The British grossly underestimated the danger of an Argentinean attack; the Argentine leadership seriously underestimated the likelihood of a British military response, and incorrectly gauged the general climate of world opinion. The story of the misperceptions and misjudgments on both sides is fascinating and instructive, but, except insofar as it sheds light on the agency of the justice motive, it is not my primary concern here.[2]

THE NATURE OF THE DISPUTE

The Falklands/Malvinas war was the product of a longstanding dispute between Britain and Argentina on the question of sovereignty over the islands. Argentina advanced a claim based primarily on historical right, while Britain countered with its own claim based largely upon the islanders' right of self-determination.[3] On their own terms, each was capable of mustering a fairly impressive case. Argentina argued that she had inherited Spain's colonial title to the islands, and that Britain had violated that title in 1833 by forcibly evicting the settled Argentine population and government.[4] The essence of the British argument was that, whatever the historical circumstances might be, the overwhelming majority of the 1,800 living Falkland Islanders (known colloquially as "Kelpers") were of British stock, had British sympathies and customs, and strongly desired to maintain their allegiance to the Crown. Thus the main philosophical battle lines were quite clearly drawn between two competing conceptions of legitimate entitlement – self-determination and historical right – from which neither side would budge before, during, or after the conflict.[5] As we shall see, this basic conflict between competing conceptions of legitimate entitlement was the overwhelming factor conditioning the outbreak of war. The war simply would not have occurred in its absence. But this can be seen most easily in retrospect, and so it will prove expedient to concentrate primarily on the proximate causes of the war. To understand those causes, it is necessary to sketch a brief history of the period leading up to the outbreak of hostilities.

Argentina never allowed its claim to the Malvinas to lapse while Britain controlled the islands, but not until 1965 did a sustained diplomatic effort to recover them get underway, spurred by United Nations Resolution 2065 calling for Argentina and the United Kingdom to negotiate a solution to their dispute. The British Foreign

Office proved remarkably accommodating: they deemed the islands themselves to be of no real economic or strategic importance; satisfying Argentina's demands seemed to the architects of British foreign policy a small price to pay if it resulted in a general improvement in relations not only between Britain and Argentina, but with Latin America as a whole, where anticolonialism remained a potent political force. Britain's national interest seemed best served by an accommodation with Argentina, even if it meant a formal transfer of sovereignty. Lest it be thought that this was merely a shameless utilitarian calculation by which the interests of the Falkland Islanders were to be sacrificed on the altar of expediency, it should be clearly noted that in the opinion of the Foreign Office, the economic future of the islands depended upon closer ties with the Argentine mainland, for straightforward logistical reasons. An accord with Argentina held out the prospect of significant welfare gains for an economically backward region that simply could not be achieved by other means. In a sense, therefore, the Foreign Office also had the best interests of the islanders at heart.[6]

The two countries negotiated a Memorandum of Understanding in August 1968, and agreed to disclose it in December.[7] The Memorandum's crucial passage stated that "The Government of the United Kingdom as part of ... a final settlement will recognise Argentina's sovereignty over the islands from a date to be agreed. This date will be agreed as soon as possible after (i) the two governments have resolved the present divergence between them as to the criteria according to which the United Kingdom Government shall consider whether the interests of the Islanders would be secured by the safeguards and guarantees to be offered by the Argentine Government, and (ii) the Government of the United Kingdom are then satisfied that those interests are so secured."[8] But while negotiations with Argentina were going smoothly, a clamor arose on the home front, where the Foreign Office found itself forced to fight a rear-guard action against a handful of Conservative members of parliament in league with representatives from the islands, constituted as the Falkland Islands Emergency Committee (later simply the Falkland Islands Committee), led by Hunter Christie, a barrister and former foreign service officer in Buenos Aires known for his hard line on the Falklands question.[9] In April 1968, a row in parliament forced the government to pledge that "the wishes [NB: not *interests*] of the islanders are an absolute condition" for any settlement with Argentina. In November, Lord Chalfont traveled to the islands in an attempt to persuade the inhabitants of the benefits of a transfer of sovereignty. He received a distinctly chilly reception.

Unable to muster the necessary support for the agreement either in Parliament or in the islands themselves, the Foreign Office reluctantly allowed it to lapse.

The Foreign Office decided that a change of strategy was in order, and placed its hopes in a gradual evolution of islander opinion: if the islanders could experience the benefits of closer association with Argentina, then perhaps they would change their minds. As Under Secretary for Dependent Territories David Scott was fond of saying, Britain would not tolerate the rape of the Falkland Islands, but would actively encourage their seduction.[10] To that end, Britain and Argentina concluded a Communications Agreement in 1971 – the high point of Anglo-Argentine diplomacy – bringing the islands regular air service to the Argentine mainland at cut rates, supplies of fresh produce, and tourists. The islanders welcomed the benefits, but remained wary of the agreement's intentions. Gradually it became apparent that the effort would fail. "The Archangel Gabriel could not have talked Mr Hunter Christie and his colleagues out of their deep suspicion of, and antagonism towards, Argentina," wrote maverick Labour M.P. Tam Dalyell. "They were intransigent. Foreign Office men who wanted the representatives of the Falkland islanders to be reasonable and accommodating towards Argentina were near despair. There was no hope of a meeting of minds. They were more British than the British."[11]

The islanders' doubts intensified with the return of Juan Perón to the Argentine presidency in 1973, which triggered an outburst of Argentine nationalism closely associated with frustration over the pace of sovereignty negotiations. In April, when Britain simply refused to discuss the subject further, negotiations came to a virtual halt. Once again the United Nations stepped in, urging the resumption of talks in Resolution 3160 (December 1973). But there was very little room for progress; Argentina continued to insist on a transfer of sovereignty, and the islanders continued to refuse to consider it.

At the end of 1975, the Argentine Ambassador to the UN, Carlos Ortiz de Rozas, ominously proclaimed that Argentina did not have unlimited patience, and voiced his frustration with Britain's obstinate and unjustified refusal to negotiate seriously on a transfer of sovereignty.[12] Britain decided to dispatch Lord Shackleton to the islands to assess their economic potential, a move that Argentina interpreted as a unilateral repudiation of further negotiations.[13] This impression was confirmed on January 17, 1976, when Derek Ashe, the new British Ambassador to Argentina, presented a note from British Foreign Minister James Callaghan to Argentine Foreign Minister Raúl Quijano calling for continued economic cooperation in the islands, but dismissing the sovereignty dispute as "unproductive." Quijano promptly recalled the Argentine ambassador to London and demanded that Ashe be withdrawn.[14]

The Argentine military coup of 1976 further lessened the islanders' interest in Argentine sovereignty, and considerably increased bilateral tensions.[15] For the next three years, there was no further progress toward resolving the dispute. The new Conservative government of Prime Minister Margaret Thatcher decided in 1979 to reconsider Britain's options. The Foreign and Commonwealth Office presented the new Minister of State, Nicholas Ridley, with three broad policy alternatives:

1. "Fortress Falklands," i.e., breaking off negotiations and preparing to defend the islands.
2. Relinquishing the islands, offering to resettle the inhabitants (an option the Foreign Office considered "politically and morally indefensible").
3. Continuing with the negotiations in search of a settlement with Argentina.[16]

The Foreign Office settled on the third option, favoring a policy called "leaseback": Britain would concede sovereignty to Argentina in return for a long lease on the Hong Kong model.[17] Ridley visited the islands in November 1980, and attempted to sell leaseback to the Kelpers. He discovered that a substantial minority strongly opposed the idea, and the rest were wary of it. Virtually no one supported it.[18]

The leaseback option – indeed, any settlement involving a transfer of sovereignty – suffered a serious political setback on December 2, 1980, when Ridley rose in the House of Commons to report on his activities:

> With permission, Mr. Speaker, I wish to make a statement on the Falkland Islands.
>
> We have no doubt about our sovereignty over the islands. The Argentines, however, continue to press their claim. The dispute is causing continuing uncertainty, emigration and economic stagnation in the islands. Following my exploratory talks with the Argentines in April, the Government have been considering possible ways of achieving a solution which would be acceptable to all parties. In this, the essential is that we should be guided by the wishes of the islanders themselves.
>
> I therefore visited the islands between 22 and 29 November in order to consult island councillors and subsequently, at their express request, all islanders on how we should proceed. Various possible bases for seeking a negotiated settlement were discussed. These

159

included both a way of freezing the dispute for a period or exchanging the title of sovereignty against a long lease of the islands back to Her Majesty's Government.

The essential elements of any solution would be that it should preserve British administration, law and way of life for the islanders while releasing the potential of the islands' economy and of their maritime resources, at present blighted by the dispute.

It is for the islanders to advise on which, if any, option should be explored in negotiations with the Argentines. I have asked them to let me have their views in due course. Any eventual settlement would have to be endorsed by the islanders and by this House.[19]

Ridley was the immediate victim of a verbal battering few British ministers have ever had the misfortune to endure.[20] As Michael Charlton puts it, "There was an immediate and conspicuous revolution of the Commons."[21] He took it from both benches. One member denounced in no uncertain terms "the shameful schemes for getting rid of these islands which have been festering in the Foreign Office for years."[22] Several sought explicit assurances that nothing would be done without the islanders' consent (assurances which, in fact, Ridley had already given). As *The Times* remarked the next day, "Seldom can a minister have had such a drubbing from all sides of the House, and Mr Ridley was left in no doubt that whatever Machiavellian intrigues he and the Foreign Office may be up to, they will come to nothing if they involve harming a hair on the heads of the islanders."[23]

The elections for the islands' legislative council on October 14, 1981, reflected a hardening of attitude against negotiations on sovereignty.[24] For all intents and purposes, leaseback was dead and buried. Britain now faced a choice between renouncing any further intention to negotiate and stringing Buenos Aires along, hoping that the issue would either go away or resolve itself in the fullness of time. Not surprisingly, Britain chose the latter.

But the men who would soon rise to power in Argentina were not willing to be strung along indefinitely. In December 1981, the commander-in-chief of the army, General Leopoldo Galtieri, with the support of Admiral Jorge Isaac Anaya, toppled President Roberto Viola in a palace coup. Together with Brigadier Basilio Lami Dozo, head of the air force, Galtieri and Anaya formed the junta that would lead Argentina into war with Britain. Anaya had a reputation as a hardliner on the Malvinas issue.[25] Lami Dozo, the junior partner in the triumvirate (the air force had always taken a back seat to the other two services in the Argentine military establishment), was considered a moderate. Galtieri fell somewhere between the other two. He told the Italian journalist Oriana Fallaci after the war that taking back the islands "was a preoccupation I always had."[26] But he had said relatively little in public on the issue before becoming President, apart from one oblique statement in an Army Day speech on May 29, 1981, that seems pregnant with significance only in retrospect. "Nobody can or will be able to say that we have not been extremely calm and patient in our handling of international problems, which in no way stem from any appetite for territory on our part," Galtieri proclaimed. "However, after a century and a half they are becoming more and more unbearable."[27]

The Malvinas question immediately rose to the top of the Argentine agenda. On January 24, 1982, Jesús Iglesias Rouco, a journalist thought to have excellent contacts in the government, predicted that Argentina would soon present Britain with a series of "firm and clear" conditions for the continuation of negotiations over the islands, with a strict deadline for their return, and that if those conditions were rejected, Argentina would break off negotiations.[28] In a subsequent article on February 7, Rouco hinted that Argentina might use military means to recover the islands if Britain proved intransigent.[29] As predicted, the Ministry of Foreign Affairs delivered a *bout de papier* to the British Ambassador on January 27, 1982, rehearsing Argentina's claim, stating that British recognition of Argentine sovereignty over the disputed islands remained a *sine qua non* for the resolution of the dispute, insisting that Argentina would never abandon its claim or relax its determination, and calling for negotiations concluding, "within a reasonable period of time and without procrastination", in the recognition of Argentinean sovereignty. The note pointed out that there had been no substantive progress to date, and that the time had come for "solutions, without further delays or dilatory arguments." To conclude an agreement "peacefully, definitively and *rapidly*," Argentina proposed establishing a permanent negotiating commission to meet in the first weeks of every month, in alternating capitals, for a duration of one year, during which period either side could withdraw at any time.[30] In reply, Britain dispatched a note asserting that it was in no doubt of its own claim to sovereignty over the islands, and refusing to accept as a premise of negotiations Argentina's position that talks must necessarily result in Britain's recognition of Argentina's claim. The note professed willingness to discuss the issue without prejudice, and expressed hope for a solution to the dispute acceptable to "all concerned, namely the British and Argentine Governments and the people of the Falkland Islands."[31]

British and Argentine representatives in New York agreed to hold a series of discussions, and issued a joint communiqué to that effect on

March 1. They agreed not to divulge the details of the negotiating framework; but, on the very same day, the Argentine Ministry of Foreign Affairs unilaterally issued a communiqué of its own:

> At the meeting held in New York on 26 and 27 February, the representatives of Argentina and Great Britain considered an Argentine proposal to establish a system of monthly meetings with a pre-established agenda, pre-arranged meeting place, and led by top-level officials. The aim of such meetings will be genuinely to speed up to the maximum the negotiations in train to achieve recognition of Argentine sovereignty over the Malvinas, South Georgia and the South Sandwich Islands, and by this means to achieve substantial results within a time which at this advanced stage of the discussions will necessarily have to be short.
>
> Argentina has negotiated with Great Britain over the solution of the sovereignty dispute over the Islands with patience, loyalty and good faith for over 15 years, within the framework indicated by the relevant United Nations Resolutions. The new system constitutes an effective step for the early solution of the dispute. However, should this not occur, Argentina reserves [the right] to terminate the working of this mechanism and to choose freely the procedure which best accords with her interests.[32]

Several Argentine officials, including Foreign Minister Nicanor Costa Méndez, disassociated themselves from the veiled threat contained in the communiqué's final sentence.[33] But, in the light of subsequent events, it seems likely to have reflected official opinion.

Lord Carrington prepared a reply and submitted it to Governor Hunt on March 8 for consideration by the Island Councils. The note expressed pleasure at the progress achieved in New York toward establishing new procedures for settling the dispute, but insisted that negotiations would have to proceed without prejudice to either side's position on the sovereignty issue; that they would have to result in an agreement satisfactory to both governments and to the Islanders; and that they could not take place against the background of threats. On March 16, the Councils unanimously supported the message as drafted, but registered their strong determination to remain British.[34] Britain did not deliver the note to Costa Méndez, as it was overtaken by events.

The immediate difficulty was an incident on South Georgia Island, 950 miles east of Port Stanley. A group of forty Argentine workers led by a scrap-metal dealer named Constantino Davidoff, under contract with a Scottish firm to salvage the remnants of an abandoned whaling station at Leith Harbour, sailed to South Georgia aboard the Argentine naval survey ship *Bahía Buen Suceso*, landing on March 19. They failed to obtain the necessary permits from British authorities twenty miles south at Grytviken, and ran up the Argentine flag. Britain protested this violation of her sovereignty, demanded that the landing party secure the necessary permits, and dispatched HMS *Endurance* to remove them if they failed to do so. All but a dozen of the workmen left the island on March 23; but the next day the Argentine naval survey ship *Bahía Paraíso* sailed into Leith bearing a detachment of marines with orders to protect the remainder of the group.

In Argentina, military activity began to gather momentum. The armed forces canceled weekend leaves and began moving supplies to the naval base at Puerto Belgrano and to the air force base at Comodoro Rivadavia. The Argentine fleet, at sea on joint maneuvers with Uruguay, turned and sailed in the direction of the Malvinas. British intelligence concluded that the risk of an invasion was high.[35] On April 2, Argentine forces seized the islands.

THE ARGENTINE DECISION TO INVADE

The invasion of the Falklands may have been intended by the junta to serve one or more of several purposes reflecting fundamentally different motivations:

- *Domestic politics (diversion)*. The invasion may have been an attempt by the junta to distract the attention of the Argentine people from the nation's economic predicament, and to boost the lagging popularity of the military regime.
- *Economic interest*. The invasion may have been intended to secure control of the economic resources of the islands and their territorial waters.
- *Strategic interest*. The junta may have been interested in securing the islands for strategic reasons, so as to enhance its military position in the South Atlantic and enable it to dominate the eastern approaches to Cape Horn.
- *Interservice rivalry*. The invasion may have been an attempt on the part of the Argentine navy to enhance its prestige and thus its influence in national politics.
- *Irredentism*. The invasion may have been intended to solve the sovereignty dispute *simpliciter* – the junta, like the rest of the nation, simply may have run out of patience with Britain's intransigence and decided to seize by force of arms what it considered rightfully Argentina's. According to this interpretation, the invasion was simply the rectification of a perceived injustice.

163

Which of these motivations were operative, and to what extent?

The diversion hypothesis represented the common wisdom in the English-speaking world during and immediately after the war itself, and was reflected in virtually every major British publication, and in all the major studies of the war by British authors unsympathetic to Argentina's claim.[36] It was also the understanding at the time of Francis Pym, Britain's new Foreign Minister, and of Alexander Haig, the American Secretary of State.[37] It is interesting to note that more recent analyses tend to downplay the diversion hypothesis in favor of irredentism. Indeed, Haig later came to believe that frustration with 150 years of futile negotiations with Britain was "the dominant factor" in the Argentine decision to invade.[38]

There is an appealing plausibility to the diversion hypothesis. In 1981, inflation in Argentina reached 130 percent; the peso fell to one-fifth of its value against the dollar; the gross national product dropped 6 percent; manufacturing output dropped 22.9 percent; real wages fell 19.2 percent; and 500,000 people out of a total work force of just under eight million were unemployed.[39] A month before the invasion La Prensa declared, "The only thing which can save this government is a war."[40] The events immediately preceding the invasion seemed to confirm this. On March 30, Argentina's labor unions attempted to stage a demonstration against the government's economic policies; the regime brutally suppressed it. Three days later, the very same people whom riot police had beaten and dispersed filled the streets demonstrating in support of the reoccupation of the Malvinas. Could the two events possibly have been coincidental? The Franks Commission thought not. "All the information, including intelligence reports, that has come to light since the invasion suggests that the decision to invade was taken by the junta at a very late date," the report concluded. "It is probable that the decision to invade was taken in the light of the development of the South Georgia situation; but it seems that the violent demonstrations in Buenos Aires on the night of 30/31 March were also a factor in the junta's decision."[41]

The diversion hypothesis suffers from several fatal weaknesses. The first is that there is simply no documentary or testimonial evidence to support it. It is not even widely maintained by opponents of the military regime in Argentina itself. Perhaps not surprisingly, it was dismissed in no uncertain terms by Galtieri in his interview with Oriana Fallaci, who accused him of invading the islands to distract public attention from Argentina's rampant inflation and massive foreign debt, to unify the country, and to bolster his own personal popularity:

I accept your argument because you are a journalist. If you were not a journalist, I promise you that I would not have permitted you to say all this. Because it hurts my principles, my good name, my military career, all that I have tried to preserve in my life. Never did I make the cold calculation you accuse me of. Never. The debt and the inflation had nothing to do with my decision. As a matter of fact, I can tell you that this conflict does not help the inflation and the debt. It is true instead that the Malvinas has helped to unify the Argentines and that it does so more and more. But the idea of obtaining this unification through war never crossed my mind, I swear and repeat.[42]

Of course, when Galtieri made these remarks, he was still the president of Argentina. If he *had* invaded the islands for domestic political reasons, he could hardly have said so, because he would have opened himself to charges that he risked Argentine lives for his own narrow political purposes. It is also interesting to notice Galtieri's choice of words: *the idea of obtaining this unification through war never crossed my mind*. He never expected war in the first place; perhaps he *did* think of obtaining unification through a successful, relatively inexpensive *fait accompli*. Nevertheless, if Galtieri were dissimulating, he must be given credit for extraordinary talent in affecting wounded pride. One should not lightly dismiss, either, his observation that the conflict did nothing to help the inflation and the debt; in fact, the war greatly aggravated Argentina's economic difficulties. If Galtieri had not anticipated a war, he would not necessarily have expected the invasion to *worsen* the economic situation; but he had no reason to expect a successful operation to *improve* matters, either. The invasion could not, therefore, have offered any reasonable prospect of countervailing the pressures the regime found itself under by virtue of the nation's economic predicament; at best, it offered a temporary distraction and a brief reprieve. What then? How would the reoccupation of the Malvinas have ensured the long-term viability of the regime? Did Galtieri expect it to boost his popularity so much that all existing grievances would be forgotten, all existing complaints forgiven? If so, he badly miscalculated in this respect as well; for although the Argentine people strongly supported the occupation of the Malvinas, they were no more favorably disposed toward the dictatorship after it than they had been before.[43] Moreover, if the invasion had been intended to divert attention from the nation's economic woes, it should have taken place *before* – not after – the March 30 demonstrations. The demonstrations had been advertised on March 20, providing plenty of time for a rapid military move.[44]

But the most impressive argument against the domestic politics hypothesis is that it does not fit with what is known about the Argentine decision-making process. All the evidence suggests that the Galtieri regime *came to power* with a conditional intention, and a very strong predilection, to invade. Their minds had been all but made up on the question well before the outbreak of domestic unrest at the end of March. The actual decision to invade was made on March 26, before the demonstrations in Buenos Aires. The timing of the invasion reflected the junta's perception of a closing window of opportunity to seize the islands without bloodshed. Domestic politics were entirely beside the point.

The key figure in the decision to invade was not Galtieri, but Admiral Jorge Anaya, commander-in-chief of the navy. Anaya had been involved in the preparation of military plans for the "recovery" of the Malvinas in the late 1960s – significantly called "Plan Goa" in honor of India's seizure of the Portuguese colony by the same name.[45] The recovery of the Malvinas obsessed Anaya. To an American officer after the war, he confessed that his "life's ambition" was "to retake the Malvinas Islands for Argentina."[46] The intensity of his passion on the issue was evident to Haig during his peace mission in April 1982. "My son is ready to die for the Malvinas," Anaya told Haig, "and it is my family's point of view that we would be proud to know his blood had mingled with this sacred soil."[47] It strains credibility to imagine that Anaya was prepared to sacrifice his son merely to distract the Argentine people from their economic hardships, especially in view of the fact that he was "not known to have further political ambitions."[48] Anaya's personal motivations on the Malvinas issue can be described much more accurately in terms of simple irredentism than narrow short-term calculations of political interest.

Galtieri needed Anaya's support to attain the presidency and retain control of the army at the same time. The navy did not carry sufficient weight to have its own man head the junta, but, as Lowell Gustafson remarks, "Anaya was savvy enough to be the kingmaker,"[49] and he exacted a price for his support. The two apparently struck a deal on December 9, 1981, whereby Galtieri received Anaya's backing in return for an understanding that Argentina would recover the Malvinas before the 150th anniversary of their seizure in January 1983 – if necessary, by means of force.[50] In late December, Costa Méndez began briefing senior journalists on the government's determination to recover the Falklands by the end of 1982, discussing in some detail the military operations that might be necessary.[51] Planning for military action began seriously in January, when the junta approved National Strategy Directive 1/82:

> The Military Committee, faced with the evident and repeated lack of progress in the negotiations with Great Britain to obtain recognition of our sovereignty over the Malvinas, Georgias and South Sandwich Islands; convinced that the prolongation of this situation affects national honour, the full exercise of sovereignty and the exploration of resources; has *resolved* to analyse the possibility of the use of military power to obtain the political objective. This resolution must be kept in strict secrecy and should be circulated only to the heads of the respective military departments.[52]

The junta charged Rear-Admiral Carlos Busser with planning "Operation Azul." "The order was not to *update* the plan but to draft a plan from *scratch*," Busser later recalled. "Argentina had made many plans in the past to recover the Malvinas, but the order we got was to make out a new plan. We started doing so in January 1982. The basic idea was to negotiate throughout 1982, but at the same time have a military plan, just in case the negotiations failed. In that case we would take the military option. But that would be only towards the end of 1982, or the beginning of 1983."[53] The junta made a deliberate decision not to threaten to use force to extract concessions from Britain in the meantime, on the ground that doing so would serve only to alert London of the danger and give the British time to reinforce the islands' defenses. If diplomacy succeeded, Argentina would recover the islands peacefully; if it failed, Britain's intransigence would be laid bare for all the world to see, facilitating a military move.[54]

On February 3, 1982, the British Ambassador in Buenos Aires picked up the scent and reported to the Foreign Office that Anaya had "got into the driving seat" on the Malvinas issue and had decided to allow a test period – perhaps up until the 150th anniversary of the British occupation – to see if negotiations got anywhere.[55] On March 1, Gustavo Figueroa, Costa Méndez's right-hand man, told reporters that if negotiations did not bear the desired fruit, "Argentina maintains the right to end the system and freely choose the procedure it may deem most convenient to its interests."[56] The very next day, Galtieri informed General Mario Benjamin Menéndez that he had been appointed Governor of Las Islas Malvinas.[57]

When Sr. Davidoff and his workers landed on South Georgia, prompting peremptory demands from London that they be removed, the junta decided to move the invasion date forward, initially to May 15.[58] The circumstances surrounding Davidoff's expedition are not entirely clear, but in retrospect it appears that the episode caught the junta by surprise.[59] There is little doubt that the navy was intimately involved in Davidoff's activities, and that it had prepared a detailed plan for establishing a military presence on South Georgia, called "Operation Alpha," in which Davidoff played a crucial if perhaps unwitting role.[60] On his first trip to South Georgia to survey the abandoned whaling station at Leith in December 1981, for instance, he traveled on the navy ice-breaker *Almirante Irizar*, which, uncharacteristically, maintained full radio silence throughout the journey, strongly indicating an ulterior purpose.[61] Moreover, Burns claims that the detachment of special forces sent to protect Davidoff and his men during their second voyage had actually sailed from the port of Ushuaia "soon after the New Year" with orders to proceed to South Georgia in late March to set up a military base in support of the civilians established there.[62] Some have therefore suspected that Davidoff's journey was an integral part of the Argentine military's plan to recover the Malvinas. Recent testimony, however – including that of Admiral Anaya – suggests that the junta were unaware of the details surrounding Davidoff's second voyage. Moreover, they were shocked by Britain's reaction to it.[63] The junta wrongly believed that Britain was trumping up the South Georgia incident as a pretext to reinforce its military presence in the South Atlantic.[64] This boded ill for a diplomatic solution, and for Galtieri, was "the straw that broke the camel's back."[65]

Beginning on March 23, the junta met every day to discuss the unfolding crisis. The local military situation was a crucial consideration in their deliberations. For the moment, the only Royal Navy vessel in the region was *Endurance*, which, fortuitously, had taken a number of marines from Port Stanley to enforce London's demands on South Georgia. But information reaching the junta suggested that British warships might be on the way. The point of a military move against the Falklands would be to seize the islands quickly and withdraw, leaving only a token force, to signal Argentina's determination to reestablish sovereignty. The junta counted on the active support of Latin America and the Non-Aligned countries, and the tacit cooperation of the United States, to persuade Britain to negotiate a transfer on the basis of the Argentine *fait accompli*.[66] It was crucial, the junta thought, to accomplish the objective without bloodshed, so as to prevent a major backlash in Britain and elsewhere.[67] No time offered a better prospect of success than the present. The junta met at 7.15 p.m. on March 26, and unanimously decided to order a military landing.[68] Thus the perception of a closing window of opportunity – not Argentine domestic politics – determined the timing of the invasion.[69] Freedman and Gamba-Stonehouse put it thus:

Our view is that it was the urgency of the dispute with Britain rather than the domestic situation which triggered the intervention. The Islands needed to be occupied before British military reinforcements, already believed to be on their way, arrived in the South Atlantic. The objective was not to hold on to the Islands indefinitely but to force Britain to engage in substantive negotiations on sovereignty, and to ensure that the United Nations and the United States took the issue seriously and helped bring the negotiations to a successful conclusion.[70]

As the Kaiser might have put it, the situation seemed to call for a little *douce violence*.

The final consideration weighing against the diversion hypothesis concerns the decentralized nature of the Argentine decision-making process, which was a source of considerable frustration for Alexander Haig in his attempt to negotiate a peaceful settlement. "If Galtieri did not hold the power of decision," Haig remarked, "neither did the junta. On every decision, the government apparently had to secure the unanimous consent of every corps commander in the army and of their equivalents in the navy and air force. Progress was made by syllables and centimeters and then vetoed by men who had never been part of the negotiations."[71] It is unclear whether or not the decision-making process leading up to the invasion was similarly fractionated; if so, it would seem even less likely that the narrow political interests of the junta were reflected in the decision, and more likely that it reflected deeply seated passions, of which irredentism was undoubtedly the strongest. Anaya's scheme would have met with little opposition – and probably considerable enthusiasm – within the relevant circles. In any event, once the decision had been made, it is clear that the decentralized nature of decision-making prevented the junta from backing away from its commitment never to relinquish sovereignty over the Malvinas and prevented compromises that might have permitted a peaceful resolution of the crisis.

There is little reason to give much weight to the economic, strategic, or interservice rivalry hypotheses.[72] The best evidence for any of these is an oblique remark made by Costa Méndez on April 15 that the "meaning of the Argentine presence in the islands" was "that Argentina controls an area in the South Atlantic, politically and economically."[73] But Costa Méndez did not speak for the junta. He was generally out of step with the regime's policy, and was not even kept fully informed of its activities and decisions.[74] National Strategy Directive 1/82 did make passing reference to "the exploration of resources;"[75] but, as we shall see below, this seems to have been at most a marginal motivation.[76]

Economically, the Falkland Islands were hardly an alluring prize. Despite frequent speculation in the 1970s that rich oil deposits might be found offshore, none had been discovered by 1982.[77] In 1976, Lord Shackleton suggested that oil production might be economically viable in the region, but concluded in 1982 that the prospects were dim.[78] Indeed, the very possibility of offshore oil concerned Buenos Aires not because Britain stood to collect the revenues rather than Argentina, but because successful development of the island's resources would complicate negotiations over sovereignty.[79] Prior to and during the war itself, the British told Haig point-blank that oil was not the issue, and he was firmly convinced that it was "the last thing on Galtieri's mind."[80] The land itself yielded nothing but peat and sheep, neither of which held out the prospect of glowing riches. The potential tourist trade of the islands was strictly limited; the inshore waters were rich only in seaweed and krill, for which there was hardly a lucrative market. And while the islands' offshore waters abounded with fish, Britain had always been willing to grant Argentina access to them as part of a comprehensive settlement. The islands therefore promised no major economic benefits that could not have been realized by means far short of outright sovereignty. It is not surprising, therefore, that Douglas Kinney concludes that neither side in the crisis "was directly motivated in its diplomacy by resource considerations."[81]

The Franks Report suggests that Argentina's interest in the Falklands increased as a result of her losing battle with Chile over title to the Beagle Channel islands.[82] The Argentine navy's southern base at Ushuaia was perilously close to the border and vulnerable to Chilean batteries; Chilean control of the Beagle Channel islands would further erode Argentina's strategic position at the tip of South America. It has been surmised that Anaya considered the Malvinas an attractive offset because "from there his navy could not only provide a southern base, it could control the Cape Horn route and stay safely clear of Chilean firepower."[83] The actual strategic value of the Falklands, however, is negligible, and it is highly unlikely that Anaya would have been attracted to them for strategic reasons. A naval base at Stanley (as the British have since found out) would be difficult to supply, expensive to maintain, and considerably more vulnerable to attack than bases on the Argentine mainland from which a fleet could operate within constant range of air cover. It is questionable whether a fleet operating from the islands could dominate the southern cape if a fleet operating from a mainland base could not; Port Stanley is too far away to provide prompt naval support, and not significantly closer than the much larger mainland base at Comodoro Rivadavia for non-time-urgent missions. Most tellingly, there is little strategic reason to worry about dominating the cape at all. While the Falklands had been strategically useful prior to the building of the Panama Canal, when important sea routes passed the islands, very little commercial traffic travels through the area today.[84] There are few targets of any value in southern Argentina attractive to the (much less powerful) Chilean navy, and none that could not be protected from a mainland base more cheaply and effectively.[85] If Argentina truly needed new naval bases to protect its southern seaboard, it could build them at a fraction of the cost at Rio Gallegos, Puerto Santa Cruz, or Puerto Deseado.[86] Thus the strategic value of the islands is negligible, and certainly not worth antagonizing a nuclear-armed Great Power.

What of the interservice rivalry hypothesis? Alexander Haig suspected that the invasion was intended at least in part to boost the fortunes and influence of the Argentine navy.[87] This is not a view that is widely held. The navy, while perhaps the most important, was by no means the sole branch involved in the recovery of the Malvinas, and it was not credited with particular responsibility for carrying out the operation. In any event, Anaya and Galtieri were on excellent terms; perhaps more than at any other previous time in Argentine history, under their leadership the army and the navy enjoyed close and cordial relations. Certainly the navy had little tangible reason to harbor serious grievances against the other branches; prior to the invasion, it had enjoyed a sustained period of growth and modernization. Of all the branches, the air force was most sorely in need of a boost in prestige. Ironically, it showed the least interest in the invasion but played the most active role in the war with Britain. To date, no serious evidence has emerged to suggest that interservice rivalries were important in the conception or execution of the operation.

That leaves irredentism, Galtieri's own explanation for the Argentine action: "Not gold, not oil, not the strategic position; the sentiment of the Argentine nation since 1833."[88] When President Reagan intervened at the eleventh hour in an attempt to persuade Galtieri not to invade, Galtieri dismissed the attempt simply by noting that Britain had refused to negotiate seriously for 150 years, and that time had finally run out.[89]

Despite the fact that it represents the official view – which political scientists are always inclined to suspect – irredentism constitutes the best explanation of the regime's behavior, although this only becomes clear once one appreciates Argentina's unusually intense nationalism, of which most Anglophone commentators were simply unaware prior to the invasion itself. On the rare occasions when Argentine nationalism has shown itself to the outside world in all its glory, few have quite believed what they have seen. Argentina's World Cup victory in 1978, for example, sent the country into paroxysms of national euphoria eclipsing anything witnessed in Europe or North America even on V-E day, and rivaling the outburst of jubilation with which Argentines greeted news of the recovery of the Malvinas in 1982.[90]

After years of frustrated attempts to regain the islands, the Argentine people had developed "a kind of collective mania about the Malvinas" which the rest of the world "failed to understand."[91] To give it a fully rational explanation is simply impossible and, for this reason, outside observers have been tempted to dismiss it as a fraud or a mask – hence the ease with which the English-speaking world discounted irredentism *per se* and embraced a cynical domestic politics explanation. But for those who cared to look, signs both of the intensity and sincerity of irredentist sentiment in Argentina were evident in abundance as early as 1968. At a news conference held for British journalists accompanying Lord Chalfont to the Falkland Islands, Ezequiel Pereyra, head of the Malvinas section of the Argentine Foreign Ministry, complained that the British did not understand how the Argentines felt about the Malvinas, and described the issue as the fundamental problem of Argentine existence.[92] Schools relentlessly drummed *Las Islas Malvinas son Argentinas* into the heads of the nation's children, and even put the slogan to music. Hastings and Jenkins note that "British ministers visiting Buenos Aires in the 1960s and 1970s were constantly baffled by the emotion the subject aroused."[93] When Ashe arrived in March 1975, for instance, he received demands for the return of the Malvinas inscribed in blood. A car bomb exploded outside the British embassy, killing two of his guards.[94]

By 1979, there were so many organizations in Argentina dedicated to the recovery of the islands that they formed an umbrella group to coordinate their activities. The government declared June 10, 1979 – the 150th anniversary of the establishment of the first Argentine government in the islands – a national holiday. Popular pressure began to build for the restitution of the islands by January 2, 1983 – the 150th anniversary of the British occupation. That date quickly developed a powerful hold on the national consciousness. It became a firm self-imposed deadline.[95]

In 1981, the Argentine press began to take the generals to task for their failure to secure sovereignty over the Malvinas.[96] The Foreign Ministry produced more and more ominous statements evincing greater and greater urgency. On July 27, 1981, a note from Foreign

172

Minister Oscar Camilión to the British Ambassador expressed "serious concern" at the lack of progress at the February round of talks, and, noting that ten years had passed since the communications agreements, declared that in the Argentine government's opinion, it was impossible "to postpone further a profound and serious discussion of the complex essential constituents of the negotiations – sovereignty and economic co-operation – in a simultaneous and global fashion with the express intention of achieving concrete results shortly. A resolute impetus must therefore be given to the negotiations. The next round of negotiations cannot be another mere exploratory exercise, but must mark the beginning of a decisive stage towards the definitive termination of the dispute."[97] The Ministry of Foreign Affairs issued a simultaneous communiqué stating that the Argentine government considered that "the acceleration of negotiations on the Malvinas, with resolution and with clear objectives in view, had become an unpostponable priority for its foreign policy."[98]

On September 22, Camilión addressed the United Nations. Referring to the "present illegal occupation" of the Malvinas, he expressed his government's hope that they would be "able to report in due course to the General Assembly that this series of negotiations concerning the Malvinas, South Georgia and South Sandwich Islands, which we hope will begin soon, was the last one."[99] After Galtieri's coup, the urgency reached a crescendo. Publications such as Haroldo Foulkes's widely read *Las Malvinas, Una Causa Nacional* made the argument that time was on Britain's side, and that if a diplomatic solution could not be found, force would have to be used.[100] The Argentine press carried on the campaign with vigor.[101] In February, a spate of articles appeared designating 1982 as the key year for the return of the islands.[102]

Galtieri and Anaya were patriotic Argentines; neither of them was immune to the enchantment of the Malvinas as a national cause.[103] Moreover, Galtieri, at least, was not a cognitively complex individual. His predecessor, General Roberto Viola, described him as a "simple and emotional" man, "a good soldier, a good commander of troops," who "knows little or nothing of politics. He is primitive."[104] Like Anaya, he, too, was entranced by the magical date of January 2, 1983. It was in such a context that Galtieri unleashed Anaya on the islands. So intense was the sense of historic injustice that when the invasion took place, the devoutly Catholic Argentine public interpreted it as an execution of Divine will, the fulfillment of a holy duty.[105]

If the Argentine people felt so intensely about the issue, why did they wait so long to redeem their beloved islands? Three considerations seem relevant here. First, throughout the nineteenth century, Argentina remained commercially dependent upon Britain and simply could not mount a plausible challenge to the Royal Navy. Indeed, not until after Thatcher's 1981 defense review, which severely weakened Britain's capability to defend distant possessions, could Argentina reasonably expect to hold its own against the British fleet. In the 1980s, for the very first time, a military option seemed to offer some hope of success.[106] Second, despite the strength of feeling over the Malvinas question, the Argentine people had not engaged in war for more than a hundred years, and had little appetite for the prospect. They considered a negotiated transfer of sovereignty preferable to a military solution, and the nation as a whole was quite willing to wait ten or fifteen years if that was the period of time required for diplomacy to work. Third, the fact of negotiations gradually intensified irredentist feeling. The very existence of negotiations gave the Argentine claims legitimacy by implying that there was something to negotiate about, and whenever the negotiations ran into an obstacle, such as islander intransigence, "Buenos Aires was enabled to feel a grievance, a sense of injustice."[107] The cumulative action of this dynamic enabled the sesquicentennial of the British occupation to assume an artificial importance as a psychic lightning rod for the collective moral outrage of the nation. After 150 years of occupation and seventeen years of futile negotiation, Argentina simply ran out of patience.[108]

The intensity of irredentist feeling rendered any compromise on the question of sovereignty impossible.[109] When Haig met Galtieri, the Argentine president told him: "In this pleasant conversation, I will say something once and then I will not repeat it again. As far as Argentina is concerned, there is no question of Argentinian sovereignty. Everything else, Argentina is disposed to negotiate ... Argentina will not step back from what it considers to be its rights."[110] Given Britain's intransigence on the question of self-determination, compromise was out of the question.[111]

What, then, can be said of the role the justice motive played in the Argentine decision to invade the Falkland Islands? Irredentism provides the simplest, least troublesome, and most persuasive explanation of the invasion. How much weight should domestic political, economic, strategic, and interservice rivalry arguments be permitted to bear?

Perhaps the Argentineans themselves might be allowed to pass judgment on this question. It is revealing that Argentine historiography explains the war simply in terms of British intransigence and "Argentina's own deep-rooted collective sentiment about the justice of the 'Malvinas' cause."[112] To an outside observer, this is cause for considerable amazement:

> Argentines are among the best-read and best-written people not just in Latin America but in the rest of the world, and yet no author or academic living in Buenos Aires at the time published a serious analysis of the political and social meaning of the war that ran contrary to the military's position. This was in striking contrast to the varied and often profound public debate about the war generated by their British counterparts ... Ernesto Sábato, one of Argentina's leading novelists who strongly opposed Perón and after the coup took a public stand against the junta, was quite literally overwhelmed by the collective emotion during the Falklands conflict. Almost inaudible between muffled sobs, Sábato declared in an interview on Spanish radio: "In Argentina it is not a military dictatorship that is fighting. It is the whole people, her women, her children, her old people, regardless of their political persuasion. Opponents to the regime like myself are fighting for our dignity, fighting to extricate the last vestiges of colonialism. Don't be mistaken, Europe; it is not a dictatorship that is fighting for the 'Malvinas'; it is the whole Nation."[113]

Even the Argentine Communist Party declared its "unequivocal support for the restoration of national sovereignty over the archipelago," and maintained that "Argentina should under no circumstances relinquish its sovereignty over the islands."[114] The Rattenbach Commission, established to investigate the junta's handling of the conflict, severely criticized Galtieri and his associates for failing to foresee the international reaction to the invasion, but did not criticize them for attempting to resolve the sovereignty dispute.[115] "It is a fact that the British never fully understood that the problem of the Islands was really very important in Argentina," said Oscar Camilión. "It is, maybe, metaphysics. From the point of view of the British it was just a far away territory. It was not a problem of the *essence, or the being, of the state*, as it was for Argentina."[116]

Finally, consider the testimony of Dr. Raúl Ricardes, Counsellor to the Argentine Mission to the United Nations – a servant of the Argentine government, but not of the Galtieri regime – given in an interview with Jeffrey Elliot:

JE: It has been said that pride, patriotism, politics, and economics motivated the Argentine invasion. To what extent is this true? Which motive was the strongest?

RR: I think you left out the most important motive – namely, principle. We sometimes forget that there are principles worth fighting for, worth dying for. Our actions in the Malvinas were motivated by principle. As I stated, what we have in the case of the Malvinas is a foreign occupation – one which took place over 150 years ago. These islands were taken by force, by the British, in 1833. They have no legitimate right to the islands. The Malvinas belong to Argentina. And it is our aim to recover our territory ...

JE: There are many who believe that, despite the claims of the Argentine Government, the sovereignty issue was quite peripheral to the war in the Malvinas. In reality, they argue, the war was a convenient way for the Argentine Government to divert attention from a deteriorating political and economic situation at home. The Malvinas, they contend, were used to unite the people and distract them from the more compelling problems which plagued Argentine society. How would you respond to such charges?

RR: Unfortunately, in conflicts of this kind, people harbor a great many misconceptions. The sovereignty issue was *the* issue which motivated our actions in the Malvinas. Otherwise, it would have been difficult, if not impossible to marshall the support necessary to prosecute the war. After all, our people are not stupid. They will not march off blindly into war. The war must be justifiable. And the people of my country are not so naive or gullible that they will believe anything they are told by their leaders. They are not willing to spill their lives and fortunes for the sake of political expediency. No, the sovereignty issue was the main force behind the war. No other issue figured into our considerations.[117]

Why should a sophisticated and literate people be so blind to the domestic political, economic, strategic, or bureaucratic causes of the conflict if these played an important role? How likely is it that a European or North American who subscribes to one of these hypotheses would be a more perceptive observer of Argentine affairs than the Argentines themselves? Virginia Gamba dismisses the domestic politics hypothesis as "the result of ignorance or misperception."[118] But the remarks of Dr. Ricardes point to a crucial fact: that even if a domestic political calculation *did* play a role in prompting the Argentine invasion, it could only have done so because such an action would give the Argentine people something that they desperately wanted. As Hastings and Jenkins remark, "Not since the days of Peron had a soldier so conspicuously implemented the popular will."[119] This popular will had nothing to do with domestic politics, with economics, or with strategy, and had everything to do with the justice motive pure and simple. If the generals sought to tap into it for their own narrow political purposes, they quickly became "prisoners of passions they themselves had helped to arouse."[120] If they did not, then they were simply prisoners of the very passions they shared with the

Argentine nation as a whole. In either case, the Argentine decision to invade the Falkland Islands provides a vivid illustration of the justice motive at work.

THE BRITISH DECISION TO RESPOND

As with the Argentine decision to invade the islands, the British decision to retake them by force of arms could plausibly have been motivated by a variety of considerations:

- *The requirements of justice.* The Argentine invasion was a blatant violation of the Falkland Islanders' right of self-determination, which the British government was morally obliged to protect.
- *Credibility.* By acquiescing in an Argentinean *fait accompli*, Britain would send a signal to the rest of the world that she was unwilling to defend her possessions and maintain her commitments, not only weakening her position in disputes over other colonies such as Gibraltar and Hong Kong, but also undermining deterrence in Central Europe.
- *Domestic politics.* A forceful response may have been necessary for the political survival of the Conservative government, which was lagging in popularity.
- *Regional economic or strategic interest.* The British government may have been eager to retain possession of the Falkland Islands for their economic and strategic value.

We can dismiss the last of these at the outset, essentially for the same reasons that weighed against the supposition that the Argentine government had been attracted to the invasion on economic or strategic grounds. Dr. Samuel Johnson, writing in the 1770s, made the point as eloquently as anyone, when he described "Falkland's Island" as "a bleak and gloomy solitude, an island thrown aside from human use, stormy in winter and barren in summer; an island which not even the southern savages have dignified with habitation; where a garrison must be kept in a state that contemplates with envy the exiles of Siberia; of which the expense will be perpetual and the use only occasional; and which, if fortune smiles upon our labours, may become a nest of smugglers in peace, and in war the refuge of future buccaneers."[121]

None of the major analyses of the Falklands war endorses the view that British actions were intended to serve economic or strategic purposes.[122] If, indeed, the islands had had any serious economic or strategic importance, then the Foreign Office would not have been so eager to be rid of them.[123] The sole reason why a transfer of

177

sovereignty never took place was that the Falkland Islanders themselves did not wish it. When *The Guardian* noted the day after the Argentine invasion that "the Falkland Islands do not represent any strategic or commercial British interest worth fighting over," it prompted one Member of Parliament to proclaim, "It is shocking that in a great newspaper such as *The Guardian* the view should be put that the only things worth fighting over are commercial matters and not the rights and freedoms of individual people."[124] As Liberal leader David Owen stated in the House of Commons, "We have made it very clear on many occasions that our retention of the administration and sovereignty of the Falkland Islands does not relate to the possibility of there being gas or oil in the region. We are not there for a commercial purpose. We are not balancing whether there is a positive or a negative trade. We are there because the islanders, successively through their legislative Council, have made it clear that they wish us to be there."[125]

Remarks such as these are typical of the dominant theme sounded both in Parliament and among the British people as a whole: Britain could not permit Argentina to get away with its seizure of the islands because of her commitment to defend the Falkland Islanders' right of self-determination. This was certainly the Prime Minister's main line of argument.[126] It was also the conviction of such figures on both sides of the House as the Leader of the Opposition, Michael Foot;[127] the former Labour Foreign Minister, Denis Healey;[128] the outgoing Conservative Foreign Minister, Lord Carrington;[129] and the Minister of Defence, John Nott.[130] In every debate on the issue, Parliament was unanimous on this point. There was a major uproar over the government's failure to foresee and prevent the Argentine invasion; there was considerable disagreement over the best means of handling the situation (whether unilaterally or through the United Nations; whether purely diplomatically, or by force or arms; whether flexibly or dogmatically) – but on this one issue alone, Parliament was united.[131] By and large, so was the rest of the country. Polls showed that an overwhelming majority of Britons were firmly committed to self-determination for the Falkland Islanders,[132] and major British newspapers – both the hysterical tabloid press and more serious publications – voiced the same opinion editorially.[133]

Despite the overwhelming preponderance of the self-determination theme, however, the question of maintaining British credibility repeatedly surfaced in Parliament and in the press. Thatcher told Haig explicitly that she felt she had to respond forcefully to the Argentine invasion so as not to give the wrong impression about the strength and determination of the West, and it was clear to Haig that the Munich analogy weighed on the Prime Minister's mind.[134] Although she shied away from leaning too heavily on the point in Parliament, she made oblique references to it from time to time.[135] This, too, was a point that enjoyed considerable bipartisan support.[136] The *Economist* found the credibility question most poignant of all, arguing that the issue was "less 1,800 islanders' wishes than the need to avoid rewarding aggression."[137]

It is clear that some of those who worried about the credibility issue had Gibraltar and Hong Kong in mind.[138] If Britain acquiesced in Argentina's coup, Spain and China might reasonably be expected to toughen their negotiating positions. But there is no evidence that anyone in Britain expected either Spain or China to behave in a similar manner, which may explain why almost all of the British formulations of the credibility problem were abstract and principled rather than concrete. Anyone who feared the immediate con-sequences of Argentina's action in Gibraltar and Hong Kong were quickly reassured by the unfolding of events. China did not attempt to exploit the situation at all. Spain kept a very close eye on the dispute, and the invasion caused some excitement on the Spanish Right, but Spain's controlling interest was its very strong desire to join NATO and the EEC, for which she needed British support. Prime Minister Leopoldo Calvo Sotelo was careful to deny an exact parallel between the Falklands and Gibraltar so as not to rock the boat.[139] So, while the credibility issue appears to have been a factor in British deliberations, specific worries about Gibraltar and Hong Kong, to the extent they existed, quickly dissipated.

The supposition that Margaret Thatcher's policy was driven by narrow calculations of domestic political interest is particularly popular among two groups: political scientists and Argentines. Thatcher's handling of the crisis clearly boosted her personal popular-ity enormously; her overwhelming election victory shortly after the war has given rise to the widespread opinion that her policy was *intended* to have precisely that effect. The supposition that Thatcher pursued a hard line, resisted compromise, and insisted on military action to cash in on a jingoistic climate of opinion is without foun-dation, however, not only because the general climate of opinion in Britain was far from jingoistic, but also because all the evidence sug-gests that Thatcher kept the task force on a tight leash until all hope of a diplomatic settlement had failed.[140]

179

Opinion polls clearly showed that the British public was ambivalent about the use of force, notwithstanding the sensationalism of the tabloid press.[141] Quite reliably over the course of the crisis, British opinion was fairly consistently divided between those who thought recovery of the islands was worth loss of life and those who thought it was not. The immediate response to the Argentine invasion was understandably bellicose, but the initial retributive impulse quickly gave way to sober second thought.[142] The ambivalence was a function of the fact that the military option carried with it two quite different risks: failure and disproportionality. Despite Thatcher's public show of confidence, it was by no means certain in April and May that Britain was capable of mounting a military expedition to dislodge a 10,000-man Argentine garrison firmly entrenched in the islands. Although the task force held significant advantages over the Argentine fleet in surface ships and submarines, and could therefore expect to control the seas, it was outnumbered in high-performance aircraft by a ratio of more than four to one and could not be assured of maintaining air superiority. The British force that defeated the Argentines on land was actually outnumbered by more than two to one; military planners generally assume as a rule of thumb that a successful offensive requires an *advantage* of three to one.[143] There were grounds, therefore, to question whether the expedition would succeed. If the expedition *did* succeed, it was by no means certain that it would do so at a morally or politically acceptable cost. The risk of disproportionality was particularly acute because the population whose rights Britain was ostensibly defending was so very small. Few would have considered the liberation of 1,800 islanders worth a heavy toll in British servicemen's lives or in the lives of islanders caught in the crossfire.[144] All but the most jingoistic would have been disturbed by the loss of Argentine lives as well.

Thatcher therefore faced a complex political problem in which a variety of considerations had to be weighed against each other, and the political benefits she reaped from her handling of the crisis were a function of the fact that she succeeded in satisfying the British public's demand for justice without reckless disregard for the peace and without an inordinate loss of life. But nothing was guaranteed in advance; she could not have known precisely what the consequences of her actions would be when she chose them. It was by no means obvious that she stood to gain politically from a hard-line stand, and for this reason, some commentators doubt that she would have suffered a devastating blow if she had opted for a purely diplomatic solution.[145]

180

If Thatcher's actions were guided by her personal political interests, then she proved to be an incredibly shrewd leader, extremely lucky, or both. But more to the point, to the extent that she allowed herself to be guided by the desires of the British people, she tacitly permitted *their* motivations to stand in for her own. Gustafson puts it thus:

> Politicians may of course do what they think is to their political advantage. But in democracies at least, the voters are willing to let them gratify their ambition as long as they serve what the voters think are their interests. Even if Thatcher did fight the war only for her political advantage, most Britons believed the war should have been fought and were willing to reward Thatcher's efficient handling of it.[146]

Given the public understanding of the stakes – defined overwhelmingly in terms of defending the rights of the Falkland Islanders – a domestic political explanation of Thatcher's behavior is in effect an explanation in terms of the justice motive merely one step removed.

Of the three plausible explanations of British behavior – moral, strategic, and domestic political – which is the most persuasive? If more than one was at work, how should we determine the appropriate weights?

The appeal to the need to defend the islanders' right of self-determination remained throughout the dominant theme, and is still the official view. The Former Counsellor and Head of Chancery of the British Mission to the United Nations, Marrack Goulding, made the point explicitly in an interview with Jeffrey Elliot:

JE: There are those who contend that this was a war that neither country wanted, fought over a place that neither country needed. Why was it so important to recover the islands?

MG: The first word that comes to mind is."principle." We cared little that these were remote islands, with few inhabitants, and that they were of little or no material value to Great Britain. These facts are relatively unimportant. This is a territory for which, and for whose inhabitants, we are responsible ... In short, we could not accept a situation in which 1,800 people, or 180 people, or 18 people should be subjected against their wishes to the domination of a foreign power which had no right to be there ...

[T]he British Government recognizes that the Argentine claim to the Falklands constitutes a problem for the United Kingdom – constitutes an obstacle to good relations with an important country in South America with whom we desire good relations. It is for this reason that we explored numerous avenues in discussions with the Argentines and the islanders. Sadly, we failed in our efforts. But it was not our fault that we failed ...

Our concern, from the very beginning, has been to resolve the problem between ourselves and Argentina in a way that would be acceptable to the islanders – I stress this point, 'in a way that would be acceptable to the islanders,' because that is the nub of the problem.[147]

An appeal to credibility would be perfectly respectable; its conspicuous absence from the official position is therefore striking, because it could well have bolstered the moral case. This suggests at least circumstantially that credibility played a significantly less important motivational role than the perceived demands of justice.

But by far the most impressive demonstration of the overwhelming importance of defending the islanders' right of self-determination is provided by Britain's negotiating behavior immediately prior to the landing in mid-May. Soon after the sinkings of the Argentine cruiser *General Belgrano* and the British destroyer *Sheffield* in the first week of May, both sides began to demonstrate eagerness to reach a peaceful settlement. Recognizing that Argentina would agree to no settlement making the wishes of the islanders "paramount," British negotiators quietly dropped the phrase. At the UN, Argentine Ambassador Enrique Ros gave both Pérez de Cuellar and British Ambassador Sir Anthony Parsons reason to believe that Argentina in turn would drop its demand that a transfer of sovereignty be stipulated ahead of time as the outcome of any further negotiation. As one British participant in the War Cabinet of May 15 put it, "We knew that if we failed to get a deal a lot of people were going to die."[148] This was also evident to the junta.

The British proposed a mutual withdrawal of forces and an interim United Nations administration for the islands, with Argentine representation. The UN administrator would be required to act within the framework of existing laws and institutions, pending the conclusion of a final agreement between the two countries, the outcome of which was not to be prejudged.[149] Britain, in effect, offered to relinquish sovereignty of the islands to an international body. In so doing, she effectively wrote off the credibility issue. Had Argentina accepted the offer, Britain would have publicly retreated from defending a commitment, and would have advertised her unwillingness to pay the price of blood to keep the British flag flying on what she claimed was British territory. As Hastings and Jenkins note, "Buenos Aires would certainly have received some reward for its aggression."[150]

The one thing that the British proposal did *not* give away was the self-determination of the islanders. By requiring the UN administrator to act within the framework of existing laws and institutions pending the conclusion of a final agreement, the proposal would have locked in British laws and customs, the system of Island Councils, restrictions on Argentine immigration, and the prohibition on Argentine acquisition of property. By insisting that the interim agreement remain in force until the conclusion of a final settlement, Britain would have been able to maintain its traditional position on the islands indefinitely: that until the islanders decided otherwise, no transfer of sovereignty could take place. Her intransigence on this point would have received international sanction to boot. No doubt the Foreign Office would have redoubled its attempts to persuade the islanders of the benefits of closer association with Argentina; but in presenting the plan to Parliament, Thatcher stated explicitly that "During the long-term negotiations we shall closely consult the islanders on their wishes and of course we believe in self-determination."[151]

The British plan did not go far enough for the junta, who objected particularly strongly to the open-endedness of the interim agreement and to the prohibitions on Argentine access and investment. It is possible that Thatcher expected an Argentine refusal and made the offer largely to demonstrate her own flexibility. But the offer itself was enough to undercut the credibility hypothesis. If Thatcher were indeed determined to demonstrate the firmness of the West and "not to allow aggression to succeed," she would never have backed away publicly from her insistence on maintaining British sovereignty over the islands and refusing to bend in the face of aggression. Thus, defending the rights of the Falkland Islanders would appear to have been a considerably more important motivation than maintaining British credibility.

It is difficult to know how much motivational weight to assign to the Conservative government's domestic political interests. The proposed agreement would undoubtedly have come under considerable criticism from the very same quarters that had successfully torpedoed a deal with Argentina for seventeen years; but this would have been offset to some degree by the undoubted popularity of preventing an unknown quantity of bloodshed. Moreover, the fact that the agreement would have secured the islanders' right of self-determination – even at the cost of formal British sovereignty – might well have satisfied the vast majority for whom securing that right was the purpose of the exercise in the first place. The government's willingness to amend the British Nationality Bill so as to grant the islanders unrestricted relocation rights in the United Kingdom further demonstrates that it had their desires and interests firmly at heart. Thus the impulse to right the wrong done to islander self-determination would appear to have been the dominant British motive. It was clearly the British public's primary concern; if the government did not fully share that concern, it at least permitted it to guide its handling of the crisis.

SOME FINAL THOUGHTS

The Falklands/Malvinas war is difficult to explain from a Realist perspective. A small non-nuclear power challenged a nuclear-armed Great Power over an issue of negligible economic or strategic value. The Great Power responded to the challenge, but not until after it had demonstrated its willingness to suffer a serious blow to its prestige. When the Great Power finally did fight, it did not do so in the name of defending its sovereign territory. In fact, it had been trying to unburden itself of that very territory for years.

For neither participant was the war economically rational. For Argentina, it gravely aggravated an already desperate economic situation. The *Economist* estimated at the time that the cost of prosecuting the war and maintaining a British garrison on the islands would eventually cost between £1.6 and £2 billion, or something in the neighborhood of £1 million for every man, woman, and child on the islands.[152] A much more cost-effective solution would have been to pay all 1,800 islanders to relocate or to accept Argentine sovereignty. The toll in lives lost was fairly small, as wars go; but for every two islanders liberated, one soldier, sailor, or airman lost his life. What was it that Argentina and Britain considered worth such a price?

The answer, quite simply, is principle. In defense of their basic moral commitments, human beings are willing to suffer exorbitant penalties. Passionless calculations would have led neither government down the paths they chose. Once those paths had been chosen, principle prevented further compromise.[153]

It is easy in retrospect to see how badly the two sides misjudged each other's commitments and intentions; it is easy to say, with hindsight, that neither side expected to pay the price it eventually had to pay. What is overlooked is the fact that the protagonists were *bound* to misjudge each other's commitments and intentions, because each was acting on the basis of a conception of justice that the other did not share, could not appreciate, and consequently discounted. To this day many Anglo-Saxon commentators believe that the Argentine junta invaded the islands to serve its own narrow political purposes, and Latin American commentators insist that Thatcher's response was a function of some similarly cynical calculation. It is evidently difficult to appreciate the sincerity and power of a moral claim that one simply does not recognize as valid.[154]

But appreciating the sincerity and power of a moral claim will not necessarily incline one to accept it. Whatever role misperceptions and misjudgments played in making war more likely, the war would not have occurred at all were it not for the central fact that Britain and Argentina advanced competing and irreconcilable claims of entitlement. Were it not for the intensity of the Argentine sense of injustice, invading the islands could have served no economic, strategic, or political purpose; were it not for the firmness of the British commitment to the self-determination of the islanders, the islands would long since have been handed over to Argentina anyway. Although the war taught both sides an important lesson about each other's commitments, it did nothing to eliminate this basic underlying conflict. "[A]lmost every Argentine believes that the Falklands belong to Argentina, and that it is a sacred national cause to 'recover' those islands," Marrack Goulding remarked after the war. "One has to recognize that, and accept it as a fact of life. Likewise, I hope that they would recognize that it is a fact of life that we are not prepared to accept the imposition of an alien and unwanted regime on 1,800 people who treasure their own way of life in territory which they regard as belonging to them and which they have inhabited for six or seven generations."[155] As long as this basic conflict between conceptions of legitimate entitlement persists, there will be no lasting peace in that remote corner of the planet.

7 JUSTICE AND INJUSTICE IN A GLOBAL CONTEXT

> Man, born in a family, is compelled to maintain society from necessity, from natural inclination, and from habit. The same creature, in his farther progress, is engaged to establish political society in order to administer justice, without which there can be no peace among them, nor safety, nor mutual intercourse.
>
> David Hume, *Essays, Moral and Political*, Essay III,
> "Of the Origin of Government," in Aiken,
> *Hume's Moral and Political Philosophy*, 311.

> [T]here is a far greater chance of conflicts in an unjust world.
> *RIO: Reshaping the International Order: A Report to the
> Club of Rome* (New York: Dutton, 1976), 122.

Of the five wars surveyed, the justice motive can only be said to have played an insignificant role in the outbreak of one: the Franco-Prussian war. The other four demonstrate that the justice motive can contribute to the outbreak of war in a complex variety of ways. Sometimes, as in the Crimean and the Falklands/Malvinas wars, hostilities can be the direct result of two conflicting and incompatible claims of justice. Russia and Turkey went to war in 1853 over the question of whether the protection of the Greek Orthodox church in the Ottoman empire lay by right with the Tsar or the Sultan. Britain and Argentina went to war in 1982 over the question of which country held legitimate title to the Falkland Islands. In the former case, the dispute could be traced ultimately to a fundamental disagreement over the proper interpretation of treaties which could – and should – have been resolved by a dispassionate examination of the treaties themselves. The Falklands/Malvinas dispute, however, was more intractable, because it ran to a deeper level: namely, whether historical right or the principle of self-determination of peoples is the appropriate criterion for determining territorial entitlements.

Similar disagreements contributed heavily to the outbreak of World War I, although primarily at the level of ultimate rather than proximate causes. The annexation of Alsace-Lorraine in 1871, for example, destroyed any possibility of a lasting and meaningful *rapprochement* between France and Germany, because France could not and would not reconcile herself to the forcible alienation of French provinces and French peoples. Enduring and irreconcilable hostility between these two countries was the single most important characteristic of pre-war European geopolitics, playing a crucial role in the conclusion of the Franco-Russian alliance, the Anglo-French *entente*, and Germany's growing fear of encirclement (and thus of her "blank cheque" to Austria). It also heavily influenced the development of Germany's highly destabilizing military plans, which significantly increased escalatory pressures in the wake of Austria's attack on Belgrade, transforming a local dispute in the Balkans into a general European war. That very local dispute may itself be traced to a conflict between two competing principles of entitlement: namely, historical dynastic right and self-determination of peoples – the latter of which was a dagger pointed at the heart of Austria-Hungary, threatening her very existence as a Great Power.

World War II also provides abundant evidence of the richness of the justice motive as an explanatory concept. The perceived injustices of the Treaty of Versailles stripped the Weimar Republic of all domestic legitimacy, provided Hitler with a vehicle for capturing public attention and public support, enabled him to tighten his grip on power, and facilitated his overthrow of the European order. They also provided the smoke screen with which Hitler masked his true objectives. More than anything else, it was Britain's sense of justice that made that smoke screen so effective for so long.

Indeed, in four of the five cases examined, the justice motive led to misperceptions and miscalculations that made war difficult or impossible to avoid. The Crimean war, World Wars I and II, and the Falklands/Malvinas war all illustrate how the failure to appreciate the strength and sincerity of an adversary's sense of justice can lead to disastrous misjudgments about the opponent's goals and resolve; they also illustrate how the sense of justice can diminish risk-aversion or cloud a leader's vision of the dangers he or she may face. Otherwise avoidable or imprudent wars may therefore sometimes be the direct result of the influence of the sense of justice on cognition and affect.

Such are some of the *ways* in which the justice motive can contribute to the outbreak of war; I have attempted to gauge the *potency* of its contribution in the analysis of each individual case. But one of the best ways of assessing the potency of the justice motive as a cause of war is to consider how likely war would have been in each case if the justice

Table 7.1. *Justice motive – modes of operation*

	Crimean war	World War I	World War II	Falklands/ Malvinas war
Issues giving rise to conflicting claims	Russian protectorate over Orthodox in Turkey; Russian occupation of Danubian Principalities	South Slavs; Alsace-Lorraine		Sovereignty over Falklands/ Malvinas
Nature of claims*	Russia: SR/PD Turkey: SR/PD	Serbia: SR/PD (before Sarajevo), FD (after) Russia: OR/FD Britain: OR/FD		Argentina: SR/PD Britain: SR/FD (Reversed 4/82)
Justice motive wrongly imputed?	No	No	YES (Hitler's, by Britain and others)	No
Adversary's justice motive under-estimated?	YES (Tsar's by Britain, France, Turkey)	YES (Britain's by Germany; Russia's by Germany and Austria-Hungary)	YES (Britain's, by Hitler, with respect to Poland)	YES (Symmetrically)
Justice motive responsible for misper-ceptions?	YES (Tsar's misreading of Allies)	No	YES (Britain blinded to Hitler's intentions)	YES (Resolve mutually under-estimated)

*OR = other-regarding; SR = self-regarding; FD = forbearance-demanding;
PD = performance-demanding

motive had not been present. While the Franco-Prussian war probably would have unfolded more or less exactly as it did in any event, the presence of the justice motive, if not always an absolutely necessary or fully sufficient condition, at least made the outbreak of war significantly more likely in each of the remaining four cases.

It is difficult to imagine that the Crimean war would have taken place at all were it not for the fact that Tsar Nicholas thought himself the victim of an intolerable injustice. The old myth about his yearning to control the Turkish straits simply does not stand up against the historical record, although it still exercises an hegemony of sorts in English-language historiography. While there is no denying the sincerity of the perception (particularly in Britain) that control of the straits was Nicholas's goal, the evidence is overwhelming that what had actually engaged and inflamed him was his mistaken belief that the Porte, with the support (and perhaps even the encouragement) of France and Britain, sought to deprive him of his right to represent the Orthodox faithful in the Ottoman dominions. Nicholas took his faith extremely seriously; he was not a calculating statesman like Bismarck, or an evil genius like Hitler. Nor was he insane – except perhaps temporarily on this one issue, which so enraged his moral sense that he was blinded to the costs of his obstinacy. The charge of the Light Brigade pales in recklessness and futility next to the course of the Tsar's headstrong diplomacy leading up to the outbreak of war. Were it not for his inflamed sense of injustice, the Tsar undoubtedly would have displayed on this occasion the good sense, fidelity, and moderation typical of his foreign policy as a whole.

World War I has come to be thought of as one of those inevitable, over-determined conflicts. But without the gaping wound left by Alsace-Lorraine in the French national consciousness, Germany's repeated overtures for *rapprochement* might well have been accepted, possibly with beneficial effects on the various elements that have collectively come to be thought of as the over-determining factors: the continental alliance structure, the level of armament, the nature of military plans and preparations, the sense of the inevitability of conflict, and the general level of hostility and suspicion. At the very least, Germany would have felt less threatened, and less dependent upon her one remaining ally, the decrepit Austro-Hungarian Empire. Without the nationalities problem in general, and Serbian nationalism in particular, that empire would not have been forced to choose in 1914 between the risk of a general European war and its own survival as a political entity. Had the Russian Tsar not undertaken to defend Serbia, he might have thought better of tangling with Austria and Germany over the bombardment of Belgrade. And if Britain had not undertaken to defend Belgian neutrality, she might well have followed her initial strong inclination to sit on the sidelines while the continental powers fought among themselves. The reasons *why* World War I was inevitable or overdetermined – if indeed it was – are all closely connected to the justice motive one way or another.

World War II cannot be said to have been the direct result of the justice motive, simply because Hitler should not be thought of as seeking a *more just* European order. For that reason, the war cannot be

189

said to have been the product of unsatisfied claims of justice. But if the Treaty of Versailles had been a just peace, the Weimar Republic (if it had existed in the first place) would have enjoyed considerably greater legitimacy, and thus considerably greater resilience in the face of domestic pressures. Hitler would have been deprived of the one issue that gave him respectability, catapulted him into the public spotlight, allowed him to solidify his domestic position once he came to power, and permitted him to keep his main antagonists – the British – off balance and off the scent for so long. Without being able to manipulate other people's senses of justice, Hitler would have had significantly greater difficulty attaining power, consolidating power, and leading his own unwilling nation into war.

Finally, it seems extremely unlikely that Britain and Argentina would have gone to war over the Falkland/Malvinas Islands in 1982 in the absence of a sovereignty dispute. The islands were of negligible economic or strategic value to either side, and even if the sole concern of the junta in invading the islands had been to distract the Argentine people from their dire economic straits, the move could have offered the junta little or no respite from domestic political pressures if the Argentine people had not thought of the islands as *terra irredenta*. The Argentine claim to the islands made all the difference: it gave the issue domestic salience and garnered some degree of international sympathy. It is difficult to imagine that the junta would have been capable of gratuitously invading what it considered to be another nation's sovereign territory; in the absence of a broadly popular and heart-felt claim to the islands, that is exactly what the operation would have amounted to not only in the eyes of the world, but also in the eyes of Argentines. Britain's response demonstrates that once Argentina had invaded, only one goal was considered worth putting the lives of soldiers and civilians at risk: righting the Argentine wrong and redeeming the islanders' right of self-determination. Thatcher's negotiating behavior indicates that she considered respect for this right her sole condition for a peaceful settlement; her willingness to relinquish sovereignty over the islands to an international body respecting that right demonstrates unequivocally that when she finally authorized military action, she did not do so to capitalize on domestic jingoism or to make a general point about British credibility. The islanders' wishes had been the sole stumbling block to a peaceful transfer of sovereignty all along; in the unfolding of events, they proved to be the only thing Britain considered worth fighting for.

The justice motive, then, seems in retrospect to have played a vital role in the outbreak of these four wars. It provides a fuller and more persuasive account of their origins at the motivational level than can be obtained from a traditional Realist analysis employing only the concepts of self-preservation and self-aggrandizement. In addition, the cases would appear to support the six hypotheses about the agency of the justice motive I proposed in Chapter 1:

Valuation

1. If an actor views a good as an entitlement, he or she will value it more highly than its strategic or economic worth warrants.

Process

2. If an actor's justice motive is engaged, he or she will accept poor gambles to restore the balance between perceived entitlements and assets.
3. If an actor's sense of injustice is engaged, he or she will exhibit insensitivity to new information and value trade-offs, and will be less amenable to negotiation and suasion through the application of carrots and sticks.
4. The justice motive will increase the likelihood of cognitive errors because of its influence on interpretation, its simplifying effect on cognitive structures, and its affective potency.

Behavior

5. An actor operating on the basis of the justice motive will be less willing to compromise in finding solutions to disputes, since the demand that entitlements be respected is a categorical one.
6. An actor operating on the basis of the justice motive will be *more* tolerant of other states' gains if they are perceived to be legitimate entitlements, and *less* tolerant of other states' gains if they are perceived to violate entitlements.

These dynamics are particularly evident in the Crimean and Falklands/ Malvinas wars, the two cases in which the justice motive played a central role as a proximate cause. But they also shed light on French policy prior to 1914 (hypothesis 1 – the inordinate importance attached to Alsace-Lorraine); British policy during the July crisis (hypothesis 5 – the categorical demand that Germany respect Belgian sovereignty); and British policy prior to World War II (hypothesis 6 – systematic misperceptions of Hitler). While these cases cannot provide a "test" of these hypotheses in any strong sense – something for which we would need to compare them with the behavior of these actors in cases that did not engage their senses of justice – it is at least suggestive that these dynamics seem to be absent in the case of the Franco-Prussian war, where none of the key actors was motivated by considerations of justice.

We should not be surprised to find that the behavior of states is influenced by philosophic psychology. Leaders, like other human beings, have senses of justice and act upon them. A vision of national entitlements and obligations can shape their policies and their choices just as powerfully as can a vision of the national interest. Not all leaders are alike in this regard; a true practitioner of *realpolitik* like Bismarck or Hitler may be guided solely or overwhelmingly by a conception of the national interest, while a Nicholas I or a Neville Chamberlain may be much more strongly guided by a sense of right and wrong. This fact represents an enormous obstacle for the development of parsimonious general theory. It would seem difficult enough to generate propositions true of both Nicholas's Russia and Bismarck's Germany, let alone of all states at all times. But recognizing the importance of the justice motive when and where it plays a role nonetheless makes possible a richer and more accurate analysis of the behavior of particular states at particular times, and enables us to explore hitherto neglected avenues for the prevention or resolution of those conflicts to which the justice motive gives rise. If the cases examined here are broadly representative, those conflicts are much more frequent than empirical political scientists hitherto have supposed. If we simply take the justice motive seriously, we may reap an enormous analytic gain, descriptively and predictively.

But merely *being aware of* the justice motive is a distant second-best to harnessing it to the service of peace, and the remainder of this chapter seeks to gauge the possibility of progress in that direction. This is, as a practical matter, ultimately the concern of leaders and diplomats; but, more immediately, it is the concern of political theorists, whose business is to help us make sense of the difficult philosophical issues involved. We move at last, therefore, from empirical questions to philosophical ones.

JUSTICE AND ORDER

In four of the five wars surveyed, the justice motive was the problem, not the solution. But there is no reason why it must always be so. The craving for justice is not the same as blood lust; it can be satisfied by means of peaceful procedures whose very existence can, in theory, contribute to the peacefulness and stability of international society.[1] This is because of the intimate connection between two concepts that students of international politics have mistakenly tended to regard as independent: namely, justice and order. By "order," I mean patterned, non-violent interaction between states, where regularity and non-violence are individually necessary and jointly sufficient.[2] Justice is a virtue of a particular type of order: namely, one which defines and protects entitlements to legitimate expectations and resolves conflicting claims through a procedure widely regarded as legitimate – what John Rawls calls a "well-ordered society."[3] The occasion for justice arises when the "circumstances of justice" obtain; namely, when actors put forward conflicting claims to goods, resources, activities, or other advantages under conditions of moderate scarcity. "Unless these circumstances existed," Rawls notes, "there would be no occasion for the virtue of justice, just as in the absence of threats of injury to life and limb there would be no occasion for physical courage."[4]

The complementarity of order and justice may easily be appreciated by noting the function justice serves in a social context. All virtues serve functions that are socially desirable:[5] for example, charity redistributes wealth; humility reduces friction; courage enhances security; and honesty supports a wide range of institutions and practices, from maintaining family cohesion to facilitating contracts. Justice has the effect of promoting social order by reducing the incidence of conflict and helping to resolve peacefully those conflicts that do occur. But while justice is *conducive* to order, it is not synonymous with it. Order can be maintained through coercion or manipulation. A hegemonic order, for example, may well be patterned and non-violent even though it lacks moral legitimacy from the perspective of its subjects. But since a hegemonic order cannot resolve – only contain – lingering grievances about what is fair, right, or just, it will survive only as long as the hegemon has the will and the resources to maintain it. It is consequently likely to be unstable and short-lived. Order and justice are therefore mutually reinforcing; order is more difficult to achieve and maintain without justice, and justice is more difficult to achieve and maintain without order. For this reason, the problems of disorder and injustice in international affairs should be understood as problems requiring a joint solution.

It is interesting to note that the common wisdom denies this, on the ground that leaders have enough difficulty merely attempting to maintaining order, and that justice is a luxury they can ill afford to

193

pursue. Indeed, attempts to pursue justice in the absence of order often succeed only in breeding chaos.[6] It is for this reason that some Realists, notably Hans Morgenthau and George Kennan, attack "moralism" on *moral* as well as prudential grounds.[7] But the fault lies not with "moralistic" foreign policies *per se*, so much as with the failure of scholars and leaders to attend to the intimate relationship between order and justice in an international context. Order may well be difficult to maintain precisely because of the lack of attention leaders pay to questions of justice; justice may well seem a luxury too costly to pursue precisely because leaders devote so much time and energy attempting to maintain a type of order that does not address basic moral grievances.

THE PROBLEM OF MORAL DIVERSITY

In most of the wars I examined in this study, the justice motive proved to be part of the problem rather than part of the solution precisely because the international society of states proved to be insufficiently well-ordered; unsatisfied claims of entitlement proved incapable of peaceful resolution. The rules, principles, and procedures apportioning entitlements between states were too weak to referee the conflicting claims advanced (for example) by France and Germany, Austria and Serbia, Argentina and Britain. Only in the case of the Crimean war was the international society of states sufficiently well-ordered to offer some hope of adjudicating the central dispute. Russia and Turkey both subscribed to the same set of rules that governed making and observing treaties; the fact that the Tsar and Nesselrode later admitted that they had not fully understood the terms of the treaties on the basis of which they advanced their claims suggests that the problem was not that the European system was insufficiently well-ordered, but that the appropriate institutions broke down.

If international society were a well-ordered society, then conceptions of legitimate entitlements would be widely shared, or some procedure would exist – itself widely regarded to be legitimate – to reconcile or choose between competing claims in any given circumstance.[8] The issues we must now address are, first, whether it is possible for an international society of states to resemble a well-ordered society so conceived; and, second, what it would look like – how the word *justice* would be understood in such a case.

A skeptic would immediately appeal to the apparent fact of cultural ethical relativism to deny the possibility of any well-ordered international society at all.[9] Consider the following observation by John Locke in his *Essay Concerning Human Understanding*:

194

He that will carefully peruse the History of Mankind, and look abroad into the several Tribes of Men, and with indifferency survey their Actions, will be able to satisfy himself, That there is scarce that Principle of Morality to be named, or *Rule* of *Vertue* to be thought on (those only excepted, that are absolutely necessary to hold Society together, which commonly too are neglected betwixt distinct Societies) which is not, somewhere or other, *slighted* and condemned by the general Fashion of *whole Societies* of Men, governed by practical Opinions, and Rules of living quite opposite to others.[10]

Beginning early in this century, with the influential works of William Graham Sumner and Edward Westermarck, anthropologists and sociologists began amassing an impressive amount of information that seemed to confirm Locke's opinion that different cultures operate on the basis of distinct moralities.[11] But the evident variety of moral beliefs and practices among various cultures has proven to be somewhat misleading, because it masks much that cultures have in common. Comparative ethicists have shown that there are no pre-moral societies; that all societies give some degree of moral value to such things as human life, sexual restraint, friendship, mutual aid, fairness, truthfulness, and generosity; and that all societies employ moral concepts such as good, bad, right, wrong, just, and unjust.[12] Despite the apparent diversity in moral beliefs, there is therefore considerable similarity in the ways in which human beings around the globe structure their moral worlds. Karl Duncker has argued that the surface diversity in moral judgments actually masks fundamental unity at a deeper level. Ethical valuations, he contends, depend upon the "pattern of situational meanings" in which they take place. The members of one society may condemn an act that another society considers morally laudable, but when the context in which their respective moral lives takes place is factored into the equation, it turns out that the act is intended to advance values that both societies share. Under different circumstances, different cultures may assign the same acts different moral valuations; but under the *same* circumstances, different cultures assign the same acts the same moral valuations.[13] Cultural differences are limited to matters of application, and do not reach the level of fundamental moral principle. Even Richard Brandt, a critic of Duncker and an adherent of ethical relativism, has succeeded in discovering only one apparent counterexample: the curious indifference of the Hopi to cruelty to animals.[14] There is evidently enough similarity in different cultures' ethical lives to enable Emile Durkheim's "science of moral facts" and Jean Piaget's psychology of moral development to bear substantial fruit. We need not despair *a priori*, therefore, of finding enough cross-cultural moral common ground on which to build a just world order.

The difficulty, however, is that while all cultures appear to share a *concept* of justice, they differ – sometimes radically – on their *conceptions*. A conception is a particular interpretation of an abstract concept. Ronald Dworkin provides the following useful illustration of this distinction:

> Suppose I tell my children that I expect them not to treat others unfairly. I no doubt have in mind examples of the conduct I mean to discourage, but I would not accept that my "meaning" was limited to these examples, for two reasons. First I would expect my children to apply my instructions to situations I had not and could not have thought about. Second, I stand ready to admit that some particular act I had thought was fair when I spoke was in fact unfair, or vice versa, if one of my children is able to convince me of that later; in that case I should want to say that my instructions covered the case he cited, not that I had changed my instructions. I might say that I meant the family to be guided by the *concept* of fairness, not by any specific *conception* of fairness I might have had in mind.[15]

In 1982, Britain and Argentina shared a concept of justice, and agreed on the abstract principle that infringement of national sovereignty is unjust because it is a violation of a legitimate entitlement; but they disagreed strongly on the appropriate criteria for determining who is entitled to exercise territorial sovereignty in any given case. The Argentines believed that the ground of legitimate title is historical right; the British believed that the controlling consideration is the wishes of the inhabitants. In different times and in different places, various other grounds have been asserted, such as common language, common descent, divine will, conquest, heredity, contract, and need. These can give rise to conflicting *conceptions* of legitimate entitlement to territory. When two conceptions clash, and when no procedure exists for resolving the dispute, war may be the result. This was certainly true in many of the other cases examined here. All of the parties in 1853 shared a concept of the right of representation, but disagreed on the nature and extent of those rights with respect to the subjects of the Ottoman dominions. All of the parties in 1914 shared concepts of sovereign authority and territorial right, but disagreed on the grounds for determining who held them. Most of the parties in 1939 shared concepts such as the right of self-determination of peoples, but disagreed on the interpretation of that right with respect to particular cases.[16]

There is room for compromise or accommodation in many cases

where claims conflict, but often the matter poses a binary choice: one claim must succeed, and one must fail. In the case of Crimea, once French policy unmasked and forced a resolution to the ambiguity in the relationships between the European powers on the one hand, and the Sultan's Christian subjects on the other, either the French or Russian claims could stand, but not both. Prior to World War I, only France or Germany could control Alsace-Lorraine, but not both. And while in 1982 Britain professed a willingness to compromise on the Falklands issue by turning the islands over to UN administration, there nonetheless remained a central issue on which compromise was simply not possible: whether the islanders themselves would have a veto over further changes in their political status.

JUSTICE AND JUSTIFICATION

If international society were a well-ordered society, then it would be possible to determine peacefully in each of these various cases which claim (if either) was the just claim. The question we must now ask is: how are we to know? To answer it, we must consider more closely the concept of justice itself.

Recall that justice is only one of a family of moral concepts whose other members include (for example) goodness, rightness, virtue, and desert. It is natural to use moral language loosely; sometimes, for instance, we call a person "just" when he or she has performed a morally laudable act not called for by the demands of justice *per se*. But here we need to be very precise about the bounds of justice. Throughout our tour of the historical record, we have been using the phrase "the justice motive" to denote the drive *to secure legitimate entitlements* or *to discharge the obligations attendant to the entitlements of others.* Thus a theory of justice is "that part of the theory of morality that deals with the legitimate structure of institutions," where by "institutions" we mean the principles, rules, norms, practices, and procedures that define entitlements and specify certain obligations.[17]

An entitlement, like a promise, presupposes the existence of an institutional substructure to give it meaning and moral authority. If there were no institution of promise-making and no practice of promise-keeping, then a promise would be nothing more than an empty utterance; it would certainly not be a promise as we know it, since there would be no reason for the listener to expect the stated undertaking to be discharged, and no reason for the promisor to feel obliged to perform it. Likewise, an entitlement presupposes the existence of an institutional context that gives a title the moral authority

197

necessary to allow it to discharge its function, i.e., to apportion rights, benefits, and obligations in a given area or on a given issue. Without the appropriate institutional context, there can be no entitlement. Thus did David Hume assert that "in the *state of nature* or that imaginary state which preceded society" there was "neither justice nor injustice,"[18] a sentiment echoed by Terry Nardin, who writes:

> Judgments of obligation and right conduct can only be made from within some body of authoritative practice, and therefore the resolution of conflicts between different bodies of authoritative practice can only be made from within one or another of them ... As its Latin origin suggests, the word "justice" (*iustitia*) stands for what is essentially a juridical concept – one of a family of ideas concerned with authoritative rules and rights (*ius*) and with the duties derived from them. The word 'justice' is therefore most at home in discourse concerning rules of morality and law that arise out of the practices of a community and prescribe forms and limits to be observed by individuals in their transactions and cooperative engagements. Just conduct is conduct responsive to the considerations comprising an authoritative moral or legal practice – that is, conduct that is lawful or right.[19]

The "moral authority" undergirding promises and entitlements must be understood in the first instance as a sociological fact, not as a philosophical sanction. It is the community's actual affirmation of the institutional substructure that permits a high enough level of compliance to preserve and promote the institutions themselves. Some people break their promises; but in most stable societies, promises are generally considered morally binding and compliance is sufficiently high that the members of society can form a reasonable expectation that they will be fulfilled. Few promises are *enforced*. There is no need. The institutions of promise-making and promise-keeping are sufficiently widely respected that they do not require the backing of power or coercion.[20]

A level of moral authority sufficient to ensure general compliance is what I mean by the term "legitimacy" (used here in its *de facto* sense).[21] A legitimate ruler is one who governs by means of authority; a tyrant is one who governs solely by means of power. What distinguishes a *just* order from a *coercive* order is exactly this. An institutional structure may be imposed upon a people against their wishes, and by means of an iron hand, a ruler can enforce compliance; but such an order will fail to win the loyalty or affirmation of those subject to it. Without moral authority, it has no legitimacy. Since a just order is one that defines and protects *legitimate entitlements*, a coercive order cannot be said to be *just*.

When we say that something is just (an act, a distribution of resources, a penalty), we are saying that it can be *justified* against the appropriate institutional background – that it is called for under the appropriate principles. If something cannot be so justified, it cannot be said to be just. It follows that if there are no such principles or no such institutional background, the adjectives "just" or "unjust" are misplaced, just as the phrase "safe at third" would be meaningless if the game of baseball did not exist (and *is* meaningless except in the context of a baseball game).

Justification, in contrast to coercion, is a species of persuasion. As Rawls puts it,

> [J]ustification is argument addressed to those who disagree with us, or to ourselves when we are of two minds. It presumes a clash of views between persons or within one person, and seeks to convince others, or ourselves, of the reasonableness of the principles upon which our claims and judgments are founded. Being designed to reconcile by reason, justification proceeds from what all parties to the discussion hold in common ... [M]ere proof is not justification. A proof simply displays logical relations between propositions. But proofs become justification once the starting points are mutually recognized, or the conclusions so comprehensive and compelling as to persuade us of the soundness of the conception expressed by their premises.[22]

It is important to note that justifications are always addressed to a particular audience for a particular reason. If the Massachusetts legislature proposes a tax increase, it will attempt to persuade the voters of Massachusetts that an increase is necessary so that it will be accepted and complied with (and, of course, to minimize the peril to incumbency). It will *not* attempt to persuade the voters of New Hampshire, or of Belgium, nor will it attempt the justification for the purpose of improving the chances that the Boston Red Sox will win the World Series. By the same token, an appeal to the demands of justice will always take place within the framework of a society that accepts the principles appealed to as legitimate (or that can be persuaded to do so, by appeal to something antecedently held), for the purpose, on the one hand, of securing a particular right or enforcing a particular obligation, and, on the other, of affirming and perpetuating the governing conception of justice itself so that it can continue to serve the function of peaceful social regulation.[23]

It is the possibility of justification in terms of the fundamental values and principles that undergird society that permits the authoritative determination of entitlements in cases of disagreement. Justification, therefore, is central to a just social order. As Nardin puts it, "Authoritative determination requires that there exist procedures for settling disputes, through the application of rules, in a manner that is recognized as binding on those concerned."[24] A just order operates through moral authority rather than coercion; it derives its legitimacy from the fact of its acceptance; and it operates through a process of justification that is always addressed to a specific audience for particular purposes.

JUSTICE BEYOND BORDERS

To this point, I have said nothing about the substantive meaning of justice in an international and intercultural context. In the remainder of this chapter, I will attempt to argue that international justice can only mean what states agree that it means; that in the absence of such an agreement, there is no such thing as international justice or injustice; and that it is unnecessary – and may even be undesirable – to attempt to think of international justice in universalistic terms. Rather, it would be more useful (at least in the short run) to think of international justice in issue- or area-specific terms, and to attempt to discipline the use of the language of justice in cases or circumstances where the necessary institutional substructures are lacking in order to prevent international differences from taking on an inflammatory moral tone. To help clarify the discussion, I will make use of three concrete theories of international justice, and draw upon the relatively straightforward Falklands/Malvinas dispute to illustrate a number of important points.

Let us begin by noting that we can ask a series of questions about any particular vision or theory of justice:

1. What is its *ground?* – i.e., what is its philosophic basis?
2. What is its *scope?* – i.e., over what body of people is it intended to be authoritative?
3. What is its *domain?* – i.e., what issue or issues is it intended to govern?[25]
4. What is its *content?* – i.e., what principles does it advance?
5. What is the *unit of analysis?* – i.e., who are the relevant moral persons? Are individuals or groups – or both – the bearers of entitlements and obligations? Who has standing to advance claims?

In addition, we can ask a series of questions about practical details, such as the institutions and procedures appropriate for the operationalization of principles; but I leave aside practical matters while I consider these more basic issues.

At the most general level, a theory of justice could be constructed upon one of three possible grounds. A *foundationalist* theory is based upon a particular metaphysic, authority, or conception of the good. Islamic justice, for example, is grounded in the Koran; a utilitarian theory of justice is grounded in some version of what John Stuart Mill called the "greatest happiness principle;"[26] and Grotius's conception of international law was grounded in a doctrine of natural law.[27] A *conventionalist* theory is based simply upon the fact of agreement: whatever can be agreed to be just *is* just simply by virtue of the agreement. Certain contractarian theories are conventionalist theories. *Constructivist* theories are neither foundationalist nor conventionalist, although they are closer to the latter than to the former. They derive moral principles by generalizing from actual moral commitments, and their moral authority rests not on *actual* agreement, but on the appropriate *hypothetical* agreement generated from the derivation.[28] In Rawls's theory, for example, principles of justice are extracted from a hypothetical choice situation (the Original Position). "Our social situation is just," Rawls writes, "if it is such that by [the appropriate] sequence of hypothetical agreements we would have contracted into the general system of rules which defines it."[29] The principles chosen, according to Rawls, will coexist in "reflective equilibrium" with considered moral judgments, and will therefore in some sense represent a generalization and abstraction of moral commitments actually held by those who choose them.[30] According to Rawls's understanding, moral theory is an "attempt to describe our moral capacity;" a theory of justice, therefore, is an attempt to describe our sense of justice, much the same way as an attempt to formulate the rules of grammar is an attempt to describe our sense of grammaticalness.[31]

Different theories of justice are intended to govern the relations among different groups of people. Some theories, particularly foundationalist ones, purport to be universal in scope – that is, to be valid for all peoples and all times. Some confine their scope to the boundaries of the individual state – usually a particular *type* of state; Rawls notes that his own theory, for example, is framed to apply to a modern constitutional democracy.[32] Canon law codifies a conception of justice for members of an ecclesiastical community; other conceptions of justice are intended to apply (for example) to sub-national political communities, sports, families, markets, and the work place.

Theories of justice also differ widely in their domain. One group of theories is often divided into theories of *political* justice, theories of *social* justice, and theories of *economic* justice. Libertarianism, for example, is a purely political theory of justice, since it is concerned solely with the definition and protection of individual rights and liberties. Welfare liberalism and socialism go further, governing distributions of wealth and access to social benefits, jobs, and services. A further distinction is often made between theories of *distributive* justice, which apportion economic resources, and theories of *retributive* justice, which deal with crime and punishment. A type of theory unique to international affairs is just-war theory, which is intended to specify the circumstances under which states may justifiably go to war, and to govern the ways in which wars may permissibly be fought.

It would be tedious to attempt to survey or even classify the contents of every possible theory of justice. Given any particular scope and domain, it is possible to imagine a broad variety of specific principles that might be advanced. More important here is the question of the unit of analysis. Some liberal theories of justice consider individual human beings the relevant moral persons – that is, the sole bearers of entitlements and obligations. Communitarianism, on the other hand, considers the central unit of analysis for political purposes to be the group or community to which individuals belong; the claims of the community as a whole are treated as prior to those of individuals. The unit of analysis has been perhaps the most controversial aspect of the philosophical debate about the meaning of international justice. The central question is whether *states*, *nations* (groups united by particular common features or experiences), or *individuals* should be treated as fundamental moral persons for the purposes of determining entitlements and obligations across borders.[33]

At this point it would be useful to discuss a few particular theories of international justice by way of illustrating diversity on these five dimensions. Let us begin with Rawls. In *A Theory of Justice*, Rawls only briefly discusses the question of justice beyond borders.[34] Applying a constructivist method, Rawls supposes that the parties to the global original position would be representatives of nations, and that they would assemble for the purpose of choosing principles to govern their relations. Rawls expects that they would choose "familiar" principles of justice:

> The basic principle of the law of nations is a principle of equality. Independent peoples organized as states have certain fundamental equal rights. This principle is analogous to the equal rights of citizens in a constitutional regime. One consequence of this equality of nations is the principle of self-determination, the right of a people to settle its own affairs without the intervention of foreign powers. Another consequence is the right of self-defense against attack, including the right to form defensive alliances to protect this right. A further principle is that treaties are to be kept, provided they are

consistent with the other principles governing the relations of states. Thus treaties for self-defense, suitably interpreted, would be binding, but agreements to cooperate in an unjustified attack are void *ab initio*.[35]

In addition, Rawls supposes that the representatives would choose principles of *jus in bello*.

The brevity of Rawls's treatment, and the fact that he makes these remarks only in the context of setting the stage for a justification of conscientious refusal, leaves many questions open. For example, Rawls writes that the parties to the international original position are representatives of "nations," and he suggests that they will affirm the principle of self-determination; yet he also claims that they will assert that "independent peoples organized *as states* have certain fundamental equal rights," leaving open the question of whether the appropriate unit of analysis is the *nation* or the *state*. (The fact that *A Theory of Justice* was written precisely for the purpose of finding a conception of justice appropriate to a pluralistic political community shows that Rawls harbors no naïve illusions about the general lack of fit between ethnic and political boundaries.) It is curious, too, that Rawls's formulation omits any principle of international distributive justice. Rawls considers distributive justice a vital part of the theory justice within the state, but since he conceives of states in rather traditional terms as fully sovereign entities, he seems to imply that distributive justice is not a fit subject for the law of nations. But one should be careful of assuming too much about Rawls's own views of international justice, since he has not addressed the subject in much detail.[36] Many others have discussed the problem of applying Rawls's method and his principles globally, and it is clear from their attempts that this is a difficult and controversial undertaking.[37]

Perhaps the most creative and provocative interpreter of Rawls on an international scale is Charles Beitz, who, like Rawls, rests his view on a hypothetical contract, but argues for a radically cosmopolitan conception of international justice, in contrast to what he calls the "morality of states" conception, whose central concern with state autonomy he regards as misplaced.[38] The essential features of Beitz's position are, first, that individual human beings, not states or intermediate political groups, are the appropriate moral persons. To the extent that it makes any sense at all to speak of the rights and obligations of states, Beitz maintains, it is only because the moral standing of states is entirely derivative of, and reducible to, the moral standing of citizens.[39] Second, the morality of states position is fatally flawed because it lacks a principle of international distributive justice.[40] Beitz insists that "the parties to the international original position would view the natural distribution of resources as morally arbitrary," and that principles of distributive justice should apply globally because economic interdependence constitutes a scheme of social cooperation.[41] "It is difficult to defend the view that state boundaries set the limits of distributive justice because it is difficult to say why differences in citizenship should count as morally relevant differences," Beitz maintains.[42] "[A] strong case can be made on contractarian grounds that persons of diverse citizenship have distributive obligations to one another analogous to those of citizens of the same state. International distributive obligations are founded on justice and not merely on mutual aid."[43]

Michael Walzer defends the "morality of states" view that Beitz attacks. His communitarian position reflects a reverence for, and deference to, communal values and ways of life that radical cosmopolitanism, or perhaps even merely a liberalism too concerned with individual rights, threatens to destroy. The central unit of analysis, on Walzer's view, is the political community, which he regards as deserving the widest possible latitude for making the choices that affect its own well-being and the lives of its members. While not denying that political communities ultimately trace their moral standing to the moral value of human life, Walzer nonetheless insists that principles of international justice cannot be indifferent to the fact that individual human beings live and die as members of distinct societies and cultures whose conceptions of justice differ. "Justice is relative to social meanings," Walzer writes:

> Indeed, the relativity of justice follows from the classic non-relative definition, giving each person his due, as much as it does from my own proposal, distributing goods for "internal" reasons. These are formal definitions that require ... historical completion. We cannot say what is due to this person or that one until we know how these people relate to one another through the things they make and distribute. There cannot be a just society until there is a society; and the adjective *just* doesn't determine, it only modifies, the substantive life of the societies it describes. There are an infinite number of possible lives, shaped by an infinite number of possible cultures, religions, political arrangements, geographical conditions, and so on. A given society is just if its substantive life is lived in a certain way – that is, in a way faithful to the shared understandings of the members.[44]

A radically cosmopolitan conception of justice, on Walzer's view, is inconceivable because humanity as a whole cannot be said to constitute a single society in the necessary sense.[45] "Politics (as distinct from mere coercion and bureaucratic manipulation) depends upon shared history, communal sentiment, accepted conventions – upon some extended version of Aristotle's 'friendship.' All this is problematic enough in the modern state; it is hardly conceivable on a global scale. Communal life and liberty requires the existence of 'relatively self-enclosed areas of political development.' Break into the enclosures and you destroy the communities. And that destruction is a loss to the individual members (unless it rescues them from massacre, enslavement, or expulsion), a loss of something valuable, which they clearly value, and to which they have a right, namely their participation in the 'development' that goes on and can only go on within the enclosure."[46]

Walzer's understanding of the proper *content* of international justice has been most thoroughly developed in his book, *Just and Unjust Wars*, which, as the title suggests, concerns itself overwhelmingly with the legitimate use of force. Walzer defends a version of what he calls the "legalist paradigm," which may be formulated in six propositions:

1. There exists an international society of independent states.
2. This international society has a law that establishes the rights of its members – above all, the rights of territorial integrity and political sovereignty.
3. Any use of force or imminent threat of force by one state against the political sovereignty or territorial integrity of another constitutes aggression and is a criminal act.
4. Aggression justifies two kinds of violent response: a war of self-defense by the victim and a war of law enforcement by the victim and any other member of international society.
5. Nothing but aggression can justify war.
6. Once the aggressor state has been militarily repulsed, it can also be punished.[47]

Like Rawls's, Walzer's vision of international justice lacks a principle of redistribution and openly embraces state autonomy and self-determination of peoples.

What can be said of these visions of justice? I noted above that the concept of justice is intimately connected with the idea of justification, and that a theory of justice is itself a fit object of justification. If we seek an account of justice capable of harnessing the justice motive to the cause of peace, we cannot be interested in theories of justice that have no hope whatsoever of enjoying substantial *de facto* legitimacy across borders. Without legitimacy there is no uncoerced compliance; without uncoerced compliance, a theory of justice can offer no hope of reducing the likelihood or incidence of conflict, since coercion itself is a

Table 7.2. *Three theories of international justice*

	Rawls	Beitz	Walzer
Ground	Constructivist	Constructivist	Foundationalist (Communal conception of human identity)
Scope	Universal?	Universal	Universal
Domain	Relations of states	Individual rights and liberties, distribution of resources	Relations of states, emphasis on regulation of war
Content	Sovereign equality of states; principle of self-determination of peoples; non-intervention; right of self-defense; *pacta sunt servanda.*	Intervention in defense of human rights; global redistribution of wealth in accordance with Rawls's difference principle.	Presumption in favor of non-intervention; self-determination; revised legalist paradigm.
Unit of analysis	State (or nation?)	Individual human being	Individual political community constituted as state or seeking statehood

form of conflict. Would Rawls's, Beitz's, or Walzer's understandings of international justice command enough international assent to make them useful?

Recall Rawls's account of justification, quoted on p. 199 above: justification is always addressed to someone who disagrees with us, or to ourselves if we are of two minds. To succeed, a justification must appeal to something that the intended audience already accepts, or can be persuaded to accept upon reflection. Any justification will have two essential features: an *intended audience* (the person or persons to whom the justification is addressed), and a *warrant* (a value or understanding – or a set of values or understandings – upon which the justification turns). A *parochial* justification is an argument that will only succeed when advanced by one member of an interpretive community to another, since it rests upon a warrant that will only command the assent of the members of that particular community.[48] We may say that the warrant of a parochial justification is itself a parochial value or understanding. A *non-parochial* justification may well succeed across the boundaries of specific interpretive communities, since it rests upon values or understandings not exclusively held by one particular interpretive community, but it may well fail if it runs afoul of other values and understandings held more dearly by the intended audience.

Most theories of justice are parochial theories.[49] Rawls's theory of justice as fairness (his *domestic* theory of justice) is self-consciously parochial, since it is intended to be persuasive only to the members of a modern constitutional democracy. Whether his understanding of international justice is parochial is certainly open to debate, although the brevity of his treatment may make that debate intractable. Beitz's theory of justice is clearly parochial because it rests upon a doctrine of individual rights peculiar to a particular strand of Western liberal thought.[50] The interpretive community to which Beitz belongs is denoted by the mysterious pronoun "we" in the following telling passages:

> ... I shall proceed on the assumption that we share some basic ideas about the nature and requirements of morality (which I call moral intuitions) and see whether international skepticism is consistent with them.[51]

> At some point, having learned what we can from the views of others, we must be prepared to acknowledge that some conception of morality is the most reasonable one available under the circumstances, and go forward to see what principles result.[52]

> [I]t is enough, in establishing standards for conduct, that we be able to regard them as the most rational choices available for anyone appropriately situated and that we be prepared to defend this view with arguments addressed to anyone who disagrees. In this way we reach decisions that are as likely to be morally right as any that are in our power to reach. We can do no more than this in matters of moral choice.[53]

Walzer is somewhat more self-conscious about the group he denotes by the pronoun "we," at least in *Just and Unjust Wars*.[54] While his argument there might therefore be thought of as parochial (being addressed to and drawing upon the moral intuitions of those the pronoun denotes), his treatment elsewhere, particularly in *Spheres of Justice*, rests on an empirical claim of general truth: namely, that community is a universal moral value, and that a conception of justice must recognize, or at least accommodate, that fact. Walzer and Rawls are likely to be somewhat more persuasive on a global scale than is Beitz, simply because, as a matter of fact, the view that communities are entitled to autonomy and self-determination is relatively widely held.[55] But it is doubtful whether Walzer or Rawls would command universal assent on very many points. What is more important for our purposes, it is unlikely that either of their conceptions of justice is detailed enough to be determinative on the kinds of issues that we have seen giving rise to international conflict, such as who holds title to the Falkland/Malvinas Islands.

At this point in the historical development of international society, no single conception of global justice enjoying the *de facto* legitimacy of the relevant actors in world affairs is determinative on the kinds of issues that our cases have proven capable of leading to the outbreak of war. To the extent that there is a legitimate conception of international justice at all, it is embodied and codified in modern international law. Nardin writes that "The moral element in international law is to be found in those general principles of international association that constitute customary international law, and above all in the most fundamental of those principles, such as the ones specifying the rights of independence, legal equality, and self-defense, and the duties to observe treaties, to respect the immunity of ambassadors, to refrain from aggression, to conduct hostilities in war in accordance with the laws of war, to respect human rights, and to cooperate in the peaceful settlement of disputes."[56] Consensus on these points, such as it is, is hardly an adequate basis for a community of justice. It may well be true that states acknowledge a duty to refrain from aggression; but what is aggression? The United Nations General Assembly declared in 1974 that aggression is "the use of armed force by a state against the sovereignty, territorial integrity or political independence of another state, or in any other manner inconsistent with the Charter of the United Nations."[57] Since neither customary international law nor the Charter of the United Nations provides any way of determining whether the Falkland Islands are rightfully British or rightfully Argentine, it is impossible to say whether the Argentine invasion counts as an instance of *aggression* (although it was clearly a use of force, which the UN Charter prohibits in the resolution of international disputes, and in that respect, at least, Argentina's action was clearly a violation of international law). The United Nations has consistently defended the right of self-determination of peoples;[58] but it has also upheld historical claims, and it has never provided criteria for deciding which peoples are eligible for self-determination, and under what circumstances the right of self-determination overrides a historical claim, or *vice versa*. To make matters even more complicated in the case of the Falklands/Malvinas, the United Nations has issued a blanket condemnation of colonialism; what, then, is the status of the islanders' *defense* of colonialism based upon the principle of self-determination of peoples?

Indeterminacy in hard cases is just one of the weaknesses of international law, both customary and positive. As a law-making body, the United Nations is beset by internal contradictions that undermine its legitimacy, not least of which is the fact that the fundamental principle on which it is founded, the sovereign equality of states, is inconsistent with the actual distribution of power within the UN itself.[59] This is not to deny that the United Nations is a useful organization, nor to demean international law as an institution. The world would be a far worse place without it. But it has not reached the level of sophistication or commanded the moral authority to constitute the basis of a well-ordered international society. It is simply inadequate to many of the tasks one would ideally like it to perform. The existing principles of justice that govern international relations today are too weak, too abstract, and enjoy too little legitimacy to be determinative in hard cases such as the Falklands/Malvinas question.

Where does this leave the question of justice in this particular case? When the institutional substructure does not exist to apportion entitlements and obligations in a situation such as the Falklands/Malvinas dispute, it does not make sense to say that there *are* any such entitlements and obligations – at least not as a matter of international justice. Neither Britain nor Argentina can claim *title* to the islands, because the institutions necessary to *confer* a title simply do not exist. With respect to the Falklands/Malvinas, Britain and Argentina remain in the proverbial state of nature.[60]

It is important to notice, however, that, although it cannot be said as a matter of international justice that either Britain or Argentina is entitled to the Falkland Islands, and hence although it cannot be said that either side's cause was *just* (bearing in mind that the word *just* is a shorthand for *justified in terms of the institutions apportioning legitimate entitlements and obligations*), it is psychologically true that each side understood its own cause as just, viewed its opponent's cause as unjust, and conceived of its claim as a claim grounded in a legitimate entitlement. The justifications they advanced in defense of those claims were parochial justifications; Britain rested its case on the self-determination of peoples, and Argentina rested its claim on historical right. In effect, each side preached to its own respective choir. Parochial conceptions of justice flowed into the gaping moral void left by the absence of an appropriate international conception.

Not surprisingly, the warrants offered, being parochial, fell on the deaf ears of those who needed to be persuaded in order for war to be avoided. Britain succeeded only in justifying its case to its own people and to those around the world who *already* gave greater moral weight to the principle of self-determination than to claims of historical right; Argentina succeeded only in justifying its case to its own people and to those around the world who already believed that historical claims trumped the principle of self-determination. Their respective

209

justifications were impressive insofar as they demonstrated the power of the justice motive as a spur to action; they were moving insofar as they illustrated fidelity to moral principles; and they were useful insofar as they mobilized domestic and international support. But they succeeded only in aggravating an already tense situation by inflaming the sense of justice in a context where justice itself was not at stake. What was true of the Falklands/Malvinas was equally true of the other cases where the justice motive contributed to the outbreak of war.

The justice motive cannot be harnessed to the cause of peace until the norms of international justice are strong enough to determine entitlements and obligations authoritatively, and until states begin to internalize those determinations and adjust their own claims and expectations accordingly. Until such time, parochial conceptions will simply continue to fill the moral void, and when those conceptions clash, conflicts will be more difficult to manage as a result. Emmerich de Vattel noted that when a state conceives of its cause as the cause of right and justice, it will "arrogate to itself all the rights of war and claim that its enemy has none ... The decision of the rights at issue will not be advanced thereby, and the contest will become more cruel, more disastrous in its effects, and more difficult of termination."[61] The justice motive, then, will continue to be part of the problem until it can become part of the solution.

TOWARD A JUST WORLD ORDER

The prevailing currents of moral thought change over time. Some see these changes as temporary or cyclical, others as inexorable and progressive.[62] *Real* conceptions of justice – those that govern actual human conduct – change over time as well. The evolution of international law, for instance, has shown that the ground of a conception of justice can change: no longer does it rest on natural law as it did in Grotius's time. Its content has also changed dramatically. The principle of self-determination of peoples, for example, is a relatively recent addition.[63] Conceptions of justice also evolve in their scope, their domain, and in their units of analysis.

In addition, different conceptions of justice with different grounds, scopes, domains, contents, and units of analysis can coexist at any given time. It is not unusual for one individual or group to be subject to (and to recognize) the moral authority of several conceptions at once. A professional athlete, for example, can simultaneously enjoy the entitlements (and shoulder the obligations) attendant to citizenship, membership in the players' union, the rules of his or her sport, and membership in a church, in a social club, or on a board of directors.

Both of these points are relevant to a useful understanding of international justice. Modern international society is very different from medieval society, or eighteenth-century international society. Some international societies have closely resembled a well-ordered society (the Concert of Europe; the OECD), while others have not (interwar Europe; post-colonial Africa). The world as a whole may evolve into a single well-ordered society, and it may not. If it does, the process may take centuries or millennia. It would be presumptuous at this stage to speculate on the details of the conceptions of justice that would govern such a society that far in the future, because it is impossible to tell what the world will look like. Nevertheless, the direction of progress is clear enough, even if the details are not. A well-ordered international society would be one in which principles of justice clearly specified entitlements and obligations, and in which the relevant actors (whatever they may be) assented to and generally behaved in conformity with those principles. Where conflicts arose, procedures that the parties to the conflicts regarded as legitimate would exist for resolving them.

We need not be dismayed by the slow pace and incremental nature of progress in that direction and, in the meantime, we must be willing to work toward it taking the world as it comes to us. At the present time, for example, we must accept as a fact of life that patriotism and nationalism lay primary claim to the political loyalties of human beings.[64] This is a matter of historical contingency; as technology and mobility have increased, intermediate kin and social units have weakened, and attachments to national groups have grown stronger.[65] But attitudes have not yet evolved to the point where they could support a strong cosmopolitan conception of justice. "The degree to which cosmopolitanism is accepted in Western countries is unclear," Nardin observes; "outside the West its appeal would appear to be small."[66]

It therefore seems difficult at the present moment to disagree with Hedley Bull's contention that "the state, whether we approve of it or not, is here to stay."[67] It also seems difficult to deny that under current conditions any principles of justice intended to have global scope will somehow have to accommodate themselves to the morality of states view. The representatives of the Third World – the very people whom Beitz would like to see benefit from a global redistribution of wealth – are the most ardent champions of state sovereignty and autonomy.[68] It is therefore highly unlikely that a cosmopolitan conception of justice would muster much assent any time in the near future. In any case, since states assert claims of entitlement and go to war over them, a conception of justice that denied them moral standing would be unlikely to be of much service to the cause of peace.[69]

By the same token, there seems little hope in the short run that a general conception of international justice will develop that includes well-defined principles of distributive entitlements and obligations, quite simply because sovereign states are loath to relinquish control of their own resources, and consider themselves the rightful arbiters of the distribution of the resources within their own borders. For the foreseeable future, the global redistribution of wealth is likely to remain in the province of mutual aid. It is also unlikely that a general conception of international justice will develop that specifies a detailed set of human rights, be they political, economic, or social, because these are questions on which there is considerable substantive disagreement between cultures.[70] If we are in search of *universal* principles of justice, therefore, we are unlikely in the short run to do much better than Rawls's rather thin consensus.

But there is no reason to be entirely skeptical of the possibility of a workable conception of international justice; after all, humans are social beings and recognize the legitimacy of social control.[71] Nor is there any particular reason why principles of justice governing international relations and defining international entitlements need to be universal in their scope, unless their domain touches universal interests or issues on which all states advance claims, none of which can be satisfied without prejudice to everyone else's. Still less is there any reason to expect principles of international justice to govern every possible domain. The universalistic impulse – a central but parochial feature of Western moral sensibility – is misplaced in an intercultural context. Until such time as international society as a whole becomes a well-ordered society (or indefinitely, if it fails to do so), there can be no grounds for complaint if a patchwork of conceptions of justice – with varied grounds, scopes, domains, contents, and units of analysis – evolves to regulate international behavior, so long as they succeed in apportioning entitlements and obligations in such a way as to satisfy those who actually advance claims. The Canada–US Free Trade Agreement, for example, defines in considerable detail the entitlements and obligations both of the two signatory states and of their respective industries, and it specifies a dispute resolution mechanism to adjudicate conflicting claims as they arise. The agreement, in short, operationalizes a conception of justice with a restricted scope and domain. Similarly, the European Community has developed institutions over time capable of defining and enforcing entitlements and obligations for its members and its nationals in a broad variety of issue areas. The Law of the Sea is an attempt to specify entitlements and obligations within a much more limited domain, but with a much larger scope; so also with the General Agreement on Tariffs and Trade.

These examples demonstrate that it is entirely appropriate to employ the concept of an international regime to the analysis of justice beyond borders. Stephen Krasner, in the now-classic formulation, defines a regime as a set of "implicit or explicit principles, norms, rules, and decision-making procedures around which actors' expectations converge in a given area of international relations."[72] While the concept of a regime has been used almost exclusively by students of international political economy, whose central activity is the empirical explication of the ways in which states pursue their conceptions of the national interest, there is nothing in the idea that disqualifies its use in normative political theory. To the contrary, Krasner respectively defines "principles" and "norms," which are both central to his definition of a regime, as "beliefs of fact, causation, *or rectitude*," and as "standards of behavior defined in terms of *rights and obligations*."[73]

Regimes do appear to have had a salutary effect on the level of international conflict in their respective domains. Robert Keohane writes:

> [R]egimes create a more favorable institutional environment for cooperation than would otherwise exist ... Such regimes are important not because they constitute centralized quasi-governments, but because they can facilitate agreements, and decentralized enforcement of agreements, among governments. They enhance the likelihood of cooperation by reducing the costs of making transactions that are consistent with the principles of the regime. They create the conditions for orderly multilateral negotiations, legitimate and delegitimate different types of state action, and facilitate linkages among issues within regimes and between regimes. They increase the symmetry and improve the quality of the information that governments receive. By clustering issues together in the same forums over a long period of time, they help to bring governments into continuing interaction with one another, reducing incentives to cheat and enhancing the value of reputation. By establishing legitimate standards of behavior for states to follow and by providing ways to monitor compliance, they create the basis for decentralized enforcement founded on the principle of reciprocity.[74]

We need not be bothered by the common wisdom that regimes are creations of self-interest rather than of the justice motive, provided that they succeed in winning the loyalty of those who participate in them. According to Hume's moral psychology, it is precisely the

213

internalization of rules of prudence that gives rise to substantive beliefs about justice in the first place.[75] The moral authority of internalized norms enables them to survive in the absence of external enforcement.[76] This is especially important in the international context, where enforcement can be weak or altogether lacking.

Ideally, of course, one would like to see the development of a regime capable of authoritatively determining such questions as who rightfully owns the Falklands. At the present moment there may seem little reason to expect one. But there is absolutely no harm done in putting the development of such a regime on the international agenda and devoting a certain amount of resources to exploring the possibility. "Whether a value-based global order is attainable, and what it might look like," writes Thomas Pogge, "is ... still an open question. Such a global order has never yet been tried ..."[77] Even if the effort yields only a partial success – for example, even if only a limited number of states sign on – the world will nonetheless be a better place for it. What Jan Narveson calls a "Moral Club" might well be the germ of a more general regime.[78] If such a club does not count among its members both Argentina and Great Britain, the question of title to the Falklands/ Malvinas cannot be settled authoritatively. But over the long run, the benefits of membership in moral clubs of various kinds might well attract those initially resistant to them, and perennial disputes may eventually find accommodation or adjudication within the institutional framework of a justice regime.[79]

International justice, then, can only mean what international actors agree it means. Not all international actors need agree on any one conception for us to speak of justice across borders; a patchwork of varied conceptions can enjoy the legitimacy of those who subscribe to them, and can efficaciously regulate international affairs. Where there are holes in the patchwork, there is neither justice nor injustice (although there may well be good or evil). Crafting, extending, repairing, and maintaining that patchwork through the development of the appropriate regimes would seem on the face of it activities worthy of the most serious attention, not only from political scientists and philosophers, but from statesmen as well. Only through their collective efforts will we discover whether it is possible to make progress toward the elusive goal of a just world order.

SOME FINAL THOUGHTS

The above discussion is unlikely to be very satisfying to anyone with a particularly strong sense of justice. We are all moral beings, and we all make moral judgments; they are almost always, however, parochial. It is disconcerting to think that projecting them into the international context may at best be inappropriate, and at worst a form of moral imperialism.

But the supposition that those judgments are likely to reflect a parochial value system is not an argument for moral skepticism. In the grand scheme of things, there may well be one and only one true conception of justice; but as human beings, our epistemic limitations prevent us even from knowing whether that is so, let alone from discovering what that one true conception may be. Moral beliefs are the province of faith, not of objective knowledge in any strong sense. The argument here – that we must be open-minded about the ground, scope, domain, content, and unit of analysis of any conception of justice defining entitlements and obligations across borders – is strictly a practical one: if we want to harness the justice motive to the cause of peace, then we must lower our philosophical sights and seek, not principles of justice that are necessarily *true* (though they may well be), but principles of justice that are *workable* – i.e., that have some hope of legitimacy in an international and intercultural context so that they can do the job we wish them to do: namely, reduce the incidence of conflict and facilitate the peaceful resolution of conflicts that arise as a consequence of the justice motive itself. As Thomas Pogge has written, a just global institutional structure "must be within reach from where we are, via a realistic transitional path not involving unacceptable moral costs."[80]

Those with more idealistic or universalistic aspirations may not agree that this is a worthy goal; they may insist that justice is too pristine a concept to be reduced to what politicians (of all people) can actually agree to. Part of the answer here is that justice, as a matter of sociological if not philosophical fact, is what people agree that it is in a given context, and that leaders – as our cases have demonstrated over and over again – are, more often than not, perfectly ordinary people. But part of the answer, too, is that justice is not the only value in the world; order is another, and justice is as difficult to secure without order as order is without justice. Justice must therefore accommodate to the essential features of the world as we know it, and thus it will have to reflect and indulge the pluralism of international society. "The best chances for world order," writes Stanley Hoffmann, "lie in the kind of pluralism that makes others share actively in the management, benefits, and burdens of international agreements or regimes and that allows us to accept their greater share precisely because they too will have a stake in preserving that order."[81]

215

Most controversial of all, undoubtedly, is the claim that in the absence of agreement on the meaning of justice in a given case, there *is* no justice or injustice. The argument rests on an understanding of justice that relies upon the institutional determination of entitlements and obligations. Where the institutions are not definitive and legitimate (i.e., morally authoritative for those subject to them), they cannot succeed in apportioning entitlements and obligations. This is not an argument for moral skepticism, either. As a matter of *psychological* fact, people will project their own moral sensibilities into situations that demand moral structure. Fidelity to one's own conception of justice will fill the void left by the absence of a determinative institutional context. I do not deny the *sincerity* of the British and Argentine claims to the Falkland Islands; I merely deny that questions of entitlement have right answers in the absence of a determinative and authoritative regime.

In the best of all possible worlds, all questions of entitlement would have a right answer, because international society would be a well-ordered society. If the best of all possible worlds is too much to hope for – and it clearly is, at least in the short run – the best we can hope to do is to discipline the use of moral language in international affairs so that the justice motive does not become engaged in situations where it does not belong. If Britain and Argentina could have been persuaded that neither of them could claim title to the Falkland Islands as a matter of justice, then their moral passions, and hence the dispute itself, might have been more easily contained. Disciplining their language might have made the difference between negotiations intended to compensate for an undeniable historical injury, and military action intended to execute the perceived demands of justice.

That, too, might be too much to hope for. It may simply be psychologically impossible to prevent parochial conceptions of justice from filling the moral void left by the absence of a determinative regime in a situation that seems to demand moral structure. If so, then the most that can be said here is that we will understand the world better if we recognize that fact and take it into account.

CONCLUSION

We will not fully understand the phenomenon of war – nor be as dexterous as we might in avoiding it – until we begin to appreciate the multidimensionality of its causes. This book demonstrates that the justice motive can contribute to the outbreak of war in a complex variety of ways, and that many wars that seem puzzling from a traditional Realist perspective emphasizing the motives of self-preservation and self-aggrandizement can be explained more satisfactorily once we appreciate the importance and the agency of moral motivations.

It seems likely that as a result of its failure to take these motivations seriously, political science has paid an enormous opportunity cost. Perhaps that cost might have been avoided if the scientific approach to international relations had supplemented, rather than rejected, the more humanistic tradition it displaced. Terry Nardin writes:

> In place of a familiar world in which people deliberated, made decisions, and acted on the basis of reasons and with reference to rules, there appeared a new world of phenomena and processes to be accounted for in terms of forces, variables, correlations, and causal laws. Theorists turned from the interpretation of "conduct" to the explanation of "behavior." It was not merely the idea of international society that had become discredited, but a whole way of looking at international relations.[1]

But the entrenchment of the scientific approach does not militate against the possibility of richer, more subtle, and more useful political science. If this study has demonstrated the possibility and the utility of using moral concepts to explain political events, then the next step is to secure and widen the beach head.

This may be done in two ways. First, empirical political science can refine our understanding of the importance of moral motivations in international politics by exploring more fully the role of the justice motive in decision making, by attempting to determine whether the justice motive has systematic effects on state behavior in specific

217

circumstances, and by gauging the strength of those effects. The cases examined here are suggestive, but they are not conclusive. While they demonstrate the possibility and usefulness of examining state behavior through normative lenses, and while they strongly suggest that the justice motive does indeed have the effects hypothesized in Chapter 1, they do not by themselves justify strong or sweeping claims about the relative importance of the justice motive as a cause of war, or about its agency. These would have to be the subjects of rather different studies.

Second, political theorists can attempt to craft conceptions of justice appropriate to particular international issues and circumstances. The cases examined here amply demonstrate the poignancy of the justice motive in the actions of the men and women who shoulder the burden of defending their nations' interests. Such men and women operate entirely in a non-ideal world. But political theorists often approach the philosophical problems of international politics from the perspective of the ideal. If indeed international justice is inescapably political – if it is shaped and determined by the interplay of cultures, as I suggest it must be – then, to give it content, we need to articulate principles and procedures that speak to the actual claims states make. The handful of cases I examine here do not provide an adequate basis for useful inductions of that kind, but they illustrate both the importance and the difficulty of that task.

If we are to bridge the empirical-normative gap, we must work from both of these directions at once. We must give the normative dimension of human behavior its due in the explanation of actual political events, and we must bring the "science of moral facts" to bear on the solution of global moral problems. Explanation and prescription need not remain forever in their present artificial isolation. Perhaps when they come together we will at last see tangible progress toward solving two of the world's most pressing problems – conflict and injustice.

Solving these problems, of course, is ultimately the task and the responsibility of practitioners, not scholars; and, as the cases I present here clearly show, leaders bring to the global stage distinctive values and viewpoints. These are difficult to transcend. Leaders are, in a sense, prisoners of the cultures that produce them.[2] Thus it is natural – perhaps even inevitable – that in a case where international society proves insufficiently well-ordered to resolve conflicting claims of justice amicably, a leader will confuse his or her parochial conception of justice with justice as such. It is natural for a leader to infer – sometimes correctly, but often wrongly – that if other states *disagree* with his or her understanding of entitlements, then their motives are ignoble, and they are therefore threats. A leader may consequently be inclined to interpret other states as grasping, rapacious, and unprincipled, even though they, too, may be motivated by the perceived demands of justice. This perception exacerbates fear and undermines trust. Thus, while the Realist account of motivation may be incomplete, Realism identifies a cardinal truth about international politics: states acting on the noblest of intentions may succeed only in kindling fear, hostility, and conflict.

The incompleteness of Realism's understanding of human nature means that Realism has difficulty explaining why the prospect of war no longer clouds the relations of so many states in the world today; it leads us to underestimate the social aspects of international society; but it perfectly models international relations where the fabric of international society is thin or torn. Keeping the fabric of international society in good repair is the preeminent goal of modern statesmanship. Wise statesmanship begins with circumspection – acknowledging that the normative lenses through which one sees the world are not necessarily the only lenses available, and recognizing that when one's own motives are principled, the motives of others may be principled, too. Even though others may not share one's own particular moral vision, they may nonetheless see the world in moral terms. They, too, may be striving for the good, and seeking to do right.

Far from being a source of fear, this should be cause for hope.

> Where an equal poise of hope and fear
> Does arbitrate th'event, my nature is
> That I incline to hope rather than fear,
> And gladly banish squint suspicion.
>
> John Milton, *Comus*, 1.410 (1634)

NOTES

INTRODUCTION

1 Hugo Grotius, *De Jure Belli ac Pacis*, trans. Francis W. Kelsey (Oxford: Clarendon Press, 1925), *passim.*; Alfred Thayer Mahan, *Armaments and Arbitration: The Place of Force in the International Relations of States* (New York: Harper, 1912), 131.
2 See generally Robert O. Keohane, ed., *Neorealism and its Critics* (New York: Columbia University Press, 1986).

THE JUSTICE MOTIVE AND WAR

1 This is not an exhaustive list of approaches, and space will not permit a comprehensive literature review here. Three recent books that include, *inter alia*, superb literature reviews are Zeev Maoz, *National Choices and International Processes* (Cambridge: Cambridge University Press, 1990); Manus I. Midlarsky, ed., *Handbook of War Studies* (Boston: Unwin Hyman, 1989); and Robert C. North, *War, Peace, Survival: Global Politics and Conceptual Synthesis* (Boulder, Colo.: Westview, 1990).
2 See the discussion, e.g., in Melvin Small and J. David Singer, *Resort to Arms: International and Civil Wars, 1816–1980* (Beverly Hills: Sage, 1982), 14–20; and Jack S. Levy, *War in the Modern Great Power System, 1495–1975* (Lexington: University Press of Kentucky, 1983), 1–7.
3 See, e.g., Morris Ginsberg, *Reason and Unreason in Society: Essays in Sociology and Social Philosophy* (Cambridge, Mass.: Harvard University Press, 1948), 177–95.
4 Cf. Benjamin A. Most and Harvey Starr, "International Relations Theory, Foreign Policy Substitutability, and 'Nice' Laws," *World Politics*, 36, No. 3 (April 1984), 383–406. By "substitutability," Most and Starr are referring to the possibility that through time and across space, similar inputs can result in different outputs (i.e. similar circumstances can generate different foreign policy acts). In international relations, the opposite may also hold: different inputs may lead to similar outputs, in which case "sometimes true" domain-specific laws may be the most that can be hoped for.
5 Bernard Brodie, *War and Politics* (New York: Macmillan, 1973), 339.
6 Quoted in Joseph S. Nye, Jr., *Nuclear Ethics* (New York: Free Press, 1986), 62.
7 See, e.g., Janice Gross Stein, "The Arab–Israeli War of 1967: Inadvertent War

Through Miscalculated Escalation," in Alexander L. George, ed., *Avoiding War: Problems of Crisis Management* (Boulder, Colo.: Westview, 1991), 126–59.

8 See, e.g., Richard Ned Lebow's analysis of the outbreak of World War I; *Between Peace and War: The Nature of International Crisis* (Baltimore: Johns Hopkins University Press, 1981), 119–47.

9 Thus we need not fear that a random computer failure could trigger World War III, because modern nuclear weapons cannot be fired unless human beings punch codes into permissive action links and turn keys to fire missiles. These involve decisions.

I do not mean to imply that only the decisions of national leaders are relevant to the understanding either of wars or of state behavior, although to avoid unnecessary complications in the remainder of this chapter I will speak as though they are. I would acknowledge that a crucial limitation on rational action is the fact that national leaders often do not know about and cannot control the actions of those under their nominal authority, yet may be forced to react to a chain of events heavily influenced by those actions. Particular dangers may arise when national leaders assume they have a degree of control over their subordinates that they do not in fact have. See Peter Douglas Feaver, *Guarding the Guardians: Civilian Control of Nuclear Weapons in the United States* (Ithaca, N.Y.: Cornell University Press, 1992). But while not all relevant actions are the consequences of decisions made by national leaders, they are nevertheless the consequences of human decisions, and national leaders are inevitably forced to decide how to respond to the actions of others.

10 See Robert Jervis, *Perception and Misperception in International Politics* (Princeton, N.J.: Princeton University Press, 1976), 356–81.

11 See, e.g., Paul Anderson and Timothy J. McKeown, "Changing Aspirations, Limited Attention, and War," *World Politics*, 40, No. 1 (October 1987), 1–29; Joseph H. de Rivera, *The Psychological Dimension of Foreign Policy* (Columbus, Ohio: Merrill, 1968); Irving Janis, *Groupthink: Psychological Studies of Policy Decisions and Fiascoes* (New York: Houghton Mifflin, 1982); Jervis, *Perception and Misperception*, and "Hypotheses on Misperception," in Klaus Knorr, ed., *Power, Strategy, and Security* (Princeton, N.J.: Princeton University Press, 1983), 152–77; Robert Jervis, Richard Ned Lebow, and Janice Gross Stein, with contributions by Patrick M. Morgan and Jack L. Snyder, *Psychology & Deterrence* (Baltimore: Johns Hopkins University Press, 1985); and Jack S. Levy, "Misperception and the Causes of War: Theoretical Linkages and Analytical Problems," *World Politics*, 36, No. 1 (October 1983), 76–99.

12 While certain cognitive biases are ubiquitous, because they result from inherent limitations in human capacities to process information, motivational psychologists argue that specific individuals are more susceptible than others to certain motivated biases (because of their individual personality structures), and that certain situations are more likely than others to result in motivated biases (because they more profoundly engage individuals' fears, anxieties, and needs). For an excellent summary, discussion, and literature review, see Richard Ned Lebow and Janice Gross Stein, "Afghanistan, Carter, and Foreign Policy Change: The Limits of Cognitive Models," in Timothy J. McKeown and Dan Caldwell, eds., *Force, Diplomacy,*

and Statecraft: Essays in Honor of Alexander L. George (Boulder, Colo.: Westview, in press).

13 The point may be illustrated by Janice Gross Stein's recent analysis of the outbreak of the 1991 Persian Gulf war, in which she argues that miscalculations played a crucial role. Stein differentiates decision-making when leaders are motivated by *need* from decision-making when leaders are motivated by *opportunity*. The crucial variable is motivation and, by means of it, Stein advances the literature on decision-making processes to the next level of generality. See Janice Gross Stein, "Deterrence and Compellence in the Gulf, 1990–91: A Failed or Impossible Task?" *International Security*, 17, No. 2 (Fall 1992), 147–79.

14 See Kjell Goldmann, "The Concept of 'Realism' as a Source of Confusion," *Cooperation and Conflict*, 23, No. 1 (1988), 2–14; and Michael Joseph Smith, *Realist Thought from Weber to Kissinger* (Baton Rouge: Louisiana State University Press, 1986), 1–22.

15 Different theorists formulate the fundamental postulates of Realism in slightly different ways. Cf., e.g., Robert O. Keohane and Joseph S. Nye, *Power and Interdependence: World Politics in Transition* (Boston: Little, Brown, 1977), chapt. 2. Realism's fundamental assumptions, according to Keohane and Nye, are (1) that states as coherent units are the dominant actors in world politics; (2) that force is a usable and effective instrument of policy; and (3) that there is a hierarchy of issues in world politics dominated by military security (pp. 23–24). These claims are either consistent with or entailed by my own formulation.

16 E.g., Stephen M. Walt, *The Origins of Alliances* (Ithaca, N.Y.: Cornell University Press, 1987); John Hertz, "Idealist Internationalism and the Security Dilemma," *World Politics*, 2, No. 2 (January 1950), 157–80; Joseph M. Grieco, "Anarchy and the Limits of Cooperation: A Realist Critique of the Newest Liberal Institutionalism," *International Organization*, 42, No. 3 (Summer 1988), 485–507.

17 Thucydides, *The Peloponnesian War*, trans. Rex Warner (Harmondsworth: Penguin, 1983), Book I, § 23 (p. 49).

18 *Ibid.*, Book V, §§ 84–116, esp. § 89 (p. 402). This latter statement – which I have paraphrased – is particularly interesting for present purposes, since it has been construed as a descriptive claim about the behavior of states in the international system; as a commentary on the limited scope for moral choice in world affairs; and as a substantive claim about the nature of international morality (namely, "might makes right"). For an excellent brief discussion of the importance of Thucydides to Realism, see Smith, *Realist Thought from Weber to Kissinger*, 4–11. Donald Kagan argues, in effect, that students of international politics have misunderstood Thucydides, and consequently misuse him. In particular, Kagan argues that Athenian power did *not* grow in the decade prior to the outbreak of the war, and that the available evidence does not suggest that the war was inevitable. *The Outbreak of the Peloponnesian War* (Ithaca, N.Y.: Cornell University Press, 1969), 345–74.

19 See Richard Schlatter, ed., *Hobbes's Thucydides* (New Brunswick, N.J.: Rutgers University Press, 1975), xi, xxvii–xxviii. In the phrase for which he is

perhaps best remembered, Hobbes wrote that life in the state of nature would be "solitary, poor, nasty, brutish, and short." *Leviathan*, ed., C.B. Macpherson (Harmondsworth: Penguin, 1968), 187–8. Although Hobbes used international politics as an example of how the state of nature would work, he was careful to distinguish relationships between individuals from relationships between states. The latter, he supposed, had sufficient weight and sufficient resources to provide a modicum of security that individuals would never have – the weakest of which, in effect, were fully capable of killing the strongest. Nevertheless, as Michael Smith writes, "His notion of the international state of nature as a state of war is shared by virtually everyone calling himself a realist." *Realist Thought from Weber to Kissinger*, 13.

20 See, e.g., Charles Beitz, *Political Theory and International Relations* (Princeton, N.J.: Princeton University Press, 1979), 27–50; Stanley Hoffmann, *Duties Beyond Borders* (Syracuse, N.Y.: Syracuse University Press, 1981), 14; and Michael Walzer, *Just and Unjust Wars* (New York: Basic Books, 1977), 3–20.

21 Most obviously, in North America, Western Europe, Scandinavia, and Australasia. Cf. Karl W. Deutsch, *Political Community and the North Atlantic Area: International Organization in the Light of Historical Experience* (Princeton, N.J.: Princeton University Press, 1957), 5, on the notion of a pluralistic security community.

22 As Robert Gilpin puts it, Realism in all its varieties assumes "the essentially conflictual nature of international affairs." Robert G. Gilpin, "The Richness of the Tradition of Political Realism," in Keohane, *Neorealism and its Critics*, 304.

23 It is possible to imagine that the peacefulness of international politics is a function of the system of deterrence: i.e., that states ensure peace through strength. The implication of this is that, if not for deterrence, wars would be epidemic. Since wars are comparatively rare events, either deterrence works remarkably well, or the Realist conception of international politics is fundamentally mistaken. Two considerations, taken together, favor the latter interpretation. First, armed conflict occurs in only a small proportion of the total number of international relationships. Second, even in relationships between known adversaries, the evidence necessary to conclude that deterrence is at work is generally missing. See Richard Ned Lebow and Janice Gross Stein, "Deterrence: The Elusive Dependent Variable," *World Politics*, 42, No. 3 (April 1990), 336–69. *A fortiori*, it would be difficult to argue that deterrence characterizes many of the non-adversarial relationships in the world, which constitute the vast majority.

24 Gilpin, "The Richness of the Tradition of Political Realism," 305.

25 Kenneth N. Waltz, "The Origin of War in Neorealist Theory," *Journal of Interdisciplinary History*, 18, No. 4 (Spring 1988), 616.

26 James Mayall, *Nationalism and International Society* (Cambridge: Cambridge University Press, 1990), 15.

27 Bruce Bueno de Mesquita, "The Contribution of Expected-Utility Theory to the Study of International Conflict," in Midlarsky, *Handbook of War Studies*, 143.

28 Robert Gilpin, "The Theory of Hegemonic War," *Journal of Interdisciplinary History*, 18, No. 4 (Spring 1988), 593.

29 Grieco, "Anarchy and the Limits of Cooperation," 487–8. See also Joseph Grieco, *Cooperation Among Nations: Europe, America, and Non-Tariff Barriers to Trade* (Ithaca, N.Y.: Cornell University Press, 1990).

30 Martin Wight, *Power Politics*, ed. Hedley Bull and Carsten Holbraad (London: Royal Institute of International Affairs, 1978), 101.

31 One strong reason for being skeptical even of this more modest claim is that civil wars occur at least as frequently as interstate wars (and much more frequently if one includes civil conflicts resulting in fewer than 1,000 battle deaths – see Small and Singer, *Resort to Arms*, 79–80, 222, 291). Unless it were stipulated that civil wars by definition break out only under conditions of (domestic) anarchy, we would have to reject even this weaker claim.

32 Jean-Jacques Rousseau, *A Lasting Peace through the Federation of Europe and the State of War*, trans. C.E. Vaughan (London: Constable, 1917), 78–9.

33 Kenneth N. Waltz, *Man, the State and War: A Theoretical Analysis* (New York: Columbia University Press, 1959), 39. For Waltz's extensive treatment of this point, see *ibid.*, 16–41.

34 See, e.g., note 25, above.

35 Hans J. Morgenthau, *Politics Among Nations: The Struggle for Power and Peace*, 5th edn. (New York: Knopf, 1978), 6.

36 *Ibid.*, 29. Morgenthau further complicates things when he writes that students of international morality "must guard against the two extremes of either overrating the influence of ethics upon international politics or underestimating it by denying that statesmen and diplomats are moved by anything but considerations of material power." *Ibid.*, 236.

37 See the discussion in Milton Friedman, "The Methodology of Positive Economics," in his *Essays in Positive Economics* (Chicago: University of Chicago Press, 1953), 3-43. For a critique of the as-if assumption in international relations theory, see Richard Ned Lebow and Janice Gross Stein, "Rational Deterrence Theory: I Think, Therefore I Deter," *World Politics*, 61, No. 2 (January 1989), 208–24.

38 I am indebted to an anonymous reader for drawing this point to my attention.

39 For further discussion, see David A. Welch, "The Organizational Process and Bureaucratic Politics Paradigms: Retrospect and Prospect," *International Security*, 17, No. 2 (Fall 1992), 112–46.

40 See, e.g., Jack Snyder, *Myths of Empire: Domestic Politics and International Ambition* (Ithaca, N.Y.: Cornell University Press, 1991).

41 Geoffrey Blainey, *The Causes of War* (New York: Free Press, 1973), 150.

42 Most theories of conflict, and especially those grounded in the dominant Realist tradition, stress that there is a special relationship between Great Power status and war. Great Powers, it is supposed, are particularly likely to be moved to war by considerations of power and prestige. Thus Levy writes, "Wars in which the Great Powers participate should be analyzed apart from wars in general because of the importance of the Great Powers and the distinctiveness of their behavior, including their war behavior." *War in the Modern Great Power System, 1495–1975*, 4.

43 As Mary Maxwell puts it, "*the impulse to moralize*, or to be concerned with the rightness and wrongness of things, is *innate*." *Morality Among Nations:*

An Evolutionary View (Albany: State University of New York Press, 1990), 5–6 (emphasis in the original).

44 Aristotle, *The Politics*, trans. Carnes Lord (Chicago: University of Chicago Press, 1984), Bk. I, chapt. II, 1253a15.

45 For a useful collection of essays on the psychology of motivation, see Gardner Lindzey, ed., *Assessment of Human Motives* (Westport, Conn.: Glenwood Press, 1979).

46 For a study of specifically moral motivation, see Laurence Thomas, *Living Morally: A Psychology of Moral Character* (Philadelphia: Temple University Press, 1989). See also Robert Folger, ed., *The Sense of Injustice: Social Psychological Perspectives* (New York: Plenum Press, 1984); Jerald Greenberg and Ronald L. Cohen, eds., *Equity and Justice in Social Behavior* (New York: Academic Press, 1982), especially the editors' survey and history in "The Justice Concept in Social Psychology," 1–41; Melvin J. Lerner, "The Justice Motive in Social Behavior: Introduction," *Journal of Social Issues*, 31, No. 3 (1975), 1–19; Melvin J. Lerner, "The Justice Motive: Some Hypotheses as to its Origins and Forms," *Journal of Personality*, 45, No. 1 (March 1977); Gerold Mikula, ed., *Justice and Social Interaction: Experimental and Theoretical Contributions from Psychological Research* (New York: Springer-Verlag, 1980); Elaine Walster, G. William Walster, and Ellen Berscheid, *Equity: Theory and Research* (Boston: Allyn and Bacon, 1978). For a critique of the supposedly objective and value-free study of moral psychology, see Edward E. Sampson, *Justice and the Critique of Pure Psychology* (New York: Plenum Press, 1983). For a less psychological and more philosophical treatment of moral psychology, see N.J.H. Dent, *The Moral Psychology of the Virtues* (Cambridge: Cambridge University Press, 1984).

47 Melvin J. Lerner, "The Justice Motive in Human Relations," in Melvin J. Lerner and Sally C. Lerner, eds., *The Justice Motive in Social Behavior: Adapting to Times of Scarcity and Change* (New York: Plenum Press, 1981), 12–13.

48 *Ibid.*, p. 13. Judith Shklar's description is more poetic: "What ... is the sense of injustice? First and foremost it is the special kind of anger we feel when we are denied promised benefits and when we do not get what we believe to be our due. It is the betrayal that we experience when others disappoint expectations that they have created in us. And it has always been with us. We hear the sense of injustice in the voices of Job and Jonah and Hesiod at the dawn of our literary history, and it still rings loud and true. Where indeed would our literature be without it? What on earth would Dickens have had to write about without the sense of injustice? He, no less than Voltaire, reminds us that we are not only aroused on our behalf but emphatically also when the indignities of injustice are experienced by other people ... When it asserts itself, the sense of injustice is unmistakable even when we refuse to acknowledge it." Judith N. Shklar, *The Faces of Injustice* (New Haven: Yale University Press, 1990), p. 83.

49 Lerner, "The Justice Motive in Human Relations," p. 13.

50 *Ibid.*, 15. For a useful discussion of the affective consequences of moral standards as a source of motivation, see Martin L. Hoffman, "Affect, Cognition, and Motivation," in Richard M. Sorrentino and E. Tory Higgins,

eds., *Handbook of Motivation and Cognition* (New York: Guilford Press, 1986), 254–80.

51 For a useful survey of various approaches to understanding the development of the sense of justice (social learning, psychoanalytic, and cognitive), see Carolyn H. Simmons, "Theoretical Issues in the Development of Social Justice," in Lerner and Lerner, eds., *The Justice Motive in Social Behavior*, 41–55.

52 The satisfaction of many demands, of course, may require both. Such is the nature of a "just compromise."

53 I discuss these issues in greater depth in Chapter 7.

54 Norman Frolich and Joe Oppenheimer, "Beyond Economic Man: Altruism, Egalitarianism, and Difference Maximizing," *Journal of Conflict Resolution*, 28, No. 1 (March 1984), 23. We should beware, however, of attempting to use such a notion of self-interest in explaining behavior, for the very reasons I discuss with reference to Blainey's claim that all conflicts are conflicts of power. See p. 17, above.

55 On the uniqueness and power of moral motivations, see C.D. Broad, "Some of the Main Problems of Ethics," in *Broad's Critical Essays in Moral Philosophy*, ed. H.D. Lewis (London: George Allen & Unwin, 1971), 223–46.

56 See, e.g., Dale T. Miller and Neil Vidmar, "The Social Psychology of Punishment Reactions," in Lerner and Lerner, eds., *The Justice Motive in Social Behavior*, 145–72.

57 Daniel Kahneman, Jack L. Knetsch, and Richard H. Thaler, "Fairness and the Assumptions of Economics," *Journal of Business*, 59, No. 4 (October 1986), S285–S300.

58 One exception is Sasson Sofer, "International Relations and the Invisibility of Ideology," *Millennium: Journal of International Studies*, 16, No. 3 (Winter 1987), 489–521, who argues that ideology can explain behavior unanalyzable in purely Realist terms.

59 Amos Yoder, *World Politics and the Causes of War since 1914* (Lanham, Md.: University Press of America, 1986), 7–8 (Table 1), 15.

60 Robert E. Osgood and Robert W. Tucker, *Force, Order, and Justice* (Baltimore: Johns Hopkins University Press, 1967), 8–9. Osgood and Tucker's list includes security; material and commercial gain; influence and dominion; status or prestige; religious or ideological supremacy. The last, of course, comes closest to the mark.

61 I am indebted to K.J. Holsti for drawing this work to my attention.

62 F.S. Northedge and M.D. Donelan, *International Disputes: The Political Aspects* (London: Europa, 1971), 35, 76.

63 Janice Gross Stein and David A. Welch, "Entitlement and Legitimacy in Decision Making," unpublished paper, October 1991.

64 Bueno de Mesquita, "The Contribution of Expected-Utility Theory," 144.

65 Later in this chapter I consider the problem of distinguishing sincere claims from insincere claims, and in chapters 2–6 I demonstrate how this may be done.

66 Paul F. Diehl and Gary Goertz, "Territorial Changes and Militarized Conflict," *Journal of Conflict Resolution*, 32, No. 1 (March 1988), 120.

67 Attention to the justice motive might also improve the usefulness of

theories of strategic interaction, which rely upon rational-actor assumptions. As Charles Glaser has recently argued, analyses of strategic interaction would benefit if they took into account adversaries' motivations. Charles L. Glaser, "Political Consequences of Military Strategy: Expanding and Refining the Spiral and Deterrence Models," *World Politics*, 44, No. 4 (July 1992), 497–538. While Glaser's primary distinction is between "greedy" and "non-greedy" adversaries, we might equally well use the labels "satisfied" and "unsatisfied" – the assignment of which may depend crucially upon the presence or absence of perceived injustices.

68 The literature on behavioral decision theory is significant. A collection of seminal papers may be found in Daniel Kahneman, Paul Slovic, and Amos Tversky, eds., *Judgment under Uncertainty: Heuristics and Biases* (Cambridge: Cambridge University Press, 1982). Two particularly important works are Daniel Kahneman and Amos Tversky, "Prospect Theory: An Analysis of Decisions under Risk," *Econometrica*, 47, No. 2 (March 1979), 263–91; and Amos Tversky and Daniel Kahneman, "The Framing of Decisions and the Psychology of Choice," *Science*, 211 (30 January 1981), 453–8. Only recently has this literature begun to filter into the study of international relations. See, e.g., the collections of essays in *International Journal*, 47, No. 2 (Spring 1992), reprinted as Janice Gross Stein and Louis W. Pauly, eds., *Choosing to Co-operate: How States Avoid Loss* (Baltimore: Johns Hopkins University Press, 1993); and in *Political Psychology*, 13, No. 2 (June 1992).

69 For example, in a question involving prospects of monetary gains, Kahneman and Tversky's subjects preferred a sure gain of 3,000 to an 80 percent chance of winning 4,000 (and a 20 percent chance of winning nothing) by a four-to-one margin. The expected utility of the preferred alternative was $3,000 \times 1.0 = 3,000$; the expected utility of the second alternative was $4,000 \times .8 = 3,200$. The same problem framed in terms of losses illustrated dramatically different preferences. By a margin of more than eleven-to-one, respondents preferred an 80 percent chance to lose 4,000 (and a 20 percent chance to lose nothing) to a sure loss of 3,000. They therefore chose the alternative with the lower expected utility (–3,200 vs. –3,000). "Prospect Theory: An Analysis of Decisions under Risk," 26. This is a good illustration of the claim that people are risk-acceptant with respect to losses, and risk-averse with respect to gains.

70 Richard Thaler, "Toward a Positive Theory of Consumer Choice," *Journal of Economic Behavior and Organization*, 1, No. 1 (March 1980), 39–60; Jack L. Sinden and J.A. Sinden, "Willingness to Pay and Compensation Demanded: Experimental Evidence of an Unexpected Disparity in Measures of Value," *Quarterly Journal of Economics*, 99, No. 3 (August 1984), 507–21; Jack L. Knetsch, "The Endowment Effect and Evidence of Non-reversible Indifference Curves," *American Economic Review*, 79, No. 5 (December 1989), 1277–84; and Daniel Kahneman, Jack L. Knetsch and Richard H. Thaler, "The Endowment Effect, Loss Aversion, and the Status Quo Bias," *Journal of Economic Perspectives*, 5, No. 1 (Winter 1991), 193–206. Anticipating this research, Robert Jervis noted in 1976 that states are willing to pay a higher price to protect what they have than to increase their values. Jervis, *Perception and Misperception*, 51.

71 See Janice Gross Stein, "International Co-operation and Loss Avoidance: Framing the Problem," *International Journal*, 47, No. 2 (Spring 1992), 215–16.

72 Subjective conceptions of entitlements will not prove fully *sufficient* for predicting references frames, in part because not all choice situations involve perceived entitlements.

73 Richard D. Anderson, Jr., "Why Competitive Politics Inhibits Learning in Soviet Foreign Policy," in George W. Breslauer and Philip E. Tetlock, eds., *Learning in U.S. and Soviet Foreign Policy* (Boulder, Colo.: Westview, 1991), 112.

74 See particularly Lebow, *Between Peace and War*; Jervis, Lebow, and Stein, *Psychology & Deterrence*; James G. Blight, *The Shattered Crystal Ball: Fear and Learning in the Cuban Missile Crisis* (Savage, Md.: Rowman and Littlefield, 1990); and Richard Ned Lebow and Janice Gross Stein, *We All Lost the Cold War* (Princeton, N.J.: Princeton University Press, forthcoming).

75 Robert Jervis, "Perceiving and Coping with Threat," in *Psychology & Deterrence*, 14–15, citing Raymond Cohen, *Threat Perception in International Crisis* (Madison: University of Wisconsin Press, 1979).

76 See, e.g., James G. Blight and David A. Welch, *On the Brink: Americans and Soviets Reexamine the Cuban Missile Crisis*, 2nd edn. (New York: Noonday, 1990), 25, 28, 120–1.

77 It is interesting to note, as we shall also see in Chapter 5, that those in Britain who came to view Hitler as a threat earliest were less impressed by the *substance* of his claims than by the manner in which he asserted them – namely, by repudiating treaties and sending in the *Wehrmacht*.

78 Janice Gross Stein, "Building Politics into Psychology: The Misperception of Threat," *Political Psychology*, 9, No. 2 (June 1988), 249–51.

79 For an excellent discussion of the general form of the "hermeneutical circle" and its treatment by Heidegger and others, see Graeme Nicholson, *Seeing and Reading* (London: Macmillan, 1984).

80 Robert Jervis, "Perceiving and Coping with Threat," in *Psychology & Deterrence*, 23.

81 See Lebow, *Between Peace and War*, 199.

82 On the effects of the evoked set, see Jervis, *Perception and Misperception*, 203–16.

83 Not all of the events that Nicholas interpreted as deliberate attempts to deny him his entitlements were deliberate. London was not even aware of some of them. This fact illustrates two other common cognitive errors: the "fundamental attribution error" (the tendency to believe that an adversary's behavior is determined by dispositional factors, while one's own is determined by situational factors); and false attribution of coherence and centralization (the tendency to assume that all of the adversary's behavior is deliberate and centrally coordinated). See Robert Mandel, "Psychological Approaches to International Relations," in Margaret G. Hermann, ed., *Political Psychology* (San Francisco: Jossey-Bass, 1986), 254–8; and Stein, "Building Politics into Psychology," 255–7.

84 For further discussion of these and other misperceptions, see Richard Smoke, "The Crimean War," in George, ed., *Avoiding War*, 36–61.

85 Philip E. Tetlock, "Learning in U.S. and Soviet Foreign Policy: In Search of

an Elusive Concept," in Breslauer and Tetlock, *Learning in U.S. and Soviet Foreign Policy*, 32. Cf. Margaret Hermann's formulation: "cognitive complexity concerns the degree of differentiation a person shows when observing or contemplating his environment"; it denotes the ability to "differentiate objects in more than dichotomous (good–bad, black–white, either–or) terms," and the willingness "to entertain the possibility that essential features of objects are not yet recognized." Margaret G. Hermann, "Leader Personality and Foreign Policy Behavior," in James N. Rosenau, ed., *Comparing Foreign Policies: Theories, Findings, and Methods* (New York: Sage, 1974), 206.

86 See, e.g., Zeev Maoz and Anat Shayer, "The Cognitive Structure of Peace and War Argumentation: Israeli Prime Ministers Versus the Knesset," *Political Psychology*, 8, No. 4 (December 1987), 575–604; Stephen G. Walker, "Personality, Situation, and Cognitive Complexity: A Revisionist Analysis of the Israeli Cases," same volume, 605–21; and Zeev Maoz, "Revisionism or Misinterpretation? A Reply to Professor Walker," same volume, 623–36.

87 Mandel, "Psychological Approaches to International Relations," 71.

88 Blight, *The Shattered Crystal Ball*; Irving L. Janis and Leon Mann, *Decision Making: A Psychological Analysis of Conflict, Choice, and Commitment* (New York: Free Press, 1977); Jervis, *Perception and Misperception*, chapt. 10 (pp. 356–81); Lebow, *Between Peace and War*, 107–11.

89 Jervis, "Perceiving and Coping with Threat," in *Psychology & Deterrence*, 18. On motivated biases, see *ibid.*, 24–7.

90 For further discussion, see Lebow and Stein, "Afghanistan, Carter, and Foreign Policy Change," and citations therein.

91 See Michael Doyle, "Liberalism and World Politics," *American Political Science Review*, 80, No. 4 (December 1986), 1151–69; and Carol R. Ember, Melvin Ember, and Bruce M. Russett, "Peace Between Participatory Polities: A Cross-Cultural Test of the 'Democracies Rarely Fight Each Other' Hypothesis," *World Politics*, 44, No. 4 (July 1992), 573–99.

92 See generally Robert Putnam, "Diplomacy and Domestic Politics: The Logic of Two-Level Games," *International Organization*, 42, No. 3 (Summer 1988), 427–60; Peter B. Evans, Dietrich Rueschemeyer, and Theda Skocpol, eds., *Bringing the State Back In* (Cambridge: Cambridge University Press, 1985); and Jack S. Levy, "Domestic Politics and War," *Journal of Interdisciplinary History*, 18, No. 4 (Spring 1988), 653–73.

93 I discuss these issues in greater detail in Chapter 7.

94 See Harry Eckstein, "Case Study and Theory in Political Science," in Fred I. Greenstein and Nelson W. Polsby, eds., *Strategies of Inquiry*, Handbook of Political Science, VII (Reading, Mass.: Addison-Wesley, 1975), 104–13. For further discussion of the limits and possibilities of case research strategies, see Alexander L. George, "Case Studies and Theory Development: The Method of Structured, Focussed Comparison," in Paul Gordon Lauren, ed., *Diplomacy: New Approaches in History, Theory, and Policy* (New York: Free Press, 1979), 43–68; and Arend Lijphart, "The Comparable Case Strategy in Comparative Research," *Comparative Political Studies*, 8, No. 2 (July 1975), 158–77.

95 See n. 42, above. A further reason for being particularly interested in Great

Power wars is that these are the conflicts that have traditionally been the most destructive. If for some reason our studies lead to conclusions that we can only believe to be valid for the wars under scrutiny, it is important to spend one's resources looking at the wars that matter most.

96 Throughout this study, I shall employ (with minor modifications) Jack Levy's identifications of Great Powers, wars involving Great Powers, Great Power wars (i.e., wars *between* two or more Great Powers), and general wars, as presented in *War in the Modern Great Power System, 1495–1975*, chapts. 2 and 3.

97 Levy defines a "general war" as one involving "nearly all the Great Powers and resulting in high levels of destruction" – operationally, involving at least two-thirds of the Great Powers and exceeding 1,000 battle deaths per million population. *Ibid.,* 75.

98 With the overthrow of communism in Eastern Europe, the dismantling of the Warsaw Pact, the precipitous decline of the Soviet Union, and the economic integration of Western Europe, the world may well have entered a new geopolitical phase. Prudence requires that we reserve judgment on the issue until we have the benefit of historical distance.

99 Only now is reliable information on Chinese motivations coming to light; see Thomas J. Christensen, "Threats, Assurances, and the Last Chance for Peace: The Lessons of Mao's Korean War Telegrams," *International Security,* 17, No. 1 (Summer 1992), 122–54. At present, we have no hard information on North Korean motivations.

100 Decision-making in the Suez conflict, however, might well provide support for the claims of this study. See Louise Richardson, "Avoiding and Incurring Losses: Decision-Making in the Suez Crisis," *International Journal,* 47, No. 2 (Spring 1992), 370–401.

101 See n. 98, above.

102 A further non-negligible consideration is the fact that the issues that gave rise to the war have not yet been settled to the satisfaction of the parties concerned; a better understanding of its causes could possibly help prevent a recurrence.

103 See, e.g., the discussion in Kagan, *The Outbreak of the Peloponnesian War,* 345 ff.

104 Many distinguish "traditional" academic history from "social-scientific" history. The division rather closely resembles the primary methodological rift in contemporary political science. My point here is not that one of these approaches is, in general, superior to the other. In either case, "the quality of an historical interpretation is critically dependent on the quality of the details out of which it is spun." Robert William Fogel and G.R. Elton, *Which Road to the Past? Two Views of History* (New Haven: Yale University Press, 1983), 125. My point is simply that interpretations of events generated by historians directly applying social scientific models that screen out normative motivations in human actions will not be of use in assessing the impact of those motivations in historical events. See generally Jacques Le Goff and Pierre Nora, eds., *Constructing the Past: Essays in Historical Methodology* (Cambridge: Cambridge University Press, 1985).

105 The Franco-Spanish War of 1823 is a case in point. See Guillaume de

Bertier de Sauvigny, *The Bourbon Restoration*, trans. Lynn M. Case (Philadelphia: University of Pennsylvania Press, 1967), 182–93; François-René, vicomte de Chateaubriand, *Congrès de Vérone; Guerre d'Espagne; Negociations: Colonies Espagnoles*, 1 (Paris: Delloyé, 1838); Martin A.S. Hume, *Modern Spain, 1788–1898* (New York: G.P. Putnam's Sons, 1903), 179–247; André Jardin and André-Jean Tudesq, *Restoration and Reaction, 1815-1848*, trans. Elborg Forster (Cambridge: Cambridge University Press, 1983); and Etienne Denis, duc Pasquier, *Histoire de Mon Temps: Mémoires du Chancelier Pasquier*, 5 (Paris: E. Plon, Nourrit, 1894), 280–303.

106 Grant Hugo defines cant as "a mode of expression, or a cast of thought, of which the effect – irrespective of the motive – is to create a misleading discrepancy between the natural meaning of words and their practical significance ... " Grant Hugo, *Appearance and Reality in International Relations* (New York: Columbia University Press, 1970), 19.

107 Waltz, *Man, the State and War*, 113.

108 The Russo-Japanese war also provides a clear illustration of this point. None of the Japanese diplomatic correspondence with Russia leading up to the war, and none of the key statements articulating Japan's goals, emphasized *wrongs* done to Japan. All of them emphasized the Russian threat to Japanese *interests*. No appeals to Japan's rights or entitlements appear in the places one would expect to see it even if there had been an intention to use it for purposes of rationalization. See, e.g., Foreign Minister Komura Jutaro's speech to the Diet on March 23, 1904: Japan, Foreign Office, *Correspondence Regarding the Negotiations between Japan and Russia (1903–1904)* (Washington, D.C.: Gibson, 1904), iii–xii; the Imperial Rescript: *Times of London*, February 11, 1904, 3; and Japan's declaration of war; Morinosuke Kajima, *The Diplomacy of Japan 1894–1922*, 2 (Tokyo: Kajima Institute of International Peace, 1978), 161–3.

109 An insurance investigator, for example, could infer causality on the basis of the following information: (1) a vehicle, braking normally, was hit from behind by a second vehicle; (2) the driver of the second vehicle was maintaining a "safe" following distance behind the first; (3) the driver of the second vehicle attempted to brake as soon as he saw the first vehicle's brake lights flash; (4) the second vehicle's brake pads were completely worn through; (5) in all other respects, the conditions of the vehicles and their drivers were the same. A logical inference would be that worn brake pads "caused" the accident; for the second vehicle should have been able to stop in time, and it is plausible to conclude that the car *would have* stopped in time had its brakes not been defective. What justifies this inference is, in part, the intuition that defective brakes make accidents more likely. Defective brakes increase a vehicle's stopping distance; requiring a longer distance in which to stop would logically seem to increase the likelihood of accidents, all other things being equal. It is for this reason that the investigator suspected the car's brakes, rather than (for example) the fact that its radio was broken: it is difficult to imagine the mechanism by means of which broken radios would cause accidents, and it is difficult to imagine that we could generalize about the propensity of broken radios to do so. But the connection between worn brakes and collisions is easy to

grasp. If the insurance investigator examined a number of accidents that occurred in circumstances under which worn brakes should *least* likely be suspected (whatever those circumstances might be), yet nonetheless concluded that worn brakes played crucial roles in many of them, he or she would then be entitled to conclude *a fortiori* that worn brakes were very probably an important cause of traffic accidents in general. What the insurance investigator *cannot* do is fix a numerical probability to the likelihood that cars with worn brake pads will have accidents for a given population of vehicles; for this, a statistical strength-of-association analysis is absolutely necessary. Yet in the absence of such a study, it would nevertheless be worthwhile to encourage drivers to maintain their brakes.

I am grateful to John Lewis Gaddis for drawing to my attention the fact that E.H. Carr used the metaphor of an automobile accident to discuss causal inference. Edward Hallett Carr, *What Is History?* (London: Macmillan, 1961), 98–101. There are those, of course, who maintain that "the only investigation of the causes of war that is intellectually respectable is that of the unique origins and causes and nature of *particular* past wars." Paul Seabury and Angelo Codevilla, *War: Ends and Means* (New York: Basic Books, 1989), 50. By way of illustration, Seabury and Codevilla note that "standard Marxist explanations for World War II stress the importance of German industrial cartels such as I.G. Farben. But how important is such an abstract factor compared with the actual presence in the Nazi party of the master rabble-rouser, Joseph Goebbels? Given that Goebbels attributes his becoming a Nazi to his mother-in-law, is *she* to be ranked as a cause, or are mothers-in-law in general?" *Ibid.*, 38. Carr notes, however, that it is possible to distinguish "rational" causes of wars (those about which we can generalize) from "accidental" causes (those about which we cannot – e.g., mothers-in-law).

THE CRIMEAN WAR

1 See, e.g., Paul W. Schroeder, *Austria, Great Britain, and the Crimean War: The Destruction of the European Concert* (Ithaca, N.Y.: Cornell University Press, 1972), xi; Alexander William Kinglake, *The Invasion of the Crimea: Its Origin and an Account of Its Progress Down to the Death of Lord Raglan*, 3rd edn., I (Edinburgh: W. Blackwood and Sons, 1863), 5; and David Wetzel, *The Crimean War: A Diplomatic History*, East European Monograph No. CXCIII (New York: Columbia University Press, 1985), v. For good general histories of the event, see Alan Palmer, *The Banner of Battle: The Story of the Crimean War* (New York: St. Martin's, 1987); and J.A.R. Marriott, *The Eastern Question: An Historical Study in European Diplomacy*, 4th edn. (Oxford: Clarendon Press, 1940). On the history of military operations, see A.J. Barker, *The War Against Russia, 1854–1856* (New York: Holt, Rinehart and Winston, 1970); and on the peace settlement, see Winfried Baumgart, *The Peace of Paris, 1856: Studies in War, Diplomacy, and Peacemaking* (Santa Barbara, Calif.: ABC-Clio, 1981).

2 Quoted in Ann Pottinger Saab, *The Origins of the Crimean Alliance* (Charlottesville: University Press of Virginia, 1977), 1. Cf. Norman Rich, *Why the*

Crimean War? A Cautionary Tale (Hanover, N.H.: University Press of New England, for Brown University, 1985), 4, 199–209.

3 Cf. Luc Monnier, *Étude sur les Origines de la Guerre de Crimée* (Geneva: Librairie Droz, 1977), 3. Temperley writes, "Had Nicholas been weak, Aberdeen strong, or Menšikov tactful, there might have been no war." Harold Temperley, *England and the Near East: The Crimea* (Hamden, Conn.: Archon Books, 1964), 305.

4 Rich, *Why the Crimean War?*, ix. Belgrade was the eastern terminus of the telegraph network in 1853; horse couriers carried diplomatic pouches back and forth across the Balkans between Belgrade and Constantinople. Monnier, *Étude sur les Origines de la Guerre de Crimée*, 5.

5 Kinglake, *The Invasion of the Crimea*, 13–14.

6 On these issues, see, e.g., *ibid.*, 108–10, and Temperley, *England and the Near East*, 232–3. The Orthodox Church in the Ottoman Empire was a largely self-governing entity in which the Patriarch of Constantinople was the most powerful figure. The essence of the ambiguity of Russia's rights in Turkey concerned the relationship between the Patriarch of Constantinople and the Tsar. In fact, the Greek Patriarch acknowledged the Tsar as his "spiritual superior." *Morning Chronicle* (London), July 9, 1853, 6. But this did not necessarily mean that the Tsar was entitled to speak on secular matters under the Patriarch's *de facto* jurisdiction. For the history of the Greek Orthodox millet in Turkey, see Saab, *The Origins of the Crimean Alliance*, 5–6n.

7 Temperley, *England and the Near East*, 287. See also 280–5 and 463–5 n. 425 for details of Orthodox and Latin conflicts at Jerusalem and their diplomatic background.

8 Temperley, *England and the Near East*, 290; Kinglake, *The Invasion of the Crimea*, 48. There is reason to believe that the evident contradiction between the two was the result of modifications to the firman made by the Russian Minister in Constantinople while he had a draft in his possession. Temperley, *England and the Near East*, 291.

9 Temperley notes that once France had raised the issue of the Capitulations of 1740, she had to seek a favorable resolution of the contradictions between the French note and the "Greek firman" to avoid giving the impression that she was allowing the treaty of 1740 to lapse. Temperley, *England and the Near East*, 294. As part of a campaign of intimidation, the French dispatched a heavy warship, the *Charlemagne*, to carry de Lavalette back to Constantinople in the summer of 1852 after a visit to Paris. *Ibid.*, 292–3. The voyage of the *Charlemagne* was delicate because it flatly contravened the Straits Convention of July 13, 1841, by the terms of which (Article I) the sultan undertook "to maintain ... the principle invariably established as the ancient rule of his Empire ... [whereby] it has at all times been prohibited for Ships of War of Foreign Powers to enter the Straits of the Dardanelles and of the Bosphorus; and ... so long as the Porte is at peace ... [to] admit no foreign Ship of War into the said Straits." In the same article, the European powers pledged "to respect this determination of the sultan, and to conform themselves to the principle above declared." In Article 2, the sultan reserved the right to grant firmans allowing the passage

NOTES TO PAGES 51–52

of light vessels of war employed in the diplomatic service of foreign powers; but the *Charlemagne* could in no way be construed as a "light vessel." See J.C. Hurewitz, "Russia and the Turkish Straits: A Reevaluation of the Origins of the Problem," *World Politics*, 14, No. 4 (July 1962), 608.

10 Temperley, *England and the Near East*, 288.

11 Kinglake, *The Invasion of the Crimea*, 51; Temperley, *England and the Near East*, 301, 303.

Fate conspired to strain relations between Russia and the Porte further by stirring up trouble in the Balkans. Upon his ascension in 1852, Prince Danilo of Montenegro sought to transform his homeland, a theocracy, into a hereditary principality, and to secularize the bishopric. He consulted Austria and Russia, both of whom received the scheme favorably; but he failed to consult the Sultan, who was nominally sovereign over the territory and refused to accept the change. The Sultan sent five Turkish armies to enforce his rights. Austria, duly fearful of nationalist or sectarian strife on its frontiers, dispatched Count Leiningen to Constantinople in February 1853 to peremptorily demand that Turkey withdraw. The Tsar, still fuming over the Holy Lands dispute, echoed Austria's ultimatum, declaring that a refusal to comply would be treated as a *casus belli*. Kinglake writes, "It may seem strange that the Czar should propose to found a declaration of war upon a grievance which was put forward by the Cabinet of Vienna, and not by himself; but he was always eager to stand forward as the protector of Christians of his own Church who had taken up arms against their Moslem rulers ..." Kinglake, *The Invasion of the Crimea*, 72. Turkey sagely withdrew, and the Tsar, somewhat mollified, canceled the purchases of horses needed to make good on his threat of war. *Ibid.*, 74–92. See also Temperley, *England and the Near East*, 221–2, 301–3; Saab, *The Origins of the Crimean Alliance*, 21–2; and Schroeder, *Austria, Great Britain, and the Crimean War*, 24. Schroeder believes that Leiningen's mission had the unfortunate effect of reinforcing Nicholas's impression that threats and ultimatums were appropriate means with which to deal with Turkey. *Ibid.*, 28.

12 Temperley, *England and the Near East*, 306. Menshikov did not seek the key to the Bethlehem Church or the removal of the silver star from the grotto, but he did seek declarations by the Turkish government that these did not confer rights of ownership upon the principal altar of the Church or any new rights over the Holy Stable of the Nativity; that no changes would be made to the ceremonies or hours of service; that the Great Gate would continue to be guarded by an Orthodox priest; and that Orthodox clerics would have precedence at the shrine of the Blessed Virgin at Gethsemane. Kinglake, *The Invasion of the Crimea*, 132–3. For further discussion of Menshikov's mission, see John Shelton Curtiss, *Russia's Crimean War* (Durham, N.C.: Duke University Press, 1979), 84–140; and Saab, *The Origins of the Crimean Alliance*, 25–49.

13 Quoted in Saab, *The Origins of the Crimean Alliance*, 27. A fuller discussion of the Russian claim may be found in Temperley, *England and the Near East*, 464–5 n. 425.

14 Rich, *Why the Crimean War?*, 38; Wetzel, *The Crimean War*, 75.

15 Curtiss, *Russia's Crimean War*, 41. The Tsar also occasionally invoked the

terms of the Treaty of Adrianople to justify his claim of a protectorate; but the only relevant passage in the text of the Treaty of Adrianople was a confirmation of existing treaties. Rich, *Why the Crimean War?*, 38.

16 Albert Seaton mistakenly believes Nicholas thought the Treat of Kutchuk-Kainardji gave him a protectorate over *all* Christians in Turkey. Albert Seaton, *The Crimean War: a Russian Chronicle* (London: Batsford, 1977), 40.

17 Paul Schroeder, for example, writes that the Russians "genuinely believed their argument that Russia had possessed and exercised this right ever since the Treaty of Kuchuk-Kainarji in 1774." Schroeder, *Austria, Great Britain, and the Crimean War*, 30. Ann Pottinger Saab writes, "In a demand that paralleled the French use of the Capitulations of 1740, the Russians tried to interpret the Treaty of Kutchuk-Kainardji as giving them a special right of intercession on behalf of the Greek Orthodox millet. (Actually, neither Nicholas nor Nesselrode had a clear recollection of the text of the treaty, and both were somewhat embarrassed later when they realized how much they had stretched it.)" Saab, *The Origins of the Crimean Alliance*, 27. Temperley flatly pronounces that "The Czar and his advisers ultimately went to war over a claim they had never troubled to examine." Temperley, *England and the Near East*, 304. See also Rich, *Why the Crimean War?*, 38–9.

18 Brison Gooch argues that Menshikov's mission may have been patterned after Austria's and France's successful attempts at bluster and intimidation. Brison D. Gooch, "A Century of Historiography on the Origins of the Crimean War," *American Historical Review*, 62, No. 1 (October 1956), 38. See n. 11 , above.

19 Kinglake, *The Invasion of the Crimea*, 94–5, 101, 105–6, 142–3.

20 See, e.g., *ibid.*, 117–25; Temperley, *England and the Near East*, 314–16. Redcliffe was not at this point authorized to call up the fleet without orders from the government.

21 Kinglake, *The Invasion of the Crimea*, 138–9.

22 For the texts of Menshikov's final note and Reshid Pasha's reply, see *ibid.*, 497–500.

23 *Ibid.*, 185.

24 *Ibid.*, 195–6.

25 *Ibid.*, 184–5. Russia had intervened militarily in Moldavia as recently as July 1848, a move sanctioned by the Treaties of Akerman and Adrianople. Temperley, *England and the Near East*, 258.

26 The Vienna note is discussed in Saab, *The Origins of the Crimean Alliance*, 51–75; Curtiss, *Russia's Crimean War*, 141–66; Temperley, *England and the Near East*, 342–4; Kinglake, *The Invasion of the Crimea*, 347–57; and is reprinted, with the Sultan's proposed modifications, in *ibid.*, 501–2. Rich argues convincingly that the "violent interpretation" was more measured and less violent than has traditionally been surmised, and that the Sultan's proposed modifications had the effect of trivializing the document. Rich, *Why the Crimean War?*, 78–80. British historians had surmised for some time that Redcliffe deliberately frustrated a peaceful settlement by counselling Turkey to reject the Vienna note; but this myth is decisively demolished in J.L. Herkless, "Stratford, The Cabinet, and the Outbreak of the Crimean War," *Historical Journal*, 18, No. 3 (September 1975), 497–523.

27 Louis Napoleon was pressing for a more active naval display, both to prevent unrest in Constantinople from getting out of hand and to further persuade Nicholas that his position was untenable. Napoleon informed the English government on July 13 that if the occupation of the Principalities did not come to an end, the French fleet could not remain at Besika Bay; on August 19 and September 21, he urged the British to order the combined squadron to Constantinople. Approaching autumn storms would force the allied fleets to seek a safer haven, and a movement *away* from Constantinople would have sent the wrong signal. Kinglake, *The Invasion of the Crimea*, 344.

28 Temperley, *England and the Near East*, 354–5.

29 Schroeder believes that by the time of Olmütz, Foreign Secretary Lord Clarendon had concluded that there was no hope of persuading Turkey to accept any proposal from Austria. Schroeder, *Austria, Great Britain, and the Crimean War*, 78. Lord John Russell also wrote Clarendon: "Of course the proposition from Olmütz is intended only to deceive"; "if Nicholas, or Nesselrode, or Buol were to act honestly all might be settled in half an hour." Russell to Clarendon, October 4 and 5, 1853, quoted in *ibid.*, 81. Cf. Temperley, *England and the Near East*, 355–6.

30 *Ibid.*, 354.

31 Kinglake, *The Invasion of the Crimea*, 354.

32 *Ibid.*, 367.

33 *Ibid.*, 358.

34 Temperley, *England and the Near East*, 371. See also Kinglake, *The Invasion of the Crimea*, 369–73.

35 Sinope and Pearl Harbor differed in important respects, of course. My point is that the emotional reactions to both events were similar. See the discussion on p. 71, below.

36 *Ibid.*, 380.

37 Curtiss, *Russia's Crimean War*, 230.

38 *Ibid.*, 231.

39 Kinglake, *The Invasion of the Crimea*, 387. Napoleon only added to the strains between Russia and France when he wrote Nicholas what he believed to be a conciliatory letter on January 29, 1854, recapitulating events as he understood them, and calling upon the Tsar to choose between peace and war. Nicholas was outraged by what he believed to be bias and selectivity in the letter, and was incensed at the fact that it was published simultaneously in the *Moniteur* – a clear violation of protocol. His reply to Napoleon stressed that it was France who had started the whole business by challenging the rights and privileges of the Orthodox Church in the Holy Land. Curtiss, *Russia's Crimean War*, 232–3.

40 Kinglake, *The Invasion of the Crimea*, 386–7. See also Temperley, *England and the Near East*, 376.

41 For details on last-minute diplomacy to avert war, see Saab, *The Origins of the Crimean Alliance*, 132–3.

42 Kinglake, *The Invasion of the Crimea*, 457–63.

43 See *ibid.*, 198–9, 326. Proof of Austria's influence came in the summer of

1854. Her threat to join the war on the side of Turkey at one stroke accomplished what Britain and France had been unable to do even by declarations of war: it persuaded the Tsar to evacuate the Danubian Principalities. On August 2, 1854, the last of the Russian troops in Moldavia and Wallachia finally re-crossed the Pruth. *Ibid.*, 434–6.

44 *Ibid.*, 32–4.

45 See, e.g., Gen. Sir Edward Hamley, *The War in the Crimea*, 7th edn. (London: Seeley & Co., 1986), 1–4.

46 See, e.g., Seaton, *The Crimean War*, 15; Wetzel, *The Crimean War*, 77; and Gooch, "A Century of Historiography on the Origins of the Crimean War," 33–5. Cf. Saab *The Origins of the Crimean Alliance*, 155–6.

47 Vernon John Puryear, *England, Russia and the Straits Question, 1844–1856* (Berkeley: University of California Press, 1931), xii. For a discussion of economic motives, see *ibid.*, 76–138; Gooch, "A Century of Historiography on the Origins of the Crimean War," 49–51; and Wetzel, *The Crimean War*, 15, 30.

48 Puryear, *England, Russia and the Straits Question*, 39.

49 G.H. Bolsover, "Nicholas I and the Partition of Turkey," *Slavonic and East European Review*, 27, No. 68 (December 1948), 144. Many in Europe in the first half of the nineteenth century feared that the collapse of the Ottoman Empire was imminent, because of the administrative, financial, judicial, and military weaknesses of the regime, as well as the latent nationalist and religious dissatisfaction of the Empire's Christian populations. Curtiss, *Russia's Crimean War*, 28.

50 Kinglake, *The Invasion of the Crimea*, 86–90; Temperley, *England and the Near East*, 276–7. Kinglake notes that the Tsar mentioned to Seymour that Russia might be forced to take temporary possession of the city under certain circumstances. For a thorough analysis of the Seymour conversations, see Gavin Burns Henderson, *Crimean War Diplomacy and Other Historical Essays* (New York: Russell & Russell, 1975), 1–14; and Curtiss, *Russia's Crimean War*, 58-83. The Tsar did not in fact use the term "sick man," but rather "sick bear." Seymour's despatch No. 87 of February 21, 1853, Foreign Office Papers 65/424, quoted in Temperley, *England and the Near East*, 272.

51 Puryear, *England, Russia and the Straits Question*, 1. Puryear argues that the agreement was "verbal," and that it was made during the Tsar's visit to England in June 1844. Puryear insists that a memorandum written by Count Nesselrode shortly after the visit is the best evidence for a secret agreement; but the memorandum itself cannot bear the weight of the claim, and the notion has since fallen into disrepute among scholars of the event. See *ibid.*, 1–74, 439–42 (in which the Nesselrode memorandum is reprinted); and Gooch, "A Century of Historiography on the Origins of the Crimean War," 53–5.

52 Temperley, *England and the Near East*, 277.

53 This claim is well documented in Puryear, *England, Russia and the Straits Question*, 11–13.

54 Curtiss, *Russia's Crimean War*, 16.

55 *Ibid.*, 19; Kinglake, *The Invasion of the Crimea*, 66.

56 Temperley, *England and the Near East*, 307.

57 See *Ibid.*, 258, 274–5.

58 *Ibid.*, 279. Temperley does not give a citation for Prokesch-Osten's remarks, but Henderson gives it as Prokesch-Osten to Ficquelmont, March 26, 1854, from *Aus den Briefen des Grafen Prokesch von Osten, 1849–1855* (Vienna, 1896), 367–70; see Henderson, *Crimean War Diplomacy and Other Historical Essays*, 13.

59 Cf. Monnier, *Étude sur les Origines de la Guerre de Crimée*, 7.

60 Cf. Kinglake, *The Invasion of the Crimea*, 173. For a rebuttal of theories of Russian aggressiveness and predation, see Curtiss, *Russia's Crimean War*, 167; for a meticulous and insightful discussion of the Tsar's attitude toward the partition of Turkey, see Hurewitz, "Russia and the Turkish Straits." Curtiss surmises that Nicholas was moved largely by fear of rebellions and insurrections, and wished to assert his control over the Christians of Turkey lest they should rebel against the sultan and unleash a revolutionary tide. Curtiss, *Russia's Crimean War*, 168–9. This view seems plausible against the backdrop of events in 1848, when liberal and nationalist revolutions swept through much of conservative Europe. But there is no evidence that this was in fact Nicholas's motivation in applying pressure on the Porte. Indeed, if it had been, he could have represented the issue accordingly and increased the likelihood that he would be supported by other European powers, especially Austria and Prussia. Moreover, during the winter of 1853–1854, after the Turkish declaration of war, Nicholas actively considered an attempt to raise the Balkan Christians in revolt against the Porte. His attempt to secure Austrian acquiescence in the scheme met with stiff resistance, and it came to naught; but it seems highly unlikely that he would even have considered the idea if Curtiss's thesis is correct. See Saab, *The Origins of the Crimean Alliance*, 134.

61 Kinglake, *The Invasion of the Crimea*, 58–9.

62 Puryear, *England, Russia and the Straits Question*, 24.

63 Kinglake, *The Invasion of the Crimea*, 60 (paraphrasing Napoleon Bonaparte).

64 Curtiss, *Russia's Crimean War*, 11.

65 Hurewitz, "Russia and the Turkish Straits: A Reevaluation of the Origins of the Problem," 607.

66 Curtiss, *Russia's Crimean War*, 18–19.

67 Gooch, "A Century of Historiography on the Origins of the Crimean War," 52; Kinglake, *The Invasion of the Crimea*, 194.

68 The best sketch of the Tsar may be found in Nicholas V. Riasanovsky, *Nicholas I and Official Nationality in Russia, 1825–1855* (Berkeley: University of California Press, 1959), 1–22.

69 Bernard Pares, *A History of Russia* (New York: Knopf, 1953), 334.

70 Riasanovsky, *Nicholas I and Official Nationality in Russia*, 15. Cf. Kinglake: "He was always ready to come forward as an eager and almost ferocious defender of his Church, and he deemed this motive to be one of such cogency that views resting on mere policy and prudence were always in danger of being overborne by it." Nicholas "had the air of a man raised above the level of common worshippers, who imagined that he was appointed to serve the cause of his Church by great imperial achievements,

and not by humble feats of morality and devotion." Kinglake, *The Invasion of the Crimea*, 69, 62–3.

71 Curtiss, *Russia's Crimean War*, 47.
72 Kinglake, *The Invasion of the Crimea*, 43.
73 Temperley, *England and the Near East*, 283.
74 Kinglake, *The Invasion of the Crimea*, 129–30.
75 Temperley, *England and the Near East*, 301.
76 Wetzel, *The Crimean War*, 41.
77 Nesselrode's circular of June 11, 1853 made clear that the demand for an affirmation of the Tsar's rights was understood *only* as a reaffirmation of the Treaty of Kutchuk-Kainardji, made necessary by the French insistence on the Capitulations of 1740. Bernadotte E. Schmitt, "The Diplomatic Preliminaries of the Crimean War," *American Historical Review*, 25, No. 1 (October 1919), 41.
78 Kinglake, *The Invasion of the Crimea*, 144–5.
79 Schmitt, "The Diplomatic Preliminaries of the Crimean War," p. 41.
80 Cf. Saab, *The Origins of the Crimean Alliance*, p. 12.
81 See Temperley, *England and the Near East*, 342.
82 Schmitt, "The Diplomatic Preliminaries of the Crimean War," 44.
83 Cf. *Ibid.*, 49.
84 E.g., Puryear, *England, Russia and the Straits Question*, 197–8; Schroeder, *Austria, Great Britain, and the Crimean War*, 23. Cf. Temperley, who squarely assigns responsibility for the genesis of the Crimean war to the dispute over the Holy Places (Temperley, *England and the Near East*, 280); and Kinglake, *The Invasion of the Crimea*, 471–2.
85 Quoted in Kinglake, *The Invasion of the Crimea*, 87.
86 *Times of London*, July 11, 1853, 5. As his war message issued in response to the Turkish declaration proclaimed, "Russia fights not for the things of this world, but for the Faith." Kinglake, *The Invasion of the Crimea*, 465.
87 It is worth noting that although the Tsar was a free agent politically, he was sensitive to the main currents of public feeling in Russia, especially as they touched religious matters. In this respect, popular reactions to events in Turkey only reinforced his own perceptions and predispositions. Events were aggravated by the popular perception in Russia that Christians under Turkish rule were severely repressed. In fact, this was generally not the case; Turkey treated its Christian populations with commendable toleration. In the other capitals of Europe, it was widely recognized that the Porte was displaying the Christian virtues of forbearance and patience; "and in proportion as men loved justice and were led by the gentle precepts of the Gospel, they inclined to the Mahometan Prince, who seemed to represent their principles, and began to think how best they could help him to make a stand against the ferocious Christianity of the Czar." Kinglake, *The Invasion of the Crimea*, 175; see also *ibid.*, 56. But the dispute with Turkey took on an unfortunate Holy War tone in the Russian peasant consciousness. The St. Petersburg correspondent for the *Times of London*, for example, described mass outrage at Turkey's "perfidy" (July 11, 1853, 5), and reported that while "the highest military and diplomatic officials are opposed to the idea of a war, it is welcomed by the lower classes

with fanatical enthusiasm. When the manifesto [posted in the churches to explain the Russian occupation of the Danubian Principalities] became publicly known here numerous Russians were seen to fall on their knees in the open street and pray for blessings on their great Czar, the defender of the Orthodox faith ..." *Times of London*, July 13, 1853, 5. Kinglake writes that, as with the Tsar himself, "love of country and devotion to the Church had become so closely welded into one engrossing sentiment, that good Muscovites could not sever the one idea from the other." "When the Emperor of Russia sought to gain or to keep for his Church the holy shrines of Palestine, he spoke on behalf of fifty millions of brave, pious, devoted subjects, of whom thousands for the sake of the cause would joyfully risk their lives. From the serf in his hut even up to the great Czar himself, the faith professed was the faith really glowing in the heart, and violently swaying the will. It was the part of wise statesmen to treat with much deference an honest and pious desire which was rooted thus deep in the bosom of the Russian people." *The Invasion of the Crimea*, 55, 43.

88 For further discussion, see, e.g., Kinglake, *The Invasion of the Crimea*, 335–6. British ships sailed back and forth between Besika Bay and Constantinople all during the summer of 1853 in violation of the Straits Convention, much to the Tsar's annoyance. Puryear, *England, Russia and the Straits Question*, 278–9. This was not, as the Tsar believed, a deliberate British signal.

89 The Tsar had in fact refused to accept Redcliffe's credentials when he was posted to St. Petersburg. Kinglake relates the Tsar's attitude toward the British Ambassador in detail, emphasizing Nicholas's fury at the thought of Redcliffe exercising *de facto* protection of Christians in Turkey through his influence with the Porte. "Men not jesting approached him with stories that the Ambassador had determined to bring over the Sultan to the Church of England. His brain was not strong enough to be safe against rumours like that." Kinglake, *The Invasion of the Crimea*, 150–1; see also 111–14, 182–3. Kinglake further suggests that "from the peace of Adrianople in 1829 down to the time of his death, the Czar would have preferred the ascendancy which Sir Stratford Canning enjoyed at Constantinople to any scheme of conquest. And, what is more, if Nicholas had succeeded in gaining this ascendancy, he would have been inclined to use it as a means of enforcing counsels somewhat similar to those which were pressed upon the Sultan by the English Ambassador; for though his first care would have been always for his own Church, it would have suited his pride and his policy to extend his protection to all the Christian subjects of the Porte." *Ibid.*, 114. See also Temperley, *England and the Near East*, 228, 321.

90 *Ibid.*, 298–9.

91 Kinglake, *The Invasion of the Crimea*, 193. Cf. *ibid.*, 189–94, 418; and Temperley, *England and the Near East*, 299–300.

92 See the discussions in *ibid.*, 350–2, and Kinglake, *The Invasion of the Crimea*, 359.

93 Saab, *The Origins of the Crimean Alliance*, 88–9.

94 See *Ibid.*, 101–2.

95 In the same interview in which Redcliffe informed the Sultan of his instructions concerning the British fleet at Malta (May 9), he urged him not

to resist the occupation of the Danubian Principalities. Temperley, *England and the Near East*, 323.

96 Puryear insists that "Russia's occupation of the Principalities did not provoke war ... The British government admitted that the Porte had no *casus belli* against Russia." Puryear, *England, Russia and the Straits Question*, 283, citing F.O. 65 Russia 423, 278. But Britain contradicted itself on this point, justifying the Turkish declaration of war on the ground that the occupation was indeed a *casus belli* (F.O. 65 Russia 438, Clarendon to Brunnow, October 1, 1853, also cited in Puryear, 297–8 n. 161); and in the House of Lords on August 12, 1853, the Foreign Secretary, the Earl of Clarendon, admitted on the record that the Russian occupation of the Danubian Principalities was a *casus belli* for the Turks. *Hansard's Parliamentary Debates*, 3rd Series, 129, col. 1633.

97 *Times of London*, July 13, 1853, 5.

98 See, e.g., *Morning Chronicle* (London), December 17, 1853, 4.

99 Saab, *The Origins of the Crimean Alliance*, 97.

100 *Ibid.*, 111.

101 Saab suggests that other factors behind the Turkish decision may have included "bitterness over the ambiguous stand of Britain and France, patriotic pride, and a serious overrating of Ottoman military capacities – plus the wish to gain something from the effort of mobilization." *Ibid.*, 92.

102 For a full discussion of divisions within the British Cabinet, see Schroeder, *Austria, Great Britain, and the Crimean War*, 32.

103 Rich, *Why the Crimean War?*, xvii.

104 Quoted in Henderson, *Crimean War Diplomacy and Other Historical Essays*, 11 (emphasis in the original); Lord Malmesbury, in an eloquent speech in the House of Lords in August, claimed that the Tsar had evident designs on Constantinople. *Hansard*, 129, col. 1609.

105 Kinglake, *The Invasion of the Crimea*, 34–6. Malmesbury provides a clear formulation of British interests in the integrity and independence of the Ottoman Empire, *Hansard*, 129, col. 1617.

106 Herbert to Clarendon, October 8, 1853; quoted in Temperley, *England and the Near East*, 358. As suggested above, Britain apparently overestimated the utility of the port of Constantinople to the Russian navy, and certainly failed to appreciate that Russia was in fact better served strategically by the status quo; but it was nonetheless true that Russian occupation of Constantinople would have increased the strains on the Royal Navy given the extra resources that would have had to have been devoted to the defense of the Mediterranean to offset a sizeable Russian naval presence.

Kinglake doubts that the cabinet had solid grounds for believing that core British interests were actually at stake in the dispute between Russia and Turkey: "No one could say that the interest which England had in the perfect independence of the Ottoman Empire was so obvious and so deep as to exclude all questioning; and even if a man were driven from that first ground, still, without being guilty of paradox, he might fairly dispute, and say that the independence of the Sultan was not really brought into peril by a form of words which, during some weeks, had received the approval of every one of the five great Powers." Kinglake, *The Invasion of the Crimea*,

415. Kinglake may be correct on the abstract point; but his view does not appear to have received much of a hearing in the cabinet itself.

107 *Ibid.*, 177, 395, 411.

108 Curtiss, *Russia's Crimean War*, 236–7.

109 Palmerston to Clarendon, April 11, 1853; quoted in Henderson, *Crimean War Diplomacy and Other Historical Essays*, 12.

110 Lord Aberdeen to the Queen, Oct. 7, 1853, PRO 28/121, Public Record Office, London.

111 Clarendon to Bloomfield, July 5, 1853; quoted in Temperley, *England and the Near East*, 344.

112 *Ibid.*, 357.

113 See, e.g., *Morning Chronicle* (London), July 9, 1853, 6. To some extent, misperceptions of the Tsar's intentions contributed to British outrage: the publication and subsequent misinterpretation of Seymour's conversations with the Tsar, and of Nesselrode's 1844 memorandum on the desirability of Anglo-Russian contingency planning in the event of a Turkish collapse, were causes of considerable scandal in Britain. See Temperley, *England and the Near East*, 278. Cf. Schroeder, *Austria, Great Britain, and the Crimean War*, 51.

114 *Morning Chronicle* (London), December 17, 1853, 4.

115 Kinglake, *The Invasion of the Crimea*, 376. "In England the indignation of the people ran to a height importing a resolve to have vengeance."

116 *Ibid.*, 377–8; see also p. 409.

117 Curtiss, *Russia's Crimean War*, 207–8.

118 See *ibid.*, 190–1.

119 Aberdeen to Sir James Graham (First Lord of the Admiralty), December 28, 1853; quoted in Schroeder, *Austria, Great Britain, and the Crimean War*, 121. Of the British and French note, Kinglake writes, "It was so framed that Lord Palmerston would know it meant war, whilst Lord Aberdeen and Mr Gladstone might be led to imagine that it was a measure rather gentle than otherwise, which would perhaps keep peace in the Euxine." Kinglake, *The Invasion of the Crimea*, 380. Aberdeen's hope seems particularly puzzling in view of his statement in October "that Russia will regard the entrance of line of battle ships into the Black Sea as a virtual declaration of war against herself." Aberdeen to the Queen, October 7, 1853, PRO 28/121.

120 For a full discussion, see, e.g., Curtiss, *Russia's Crimean War*, 191–2.

121 *Hansard*, 129, col. 1619. A particularly clear statement of the Russian injustice perpetrated against the Turks was made by Mr. Layard in the House of Commons on July 22, 1853; *Hansard*, 129, cols. 647–50.

122 Kinglake, *The Invasion of the Crimea*, 465. Clear statements of the multiplicity of British motivations were made by Clarendon in the House of Lords, *Hansard*, 132, cols. 140–53 (March 31, 1854); and by Russell in the House of Commons, *ibid.*, cols. 198–217.

123 Gooch, "A Century of Historiography on the Origins of the Crimean War," 36–7; Temperley, *England and the Near East*, 280, 286. Indeed, only in 1847 did Pope Pius IX appoint a Latin patriarch of Jerusalem and actually require him to live there. *Ibid.*, 284. Kinglake's interpretation is similar:

"Neither the interest nor the honour of France required that in the Eastern Question she should stand more forward than any other of the remonstrant States; but the personal interest of the new Emperor and his December friends did not at all coincide with the interest of France; for what he and his associates wanted, and in truth what they really needed, was to thrust France into a conflict which might be either diplomatic or warlike, but which was at all events to be of a conspicuous sort, tending to ward off the peril of home politics, and give to the fabric of the 2d of December something like station and celebrity in Europe. In order to achieve this, it clearly would not suffice for France to be merely one of a conference of four great Powers quietly and temperately engaged in repressing the encroachment of the Czar ... [A] close, separate, and significant alliance with England, and with England alone, to the exclusion of the rest of the four Powers, would not only bring about the conflict which was needed for the safety and comfort of the Tuileries, but would seem in the eyes of the mistaken world to give the sanction of the Queen's pure name to the acts of the December night and the Thursday the day of blood." Kinglake, *The Invasion of the Crimea*, 322–3. Kinglake's analysis of the intentions and role of Napoleon III has long been controversial. Kinglake blames the war almost entirely on the French Emperor. The received wisdom among historians is that Kinglake's indictment was heavily influenced by personal animosity toward Napoleon traceable to a romantic rivalry. See Gooch, "A Century of Historiography on the Origins of the Crimean War," 44–9.

124 Curtiss, *Russia's Crimean War*, 43.
125 *Ibid.*, 40. Wetzel, offering a similar interpretation, argues that Napoleon was motivated simply by considerations of prestige. Wetzel, *The Crimean War*, 40.
126 Monnier, *Étude sur les Origines de la Guerre de Crimée*, 22.
127 See, e.g., Saab, *The Origins of the Crimean Alliance*, 156. Some, such as Puryear, interpret the religious issue as a "challenge Napoleon was offering for political supremacy in the Ottoman Empire." Puryear, *England, Russia and the Straits Question*, 197. Some support for this thesis may be gleaned from a passage (later crossed out) written by the French Foreign Minister, de la Hitte, to General Aupick at the time France originally put forth her claim: "Finally, there is another consideration of great weight in our eyes because it is connected with still higher interests yet, that is ... the utility that there is for the Porte itself that our influence in the Orient be adequate to counterbalance the always growing [influence] of Russia." Saab, *The Origins of the Crimean Alliance*, 10. But Puryear's interpretation seems unlikely given the fact that France had limited its claim of protection to "the Pope, his rights in the East and European Roman Catholic ecclesiastical establishments." When asked by the Porte if he claimed a protectorate over Catholic subjects as a whole within the Ottoman Empire, Ambassador de Lavalette replied, "Certainly not." Temperley, *England and the Near East*, 295–6. France was therefore demanding influence over a very small constituency in Turkey, hardly large enough to give

243

it "political supremacy." Moreover, the roughness with which France asserted its claims, and the difficulties in which it put the Sultan, could hardly have been calculated to endear France to the Porte.

128 See the discussion in Saab, *The Origins of the Crimean Alliance*, 126–7.

129 See Kinglake, *The Invasion of the Crimea*, 468–85; cf. Schroeder, *Austria, Great Britain, and the Crimean War*, xiii. This is not, of course, a motivational factor.

130 Schroeder emphasizes British frustration with Austria's attempt to deal with the unfolding crisis in the traditional diplomatic manner of the Concert, "primarily because no such solution could bring the defeat for Russia and the victory for Britain and her principles that Palmerston and liberal opinion demanded." Schroeder, *Austria, Great Britain, and the Crimean War*, xii.

131 *The Crimean War*, 13.

132 See the excellent analysis in J.C. Hurewitz, "Ottoman Diplomacy and the European State System," *Middle East Journal*, 15, No. 2 (Spring 1961), 141–52.

133 Kinglake, *The Invasion of the Crimea*, 40.

THE FRANCO-PRUSSIAN WAR

1 Michael Howard, *The Franco-Prussian War: The German Invasion of France, 1870–1871* (New York: Macmillan, 1962), 1.

2 Lawrence D. Steefel, *Bismarck, the Hohenzollern Candidacy, and the Origins of the Franco-German War of 1870* (Cambridge: Harvard University Press, 1962), 1.

3 G.P. Gooch, "Foreword," in Georges Bonnin, ed. *Bismarck and the Hohenzollern Candidature for the Spanish Throne: The Documents in the German Archives*, trans. Isabella M. Massey (London: Chatto & Windus, 1957), 9.

4 Steefel, *Bismarck, the Hohenzollern Candidacy, and the Origins of the Franco-German War of 1870*, gives a thorough account of the diplomacy leading up the outbreak of the war, while Howard, *The Franco-Prussian War*, provides perhaps the best general history of the event as a whole, and is particularly strong on the military aspects of the conflict. A useful brief diplomatic history may be found in John Emerich Edward Dalberg-Acton, First Baron Acton, "The Causes of the Franco-Prussian War," *Historical Essays and Studies*, ed. John Neville Figgis and Reginald Vere Laurence (London: Macmillan, 1908); more detailed general diplomatic histories include Pierre Lehautcourt (Général Palat), *Les Origines de la Guerre de 1870: La Candidature Hohenzollern, 1868–1870* (Paris: Berger-Levrault, 1912); Robert Howard Lord, *The Origins of the War of 1870: New Documents from the German Archives* (New York: Russell & Russell, 1966), 3–117; and Albert Sorel, *Histoire Diplomatique de la Guerre Franco-Allemande*, I (Paris: E. Plon, 1875), 1–59. Two accounts by the architects of French policy give the French version of events: Le Duc de Gramont, *La France et la Prusse Avant la Guerre* (Paris: E. Dentu, 1872), is tight-lipped and defensive; more informative are the thirteenth and fourteenth volumes of Émile Ollivier's monumental *L'Empire Libéral: Études, Récits, Souvenirs*, usefully condensed and beautifully translated by George

Burnham Ives and published as Émile Ollivier, *The Franco-Prussian War and its Hidden Causes* (London: Sir Isaac Pitman & Sons, 1913). Bismarck's memoirs are thin and notoriously unreliable – see Lord, *The Origins of the War of 1870*, v – but they nevertheless give what was the official German version of events for many years after the war: Otto Fürst von Bismarck, *Bismarck, the Man and the Statesman: Being the Reflections and Reminiscences of Otto, Prince von Bismarck, Written and Dictated by Himself after His Retirement from Office*, II, trans. A.J. Butler (New York: Harper & Brothers, 1898); W.R. Fryer, "The War of 1870 in the Pattern of Franco-German Relations," *Renaissance and Modern Studies*, 18 (1974), 77–125, places the war in a broader historical context; Helmuth von Moltke, *The Franco-German War of 1870-71*, trans. Clara Bell and Henry W. Fischer (New York: Harper & Brothers, 1901), gives a detailed history of the military operations of the war; Jules Favre, *The Government of the National Defence, from the 30th of June to the 31st of October 1870*, trans. H. Clark (New York: AMS Press, 1974), provides a balanced and informative account from a participant's perspective of the diplomacy and politics following the French collapse on the battlefield. For further sources, see William E. Echard, ed., *Foreign Policy of the French Second Empire: A Bibliography* (New York: Greenwood Press, 1988).

5 Lord writes, "With all due sympathy for the German unifying movement, it is not to be wondered at that the French people felt alarmed at a revolution so contrary to all the traditions of French policy, and at the menace to their security implied in the sudden appearance at their gates of an immensely aggrandized power, of vast military strength and with still unsatiated ambitions." Hence, in part, the impression in France that Austria's defeat had in fact been a French defeat, and the popular clamor for "revenge for Sadowa." Lord, *The Origins of the War of 1870*, 10. See also F. Darmstaedter, *Bismarck and the Creation of the Second Reich* (New York: Russell & Russell, 1965), 303–4, 309.

6 This is a recollection generally credited by historians. See Steefel, *Bismarck, the Hohenzollern Candidacy, and the Origins of the Franco-German War of 1870*, 9, 220; and Lord, *The Origins of the War of 1870*, 3, 6, 12. Cf. Ollivier, *The Franco-Prussian War and its Hidden Causes*, 5.

7 Cf. Lord, *The Origins of the War of 1870*, 4.

8 The Duchy had been included in the German confederation in 1815, and had joined the *Zollverein* in 1842; it had not joined the North German Confederation in 1866, but was garrisoned by Prussian forces.

9 Frustrated with his inability to deal with Prussia, Napoleon at one point turned directly to the King of Holland with an offer to purchase Luxembourg. The King was willing to sell, but only with Prussian approval. Bismarck refused to give his consent, and only a last-minute compromise neutralizing and demilitarizing Luxembourg averted a rupture with France. See Steefel, *Bismarck, the Hohenzollern Candidacy, and the Origins of the Franco-German War of 1870*, 4–6; Lord, *The Origins of the War of 1870*, 11; Darmstaedter, *Bismarck and the Creation of the Second Reich*, 306–7, 343–8.

10 Lynn M. Case, *French Opinion on War and Diplomacy during the Second Empire* (Philadelphia: University of Pennsylvania Press, 1954), 213–17.

11 Steefel, *Bismarck, the Hohenzollern Candidacy, and the Origins of the Franco-German War of 1870*, 3.

12 Theodore Zeldin, *Émile Ollivier and the Liberal Empire of Napoleon III* (Oxford: Clarendon Press, 1963), 171. Ollivier and Napoleon appear to have understood the principle of nationalities quite differently. For Ollivier, it was equivalent to the principle of self-determination of peoples. If the German people as a whole chose to form a single German polity, then the principle would sanction unification; but if the Germans as a nation chose to live in smaller, separate units, that, too, could be justified by the principle. Napoleon, on the other hand, appears to have understood it to require a one-to-one correspondence between nations and states. Cf. Ollivier, *The Franco-Prussian War and Its Hidden Causes*, 5–8.

13 *Ibid.*, 11.

14 Zeldin, *Émile Ollivier and the Liberal Empire of Napoleon III*, 169–70.

15 See Darmstaedter, *Bismarck and the Creation of the Second Reich*, 344.

16 *Ibid.*, 304.

17 See *ibid.*, 344.

18 A small minority of German historiographers has argued that Napoleon's territorial ambitions on the west bank of the Rhine were the ultimate causes of the war. This line of interpretation permits a convenient and rather suspicious assignment of blame. See, e.g., Hermann Oncken, *Napoleon III and the Rhine: The Origin of the War of 1870–1871*, trans. Edwin H. Zeydel (New York: Russell & Russell, 1967). Napoleon probably did want marginal adjustments to the frontier in France's favor, including restoration of the districts that had been taken by the second Peace of Paris in 1815 – and, if he could get them, Belgium and Luxembourg. See Steefel, *Bismarck, the Hohenzollern Candidacy, and the Origins of the Franco-German War of 1870*, 4. And there is no denying the fact that, in addition to providing a more defensible frontier, French control of territory on the west bank of the Rhine – especially the coal fields of the Saar – would have been tremendously valuable to France in a period of rapid industrialization. See Paul Bernstein, "The Economic Aspects of Napoleon III's Rhine Policy," *French Historical Studies*, 1, No. 3 (Spring 1960), 335–47. But while economic considerations may have reinforced Napoleon's interest, he always framed his claims in political terms and quickly retreated from his proposal for concessions in the Saar. Moreover, it is difficult to imagine why Napoleon would have waited until after 1866 to pursue an expansionist policy, when a favorable military balance suddenly shifted against him. It seems more likely that Prussia's gains provided both the need and the justification for France's demands.

19 On the Spanish Revolution of 1868, see Willard A. Smith, "The Background of the Spanish Revolution of 1868," *American Historical Review*, 55, No. 4 (July 1950), 787–810; Ollivier, *The Franco-Prussian War and its Hidden Causes*, Appendix B, 419–21; Pierre de la Gorce, *Histoire du Second Empire*, VI (Paris: Librairie Plon, 1912), 189–202.

20 Montpensier was also strongly opposed by Napoleon. See Willard A. Smith, "Napoleon III and the Spanish Revolution of 1868," *Journal of Modern History*, 25, No. 3 (September 1953), 221.

21 On the Hohenzollern candidacy, see Michel Dacier, "La Candidature Hohenzollern," *Écrits de Paris*, No. 295 (September 1970), 3–12; Sorel, *Histoire Diplomatique de la Guerre Franco-Allemande*, I, 60–87; and Steefel, *Bismarck, the Hohenzollern Candidacy, and the Origins of the Franco-German War of 1870*, 111–43.

22 Steefel, *Bismarck, the Hohenzollern Candidacy, and the Origins of the Franco-German War of 1870*, 14–15.

23 For the texts of Prim's diplomatic overtures and the early Prussian responses, see Bonnin, *Bismarck and the Hohenzollern Candidature for the Spanish Throne*, 59–68. At one point, when Leopold seemed dead set against accepting the candidacy for the crown, Prim considered his younger brother, Prince Frederick. The younger prince, like the elder, was inclined to refuse, but consented to accept if so commanded by the King. William's marginalia on Karl Anton's message of March 28, demonstrate his unwillingness to issue such a command. *Ibid.*, 101–2.

24 See Steefel, *Bismarck, the Hohenzollern Candidacy, and the Origins of the Franco-German War of 1870*, 62–4.

25 Bonnin, *Bismarck and the Hohenzollern Candidature for the Spanish Throne*, 68–73.

26 Bismarck to Karl Anton, May 28, 1870; Karl Anton to Bismarck, May 31, 1870. *Ibid.*, 158, 162–3.

27 William to Karl Anton, June 21, 1870; quoted in *ibid.*, 198–9 (emphasis in the original). Cf. also King William to Leopold, June 21, 1870, in which he consents, but "with a very heavy heart." *Ibid.*, 197–8.

28 *Ibid.*, 194.

29 Steefel, *Bismarck, the Hohenzollern Candidacy, and the Origins of the Franco-German War of 1870*, 99.

30 On the French reaction to the Hohenzollern candidacy, see la Gorce, *Histoire du Second Empire*, VI, 216–23.

31 Quoted in Lord, *The Origins of the War of 1870*, 42; see also Ollivier, *The Franco-Prussian War and its Hidden Causes*, 92–3; and Steefel, *Bismarck, the Hohenzollern Candidacy, and the Origins of the Franco-German War of 1870*, 114.

32 Lord, *The Origins of the War of 1870*, 48. Gramont instructed Count Benedetti on July 7 to secure a declaration from King William disavowing the candidacy and ordering Leopold to withdraw it. He ordered Benedetti to invoke precedents to justify the demand, and urged him to act speedily, since the preparation of military contingencies would have to begin within a matter of days. "If you secure from the King that he revokes the acceptance of the prince of Hohenzollern, it will be an immense success and a great service. The King, on his part, will have assured the peace of Europe. Otherwise, it is war." Quoted in Steefel, *Bismarck, the Hohenzollern Candidacy, and the Origins of the Franco-German War of 1870*, 126. For the texts of Gramont's communications, see *Les Origines Diplomatiques de la Guerre de 1870*, XXVIII (Paris: Imprimerie Nationale, 1931), 87–90 and 90–91. To the French Ambassador in St. Petersburg, Count Fleury, Gramont telegraphed instructions to inform the Russian Foreign Minister, Prince Gorchakov, that if Prussia insisted on the Hohenzollern candidacy, "it will be war." *Ibid.*, 64–5.

33 Lord, *The Origins of the War of 1870*, 35.

34 Ollivier believed the Hohenzollern candidacy was from first to last a Prussian ruse, in part because it was not the Prussian custom to admit a distinction between the King and the state. Accordingly, he found it difficult to take seriously an attempt to draw a distinction between the king as king and the king as head of the House of Hohenzollern. "It was our impression," Ollivier maintained, "that the King was playing with us." See Ollivier, *The Franco-Prussian War and its Hidden Causes*, 148, 151.

35 Karl Anton to Abeken, July 8, 1870; in Bonnin, *Bismarck and the Hohenzollern Candidature for the Spanish Throne*, 229–31.

36 In response to Karl Anton's withdrawal of his son's candidacy, King William wrote his wife, "A stone has been lifted from my heart!" William to Augusta, July 12, quoted in Lord, *The Origins of the War of 1870*, 67.

37 Quoted in Bonnin, *Bismarck and the Hohenzollern Candidature for the Spanish Throne*, 252.

38 *Ibid.*, 133.

39 Ollivier, *The Franco-Prussian War and its Hidden Causes*, 233.

40 See *Ibid.*, 218–19; Sorel, *Histoire Diplomatique de la Guerre Franco-Allemande*, I, 124–98; and Steefel, *Bismarck, the Hohenzollern Candidacy, and the Origins of the Franco-German War of 1870*, 144–64, esp. p. 149. For details of the Ems negotiations, see Le Comte Benedetti, *Ma Mission en Prusse* (Paris: Henri Plon, 1871); and Sorel, *Histoire Diplomatique de la Guerre Franco-Allemande*, I, 88–123.

41 Quoted in Steefel, *Bismarck, the Hohenzollern Candidacy, and the Origins of the Franco-German War of 1870*, 185. See also *ibid.*, 153. There was in fact no demand for an apology, and either Werther or Abeken misrepresented the proposal. Ollivier, *The Franco-Prussian War and its Hidden Causes*, 213.

42 For Abeken's original text, see Bismarck, *Bismarck, the Man and the Statesman*, 97n; for Bismarck's version, see *ibid.*, 100–1. For Bismarck's own account, see *ibid.*, chapt. 22, 87–103, esp. pp. 96–102. William Langer casts doubt on the accuracy of Bismarck's version. William L. Langer, "Bismarck as a Dramatist," in A.O. Sarkissian, ed., *Studies in Diplomatic History and Historiography in Honour of G.P.Gooch* (London: Longman's, 1961), 199–216. See also Lord, *The Origins of the War of 1870*, 100–6; and Steefel, *Bismarck, the Hohenzollern Candidacy, and the Origins of the Franco-German War of 1870*, 183–94.

43 Ollivier, *The Franco-Prussian War and its Hidden Causes*, 309.

44 *Ibid.*, 251; Steefel, *Bismarck, the Hohenzollern Candidacy, and the Origins of the Franco-German War of 1870*, 198–200.

45 On the climax of the crisis, see la Gorce, *Histoire du Second Empire*, VI, 256–314; Ollivier, *The Franco-Prussian War and its Hidden Causes*, 308–365; and Steefel, *Bismarck, the Hohenzollern Candidacy, and the Origins of the Franco-German War of 1870*, 208–19.

46 Quoted in *ibid.*, 210–13.

47 Cf. Smith, "Napoleon III and the Spanish Revolution of 1868," 211; Lord, *The Origins of the War of 1870*, 27; Ollivier, *The Franco-Prussian War and its Hidden Causes*, 70.

48 See Gramont, *La France et la Prusse Avant la Guerre*, 10; Ollivier, *The Franco-Prussian War and its Hidden Causes*, 298; and Steefel, *Bismarck, the Hohenzollern Candidacy, and the Origins of the Franco-German War of 1870*, 230 n. 23.

49 See, e.g., Case, *French Opinion on War and Diplomacy during the Second Empire*, 225–62; Aimé Dupuy, *1870–1871: La Guerre, la Commune, et la Presse* (Paris: Armand Colin, 1959); La Gorce, *Histoire du Second Empire*, VI, 229-32; Lehautcourt, *Les Origines de la Guerre de 1870*, 481; and Steefel, *Bismarck, the Hohenzollern Candidacy, and the Origins of the Franco-German War of 1870*, 135.

50 J. Stengers, "Aux Origines de la Guerre de 1870: Gouvernement et Opinion Publique," *Revue Belge de Philologie et d'Histoire*, 34, No. 3 (1956), 745. See also Case, *French Opinion on War and Diplomacy during the Second Empire*, 251–9; Fernand Giraudeau, *La Verité sur la Campagne de 1870: Examen Raisonné des Causes de la Guerre et de Nos Reverses* (Marseille: Typographie Marius Olive, 1871); and Ollivier, *The Franco-Prussian War and its Hidden Causes*, 216, who notes the extent to which his own decisions were influenced by public opinion. Cf. E. Malcolm Carroll, "French Public Opinion on War with Prussia in 1870," *American Historical Review*, 31, No. 4 (July 1926), 679–700. Carroll denies that public opinion was clearly in favor of war, argues that the government led it rather than followed it, and maintains that Paris was not inflamed by the Ems Telegram. Carroll's argument is not given much credence by historians today.

51 See, e.g., Ollivier, *The Franco-Prussian War and its Hidden Causes*, 80, 164, 197, 225.

52 *Ibid.*, 321.

53 Ollivier to Princess Wittgenstein, July 10, 1863; quoted in Zeldin, *Émile Ollivier and the Liberal Empire of Napoleon III*, 175.

54 See, e.g., the July 6 declaration, quoted on p. 83, above; and Lord Lyons's July 5 report of his conversation with Gramont, quoted in Steefel, *Bismarck, the Hohenzollern Candidacy, and the Origins of the Franco-German War of 1870*, 121.

55 Quoted in Darmstaedter, *Bismarck and the Creation of the Second Reich*, 344.

56 Lord, *The Origins of the War of 1870*, 28; Ollivier, *The Franco-Prussian War and its Hidden Causes*, 80.

57 Steefel, *Bismarck, the Hohenzollern Candidacy, and the Origins of the Franco-German War of 1870*, 152. Cf. Ollivier, *The Franco-Prussian War and its Hidden Causes*, 207. For the text of Karl Anton's message, see p. 84, above.

58 Quoted in *ibid.*, 97.

59 See Giovanni Sartori, "Concept Misformation in Comparative Politics," *American Political Science Review*, 64, No. 4 (December 1970), 1033–53. The result of conceptual stretching, Sartori writes, is that "our gains in extensional coverage tend to be matched by losses in connotative precision. It appears that we can cover more ... only by saying less, and by saying less in a far less precise manner." *Ibid.*, 1035.

60 Ollivier, *The Franco-Prussian War and its Hidden Causes*, 121–2, and Appendix F, pp. 445–50. See also Lord, *The Origins of the War of 1870*, 78.

61 Ollivier, *The Franco-Prussian War and its Hidden Causes*, 150.

62 See Pierre Saint Marc, *Émile Ollivier* (Paris: Plon, 1950), *passim.*; Ollivier, *The Franco-Prussian War and its Hidden Causes*, 76, 100; Zeldin, *Émile Ollivier and the Liberal Empire of Napoleon III*, 174.

63 Since 1866, France had attempted to conclude alliances with Austria and Italy directed against Prussia. These attempts had failed or were incom-

plete at the outbreak of war. See la Gorce, *Histoire du Second Empire*, VI, 148–57.

64 Steefel, *Bismarck, the Hohenzollern Candidacy, and the Origins of the Franco-German War of 1870*, 116. See also Bismarck, *Bismarck, the Man and the Statesman*, 93.

65 Among those who conclude that Bismarck actively engineered a French declaration of war are S. William Halperin, "The Origins of the Franco-Prussian War Revisited: Bismarck and the Hohenzollern Candidature for the Spanish Throne," *Journal of Modern History*, 45, No. 1 (March 1973), 83–91 (a negative review of Eberhard Kolb, *Der Kriegsausbruch 1870: Politische Entscheidungsprozesse und Verantworlichkeiten in der Julikrise 1870* (Göttingen: Vandenhoeck & Ruprecht, 1970), itself an apology for Bismarck); Lord, *The Origins of the War of 1870*, 5; and Frank Spencer, "Historical Revision No. 122: Bismarck and the Franco-Prussian War," *History*, 40, No. 140 (October 1955), 319–25.

66 Bismarck, *Bismarck, the Man and the Statesman*, 89.

67 Quoted in Steefel, *Bismarck, the Hohenzollern Candidacy, and the Origins of the Franco-German War of 1870*, 240.

68 Bismarck to Reuss, March 9, 1869, quoted in Chester W. Clark, "Bismarck, Russia, and the War of 1870," *Journal of Modern History*, 14, No. 2 (June 1942), 197.

69 Steefel, *Bismarck, the Hohenzollern Candidacy, and the Origins of the Franco-German War of 1870*, 21–2, 239; Bonnin, *Bismarck and the Hohenzollern Candidature for the Spanish Throne*, 27.

70 See Lord, *The Origins of the War of 1870*, 9.

71 *Ibid.*, 71, 95.

72 Bismarck, *Bismarck, the Man and the Statesman*, 98–100.

73 Lord, *The Origins of the War of 1870*, 39; and William to Augusta, July 7, 1870, quoted in Steefel, *Bismarck, the Hohenzollern Candidacy, and the Origins of the Franco-German War of 1870*, 120.

74 *Ibid.*, 109.

75 Ollivier, *The Franco-Prussian War and its Hidden Causes*, 378; see also p. 275.

76 "Bismarck deliberately embarked on a project which, whatever its primary aim may have been, did involve placing Napoleon in a position where he might either have to fight or to accept another grave defeat that might involve the downfall of his tottering dynasty. And France then tried to turn the tables by forcing Prussia to confront the alternative of war or a humiliating backdown ..." Lord, *The Origins of the War of 1870*, 9.

77 See, e.g. Henk Houweling and Jan G. Siccama, "Power Transitions as a Cause of War," *Journal of Conflict Resolution*, 32, No. 1 (March 1988), 87–102; Robert G. Gilpin, *War and Change in World Politics* (Cambridge: Cambridge University Press, 1981); Gilpin, "The Theory of Hegemonic War;" and Jack Levy, "Declining Power and the Preventive Motive for War," *World Politics* 40, No. 1 (October 1987), 82–107.

78 France and Prussia signed the Treaty of Frankfurt on May 10, 1871, and exchanged ratifications on May 21. For details of the peace negotiations, see Howard, *The Franco-Prussian War*, 432–56.

79 Quoted in Darmstaedter, *Bismarck and the Creation of the Second Reich*, 370. See also Sorel, *Histoire Diplomatique de la Guerre Franco-Allemande*, II, 10–11.

80 See Emanuel Gutmann, "Concealed or Conjured Irredentism: The Case of Alsace," in Naomi Chazan, ed., *Irredentism and International Politics* (Boulder, Colo.: Lynn Rienner, 1991), 37–50.

81 Bismarck was not particularly enthusiastic about annexing Metz, a purely French enclave. But Moltke insisted that possession of the fortress at Metz was militarily equivalent to fielding an army of 120,000, and Bismarck did not contend the point. Howard, *The Franco-Prussian War*, 447–8.

82 *The War Diary of the Emperor Frederick III, 1870–1871*, trans. and ed. A.R. Allinson (New York: Howard Fertig, 1988), 289.

83 Heinrich von Treitschke, *Germany, France, Russia, & Islam*, trans. George Haven Putnam (New York: G.P. Putnam's Sons, 1915), 98–9, 104–5, 129. Well might we ponder Putnam's suggestion: "With reference to Treitschke's claim, which was confirmed as the claim of Germany, that the appropriation of Alsace and Lorraine constituted a 'restitution' of German territory and of peoples that had been stolen from Germany, it may be in order to ask whether there does not apply, or whether there ought not to apply, to issues between nations as to those between individuals, some statute of limitations? A period of one hundred years, for instance, in which time three generations of men have come into activity, might properly be accepted, under a common-sense code of international relations, as sufficiently long to bar out grievances or appropriations that were back of the birth of the great-grandfathers of living men." Translator's foreword, *ibid.*, vi.

84 Henri Welschinger, *La Guerre de 1870: Causes et Responsabilités*, II, 2nd edn. (Paris: Plon-Nourrit, 1910), 313–16.

85 Quoted in Howard, *The Franco-Prussian War*, 446.

86 *Ibid.*, 449.

87 Ollivier, *The Franco-Prussian War and its Hidden Causes*, 8.

WORLD WAR I

1 Rt. Hon. Herbert Henry Asquith, *The Genesis of the War* (New York: George H. Doran, 1923), 16.

2 Bethmann Hollweg to Berchtold, in Imanuel Geiss, ed., *July 1914: The Outbreak of the First World War: Selected Documents* (New York: Charles Scribner's Sons, 1967), 44. For an excellent brief treatment of the background to the war see Joachim Remak, *The Origins of World War I, 1874–1914* (New York: Holt, Rinehart & Winston, 1967).

3 After the outbreak of war, when Prince von Bülow asked his successor how it all had happened, Bethmann Hollweg replied, "Oh – if only I knew!" Bernhard Heinrich Martin Karl fürst von Bülow, *Memoirs of Prince von Bülow*, III (Boston: Little, Brown, 1932), 166. In view of his accurate prediction, Bethmann Hollweg's remark is better interpreted as a confession of impotence than of ignorance.

4 On mobilization pressures, see esp. Jack S. Levy, "Organizational Routines and the Causes of War," *International Studies Quarterly*, 30, No. 2 (June 1986),

193–222; and L.C.F. Turner, *Origins of the First World War* (New York: Norton, 1970). See also Steven Van Evera, "The Cult of the Offensive and the Origins of the First World War," in Steven E. Miller, ed., *Military Strategy and the Origins of the First World War* (Princeton, N.J.: Princeton University Press, 1985), 58–107; and Jehuda L. Wallach, *The Dogma of the Battle of Annihilation: The Theories of Clausewitz and Schlieffen and their Impact on the German Conduct of Two World Wars* (Westport, Conn.: Greenwood Press, 1986), 54–60 (for a description and critique of the Schlieffen plan). For a persuasive argument that, contrary to popular belief, mobilization in 1914 was *not* tantamount to war and did not make war inevitable, see Marc Trachtenberg, "The Meaning of Mobilization in 1914," *International Security*, 15, No. 3 (Winter 1990/91), 120–50.

5 Sean Lynn-Jones, for example, argues that the Anglo-German détente immediately prior to the war led the German government to believe that it could count on British neutrality in the event of a continental conflict. See Sean M. Lynn-Jones, "Détente and Deterrence: Anglo-German Relations, 1911–1914," *International Security*, 11, No. 2 (Fall 1986), 121–50, and citations therein; see also R.J. Crampton, *The Hollow Detente: Anglo-German Relations in the Balkans, 1911–1914* (London: George Prior, n.d.). On German cognitive impairment and miscalculation in the July crisis, see Lebow, *Between Peace and War*, 119–47.

6 The Kaiser's biographer, Michael Balfour, writes that William was undoubtedly intelligent, but nervous, impetuous, and weak. "The simple truth about the Kaiser is that, for all his undoubted gifts, he was not up to the outsize job which destiny had assigned to him." Michael Balfour, *The Kaiser and His Times* (Boston: Houghton Mifflin, 1964), 434. See also Luigi Albertini, *The Origins of the War of 1914*, I, trans. and ed. Isabella M. Massey (London: Oxford University Press, 1952), 73n, 159–60; G.P. Gooch, *Recent Revelations of European Diplomacy* (London: Longmans, Green, 1927), 2; and G.P. Gooch, *Before the War: Studies in Diplomacy*, II (London: Longmans, Green, 1936), 233–34. Erich Brandenburg, who sought to blame French and Russian policy for the outbreak of the war, frankly condemned German statesmen for unskilled diplomacy and the failure to seize timely diplomatic opportunities. *From Bismarck to the World War: A History of German Foreign Policy, 1870–1914*, trans. Annie Elizabeth Adams (London: Oxford University Press, 1927).

7 In November 1913, for example, the Belgian King visited Potsdam and was alarmed to discover that the Kaiser had come to believe that a European war was inevitable. Gooch, *Before the War*, II, 263.

8 Useful brief historiographical essays may be found in James Joll, *The Origins of the First World War* (London: Longman, 1984), 1–8; and Geiss's introduction to *July 1914*, 9–16. For more detailed treatments, see H.W. Koch, ed., *The Origins of the First World War: Great Power Rivalry and German War Aims*, 2nd edn. (Basingstoke, Hampshire: Macmillan, 1984); and Dwight E. Lee, ed., *The Outbreak of the First World War: Who Was Responsible?* (Boston: D.C. Heath, 1958). The classic apologia for Germany and Austria is Count Max Montgelas, *The Case for the Central Powers: An Impeachment of the Versailles Verdict*, trans. Constance Vesey (New York: Knopf, 1925), heavily sup-

ported by Harry Elmer Barnes, *In Quest of Truth and Justice: De-Bunking the War Guilt Myth* (Chicago: National Historical Society, 1928). The most widely read indictments of German policy are Fritz Fischer's *Griff nach der Weltmacht* and *Krieg der Illusionen*, published in English as *Germany's Aims in the First World War* (New York: Norton, 1967) and *War of Illusions: German Policies from 1911 to 1914*, trans. Marian Jackson (London: Chatto & Windus, 1975). For discussion, see John A. Moses, *The Politics of Illusion: The Fischer Controversy in German Historiography* (London: George Prior, 1975); and Fischer's response to his critics, *World Power or Decline: The Controversy Over Germany's Aims in the First World War*, trans. Lancelot L. Farrar, Robert Kimber, and Rita Kimber (New York: Norton, 1974).

9 Sidney Bradshaw Fay, *The Origins of the World War*, 2nd edn., I (New York: Free Press, 1966), 34. By "militarism," Fay means both the existence of large standing armed forces and the fear they engender, and certain attitudes of the military classes "who tend to dominate, especially at a time of political crisis, over the civilian authorities." *Ibid.*, 39. Fay writes that "Nationalism... must be accounted one of the major underlying causes of the War. In its chronic form of Pan-Germanism, Pan-Slavism and *revanche*, it nourished hatred between Germany and her two neighbors on the East and West. It worked in curious and devious ways. It had contributed happily to the unification of Germany and Italy. On the other hand, it had disrupted the Ottoman Empire and threatened to disrupt the Hapsburg Monarchy." *Ibid.*, 44.

10 Quoted in Geiss, *July 1914*, 21.

11 For a fuller discussion of the pre-war power relationships, see Paul M. Kennedy, "The First World War and the International Power System," in Miller, *Military Strategy and the Origins of the First World War*, 7–40.

12 Quoted in Geiss, *July 1914*, 21.

13 Quoted in Jonathan Steinberg, "The Copenhagen Complex," in Walter Laqueur and George L. Mosse, eds., *1914: The Coming of the First World War* (New York: Harper & Row, 1966), 25.

14 Geiss, *July 1914*, 33–4; and Wolfgang J. Mommsen, "The Debate on German War Aims," in Laqueur and Mosse, *1914: The Coming of the First World War*, 77.

15 In May 1913, on a dispatch from Count Pourtalès, German Ambassador to St. Petersburg, the Kaiser wrote, "The struggle between Slavs and Germans is inevitable. When? We shall see." Quoted in Gooch, *Before the War*, II, 340. His obsession with Houston Chamberlain's *The Foundations of the Nineteenth Century*, a work of purest Social Darwinism, was widely known. Asquith, *The Genesis of the War*, 80–1, 87–8. But William appears not to have understood it. Chamberlain attributed the development of modern civilization to the genius of the "Teutons," by which he meant, *inter alia*, the Slavs. Houston Stewart Chamberlain, *Foundations of the Nineteenth Century*, 2 vols., trans. John Lees (New York: John Lane, 1913).

16 In February 1913, Moltke wrote his Austrian counterpart, Conrad von Hötzendorf, "that a European war is bound to come sooner or later, in which the issue will be one of a struggle between Germandom and Slavdom," and that "[t]o prepare themselves for that contingency is the

duty of all states which are the champions of Germanic ideas and culture."
Quoted in Geiss, *July 1914*, 43.

17 For evidence of the relationship between the Kaiser's racial views and his
support for Austria's Serbian policy, see Berchtold's memorandum of conversation, October 28, 1913, and the report of the Austro-Hungarian Chargé
d'Affaires in Munich to Berchtold, December 16, 1913, reprinted in R.W.
Seton-Watson, "William II's Balkan Policy," *The Slavonic and East European
Review*, 7, No. 19 (June 1928), 24–7 and 28–9.

18 On Pan-Germanism generally, see R.W. Seton-Watson, *German, Slav, and
Magyar: A Study in the Origins of the Great War* (London: Williams and
Norgate, 1916), 121–87; on the Pan-German League in particular, see
Mildred S. Wertheimer, *The Pan-German League, 1890–1914*, Columbia Uni-
versity Studies in History, Economics and Public Law, 112, No. 2 (New
York: Longmans, Green, 1924), esp. 94–5.

19 *Ibid.*, 200–1. Harry Elmer Barnes writes, "Even in official circles the Pan-
German League was laughed at as a noisy nuisance." *The Genesis of the
World War: An Introduction to the Problem of War Guilt* (New York: Knopf,
1929), 52.

20 On the tension between supporters of national self-sufficiency and German
imperialists, see Mommsen, "The Debate on German War Aims," 46–7.

21 For background on *Weltpolitik*, see David P. Calleo, *The German Problem
Reconsidered: Germany and the World Order, 1870 to the Present* (Cambridge:
Cambridge University Press, 1978), 18–22; cf. Fischer, *Germany's Aims in the
First World War*, 3–49.

22 Bülow, *Memoirs*, I, 480–2; and *Imperial Germany*, trans. Marie A. Lewenz
(New York: Dodd, Mead, 1917), 1–15.

23 David E. Kaiser, "Germany and the Origins of the First World War," *Journal
of Modern History*, 55, No. 3 (September 1983), 451.

24 On the Anglo-German naval rivalry, see Zara S. Steiner, *Britain and the
Origins of the First World War* (New York: St. Martin's, 1977), 48–59.

25 Grand Admiral Alfred von Tirpitz, *My Memoirs*, I (New York: Dodd, Mead,
1919), 77–88.

26 Bülow, *Memoirs*, I, 482; III, 379.

27 On the "risk fleet" theory and its underlying political and strategic miscalculations, see Paul M. Kennedy, *The Rise of the Anglo-German Antagonism
1860–1914* (London: Allen & Unwin, 1980), 417–18.

28 Kaiser, "Germany and the Origins of the First World War," 450–7.

29 Paul Kennedy traces the underlying source of antagonism between Britain
and Germany to economic factors. Kennedy, *The Rise of the Anglo-German
Antagonism*. But, as James Joll puts it, "It is hard to find evidence that this
particular war at this particular moment was directly the consequence of
economic pressures or immediate economic needs." Joll, *The Origins of the
First World War*, 144. Indeed, the business community was among the least
enthusiastic supporters of war in 1914. "Generally speaking," writes Sidney
Fay, "economic imperialism is usually exaggerated as one of the underlying
causes of the war." Fay, *The Origins of the World War*, I, 46.

30 Steiner, *Britain and the Origins of the First World War*, 44–5.

31 Grey to Bertie, November 12, 1908, *British Documents on the Origins of the*

War, VI, ed. G.P. Gooch and Harold Temperley (London: His Majesty's Stationery Office, 1930), 216–17.

32 Asquith, *The Genesis of the War*, 74–5.

33 Geiss, *July 1914*, 31–2.

34 Grey to Bertie, July 20, 1911, quoted in Gooch, *Before the War*, II, 74.

35 *Ibid.*, II, 117. Britain also accommodated Germany on the Baghdad railway question. Viscount Edward Grey of Fallodon, *Twenty-Five Years, 1892–1916*, I (New York: Frederick A. Stokes, 1925), 292–3.

36 Camille Bloch, *The Causes of the World War: An Historical Summary* (London: George Allen & Unwin, 1935), 29. Jonathan Steinberg writes that Germany's *weltpolitische angst* defies the "normal techniques of historical analysis," because of Germany's obvious strength. Steinberg, "The Copenhagen Complex," 39.

37 David Lloyd George, *War Memoirs of David Lloyd George*, I (Boston: Little, Brown, 1933), 28.

38 Geiss, *July 1914*, 36–7. Geiss doubts that the German leadership was as afraid of encirclement as many have come to believe; but see note 139, below.

39 Quoted in Gooch, *Before the War*, II, 264.

40 See Albertini, *The Origins of the War of 1914*, I, 550.

41 On German discussion of a preventive war, see Geiss, *July 1914*, 38–48. Bethmann Hollweg saw in the July crisis an opportunity to improve Germany's international position, by peace if possible (driving a wedge between the Triple Entente powers), and by war if necessary. He expressed his fears of encirclement to Riezler on July 7, 1914, evidently concerned in particular by Russia's program of railway construction. Kaiser, "Germany and the Origins of the First World War," 467.

42 Theobald von Bethmann Hollweg, *Reflections on the World War*, trans. George Young (London: Thornton Butterworth, 1920), 163.

43 Calleo, *The German Problem Reconsidered*, 28. This is not to suggest that German leaders had no real interest in colonialism. Quite the contrary. Bethmann Hollweg tipped his hand to the British Ambassador to Berlin, Sir Edward Goschen, when, on July 29, 1914, in making a bid for British neutrality in the event of a Franco-German war, he refused to disavow territorial designs on France's overseas colonies. Kaiser, "Germany and the Origins of the First World War," 467–8. Bethmann Hollweg did not hide his interest in acquiring territory in Central Africa and Asia Minor. He told the French Ambassador Jules Cambon in early 1914 that Germany "needs a place in the sun" and "is in a sense condemned to spread outwards." *Ibid.*, 463. Fritz Fischer interprets Bethmann Hollweg's September Programme, which envisaged the creation of a greater "Mitteleuropa" under German control, as evidence of an intention to dominate the continent of Europe. Fischer, *Germany's Aims in the First World War*, 104–5. But as L.C.F. Turner notes, one cannot use war aims formulated *after* the outbreak of hostilities as reliable guides to leaders' intentions *prior* to the war. Turner, *Origins of the First World War*, 113.

44 See, e.g., Fay, *The Origins of the World War*, I, 53; and Barnes, *The Genesis of the World War*, 78: "Of all the underlying political and diplomatic causes of the World War the French hope of avenging 1870 must be held to be,

beyond all comparison, the most important." Coleman Phillipson writes that the main cause of the powder keg on which Europe sat in 1914 was the "irreconcilable character of the relationships between France and Germany," caused by the issue of Alsace-Lorraine. Coleman Phillipson, *Alsace-Lorraine: Past, Present, and Future* (New York: Dutton, 1918), 28.

45 See generally Barry Cerf, *Alsace-Lorraine since 1870* (New York: Macmillan, 1919); and Charles Downer Hazen, *Alsace-Lorraine under German Rule* (New York: Henry Holt, 1917).

46 Fay, *The Origins of the World War*, I, 51; see also Albertini, *The Origins of the War of 1914*, I, 104n; Charles Seymour, *The Diplomatic Background of the War, 1870–1914* (New Haven: Yale University Press, 1916), 14–15. Victor Hugo wrote: "France will have but one thought: to reconstitute her forces, gather her energy, nourish her sacred anger, raise her young generation to form an army of the whole people, to work without cease, to study the methods and skills of our enemies, to become again a great France, the France of 1792, the France of an idea with a sword. Then one day she will be irresistible. Then she will take back Alsace-Lorraine." Quoted in Barbara W. Tuchman, *The Guns of August* (New York: Macmillan, 1962), 30.

47 Raymond Poincaré, *Les Origines de la Guerre* (Paris: Librairie Plon, 1921), 21. Poincaré himself once remarked after the war, "I saw no reason for my generation to go on living than the hope of recovering our lost provinces." Bernadotte Everly Schmitt, *The Coming of the War, 1914* (New York: Charles Scribner's Sons, 1930), I, 64.

48 George F. Kennan, *The Fateful Alliance: France, Russia, and the Coming of the First World War* (Manchester: Manchester University Press, 1984), 117. Bismarck even tried to buy the friendship of France by offering her a free hand in Tunisia, prompting Leon Gambetta to remark, "France must not indulge in conquests or adventures before having reclaimed and restored to the Republic the lost provinces of Alsace and Lorraine." Quoted in Albertini, *The Origins of the War of 1914*, I, 29.

49 Baron Courcel to Jules Ferry, December 3, 1884; quoted in Fay, *The Origins of the World War*, I, 99–100. The French Historian Ernest Lavisse wrote that "Between Germany and France a direct conversation is impossible. Each has its reasons which the other is not willing to understand. France does not admit the sinister Bismarckian doctrine – Alsace, *'glacis'* of the Empire sacrificed to the necessity of maintaining German cohesion by the fear of the French pretensions; it does not admit the argument of ethnography, nor that force is sufficient to create rights over the spirits. And the Germans will never, never, never understand that we are attached to Alsace-Lorraine by an obligation of honor; the injuries and blows which it receives, we receive; we suffer in it as one suffers in an amputated member." Quoted in Schmitt, *The Coming of the War, 1914*, I, 67.

50 Seymour, *The Diplomatic Background of the War*, 22–3.

51 Gordon Martel, *The Origins of the First World War* (London: Longman, 1987), 32. General Boulanger was a fiery champion of the recovery of the lost provinces, too popular – and thus too dangerous – to be left out of the many French cabinets of the late 1880s. He was appointed Minister of War in 1886, and enflamed German fears with his fondness for such pronounce-

ments as, "We remember that they are waiting for us in Alsace and Lorraine." Fay, *The Origins of the World War*, I, 100–1.

52 Schmitt, *The Coming of the War, 1914*, I, 67–8n.

53 Quoted in *ibid.*, 68.

54 Bloch, *The Causes of the World War*, 31.

55 Quoted in Gooch, *Before the War*, II, 152. Cf. also Albertini, *The Origins of the War of 1914*, I, 132; Kennan, *The Fateful Alliance*, 117–19; and Schmitt, *The Coming of the War, 1914*, I, 66.

56 Quoted in Gooch, *Before the War*, II, 264.

57 John F.V. Keiger, *France and the Origins of the First World War* (London: Macmillan, 1983), 5.

58 Joll, *The Origins of the First World War*, 98–9.

59 H. Maringer, *Force au Droit: Le Problème d'Alsace-Lorraine* (Paris: Berger-Levrault, 1913).

60 Kennan, *The Fateful Alliance*, 135, 249; Gordon Brook-Shepherd, *Royal Sunset: The European Dynasties and the Great War* (Garden City, N.Y: Doubleday, 1987), 189.

61 Kennan, *The Fateful Alliance*, 95.

62 Andrew continues: "Faure repeated this warning during the visits to France by the Tsar in 1896 and by Muraviev a year later. Delcassé, however, hoped that France might win back the lost provinces without a war. He told the Russian ambassador soon after he became foreign minister in 1898 that France would never endanger the peace of Europe to recover Alsace-Lorraine – 'but may not circumstances come about which will spontaneously make a just solution possible?'" Christopher Andrew, "The Reshaping of the Dual Alliance," in Laqueur and Mosse, *1914: The Coming of the First World War*, 141.

It is common for historians of the First World War to blame German statesmen for permitting France and Russia to conclude a military alliance – something, we are told, Bismarck would never have done. It is conceivable that if Count Leo von Caprivi had not permitted the lapse of the Reinsurance Treaty, Russia would never have felt the need to seek an ally in France. But one should not forget that France, too, was in search of an ally, and might well have succeeded in wooing Russia in any case.

63 See Gerhard Ritter, *The Schlieffen Plan: Critique of a Myth* (London: Oswald Wolff, 1958), 17–21, 23, 39, 134–48; and Tuchman, *The Guns of August*, 21. Ironically, in 1911, the younger Moltke expected France to remain on the defensive behind her elaborate fortifications facing Lorraine in the event of war, and yet he insisted on weakening the right wing to reinforce the left. Ritter, *The Schlieffen Plan*, 165. Events would prove both Schlieffen and Moltke incorrect. The French operational plan *did* call for an offensive thrust into Lorraine, but strictly for military reasons. The prevailing attitude in the French military establishment was that the lost provinces could only be recovered after a decisive defeat of the whole of the German army, not a single successful drive to the west bank of the Rhine. See Jack Snyder, *The Ideology of the Offensive: Military Decision-making and the Disasters of 1914* (Ithaca, N.Y.: Cornell University Press, 1984), 19, 41–2.

64 See Wallach, *The Dogma of the Battle of Annihilation*, 38.

65 Karl Kautsky, *The Guilt of William Hohenzollern* (London: Skeffington & Son, n.d.), 233.

66 Cf. Laurence Lafore, *The Long Fuse: An Interpretation of the Origins of World War I* (Philadelphia: Lippincott, 1965), 17; and Seton-Watson, *German, Slav, and Magyar*, 47.

67 See generally Albertini, *The Origins of the War of 1914*, I, 2–7; Bloch, *The Causes of the World War*, 8–19; Seton-Watson, *German, Slav, and Magyar*, 82–120; and R.W. Seton-Watson, *The Southern Slav Question and the Hapsburg Monarchy* (New York: Howard Fertig, 1969).

68 Albertini, *The Origins of the War of 1914*, I, 7–12; Seton-Watson, *German, Slav, and Magyar*, 48–81.

69 A commercial treaty signed on May 6, 1881, for example, gave Austria the lion's share of Serbia's import and export trade, and thus a virtual economic stranglehold on her smaller neighbor. Albertini, *The Origins of the War of 1914*, I, 31n.

70 *Ibid.*, 139.

71 *Ibid.*, 142.

72 Gooch, *Before the War*, I, 393.

73 Using an idiom commonplace in references to Alsace-Lorraine, the German Minister in Belgrade wrote in July 1914 that the annexation of Bosnia-Herzegovina had "inflicted on the Serbian soul a wound which has never healed." Quoted in Bloch, *The Causes of the World War*, 20.

74 Albertini, *The Origins of the War of 1914*, I, 222; see also p. 15, and for detailed discussion, 190–300.

75 M. Bogitshevich, *Causes of the War: An Examination into the Causes of the European War with Special Reference to Russia and Serbia* (Amsterdam: C.L. Van Langenhuysen, 1919), 25–6.

76 Gooch, *Before the War*, I, 404.

77 Albertini, *The Origins of the War of 1914*, I, 222.

78 See *ibid.*, 297–8.

79 Quoted in Gooch, *Before the War*, I, 414–15.

80 See Schmitt, *The Coming of the War, 1914*, I, 185–209, 298, esp. 190, 198, 204.

81 Gooch, *Before the War*, I, 420.

82 On September 27, 1912, Berchtold told the German Chargé d'Affaires that Austria would not tolerate Serbian expansion into the Sanjak, precisely for this reason. Albertini, *The Origins of the War of 1914*, I, 385; Gooch, *Before the War*, II, 385. Cf. 405. Serbia and Montenegro actively explored the possibility of union in the winter of 1913–1914. *Ibid.*, I, 511; see generally 509–18.

83 Gooch, *Before the War*, I, 417. In August 1912, Berchtold drafted a memorandum on Balkan policy for his ambassadors in Berlin and Rome in which he argued that a war between Austria and Serbia was inevitable. Albertini, *The Origins of the War of 1914*, I, 463.

84 Albertini, *The Origins of the War of 1914*, I, 391; Fay, *The Origins of the World War*, I, 445. For an excellent brief summary of the Balkan wars, see *ibid.*, 438–47.

85 Gooch, *Before the War*, II, 394.

86 Berchtold, of course, was concerned about the prospect of a Serbian naval presence on the Adriatic. *Ibid.*, 390.

87 Quoted in *ibid.*, 333.

88 See Albertini, *The Origins of the War of 1914*, I, 486–7. The Serbian representative delivered news of the Austrian declaration of war to Sazonov on July 28, 1914 thus: "I have the honour to inform Your Excellency of this regrettable act, which the Great Power had the courage to commit against a small Slav country which only emerged from a long series of heroic but exhausting battles, and I beg leave on this occasion of deep gravity for my country, to express the hope that this act, which disturbs the peace of Europe and revolts her conscience, will be condemned by the whole civilized world and severely punished by Russia, the protector of Serbia." *Collected Diplomatic Documents Relating to the Outbreak of the European War* (London: His Majesty's Stationery Office, 1915), 392.

German policy during the Balkan wars had been moderate and farsighted. Bethmann Hollweg cooperated with British Foreign Secretary Sir Edward Grey in making possible a cooperative international solution that effectively contained the Austro-Serbian conflict. But his sympathies were unambiguous, and his fears quite revealing: although he insisted that Austria had vital interests in the region, "unlike the purely sentimental interest which was all that Russia could claim," he expressed his fears in a letter to Berchtold that a weak-willed Tsar would be stampeded into intervention by Pan-Slav sentiment if Austria should attack Serbia. Gooch, *Before the War*, II, 251, 253. Bethmann Hollweg therefore discounted the sincerity and force of Russia's moral commitment to Serbia. But his concern about the Tsar's susceptibility to public pressure raises serious questions about the grounds upon which, in a situation considerably more threatening to Serbia two years later, he calculated Russia would not intervene.

89 Quoted in Gooch, *Before the War*, II, 418. Even while Pašić was in Vienna in October 1913 offering an olive branch and attempting to reach an understanding, Berchtold concluded, "That the Serbs at a later moment have the intention of disputing our possession of our southern provinces, is of course beyond all doubt." Quoted in Albertini, *The Origins of the War of 1914*, I, 477. Cf. also Berchtold's conversation with the German Ambassador, von Tschirschky, on March 13, 1913, as related by Gooch: "In exchanging St. Petersburg for the Ballplatz he had brought with him no general political programme. But his first aim had been to reach good relations with Servia, since as Ambassador in Russia he had tasted the evil consequences and the chronic unpleasantness in Austro-Russian relations arising from the friction between Vienna and Belgrad. To his great regret a year's work as Foreign Minister had shown that all attempts were in vain, and that neither the Servian dynasty nor people desired to make an honorable peace. The Serbs, like most other Slavs, dreamed of a Great Servian realm. Their decisions were directed towards its realisation, and never – at any rate as the result of peaceful argument – would they renounce the idea of adding to it Austria's Southern Slav provinces." Gooch, *Before the War*, II, 406; see also 414–15.

90 Quoted in Joll, *The Origins of the First World War*, 74.

91 Quoted in Fay, *The Origins of the World War*, I, 445–6.

92 Bloch, *The Causes of the World War*, 23.

93 Gooch, *Before the War*, II, 210–11.
94 Quoted in D.C.B. Lieven, *Russia and the Origins of the First World War* (New York: St. Martin's, 1983), 125.
95 Quoted in Gooch, *Before the War*, II, 248. On December 2, 1912, Bethmann Hollweg gave a speech in which he said that the conflicting claims of the parties affected by the Balkan dispute would be settled, if possible, by peaceful means. If, however, irreconcilable differences emerged and it proved necessary for the Powers to assert their will, Germany would stand by Austria. "If ... in this process of securing their interests they, contrary to all expectation, are attacked from a third side and thereby threatened in their existence, we, true to our duty as an ally, would have to stand resolutely at their side. And then we should fight for the preservation of our own position in Europe, for the defence of our own future and safety. I am firmly convinced that for such a policy we should have the whole people behind us." Quoted in *ibid.*, 249. Cf. also his report to the Kaiser, April 8, 1913: "In accordance with His Majesty's directions we have stood loyally at the side of our Austrian ally throughout the crisis. Austria's interest forbids a Slav advance to the Adriatic ... It is owing chiefly to our support that this has been prevented, and Servia's Adriatic efforts limited to the use of a commercial harbour ... The Albanian buffer state is Austria's only gain from the shipwreck of her Balkan aspirations. If even this modest advantage slips from her grasp at the eleventh hour, her policy would suffer a bankruptcy which would shatter her international status and gravely imperil her national cohesion. To avert the weakening of Germany through the humiliation of Austria is our chief task at this moment. The prospect of performing it peacefully increases with the resolution and strength of our association with our ally." *Ibid.*, 253–4.
96 Quoted in Schmitt, *The Coming of the War, 1914*, II, 20.
97 Quoted in Pierre Renouvin, *The Immediate Origins of the War (28th June – 4th August 1914)*, trans. Theodore Carswell Hume (New Haven: Yale University Press, 1928), 18.
98 *Ibid.*, 19.
99 On this question, which is a matter of considerable controversy, see Albertini, *The Origins of the War of 1914*, II, 120–80; and Schmitt, *The Coming of the War, 1914*, I, 230–6.
100 See Gooch, *Recent Revelations of European Diplomacy*, 73. Conrad understood Sarajevo to be Serbia's declaration of war, and maintained that it could only be answered by a declaration of war in return. Gooch, *Before the War*, II, 434. The Emperor Francis Joseph wrote the following to Kaiser William: "The attack on my poor nephew is the direct result of the agitation of Russian and Servian Panslavs, the sole aim of which is the weakening of the Triple Alliance and the dissolution of my Empire. The bloody deed was not the work of a single individual, but a well organised plot whose threads extend to Belgrad. Though it may be impossible to establish the complicity of the Servian Government, no one can doubt that its policy of uniting all Southern Slavs under the Servian flag encourages such crimes, and that the continuation of this situation is a chronic peril for my House and my territories ... The aim of my Government in future

must be the isolation and diminution of Servia." Quoted in *ibid.*, 434–5. Ironically, the government at first made an attempt to incite popular indignation against Serbia, but soon found itself having to put a check upon it. John Ewart Wallace Sterling, "Diplomacy and the Newspaper Press in Austria-Hungary, Midsummer 1914," Diss. Stanford 1937.

101 See, e.g., Geiss, *July 1914*, 83; and Norman Stone, "Hungary and the Crisis of July 1914," in Laqueur and Mosse, *1914: The Coming of the First World War*, 147. For background, see Albertini, *The Origins of the War of 1914*, II, 120–80; and Alfred Francis Pribram, *Austrian Foreign Policy, 1908–1918* (London: George Allen & Unwin, 1923).

102 See Geiss, *July 1914*, 80–7. The Emperor agreed with Berchtold that a peaceful solution would be worthless unless Belgrade could guarantee to suppress the Pan-Serb movement – something of which he was evidently skeptical. Macchio to Tisza, July 9, *ibid.*, 103–4. The Council met again on July 19 to discuss details of the forthcoming *démarche*. For minutes of the meeting and the text of the ultimatum to Serbia, see *ibid.*, 139–46.

Austria chose July 23 as the date on which to deliver the ultimatum. The delay was calculated to minimize the danger of an adverse Russian reaction: the French President and Prime Minister, Raymond Poincaré and René Viviani, were paying a state visit to the Tsar, and were scheduled to sail from St. Petersburg that very day. It would be imprudent to make it easy for France and Russia to coordinate their responses. "[W]e should consider it unwise to undertake the threatening step in Belgrade at the very time when the peaceloving, reserved Czar Nicolas and undeniably cautious Herr Sazonov, are under the influence of the two, who are always for war, [Russian Ambassador to Paris Alexander Petrovich] Isvolsky and Poincaré." Berchtold to Count Szögyény, Austro-Hungarian Ambassador in Berlin, July 15, in Geiss, *July 1914*, 116–17.

103 On July 14 the Serbian Minister at Vienna reported on an article in the *Neue Freie Presse* that proclaimed, "We have to settle matters with Serbia by war; it is evident that peaceable means are of no avail. And if it must come to war sooner or later, then it is better to see the matter through now." Jovanović to Pašić, July 14, *Collected Diplomatic Documents Relating to the Outbreak of the European War*, 380. See also Bloch, *The Causes of the World War*, 49–51. One of the reasons why the time was considered favorable was that in July 1914, Serbia was in serious domestic difficulty. The Balkan wars had exhausted the nation; civil-military relations were approaching a nadir; Pašić and the Black Hand were at loggerheads; and the government was fighting for its life in a bitter election campaign. See Albertini, *The Origins of the War of 1914*, II, 350–3; Geiss, *July 1914*, 51; and Joll, *The Origins of the First World War*, 72–5.

104 Quoted in Gooch, *Before the War*, II, 441.

105 *Collected Diplomatic Documents Relating to the Outbreak of the European War*, 387.

106 Pašić, Secretary General of the Foreign Office Slavko Gruić, and Minister of Public Instruction Ljuba Jovanović all testified that they understood the ultimatum to mean that Austria-Hungary was bent on war. Albertini, *The Origins of the War of 1914*, II, 346–7; and Bloch, *The Causes of the World War*, 81.

107 Renouvin, *The Immediate Origins of the War*, 96.

108 Even the Kaiser was impressed: "After reading over the Serbian reply, which I received this morning, I am convinced that on the whole the wishes of the Danube Monarchy have been acceded to. The few reservations that Serbia makes in regard to individual points could, according to my opinion, be settled by negotiation. But it contains the announcement *orbi et urbi* of a capitulation of the most humiliating kind, and as a result, *every cause for war* falls to the ground." But this favorable reaction was not enough to make the Kaiser counsel Austria to back down. "Nevertheless," he continued, "the piece of paper, like its contents, can be considered as of little value so long as it is not translated into *deeds*. The Serbs are Orientals, therefore liars, tricksters, and masters of evasion. In order that these beautiful promises may be turned to truth and facts, a *douce violence* must be exercised. This should be so arranged that Austria would receive a *hostage* (Belgrade), as a guaranty for the enforcement and carrying out of the promises, and should occupy it until the *petita* had *actually* been complied with. This is also necessary in order to give the army, now *unnecessarily* mobilized for the third time, the external *satisfaction d'honneur* of an ostensible success in the eyes of the world, and to make it possible for it to feel that it had at least stood on foreign soil. Unless this were done, the abandonment of the campaign might be the cause of a wave of bad feeling against the Monarchy, which would be dangerous in the highest degree." William to Jagow, July 28, in Geiss, *July 1914*, 256.

For the text of the Serbian reply to the Austrian ultimatum, see *ibid.*, 201–4. Albertini argues that Pašić would have accepted the Austrian ultimatum *in toto* with merely a small reservation on point 6 (since he was frightened of disclosures that the Serbian government knew about or was actively involved in the plot to assassinate Francis Ferdinand), but that assurances of Russian support led him to take a bolder course and reject point 6 outright. Albertini, *The Origins of the War of 1914*, II, 353–61. But cf. R.W. Seton-Watson, *Sarajevo: A Study in the Origins of the Great War* (London: Hutchinson, 1926), 257.

109 Pašić's overtures to Russia predate the delivery of Austria's ultimatum, demonstrating that he expected an ominous turn of events. See, e.g., Gooch, *Before the War*, II, 363. Prince Alexander of Serbia's message to Tsar Nicholas II of July 29 is instructive because it plays on the Tsar's obligations not only as protector of the Serbs, but also as champion of the Slavs and Orthodox. *Collected Diplomatic Documents Relating to the Outbreak of the European War*, 286.

110 See *How the War Began in 1914: Being the Diary of the Russian Foreign Office from the 3rd to the 20th (Old Style) of July, 1914*, trans. Maj. W. Cyprian Bridge (London: George Allen & Unwin, 1925). See also, e.g., Gooch, *Before the War*, II, 366.

111 See, e.g., Renouvin, *The Immediate Origins of the War*, 339.

112 Gooch, *Before the War*, II, 184. Ironically, Sazonov explained in October 1912 to Count Benckendorff, Russian Ambassador to London, that his aim in forming the Balkan League was to end the Bulgar-Serb rivalry, which he understood to be vital to the stabilization of the Balkans. Instead, once

joined together, Serbia and Bulgaria *destabilized* the region. *Ibid.*, 323. For a useful discussion of the Russian tight rope in Balkan policy, see *ibid.*, 324–9.

113 Pourtalès to Bethmann Hollweg, July 25, quoted in Fay, *The Origins of the World War*, II, 300.

114 Szápáry to Berchtold, July 24, in Geiss, *July 1914*, 178. See also, e.g., Schmitt, *The Coming of the War, 1914*, II, 253, on Sazonov's concern with the balance of power.

115 Lieven, *Russia and the Origins of the First World War*, 142.

116 Pourtalès to Jagow, July 25, Geiss, *July 1914*, 185.

117 Sazonov circulated a note to the Russian missions in Vienna, Berlin, Paris, London, Rome and Bucharest on July 24 informing them of his attempt to persuade Austria to extend the deadline so that the Powers could study it and advise Serbia how to respond. "The rejection by Austria of our proposal for dealing with the matter," Sazonov announced, "would rob the declaration made by her today of all meaning and openly at variance with international ethics." *Ibid.*, 188.

118 "If Serbia is really in such a helpless condition as to leave no doubt regarding the result of an armed struggle with Austria, it would perhaps be better that in the event of an invasion by Austria the Serbs should make no attempt whatever to offer resistance, but should retire and, allowing the enemy to occupy their territory without fighting, appeal to the Powers. In this appeal the Serbs, after pointing out the difficulty of their position after the recent war during which they gained the recognition of Europe by their moderation, might allude to the impossibility of their maintaining an unequal struggle, and ask for the protection of the powers based upon a sense of justice." Sazonov to Chargé d'Affaires Strandtmann, July 24; *ibid.*, 187–8.

119 Serge Sazonov, *Fateful Years, 1909–1916: The Reminiscences of Serge Sazonov* (New York: Frederick A. Stokes, 1928), 149; see also pp. 165, 179. With the exception of these few references, Sazonov's memoirs provide little guidance to his motivations in the July crisis. More often than not, Sazonov did not pay careful attention to the grounds of his policies, and therefore did not take the trouble to sort them out in his own mind. In his draft report to Nicholas II of July 25, which was intended to form the basis of a reply to a message from the King of England, Sazonov wrote, "If Austria persists any longer with this line of policy, Russia will not be able to remain indifferent and the possibility of grave international complications will have to be taken into account. It is to be hoped that in this event Russia and England will both find themselves on the side of right and justice and that the disinterested policies of Russia, whose sole aim is to prevent the establishment of Austrian hegemony in the Balkans will find active support on the part of England." Geiss, *July 1914*, 209. Without further elaboration, it is difficult to imagine how the sole aim of preventing Austrian hegemony in the Balkans all by itself put Russia on the side of right and justice.

120 To King George V, Nicholas wrote on August 1 that the object of Austria's action was "to crush Servia and make her a vassal state of Austria. Effect of this would have been to upset balance of power in Balkans, which is of

such vital interest to my empire." *Collected Diplomatic Documents Relating to the Outbreak of the European War*, 537. The reference to the importance of the balance of power in this case, however, may have been calculated to appeal to the intended audience.

121 See, e.g., Renouvin, *The Immediate Origins of the War*, 153–4.

122 Geiss, *July 1914*, 311.

123 E.g., Nicholas II to William II, July 29: "Am glad you are back. In this most serious moment I appeal to you to help me. An ignoble war has been declared on a weak country. The indignation in Russia, shared fully by me, is enormous. I foresee that very soon I shall be overwhelmed by the pressure brought upon me, and be forced to take extreme measures which will lead to war. To try and avoid such a calamity as a European war, I beg you in the name of our old friendship to do what you can to stop your allies from going too far." Geiss, *July 1914*, 260–1.

124 Lieven, *Russia and the Origins of the First World War*, 144.

125 Schmitt, *The Coming of the War, 1914*, II, 22–3; Lieven, *Russia and the Origins of the First World War*, 131–4.

126 Maurice Paléologue, *An Ambassador's Memoirs*, I, 6th edn., trans. F.A. Holt (New York, George H. Doran, 1924), 43–4. "The liberation of the Slav and Christian peoples of the Balkans from foreign domination was ardently desired by wide circles, and the Tsar's government could never ignore this sentiment; it had, in 1908–1909 and 1912–1913, only with difficulty resisted the pressure of the Pan-Slavists for war in behalf of Serbia and Montenegro. As late as 23 May, 1914, the foreign minister, S.D. Sazonov, had proclaimed in the Duma the principle of 'the Balkans for the Balkan peoples.' If the Austro-Hungarian action threatened the vital interests of Serbia, he would unquestionably be called on to make good his words." Schmitt, *The Coming of the War, 1914*, I, 440–1.

127 Bienvenu-Martin to Viviani, July 26; Quoted in Fay, *The Origins of the World War*, II, 306–7.

128 Many in Germany, however, also believed that a war with Russia was inevitable. Hence the immediate risk of war on favorable terms seemed palatable in contrast to the apparent certainty of a later war on less favorable terms. See Albertini, *The Origins of the War of 1914*, I, 577; Szögyény to Berchtold, July 5, in Geiss, *July 1914*, 76–7; Szögyény to Berchtold, July 12, *ibid.*, 110–11; and Jagow to Lichnowsky, private letter, July 18, *ibid.*, 123. In any case, it was widely believed that at the present time, the Tsar could be persuaded not to intervene against Austria-Hungary by playing on his monarchical sympathies – an appeal that fell on entirely deaf ears. On July 21, Bethmann Hollweg instructed Pourtalès to "call the attention of Sazonoff to the grave consequences to the monarchical idea if the monarchical Powers, putting aside their national sympathies and political points of view, do not stand squarely at the side of Austria. For the political radicalism which rules in Servia, and which does not stop short of crimes against its own royal family, must be crushed. In this task Russia is as much interested as Germany." Gooch, *Before the War*, II, 272–3.

129 The Russian Ambassador to Vienna called on Berchtold on August 1 and

explained, in what Berchtold dismissively considered "a purely academical fashion," that Russia had obligations "as an orthodox and Slav state" and that her policy was dependent upon "certain sentimental characteristics of the Russian people." Geiss, *July 1914*, 343.

130 Albertini, *The Origins of the War of 1914*, I, 516; Gooch, *Before the War*, II, 247.
131 Quoted in Schmitt, *The Coming of the War, 1914*, I, 288–9.
132 Gooch notes that in 1913, William began to shed his conservative attitude and actively encouraged both Conrad and Berchtold to deal decisively with Serbia. Gooch, *Before the War*, II, 255–6. Jagow's circular of July 30 justified Austria's actions against Serbia in terms of the need to crush "Greater Serbian chauvinism." Geiss, *July 1914*, 306. William's marginal comments on diplomatic correspondence are quite revealing; consider, for example, Tschirschky to Bethmann Hollweg, June 30, 1914 (italicized phrases underlined by the Kaiser): "Count Berchtold told me today that *everything* pointed to the fact that the threads of the conspiracy to which the Archduke fell a sacrifice, *ran together at Belgrade*. The affair was so well thought out that very young men were intentionally selected for the perpetration of the crime, against whom *only a mild punishment could be decreed*. [William's marginal comment: I hope not.] The Minister spoke very bitterly about the Serbian plots.

"I frequently hear expressed here, even among serious people, the wish that at *last a final and fundamental reckoning should be had with the Serbs*. [William: Now or never.] The Serbs should first be presented with a number of demands, and in case they should not accept these, energetic measures should be taken. *I take opportunity of every such occasion to advise quietly but very impressively and seriously against too hasty steps*. [William: Who authorized him to act that way? That is very stupid! It is none of his business, as it is solely the affair of Austria, what she plans to do in this case. Later, if plans go wrong, it will be said that Germany did not want it! Let Tschirschky be good enough to drop this nonsense! The Serbs must be disposed of, *and* that right *soon!*]" Geiss, *July 1914*, 64–5.

Tschirschky to Jagow, July 10, is also revealing: "His Majesty had shown himself more inclined to the view that *concrete demands should be levelled at Serbia*. [William: Very much so! And unambiguous ones!] ... The respite allowed for the reply must be made as brief as possible, say forty-eight hours. It is true, that even so short a respite would suffice to enable Belgrade to get advice from St Petersburg. If the Serbs should accept all the demands made on them, it would prove a solution which would be 'very disagreeable' to him, and he was still considering what *demands* could *be put* that would be *wholly impossible for the Serbs to accept*. [William: Evacuate the Sanjac! Then the row would be on at once! Austria must absolutely get that back at once, in order to prevent the union of Serbia and Montenegro and the gaining of the seacoast by the Serbians! To act like 'gentlemen' to murderers, after what has happened! Idiocy!]" *Ibid.*, 107–8.

Moltke appears to have been of a similar mind: "For more than five years Serbia has been the cause of a European tension which has been pressing with simply intolerable weight on the political and economic existence of nations. With a patience approaching weakness, Austria has up to the present borne the continuous provocations and the political machinations aimed at the disruption of her own national stability by a people who proceeded from regicide at home to the murder of princes in a neighbouring land. It was only after the last despicable crime that she took to extreme measures, in order to burn out with a glowing iron a cancer that has constantly threatened to poison the body of Europe. One would think that all of Europe would be grateful to her." Moltke to Bethmann Hollweg, July 29, *ibid.*, 282.

133 See, e.g., his marginal comments on Jagow's report of Lichnowsky's communication, July 23, in *ibid.*, 170–1.

134 "[T]he Slavs are not born to command, but to obey. They must be reminded of the fact; and if they think that salvation will come to them from Belgrade, they must be shown that they are wrong." Quoted in Bloch, *The Causes of the World War*, 30.

135 See, e.g., Tschirschky to Bethmann Hollweg, July 14; in Geiss, *July 1914*, 114.

136 *Ibid.*, 284. Germany was not actually obliged to come to Austria's support in 1914 by the terms of the Fifth Treaty of the Triple Alliance, signed in 1912. The operative article (Art. III) stated, "If one, or two, of the High Contracting Parties, without direct provocation on their part, should chance to be attacked and to be engaged in a war with two or more Great Powers nonsignatory to the present Treaty, the *casus foederis* will arise simultaneously for all the High Contracting Parties." When Germany declared war against Russia on August 1, these conditions had not been fulfilled. See Alfred Francis Pribram, *The Secret Treaties of Austria-Hungary, 1879–1914*, trans. J.G. d'Arcy Paul and Denys P. Myers (New York: Howard Fertig, 1967), I, 247.

137 See note 132, above.

138 Germany's main approach to crisis management was an attempt to localize the conflict. Part of that task involved preventing the question of Alsace-Lorraine from complicating matters. Bethmann Hollweg sent the following message to the Secretary of State for Alsace-Lorraine on July 16: "You will already have seen, from your reading of the papers, that the European situation is not at present free from dangers. In the event of an Austro-Serbian conflict it will be of the utmost importance to localise this difference. We have reason for doubting, and sincerely trust that France, burdened at the present time by all sorts of troubles, will do everything she can to prevent Russia from intervening. This task will be made materially easier for the present authorities at Paris if the French nationalists find no cause for agitation of which to make capital during the next few weeks; I have therefore arranged at Berlin that all press polemics with France shall be cut out as far as possible during the next few weeks, and I would ask you to do the same thing at Strasbourg. It would also be advisable to postpone for a few weeks any administrative measures which have possibly been arranged for, which might be made use of in France for purposes of agitation. If we are successful not only in keeping France quiet but in having St Petersburg admonished to keep the peace, it would have

what would be for us a most favourable effect on the Franco-Russian alliance." Geiss, *July 1914*, 118.

139 The Kaiser's long marginal comment at the end of Pourtalès's telegram to Jagow, July 30, is quite revealing: " ... I have no doubt left about it: England, Russia and France have *agreed* among themselves – after laying the foundation of the *casus foederis* for us through Austria – to take the Austro-Serbian conflict for an *excuse* for waging a *war of extermination* against us. Hence Grey's cynical observation to Lichnowsky 'as long as the war is *confined* to Russia and Austria, England would sit quiet, only when we and France *are mixed up* in it would he be compelled to make an active move against us'; i.e., either we are shamefully to betray our allies, *sacrifice* them to Russia – thereby breaking up the Triple Alliance, or we are to be attacked in common by the Triple Entente for our *fidelity to our allies* and punished, whereby they will satisfy their jealousy by joining in totally *ruining* us. That is the real naked situation *in nuce*, which, slowly and cleverly set going, certainly by Edward VII, has been carried on, and systematically built up by disowned conferences between England and Paris and St Petersburg; finally brought to a conclusion by George V and set to work. And thereby the stupidity and ineptitude of our ally is turned into a snare for us. So the famous *'encirclement'* of Germany has finally become a complete fact, despite every effort of our politicians and diplomats to prevent it. The net has been suddenly thrown over our head, and England sneeringly reaps the most brilliant success of her persistently prosecuted purely *anti-German world-policy*, against which we have proven ourselves helpless, while she twists the noose of our political and economic destruction out of our fidelity to Austria, as we squirm *isolated* in the net. A great achievement, which arouses even the admiration of him who is to be destroyed as its result! Edward VII is stronger after his death than I who am still alive!" Geiss, *July 1914*, 293–5 (emphasis in the original).

140 In so far as this analysis sheds light on the question of war guilt, it tends to support the conclusions of Konrad Jarausch and Pierre Renouvin; namely, that Germany's leaders were willing to accept a local war, feared a continental war but accepted the risk, and abhorred the idea of a world war. Konrad H. Jarausch, "The Illusion of Limited War: Chancellor Bethmann Hollweg's Calculated Risk, July 1914," *Central European History*, 2, No. 1 (March 1969), 48–76; Renouvin, *The Immediate Origins of the War*, 51.

141 Quoted in Albertini, *The Origins of the War of 1914*, II, 605–6.

142 Paléologue, *An Ambassador's Memoirs*, I, 45–6. Baron von Schilling's diary entry for July 28 confirms Paléologue's communication of the French government's readiness to fulfill its obligations in case of necessity. (Schilling was the Head of Chancery at the Russian Ministry of Foreign Affairs.) Albertini, *The Origins of the War of 1914*, II, 537. There is some question whether Paléologue had gone beyond his instructions and deliberately acted as an *agent-provocateur*. See *ibid.*, 534–9.

143 Schmitt, *The Coming of the War, 1914*, II, 17

144 Many of these were incorrect. Albertini, *The Origins of the War of 1914*, III, 67.

145 Schmitt, *The Coming of the War, 1914*, II, 334. This is not to suggest that France made *no* efforts to minimize escalatory pressures. On July 30, for example, French troops were ordered to withdraw to a distance of approximately ten kilometers from the German frontier. Geiss, *July 1914*, 274.

146 Poincaré, *Les Origines de la Guerre*, 252.

147 *Ibid.*, 227.

148 Geiss, *July 1914*, 325. As Schoen later remarked, "From a purely military standpoint the demand for a guarantee of neutrality may be correct, from a political point of view it was a mistake. As matters stood, France's neutrality would have been such an immense advantage to us that we should have had more reason for offering than for demanding something for its maintenance." Freiherr von Schoen, *The Memoirs of An Ambassador: A Contribution to the Political History of Modern Times*, trans. Constance Vesey (London: George Allen & Unwin, 1922), 195.

149 The occasion for the contingency did not arise. When Schoen inquired about France's intentions, Viviani responded merely that France would be guided by her interests. Poincaré claims that this response was deliberately ambiguous; it was feared that too strong a statement in one direction would "betray our ally," and too strong a statement in the other would constitute a provocation. Poincaré, *Les Origines de la Guerre*, 266. Barbara Tuchman claims that France had intercepted and decoded Schoen's instruction and knew of the pledge demand; *The Guns of August*, 76.

150 *Collected Diplomatic Documents Relating to the Outbreak of the European War*, 253–5 and 255–64.

151 Quoted in Albertini, *The Origins of the War of 1914*, III, 82.

152 Gooch, *Recent Revelations of European Diplomacy*, 209. See also Gooch, *Before the War*, II, 151, 197. Albertini raises questions about Poincaré's commitment to peace, invoking "the passion which glowed in the hearts of so many Frenchmen and in few more intensely than that of Poincaré, the man of Lorraine, a passion which might well tempt him not to let slip a favorable chance of recovering the lost provinces." Albertini, *The Origins of the War of 1914*, II, 606. See also *ibid.*, III, 80–1.3

153 Tuchman, *The Guns of August*, 125.

154 Asquith, *The Genesis of the War*, 311.

155 Grey wrote: "The Germans do not realise that England has always drifted or deliberately gone into opposition to any Power which establishes a hegemony in Europe." Quoted in Gooch, *Before the War*, II, 34.

156 Quoted in *ibid.*, 17.

157 Crowe's minute on Buchanan to Grey, July 24; Geiss, *July 1914*, 198.

158 Grey, *Twenty-Five Years*, I, 302–3.

159 See Albertini, *The Origins of the War of 1914*, III, 364–411; Winston S. Churchill, *The World Crisis*, I (New York: Charles Scribner's Sons, 1923), 228-36; and Schmitt, *The Coming of the War, 1914*, II, 280.

160 On July 31, the Clerk of the Privy Council wrote, "in spite of Edward Grey's misgivings and the more strongly expressed dissent of Winston Churchill, no decision was reached in favour of any further precautionary steps. Indeed the disposition of Ministers was hardening into resistance to the

demand for mobilization, the large majority being wholly opposed to such a step." Quoted in Schmitt, *The Coming of the War, 1914*, II, 286.

161 *Ibid.*, 340–1.

162 Grey, *Twenty-Five Years*, I, 323–5.

163 Geiss, *July 1914*, 327–8.

164 Michael G. Ekstein and Zara Steiner, "The Sarajevo Crisis," in F.H. Hinsley, ed., *British Foreign Policy Under Sir Edward Grey* (Cambridge: Cambridge University Press, 1977), 404.

165 Grey, *Twenty-Five Years*, II, 4–8.

166 FO 93 14/4, Public Record Office, London.

167 CAB 41/35/22, July 30, 1914, p. 2; PRO, London.

168 CAB 37/120 95, PRO, London. On August 2, 1914, Lord Crewe wrote to the King, "As regards Belgium it was agreed, without any attempt to state a formula, that it would be made evident that a substantial violation of the neutrality of that country would place us in the situation contemplated as possible by W. Gladstone in 1870, when interference with Belgian independence was held to compel us to take action." CAB 41/35/23, PRO, London.

169 *Hansard*, vol. CCII, p. 1787, Aug. 10, 1870; quoted in CAB 37/120 95.

170 CAB 41/35/23, PRO, London.

171 Gooch, *Before the War*, II, 127; Grey to Goschen, August 1, in *Collected Diplomatic Documents Relating to the Outbreak of the European War*, 93.

172 Lichnowsky to Foreign Office, August 4, quoted in Schmitt, *The Coming of the War, 1914*, II, 401. See also Grey, *Twenty-Five Years*, I, 331.

173 He adds, in his memoir, "That was the British *casus belli*." Asquith, *The Genesis of the War*, 315.

174 See, e.g., *ibid.*, 316. Grey, for example, explained his actions to the American Ambassador, upon the rupture of relations with Berlin, by appealing first to Britain's moral duty to defend the rights of Belgium, and then to the importance of maintaining the European equilibrium. Gooch, *Before the War*, II, 130–1. Zara Steiner argues that the treaty obligation to Belgium provided a rationalization for the British interest in resisting Germany's attack on France, and that "Belgium proved to be a catalyst which unleashed the many emotions, rationalisations and glorifications of war which had long been part of the British climate of opinion. Having a moral cause, all the latent anti-German feeling, fed by years of naval rivalry and assumed enmity, rose to the surface." Steiner, *Britain and the Origins of the First World War*, 237, 233. See also Ekstein and Steiner, "The Sarajevo Crisis," 407. It may well be that the violation tapped a wellspring of anti-Germanism, but it is difficult to credit the suggestion – if the suggestion is intended – that the profession of British moral indignation was somehow insincere and merely provided a convenient excuse for entering the war. The prospect of entering the war was not widely popular; nor, for that matter, did Britain need an excuse to intervene if she so desired. A simple invocation of the national interest, or an appeal to the importance of the Entente, would have sufficed.

175 Lichnowsky to Jagow, August 1, reports Grey's comments on Belgian neutrality, eliciting skeptical marginalia from the Kaiser. Geiss, *July 1914*,

345–7. Interestingly, Bethmann Hollweg acknowledged the wrong of violating Belgian territory in his speech before the Reichstag on August 4: "Gentlemen, we are now in a state of necessity, and necessity knows no law. Our troops have occupied Luxembourg and perhaps have already entered Belgian territory. Gentlemen, that is a breach of international law .... The wrong – I speak openly – the wrong we thereby commit we will try to make good as soon as our military aims have been obtained." *Collected Diplomatic Documents Relating to the Outbreak of the European War*, 438. Schoen also condemned the violation of Belgian neutrality; *The Memoirs of an Ambassador*, 248–9.

176 Goschen to Grey, August 6, quoted in Schmitt, *The Coming of the War, 1914*, II, 406–7.

177 Quoted in Gooch, *Before the War*, II, 126.

178 Grey, *Twenty-Five Years*, II, 2–3. On Anglo-French military cooperation generally, see Samuel R. Williamson, Jr., *The Politics of Grand Strategy: Britain and France Prepare for War, 1904–1914* (Cambridge, Mass.: Harvard University Press, 1969). Not everyone understood the last point in purely moral terms; Lord Crewe, for example, wrote the King that "the practical protection of the French coasts ... is not only a recognition of our friendship with France, but is also imperatively required to preserve British interests." CAB 41/35/23, Aug. 2, 1914, PRO, London.

179 Grey, *Twenty-Five Years*, I, 302–3.

180 Geiss, *July 1914*, 331.

181 Albertini, *The Origins of the War of 1914*, II, 363.

182 *Ibid.*, 470–4. For evidence of Germany's conscious attempt to make Russia look responsible for the outbreak of war see Bethmann Hollweg to William II, July 28, in Geiss, *July 1914*, 258.

183 At 11 p.m. on August 1, Isvolsky informed Poincaré that Germany had declared war on Russia, and inquired about the attitude of France. Poincaré declared that France would honor her treaty obligations, which required her to declare war on Germany; but he deemed it vital to ensure that Germany declare war on France first, so as not to jeopardize his attempt to bring Britain in on the side of Russia and France. Schmitt, *The Coming of the War, 1914*, II, 338.

WORLD WAR II

1 My discussion will be confined to the outbreak of war in the European theater, in part so as to keep it comparatively brief, but also because it may well be debated whether the war in the Pacific was *sui generis* – i.e., whether it would have occurred in the absence of an ongoing war in which both the Soviet Union and Britain, two important Pacific powers, were already engaged.

2 *The Treaty of Peace Between the Allied and Associated Powers and Germany, The Protocol thereto, the Agreement respecting the military occupation of the Rhine, and the Treaty Between France and Great Britain respecting Assistance to France in the event of unprovoked aggression by Germany, Signed at Versailles, June 28th, 1919* (London: His Majesty's Stationery Office, 1919); E.H. Carr, *Inter-*

national Relations Between the Two World Wars (1919–1939) (London: Macmillan, 1963), 6–9.

3 Paul von Hindenburg first advanced the "stab in the back" thesis in testimony before the Allied committee charged with examining the question of responsibility for war on November 18, 1919; *Official German Documents Relating to the World War*, II (New York: Oxford University Press, 1923), 855.

4 Carr, *International Relations Between the Two World Wars*, 4–5. On the war guilt clause, Carr writes, "The Allied governments, in the passion of the moment, failed to realise that this extorted admission of guilt could prove nothing, and must excite bitter resentment in German minds. German men of learning set to work to demonstrate the guiltlessness of their country, fondly believing that, if this could be established, the whole fabric of the treaty would collapse." *Ibid.*, 46.

5 A.J.P. Taylor, *The Origins of the Second World War* (New York: Atheneum, 1962), 18–19.

6 *Ibid.*, 68.

7 For useful debate on Taylor's thesis, see E.M. Robertson, ed., *The Origins of the Second World War: Historical Interpretations* (London: Macmillan, 1971), and Gordon Martel, ed., *The Origins of the Second World War Reconsidered: The A.J.P. Taylor Debate after Twenty-Five Years* (Boston: Allen & Unwin, 1986), especially the essay by Norman Rich, "Hitler's Foreign Policy," 119–39, which is a scathing response to Taylor.

8 On why Hitler was different, see the excellent discussion in John Mueller, *Retreat from Doomsday: The Obsolescence of Major War* (New York: Basic Books, 1989), 64–71.

9 See Alan Bullock, "Hitler and the Origins of the Second World War," in Hans W. Gatzke, ed., *European Diplomacy Between Two Wars, 1919–1939* (Chicago: Quadrangle, 1972), 221–46.

10 See, e.g., E.M. Robertson, *Hitler's Pre-war Policy and Military Plans, 1933–1939* (London: Longmans, 1963); and Donald Cameron Watt, *How War Came: The Immediate Origins of the Second World War, 1938–1939* (New York: Pantheon, 1989), 440–1. Well before he became Chancellor, Hitler spoke in excited and violent terms about "the next war." Alan Bullock, *Hitler: A Study in Tyranny*, abr. edn. (New York: Harper & Row, 1971), 121. Cf. also Leonidas Hill, "Three Crises, 1938–39," *Journal of Contemporary History*, 3, No. 1 (January 1968), 113–44, who argues that the papers of Ernst von Weiszäcker, State Secretary in the German Foreign Office from 1938–43, suggest that in the last years of peace Hitler was clearly driven by war lust, and that he was operating on a definite timetable determined largely by military considerations.

11 "The Power of Germany was directed by Adolf Hitler. Careful analyses by scholars have revealed internal divisions, organizational confusions, jurisdictional battles, institutional rivalries, and local deviations behind the façade of monolithic unity that the Third Reich liked to present to its citizens and to the world in word and picture. The fact remains, however, that the broad lines of policy were determined in all cases by Hitler himself." Gerhard L. Weinberg, *The Foreign Policy of Hitler's Germany: Starting World War II, 1937–1939* (Chicago: University of Chicago Press, 1980), 657.

12 See, e.g., Bullock, *Hitler*, 190; and John Toland, *Adolf Hitler* (Garden City, N.Y.: Doubleday, 1976), 467.

13 *Ibid.*, 468–9.

14 Sidney Aster, *1939: The Making of the Second World War* (New York: Simon and Schuster, 1973), 235.

15 World War II is, of course, one of the most extensively studied events of all time. Useful guides to available scholarship include Helen Kehr and Janet Langmaid, *The Nazi Era, 1919–1945: A Select Bibliography of Published Works from the Early Roots to 1980* (London: Mansell, 1982); Louis Leo Snyder, *The Third Reich, 1933–1945: A Bibliographical Guide to German National Socialism* (New York: Garland, 1987); and Peter D. Stachura, *The Weimar Era and Hitler, 1918–1933: A Critical Bibliography* (Oxford: Clio Press, 1977).

16 Taylor, *The Origins of the Second World War*, 108.

17 Quoted in Bullock, *Hitler*, 173.

18 Arnold Wolfers, *Britain and France Between Two Wars: Conflicting Strategies of Peace since Versailles* (New York: Harcourt, Brace, 1940), 216–17, 217–18n.

19 A. Lentin, *Lloyd George, Woodrow Wilson and the Guilt of Germany: An Essay in the Pre-history of Appeasement* (Leicester: Leicester University Press, 1984), 134.

20 Hitler heard of the armistice while in hospital undergoing treatment for gas exposure; his outrage at those who had "stabbed Germany in the back" was so profound that he resolved then and there to become a politician. Adolf Hitler, *Mein Kampf* (New York: Reynal & Hitchcock, 1939), 266–9.

21 Bullock, *Hitler*, 48, 62.

22 Hitler, *Mein Kampf*, 978. See also *ibid.*, 696, 925–6.

23 *Ibid.*, 309.

24 Hitler's speech to the Industry Club, Düsseldorf, January 27, 1932; quoted in Bullock, *Hitler*, 101-3.

25 In 1923 – perhaps not surprisingly – Houston Chamberlain professed himself to be an ardent admirer of Adolf Hitler. Rohan d'O. Butler, *The Roots of National Socialism, 1783–1933* (New York: Howard Fertig, 1968), 223–4.

26 For a thorough intellectual history and analysis of National Socialism, see Kurt London, *Backgrounds of Conflict: Ideas and Forms in World Politics* (New York, Macmillan, 1945), 36–129.

27 Robert G.L. Waite, "Adolf Hitler's Anti-Semitism: A Study in History and Psychoanalysis," in Benjamin B. Wolman, ed., *The Psychoanalytic Interpretation of History* (New York: Basic Books, 1971), 196.

28 Hitler, *Mein Kampf*, 288–9 (emphasis in the original). Hitler's reference to the Creator is interesting; most commentators insist that he was an atheist.

29 See Hans Staudinger, *The Inner Nazi: A Critical Analysis of* Mein Kampf, ed. Peter M. Rutkoff and William B. Scott (Baton Rouge: Louisiana State University Press, 1981), 31–52. See also Toland, *Adolf Hitler*, 397.

30 One of the few references to this may be found in his speech to the Reichstag, February 20, 1938; Adolf Hitler, *My New Order*, ed. Raoul de Roussy de Sales (New York: Reynal & Hitchcock, 1941), 435.

31 See H.R. Trevor-Roper, "The Mind of Adolf Hitler," introductory essay to

Hitler's Secret Conversations 1941–1944 (New York: Farrar, Straus & Young, 1953), xxiii. Cf. Toland, *Adolf Hitler*, 221.

32 Hitler, *Mein Kampf*, 601.

33 In 1936, he dictated a memorandum analyzing the world situation in which he emphasized the threat of Bolshevism and the need for *lebensraum*. The memorandum concluded with the following statement: "I thus set the following tasks: I. The German armed forces must be operational within four years. II. The German economy must be fit for war within four years." Jeremy Noakes and Geoffrey Pridham, *Documents on Nazism, 1919–1945* (New York: Viking, 1975), 408. And in November 1937, Hitler told Germany's civilian and military leaders, "The aim of German policy was to make secure and preserve the racial community and to enlarge it. It was therefore a question of space . . . . Germany's problem could only be solved by means of force and this was never without attendant risks." Minutes of the Conference in the Reich Chancellery, Berlin, November 5, 1937 ("Hossbach Memorandum"); Germany, Auswärtiges Amt, *Documents on German Foreign Policy, 1918–1945* (Washington, D.C.: United States Government Printing Office, 1949-), Ser. D, I, November 10, 1937, 29–39; 29, 34.

34 Hitler, *Mein Kampf*, 947 (emphasis in the original).

35 Bullock, *Hitler*, 487. Bullock describes Hitler as "a man who believed neither in God not in conscience ('a Jewish invention, a blemish like circumcision')," who thought of himself as "the Siegfried come to reawaken Germany to greatness, for whom morality and suffering were irrelevant." *Ibid.*, 216.

36 Hitler, *Mein Kampf*, 949. Hitler's single-minded pursuit of *lebensraum*, and (in contrast to Treitschke) his indifference to the fate of Alsace and Lorraine, account for his satisfaction with Germany's western border, but his unwillingness to accept as permanent her eastern frontiers. Cf. Carr, *International Relations Between the Two World Wars (1919–1939)*, 95; and Taylor, *The Origins of the Second World War*, 54.

37 Hitler, *Mein Kampf*, 887–8.

38 Bullock, *Hitler*, 283. "The passions which ruled Hitler's mind were ignoble: hatred, resentment, the lust to dominate, and, where he could not dominate, to destroy. His career did not exalt but debased the human condition, and his twelve years' dictatorship was barren of all ideas save one – the further extension of his own power and that of the nation with which he had identified himself. Even power he conceived of in the crudest terms: an endless vista of military roads, S.S. garrisons, and concentration camps to sustain the rule of the Aryan 'master race' over the degraded subject peoples of his new empire in the east." *Ibid.*, 487.

39 While the following discussion is intended primarily to develop a single line of argument, it attempts to be sensitive to the multicausality of the collapse of the Weimar Republic, and to the irreducible element of mystery surrounding a civilized people's embrace of a fundamentally uncivilized creed. See generally John Hiden and John Farquharson, *Explaining Hitler's Germany: Historians and the Third Reich* (Totowa, N.J.: Barnes & Noble, 1983), esp. Chapter 7, "National Socialism: The Problem of a General Interpretation," 152–70.

40 Noakes and Pridham, *Documents on Nazism*, 37–8.

41 It should be noted that the third plank appears to represent a demand for the return of Germany's lost colonies. This ambiguity might have been intended to mask the demand for *lebensraum* by representing it, too, as a question of the injustice of Versailles. However, the subsequent publication of *Mein Kampf* should have dispelled any illusions on this point. See p. 133, above.

42 Appendix to volume I of *Mein Kampf*, 517–59. For a typical assault on Versailles, see, e.g., Hitler's speech of August 1, 1923 in Munich; in Hitler, *My New Order*, 64–6.

43 Toland, *Adolf Hitler*, 123.

44 Maurice Baumont, "The Role of Foreign Policy in the Success of the National-Socialist Party," in Maurice Baumont, John H.E. Fried, and Edmond Vermeil, eds., *The Third Reich* (New York: Praeger, 1955), 456, 472.

45 *Ibid.* Cf. Eliot Barculo Wheaton, *Prelude to Calamity: The Nazi Revolution, 1933–35* (Garden City, N.Y.: Doubleday, 1968), 7.

46 Wolfers, *Britain and France Between Two Wars*, 63.

47 It was especially difficult for Hitler to portray himself as a critic of the government when the government itself was actively working to revise the status quo. See Annelise Thimme, "Stresemann and Locarno," in Gatzke, ed., *European Diplomacy Between Two Wars, 1919–1939*, 73–93; and Wolfers, *Britain and France Between Two Wars*, 64–5.

48 Hitler's frustration with his inability to woo the Right to his cause led him to write a sequel to *Mein Kampf* in 1928 that focussed primarily on the one area in which Hitler could expect to find sympathetic conservative ears: foreign policy. This book was never published, possibly because it was overtaken by events. See Adolf Hitler, *Hitler's Secret Book*, trans. Salvator Attanasio (New York: Grove Press, 1961).

49 Bullock, *Hitler*, 74–6.

50 See Wheaton, *Prelude to Calamity*, 23.

51 *Ibid.*, 100.

52 Richard F. Hamilton, *Who Voted for Hitler?* (Princeton, N.J.: Princeton University Press, 1982), esp. 420–3; Toland, *Adolf Hitler*, 243–4.

53 Bullock, *Hitler*, 82.

54 See Taylor, *The Origins of the Second World War*, 44.

55 Bullock, *Hitler*, 139.

56 See Eric Matthias, "The Influence of the Versailles Treaty on the Internal Development of the Weimar Republic," in Anthony Nicholls and Eric Matthias, eds., *German Democracy and the Triumph of Hitler* (New York: St. Martin's, 1971), 13–28.

57 For extensive treatments, see Gerhard L. Weinberg, *The Foreign Policy of Hitler's Germany: Diplomatic Revolution in Europe, 1933–36* (Chicago: University of Chicago Press, 1970); and Weinberg, *The Foreign Policy of Hitler's Germany: Starting World War II, 1937–1939*.

58 One might wonder why popular support was important after 1933, given Hitler's ability to eliminate his political rivals. In part, the answer is that Hitler needed to persuade the public to acquiesce in the creation of a one-party dictatorship given the comparatively small number of ideologically committed Nazis. But it was also important for the satisfaction of

Hitler's psychological needs that he win the approval and adoration of the people. As Bullock notes, he was "careful to insist that his power was rooted in the people; his was a plebiscitary and popular dictatorship, a democratic Caesarism. It is obvious that Hitler felt – and not without justification – that his power, despite the Gestapo and the concentration camps, was founded on popular support to a large degree." Bullock, *Hitler*, 228.

59 *Ibid.*, 178.

60 Toland, *Adolf Hitler*, 321.

61 March 7, 1936; see Hitler, *My New Order*, 362–84. See also his speech of March 20 in Hamburg, *ibid.*, 384–6. For a full account of the remilitarization, see Éva H. Haraszti, *The Invaders: Hitler Occupies the Rhineland*, trans. Zsófia László; translation revised by Brian McLean (Budapest: Akadémiai Kiadó, 1983).

62 Quoted in Toland, *Adolf Hitler*, 388. It is generally believed that Hitler had instructed German troops to offer no resistance to a French response; but Donald Cameron Watt argues that the order to effect "a strategic withdrawal" to the east bank of the Rhine would have entailed military action and loss of life. Donald Cameron Watt, "German Plans for the Reoccupation of the Rhineland," *Journal of Contemporary History*, 1, No. 4 (October 1966), 193–9.

63 Toland, *Adolf Hitler*, 389. Bullock insists that there was a certain amount of fraud and intimidation during the balloting, but concedes that the overwhelmingly positive result clearly indicated that Hitler's bold stroke had the support of the German people. Bullock, *Hitler*, 192.

64 Bullock, *Hitler*, 197.

65 The agreement permitted Germany to build a fleet of gross tonnage 35 percent that of Britain's, and an equal number of submarines. By concluding the agreement, Britain implicitly freed Germany from the naval restriction of the Treaty of Versailles.

66 See his speech to the Reichstag of February 20, 1938; in Hitler, *My New Order*, 443–96. Hitler warned third parties not "to exert an influence on the shaping of the situation in Austria which would be incompatible with the right to self-determination of the German people." Foreign Ministry to various German Diplomatic Missions, March 12, 1938; *Documents on German Foreign Policy, 1918–1945*, Ser. D, I, No. 366, 586–7.

67 Since 1935, the German Foreign Office had been funding the Nazi Sudeten German Party, under the leadership of Karl Henlein, which spearheaded the cause of union. Bullock, *Hitler*, 253.

68 *Times of London*, March 14, 1938, 14.

69 In one of his less graceful extemporizations, Hitler declared in Nuremberg on September 12, 1938 that "more than 3,500,000 people were robbed in the name of the right of self-determination of a certain Mr. Wilson of their self-determination and of their right to self-determination." Hitler, *My New Order*, 506.

70 See the discussion below, pp. 145–7.

71 For the text of the agreement, see Noakes and Pridham, *Documents on Nazism*, 547–8. Given the size and quality of the Czechoslovak army, and

Germany's incomplete rearmament, Prague almost certainly could have put up a decent fight even without French support if war had broken out in 1938. But Czechoslovakia was so wedded to the necessity of Western support that she was psychologically incapable of offering any resistance. See David Vital, "Czechoslovakia and the Powers, September 1938," *Journal of Contemporary History*, 1, No. 4 (October 1966), 37–67.

72 François-Poncet to Bonnet, October 4, 1938, in France, Ministère des Affaires Étrangères, *The French Yellow Book: Diplomatic Documents (1938–1939): Papers Relative to the Events and Negotiations which Preceded the Opening of Hostilities between Germany on the One Hand, and Poland, Great Britain and France on the Other* (New York: Reynal & Hitchcock, 1940), 16.

73 Quoted in Toland, *Adolf Hitler*, 407.

74 In a speech in Wilhelmshaven on April 1, 1939, Hitler justified the takeover of Czechoslovakia on strategic grounds, only incidentally invoking allegations that Czechoslovakia had abused ethnic Germans. Hitler, *My New Order*, 615–28.

75 See, e.g., Wolfers, *Britain and France Between Two Wars*, 5.

76 *Ibid.*, 90n. "On the whole," writes Wolfers, "the British seem to have had more sympathy and understanding for the psychological reactions of the Germans than of the French. French fears they considered exaggerated, while German resentment appeared justified. The fact that the war spirit did not disappear was generally attributed to the provocative policy of the French and to the injustice of some of the provisions of the Treaty of Versailles. The Germans were the ones who were being provoked." *Ibid.*, 244–5.

77 France and Britain were the only two Powers between the wars who were in a position to check Hitler. The United States' repudiation of the Treaty, the League, and Wilsonian internationalism heralded a return to isolation that the Depression powerfully reinforced; it had neither the will nor the means to offer Hitler any serious resistance (see also n. 79, below). The Soviet Union was too preoccupied with collectivization, and too weakened by Stalin's military purges, to play an active role in European diplomacy; she was also covertly helping Germany rearm in return for industrial assistance. Italy – more of a Great Power in style than in substance – was in no position to object to the expansion of Germany into ethnically contiguous territory when her own forces were attempting to subjugate Ethiopia.

78 John Maynard Keynes, *The Economic Consequences of the Peace* (New York: Harcourt, Brace and Howe, 1920). See, e.g., p. 225.

79 According to Arnold Wolfers, "These 'principles of justice' might influence British governmental policy directly, or in an indirect way, by their effect on public opinion. To the continental observer of British affairs, naturally skeptical, nothing was more amazing than the hold which the Wilsonian principles were able to gain on public opinion throughout the British Isles and the Dominions, particularly on Leftist opinion. The result was that even in cases where the government did not approve of making these principles the basis of practical policies, it was constantly under great pressure to take them into consideration. How influential this factor must

have been in Britain was apparent from the importance Germany attached to it in presenting her case. Hitler, whose realism even the cynics may be willing to admit, did not abandon the German practice of appealing to the sense of justice of British public opinion and of basing German claims on Wilsonian principles." Wolfers, *Britain and France Between Two Wars*, 216–17. Bullock writes: "This invoked sympathy for Germany, allowed Hitler to appear as the representative of reason and justice, protesting against the unreasonableness and injustice of Germany's former opponents, and enabled him to turn round and use with great effect against the supporters of the League of Nations all the slogans of Wilsonian idealism, from self-determination to a peace founded upon justice." Bullock, *Hitler*, 177. Hitler's arguments also had an effect on American opinion; see Selig Adler, "The War Guilt Question and American Disillusionment, 1918–1928," *Journal of Modern History*, 23, No. 1 (March 1951), 1–28.

80 See, e.g., p. 145, below. Since no records were kept of the proceedings of Third Republic cabinet meetings, it is somewhat difficult to reconstruct the motivations of French statesmen during this period, especially in view of the fact that relatively few of the key players left memoirs. The richest trove of information is *Documents Diplomatiques Français 1932–1939* (Paris: Imprimerie Nationale, 1963–1986), published by the Commission de Publication des Documents Relatifs aux Origines de la Guerre 1939–1945. Most of the key documents appear also in the *French Yellow Book*, although its selection of documents reflects a conscious attempt to put the best face on French policy.

81 See, e.g., Albert Carl Gay, Jr., "The Daladier Administration, 1938–1940," Diss. University of North Carolina 1970. British Prime Minister Sir Neville Chamberlain was well aware of this, and lamented it. "France's weakness," he wrote, "is a public danger just when she ought to be a source of strength and confidence, and as a friend she has two faults which destroy half her value. She can never keep a secret for more than half an hour, nor a government for more than nine months!" Letter to Mrs. Morton Prince, January 16, 1938; quoted in Keith Feiling, *The Life of Neville Chamberlain* (London: Macmillan, 1947), 323.

82 The one occasion on which France attempted to influence German policy unilaterally was in 1923, when French troops occupied the Ruhr to enforce the delivery of reparations. For this she was universally condemned. The French Right never fully recovered from the setback, and the country retreated into a policy of *rapprochement* which, under the leadership of Aristide Briand, substantially improved the climate of Franco-German relations for a period of time. Wolfers, *Britain and France Between Two Wars*, 57–62. But although Stresemann and Briand both pursued a policy of *rapprochement*, they operated on different assumptions that were destined to ruin any lasting reconciliation. For Stresemann, *rapprochement* was a means of cultivating French good will and thus her eventual acquiescence in a major revision of the Versailles system; for Briand, it was a means of reconciling Germany with the *status quo*. *Ibid.*, 64–5.

83 By the terms of the Pact of Locarno (1925), Britain and Italy guaranteed the frontiers of Belgium and France against German attack, and the frontiers of

Germany against French attack. Germany recognized her western borders as final, and reaffirmed her commitment to the demilitarization of the Rhineland.

84 See Anthony Adamthwaite, *France and the Coming of the Second World War* (London: Frank Cass, 1977), 37–41; and John C. Cairns, "March 7, 1936, Again: The View from Paris," in Gatzke, ed., *European Diplomacy Between Two Wars, 1919–1939*, 172–92.

85 See P.M.H. Bell, *The Origins of the Second World War in Europe* (London: Longman, 1986), 90–100; and Jean-Baptiste Duroselle, "France and the Crisis of March 1936," in Evelyn M. Acomb and Marvin L. Brown, Jr., eds., *French Society and Culture Since the Old Regime* (New York: Holt, Rinehart and Winston, 1966), 258–65.

86 Weinberg, *The Foreign Policy of Hitler's Germany: Diplomatic Revolution in Europe, 1933–36*, 243. For a discussion of the French preoccupation with the defensive, see Gay, "The Daladier Administration, 1938–1940," 23–42.

87 According to Williamson Murray's excellent survey of the strategic and economic situation, Britain and France consistently overestimated German capabilities and underestimated their own. See Williamson Murray, *The Change in the European Balance of Power, 1938–1939: The Path to Ruin* (Princeton, N.J.: Princeton University Press, 1984).

88 Duroselle, "France and the Crisis of March 1936," 256. General Maurin, Minister of War, wrote on February 17, in anticipation of the German move, that "to use our right to occupy the demilitarized zone runs the risk of being contrary to French interests" because "[w]e risk appearing as the aggressor and finding ourselves left to face Germany alone." Quoted in *ibid.*, 251.

89 Blum drifted from outright pacifism early in the interwar period to advocating a strong policy against Germany. His odyssey reflects both a realistic assessment of the threat posed by Hitler, and a self-identification as "Frenchman, Socialist, and Jew." Bell, *The Origins of the Second World War in Europe*, 99–100.

90 Gay, "The Daladier Administration, 1938–1940," 222.

91 On March 15, 1938, the French Permanent Committee of National Defense met to consider what help could be given to Prague in the event of a German attack, in fulfillment of her treaty obligations. The committee concluded that nothing could be done without the danger of a lengthy war; General Vuillemin, Chief of Air Staff, baldly confessed his opinion that, in a Franco-German war, the French air force would last a mere fifteen days. Yet on April 29 – not two months later – Premier Edouard Daladier told British Prime Minister Neville Chamberlain that "war could only be avoided if Great Britain and France made their determination quite clear to maintain the peace of Europe." Adamthwaite, *France and the Coming of the Second World War*, 87–8, 180.

92 Quoted in Gay, "The Daladier Administration, 1938–1940," 96–7.

93 Daladier attempted to rationalize his complicity in the dismemberment of Czechoslovakia by insisting to President Eduard Beneš that his first thought had been "to save the Czechoslovak nation from the more redoubtable trial of war." Daladier to Bonnet, September 30, 1938, in *The French*

Yellow Book, 12. On French public opinion before and after Munich, see Geneviève Vallette and Jacques Bouillon, *Munich, 1938* (Paris: Armand Colin, 1964). See also Gay, "The Daladier Administration, 1938–1940," 257–8.

94 Lentin, *Lloyd George, Woodrow Wilson and the Guilt of Germany*, 135.

95 Wolfers, *Britain and France Between Two Wars*, 212–13.

96 William Rock defines appeasement as a policy of "identifying the basic grievances of disgruntled powers, particularly Germany and Italy, and attempting to negotiate removal of those grievances through reasonable concessions in the face of legitimate demands, thus opening the way for a general settlement that would ensure the continuation of peace for all." Rock insists that appeasement "was not undertaken from cowardice or fear, but from a strong sense of mission impelled by a variety of practical considerations and tempered by the combination of guilty conscience and superior morality. In its earlier phases, it embodied the political sentiment of a strong majority of Englishmen." William R. Rock, *British Appeasement in the 1930s* (London: Edward Arnold, 1977), 30.

97 See, e.g., Foreign Secretary Anthony Eden's remarks in the House of Commons, which reveal that his primary concern was "that this amounts to the unilateral repudiation of a treaty freely negotiated and freely signed" – a remark, incidentally, that implied a crucial distinction on this score between Locarno and Versailles. *Parliamentary Debates Official Report*, 309, Fifth Series, Commons, col. 1810 (hereafter cited as 309 H.C. Deb. 5 s., col. 1810). See also Haraszti, *The Invaders*, 144–52.

98 Toland, *Adolf Hitler*, 388; Haraszti, *The Invaders*, 114. A.J.P. Taylor maintains that "there was almost unanimous approval in Great Britain that the Germans had liberated their own territory," and that the Prime Minister, Stanley Baldwin, "agreed with this public opinion." Taylor, *The Origins of the Second World War*, 99. Cf. also Keith Middlemas and John Barnes, *Baldwin: A Biography* (New York: Macmillan, 1969), 914. Ambassador von Hoesch submitted a report to the German Foreign Office on March 10, 1936, in which he wrote that "the broad mass of people ... are the most favourably disposed towards the action taken by the Reich Government. The so-called 'man in the street' generally takes the view that he does not care a damn if the Germans occupy their own territory with military forces, which is a thing all other states do anyway." *Documents on German Foreign Policy, 1918–1945*, Series C, V, No. 66, 92–5; 92.

99 March 9, 1936, 15. This view is echoed, e.g., in Dalton's speech of March 26, 310 H.C. Deb. 5 s., col. 1454. Cf. the remarks of Sir Archibald Sinclair, who would later become a staunch advocate of a vigorous policy against Hitler: "For too long we refused to recognize the equality of Germany. Hitlerism is a revolt against humiliation, an expression of economic despair and a passionate demand for German equality of rights, status and opportunity with other nations. Nor, while we must condemn any violation of treaties, can we regard the occupation of German territory by German troops as so clearly indefensible, as an aggression against the territory of a member of the League." 309 H.C. Deb. 5 s., col. 1863.

100 See Chamberlain's statement to the House of Commons, March 14, 1938,

333 H.C. Deb. 5 s., cols. 45–52; and the *Times of London*, March 15, 1938, 15: "The employment of violent means, under any conditions, to secure an end, *even a legitimate end*, is bound to move the British Government and people to instinctive resentment and condemnation." Emphasis added.

101 *Times of London*, March 14, 1938, 15.

102 March 14, 1938; 333 H.C. Deb. 5 s., col. 61.

103 See, e.g., the *Times of London* editorial of September 27, 1938 (p. 13), which noted that "the right of the Sudeten Germans to be united with the Reich" was "admitted to be a perfectly reasonable case."

104 Taylor, *The Origins of the Second World War*, 157–8.

105 See Dirksen to Foreign Ministry, Political report on Anglo-German relations, July 18, 1938, *Documents on German Foreign Policy, 1918–1945*, Ser. D, I, No. 793, 1153–9. Dirksen noted that the British Cabinet "is showing growing understanding for the demands of Germany in the Sudeten question. It would be willing to make great sacrifices to satisfy Germany's other legitimate demands – on the *one* condition that these objectives are sought by peaceful means." *Ibid.*, 1159.

106 On September 21, 1938, Runciman wrote to Beneš that he had "much sympathy" with the Sudeten case. "It is a hard thing to be ruled by an alien race," he noted, and although he conceded that Czech rule had not been "actively oppressive" or "terroristic," it had been "marked by tactlessness, lack of understanding, petty intolerance and discrimination." Great Britain, Foreign Office, *Documents on British Foreign Policy, 1919–1939* (London: His Majesty's Stationery Office, 1946–1986), 3rd Ser., II, 675–9; 676.

107 Record of Anglo-French conversations held at No. 10 Downing St., September 18, 1938, *Documents on British Foreign Policy, 1919–1939*, 3rd Ser., II, No. 928, 380.

108 *Ibid.*

109 Daladier feared "that Germany's real aim was the disintegration of Czechoslovakia and the realisation of pan-German ideals through a march to the East," and that eventually, he would turn on Britain and France. *Ibid.*, 380-4.

110 *Ibid.*, 386. Cf. also Chamberlain's statement to the House, September 28, 1938; 339 H.C. Deb. 5 s., col. 15.

111 Feiling, *The Life of Neville Chamberlain*, 359–60. Iain Macleod's account is similar; *Neville Chamberlain* (London: Frederick Muller, 1961).

112 Macleod, *Neville Chamberlain*, 240. See also Taylor, *The Origins of the Second World War*, 135. Chamberlain's moral sensibilities, of course, pulled him in opposite directions. While he profoundly abhorred Nazism, he had a very strong aversion to war and a strong desire to do justice to the German people – all of which Feiling clearly recognized. See, e.g. *The Life of Neville Chamberlain*, 320–2. The story of Chamberlain's policy toward Hitler from Munich to Poland is in essence the story of a shifting moral center of gravity – a growing realization that the evil of Nazism was greater than the evil of bloodshed, a dawning recognition that the demands of justice required resisting Hitler, not appeasing him. Thus Chamberlain, champion of the peace, was ultimately able, in good conscience, to bring his nation into war.

113 Feiling, *The Life of Neville Chamberlain*, 323. See also *ibid.*, 341, 354. Note the irony of Duff Cooper's remarks in the House of Commons on September 28, 1938: "The Prime Minister has believed in addressing Herr Hitler through the language of sweet reasonableness. I have believed that he was more open to the language of the mailed fist." 339 H.C. Deb. 5 s., col. 34.

114 September 28, 1938; 339 H.C. Deb. 5 s., cols. 24–5. In a sense, Hitler did mean what he said; but the conditions he ultimately laid down for agreeing to guarantee Czechoslovakia's frontiers would have had the effect of reducing her to a vassal state. See Lacroix to Bonnet, February 18, 1939, *The French Yellow Book*, 60–1. The question of the German guarantee provides a striking and sobering reminder that Hitler's agenda was not what it seemed to the Western powers. On February 7, 1939, the French Ambassador in Prague reported a conversation with the Czech Foreign Minister, who had recently returned from Berlin: "What appears to have impressed him most was the importance which Herr Hitler and Herr von Ribbentrop attach to the Jewish question – absolutely out of proportion to the importance given to the other questions dealt with. The Foreign Minister of the Reich, as well as the Chancellor, are said to have stated emphatically that it was not possible to [give] a German guarantee to a state which does not eliminate the Jews." Lacroix to Bonnet, February 7, 1939, *ibid.*, 56.

115 Quoted in Macleod, *Neville Chamberlain*, 248.

116 Historians have not overlooked the influence of Nevile Henderson, Chamberlain's Ambassador in Berlin, whose sympathies with Germany's territorial claims were well-known (see, e.g., Aster, *1939*, 202). Donald Cameron Watt insists that Henderson "misrepresented Britain to Hitler and Hitler to Britain; and not only to Britain, but to Britain's partners in the Commonwealth, who then fed back his views of German reasonableness as pressure on the British Cabinet to seek accommodation with Germany. It can hardly be a coincidence that a decisive turn in the Cabinet's perception of Hitler occurred during his absence in Britain from November 1938 to February 1939." Watt, *How War Came*, 614. Even after Prague, Henderson clung to the importance of satisfying Germany's legitimate grievances. He wrote to Horace Wilson on May 24, 1939, "The Prague coup has affected our whole outlook towards Hitler but it has not altered the merits of the Danzig-Corridor case in themselves. I may be wrong but I am personally convinced that there can be no permanent peace in Europe until Danzig has reverted to Germany. The Poles cannot be master of the 400,000 Germans in Danzig – ergo Germany must be. I am sorry that I feel that way, but I fear that we are again on a bad wicket as we were over the Sudeten. By all means be firm and say 'No' to the Dictators: I am all for that on two conditions (a) that we have the force to back up our 'No' if need be, and (b) that we supplement it by the fair and just solution. Granted that the first condition is fulfilled, are we going to see or be able to insist that the second is? It is my doubt as to the answer to the second question which makes me pessimistic." Quoted in Simon Newman, *March 1939: The British Guarantee to Poland: A Study in the Continuity of British Foreign Policy* (Oxford: Clarendon Press, 1976), 214.

117 Wolfers argues that British policy was the product of "national interests, reasonableness, and a sense of justice, all working together ..." Wolfers, *Britain and France Between Two Wars*, 248–9.

118 Taylor writes: "Morality did not enter French calculations, or entered only to be discarded. The French recognized that it was their duty to assist Czechoslovakia; they rejected this duty as either too dangerous or too difficult. Léon Blum expressed French feeling best when he welcomed the agreement of Munich with a mixture of shame and relief. With the British, on the other hand, morality counted for a great deal. The British statesmen used practical arguments: the danger from air attack; the backwardness of their re-armament; the impossibility, even if adequately armed, of helping Czechoslovakia. But these arguments were used to reinforce morality, not to silence it. British policy over Czechoslovakia originated in the belief that Germany had a moral right to the Sudeten German territory, on grounds of national principle; and it drew the further corollary that this victory for self-determination would provide a stabler, more permanent peace in Europe." Taylor, *The Origins of the Second World War*, 189. Cf. also Lentin, *Lloyd George, Woodrow Wilson and the Guilt of Germany*, 132–54.

It is interesting to note the German perception that appeals to self-determination had had the desired effect on the French. For example, the German Ambassador in Paris filed the following report on June 5, 1939, noting that the French were simply unable to understand the idea of *lebensraum*: "For the French mind it represents something like a moral wilderness or political jungle. For them the right to 'living space' is the right to brutality and force, a relapse into barbarism. Daladier, in his latest speech, on June 4, displayed suitable horror at this bogey and repudiated the concept with violent gestures as inconceivable to him. For him there can be no sort of discussion on this subject. It was quite another matter, a short time ago, with the concept of 'right to self-determination.'" Welczeck to Foreign Ministry, June 5, 1939; *Documents on German Foreign Policy, 1918–1945*, Ser. D, VI, No. 477, 641–2.

119 Taylor, *The Origins of the Second World War*, 203.

120 See Chamberlain's speech in the House, March 15, 1938, 345 H.C. Deb. 5 s., col. 440; the editorial in the *Times of London*, March 15, 1939, 15; and Aster, *1939*, 29.

121 Wolfers, *Britain and France Between Two Wars*, 292–3. Although it is generally recognized that appeasement was an *ineffective* policy – because Hitler was unappeasable – there are those who still defend Chamberlain's policy by noting that the principle of self-determination was indeed at issue in Czechoslovakia in 1938, and by pointing out that this was a crucial difference between the Czech and Polish cases. The implication is that Chamberlain's desertion of appeasement in March 1939 was just as appropriate as his pursuit of it in 1938. See, e.g., Roy Douglas, *In the Year of Munich* (New York: St. Martin's, 1977), 130.

122 H.C. Deb. 5 s., col. 437.

123 Bonnet to Corbin, March 16, 1939, *The French Yellow Book*, 87.

124 345 H.C. Deb. 5 s., col. 2415.

125 *The French Yellow Book*, 124.

126 Bullock, *Hitler*, 313.
127 For a thorough reconstruction of the events during this period, see Aster, *1939*; Nicholas Fleming, *August 1939: The Last Days of Peace* (London: Peter Davies, 1979); Newman, *March 1939*; and Anita Prazmowska, *Britain, Poland, and the Eastern Front, 1939* (Cambridge: Cambridge University Press, 1987).
128 Toland, *Adolf Hitler*, 524.
129 *Documents on German Foreign Policy, 1918–1945*, Ser. D, VI, No. 433, 574–80; 575, 576; emphasis in the original.
130 See pp. 133–5, above.
131 See Hitler's speech to his Commanders-in-Chief, August 22, 1939; Noakes and Pridham, *Documents on Nazism*, 562–8, esp. 565–7. While Hitler's analysis suggested that he believed war with the Western Powers was *inevitable*, he evidently had concluded that it was not *imminent*. See also Watt, *How War Came*, 444–6. French Foreign Minister Georges Bonnet attempted on several occasions to convince his German counterpart, Joachim von Ribbentrop, that France would indeed support Poland in the event of a German attack; Note by Bonnet on his interview with Count von Welczeck, July 1, 1939, *The French Yellow Book*, 193–7; Bonnet to Ribbentrop, July 21, 1939, *ibid.*, 221–4; Bonnet to Ribbentrop, September 1, 1939, *ibid.*, 377–8. But Hitler had seen little evidence in the previous years that France took her commitments seriously. Bonnet's messages simply lacked credibility. As the crisis reached a crescendo, Daladier made a direct appeal to Hitler: "Unless you attribute to the French people a conception of national honour less high than that which I myself recognize in the German people, you cannot doubt either that France will be true to her solemn promises to other nations, such as Poland ... " But in the very next breath, Daladier undercut the force of his warning: "In so serious an hour I sincerely believe that no man endowed with human feelings could understand that a war of destruction should be allowed to break out without a last attempt at a pacific adjustment between Germany and Poland." Bonnet to Coulondre, August 26, 1939, *ibid.*, 311–12. In response, Hitler trotted out his tired appeal to the injustice of the "*Diktat* of Versailles." Coulondre to Bonnet, August 27, 1939, *ibid.*, 322.
132 Noël to Bonnet, April 29, 1939, *ibid.*, 132.
133 Vaux Saint-Cyr to Bonnet, March 30, 1939, *ibid.*, 110–11.
134 Noël to Bonnet, May 15, 1939, *ibid.*, 159–62.
135 Noël to Bonnet, August 12, 1939, *ibid.*, 261–2.
136 See, e.g, Bonnet to Cambon, August 24, 1939, *ibid.*, 290; Bonnet to Noël, August 24, 1939, *ibid.*, 293.
137 Coulondre to Bonnet, August 26, 1939, *ibid.*, 307.
138 *Ibid.*, 388.
139 September 3, 1939; *ibid.*, 401–2.
140 *Ibid.*, 384–92; 389. Albert Lebrun, President of the Republic, made a similar link when he justified war with Germany by appeal to France's "own safety and her faithfulness to her obligations." Address to the French Parliament, September 2, 1939, *ibid.*, 383–4.
141 As Daladier put it in his address to the nation on September 3: Germany

"desires the destruction of Poland, so as to be able to dominate Europe quickly and to enslave France." *Ibid.*, 403.

142 Quoted in Aster, *1939*, 33; see also *ibid.*, 104. On March 27, in a meeting of the Cabinet Foreign Policy Committee, Halifax declared that "there was probably no way in which France and ourselves could prevent Poland and Roumania from being overrun. We were faced with the dilemma of doing nothing, or entering into a devastating war. If we did nothing this in itself would mean a great accession to Germany's strength and a great loss to ourselves of sympathy and support in the United States, in the Balkan countries, and in other parts of the world. In those circumstances if we had to choose between two great evils he favoured our going to war." Quoted in Newman, *March 1939*, 152–3. In Cabinet on March 30, 1939, Halifax insisted that "plans had been prepared by Germany for a number of adventures, including an attack on Poland. The real question was which adventure Germany proposed to undertake next and at what date." *Ibid.*, 193.

143 *Ibid.*, 152.

144 *Ibid.*, 155.

145 *Ibid.*, 204.

146 Aster, *1939*, 191.

147 Wolfers, *Britain and France Between Two Wars*, 298.

148 CAB 23/100, Septemter 1, 1939, Public Record Office, London.

149 Quoted in Aster, *1939*, 369.

150 September 1, 1939; 351 H.C. Deb. 5 s., cols. 133–5: "There is a view among those who are now our enemies that might is right. I believe that right is might ... There is in the human spirit something which may be tortured and which may be temporarily suppressed but which can never be destroyed, and that is its determination to keep alive and keep fully aflame the lamp of liberty." Col. 135.

151 September 3, 1939; 351 H.C. Deb. 5 s., col. 295.

152 September 2, 1939, 11.

153 Cabinet 47(39)–49(39), CAB 23/100, September 1–3, 1939, PRO, London.

154 Bell, *The Origins of the Second World War in Europe*, 109.

155 The Cabinet was way out in front of Chamberlain, demanding that Britain issue Hitler a clear ultimatum to evacuate Poland with a strict time limit. Chamberlain's reluctance to attach a time limit to his demand that Germany evacuate Polish territory nearly prompted a ministerial revolt. Aster, *1939*, 376–85. See also Chamberlain's statement to the House, 1 September; 351 H.C. Deb. 5 s., cols. 126–33.

156 Chamberlain's declaration of war, September 3, 1939; 351 H.C. Deb. 5 s., col. 292.

157 Feiling, *The Life of Neville Chamberlain*, 415–16.

THE FALKLANDS/MALVINAS WAR

1 The English-language literature on the Falklands/Malvinas war is already considerable. Early general accounts and analyses include Peter Calvert, *The Falklands Crisis: The Rights and the Wrongs* (London: Frances Pinter,

1982); Alberto R. Coll and Anthony C. Arend, eds., *The Falklands War: Lessons for Strategy, Diplomacy, and International Law* (Boston: George Allen & Unwin, 1985); Christopher Dobson, John Miller, and Ronald Payne, *The Falklands Conflict* (London: Coronet, 1982); Paul Eddy, Magnus Linklater, Peter Gillman, and the Sunday Times Insight Team, *The Falklands War* (London: André Deutsch, 1982); Max Hastings and Simon Jenkins, *The Battle for the Falklands* (New York: Norton, 1984); and R. Reginald and Dr. Jeffrey M. Elliot, *Tempest in a Teapot: The Falkland Islands War* (San Bernardino, Calif.: Borgo Press, 1983). More recent works include Peter Beck, *The Falkland Islands as an International Problem* (London: Routledge, 1988); Michael Charlton, *The Little Platoon: Diplomacy and the Falklands Dispute* (London: Basil Blackwell, 1989); Alex Danchev, ed., *International Perspectives on the Falklands Conflict* (New York: St. Martin's, 1992); G.M. Dillon, *The Falklands, Politics and War* (London: Macmillan, 1989); Lawrence Freedman, *Britain and the Falklands War* (Oxford: Basil Blackwell, 1988); Lawrence Freedman and Virginia Gamba-Stonehouse, *Signals of War: The Falklands Conflict of 1982* (London: Faber and Faber, 1990); Lowell S. Gustafson, *The Sovereignty Dispute over the Falkland (Malvinas) Islands* (New York: Oxford University Press, 1988); Douglas Kinney, *National Interest/National Honor: The Diplomacy of the Falklands Crisis* (New York: Praeger, 1989); and, from an Argentine perspective, Rubén O. Moro, *The History of the South Atlantic Conflict*, trans. Michael Valeur (New York: Praeger, 1989). For a detailed military history, see Martin Middlebrook, *Operation Corporate: The Falklands War, 1982* (London: Viking, 1985). Useful guides to works written prior to and immediately after the war include the Argentine Ministry of Education's *Bibliografía Sobre Las Islas Malvinas* (Buenos Aires: Centro Nacional de Documentación e Información Educativa, 1982); Federico A. Daus and Raúl C. Rey Balmaceda, *Islas Malvinas: Geografía-Bibliografía* (Buenos Aires: OIKOS, Asociación para la Promoción de los Estudios Territoriales y Ambientales, 1982); and Sara de Mundo Lo, *The Falkland/Malvinas Islands: A Bibliography of Books (1619–1982)* (Urbana, Ill.: Albatross, 1983).

2 Most of the general works cited in n. 1 above deal with the question of misperceptions in considerable detail. Specifically on the issue, see also *Economist*, June 19, 1982, 35–43; Virginia Gamba, *The Falklands/Malvinas War: A Model for North-South Crisis Prevention* (Boston: Allen & Unwin, 1987); and Richard Ned Lebow, "Miscalculation in the South Atlantic: The Origins of the Falklands War," in Jervis, Lebow, and Stein, *Psychology & Deterrence*, 89–124.

3 The actual dispute was more complicated than this. Among the other issues involved were decolonization and acquisitive prescription. Moreover, Britain's assertion of the islanders' right of self-determination was qualified: Britain defended their *internal* rather than *external* self-determination (i.e., Britain did not claim that the islanders were sovereign). For extensive discussion and analysis of these subtle and complex issues, see especially Gustafson, *The Sovereignty Dispute over the Falkland (Malvinas) Islands*.

4 This point has been conceded by British officials at various times, although never publicly. For example, Gaston de Berhardt, a member of the Foreign Office's research department, prepared a memorandum on the sovereignty

dispute in 1910 that prompted the head of the American department, Sidney Spicer, to comment, "it is difficult to avoid the conclusion that the Argentine government's attitude is not altogether unjustified and that our action has been somewhat high-handed." A 1946 Foreign Office paper described the occupation of 1833 quite simply as "an act of unjustifiable aggression." Eddy *et al., The Falklands War*, 40–1.

5 Britain advanced an historical counter-claim, of course, and Argentina took pains to deflect the argument from self-determination, by arguing (among other things) that the principle should carry no more weight in 1982 than it did in 1833; that the population of the islands was too small for self-govern-ment; and that, since the Falkland Islands Company employed a third of the islands' work force, owned 46 percent of the land, and controlled almost all of the islands' services, "the Falkland islanders cannot determine by themselves what they want to do, because they are actually a factory which has been colonized and exploited by a monopoly which does not permit any freedom to the islanders." Laurio H. Destefani, *The Malvinas, the South Georgias and the South Sandwich Islands: The Conflict with Britain* (Buenos Aires: Edipress, 1982), 108, quoting Argentina's Extraordinary Ambassador to the UN and chief of the Argentine delegation to the commit-tee on decolonization, Bonifacio del Carril. See also Fritz L. Hoffmann and Olga Mingo Hoffmann, *Sovereignty Dispute: The Falklands/Malvinas, 1493–1982* (Boulder, Colo.: Westview, 1984), 12, 103. The sovereignty dispute was therefore not merely a dialogue of the deaf, but a full-fledged debate.

All major works on the conflict deal with the history of the dispute; many of those written in English are understandably sympathetic to Britain. Two exceptions are Hoffmann and Hoffmann, *Sovereignty Dispute*, and Federico Meléndez, *The Falklands: A Study in International Confrontation* (Carlsbad, Calif.: Arcadia Publications, 1984). The official Argentine case may be found in Destefani, *The Malvinas, the South Georgias and the South Sandwich Islands*, esp. 37–110. A concise analysis from the British perspective may be found in J.C.J. Metford, "Falklands or Malvinas? The Background to the Dispute," *International Affairs*, 44, No. 3 (July 1968), 463–81. The official British case is contained in two Foreign and Commonwealth Office publications: *The Disputed Islands: The Falkland Crisis: A History & Background* (London: Her Majesty's Stationery Office, 1982), 29–36; and *The Falkland Islands: The Facts*, rev. edn. (London: Her Majesty's Stationery Office, 1982). For a balanced discussion of both cases, see Alfred Rubin, "Historical and Legal Back-ground of the Falkland/Malvinas Dispute," in Coll and Arend, *The Falklands War*, 9–21. For a summary of the cases, and all major relevant documents, see Raphael Perl, *The Falkland Islands Dispute in International Law and Politics: A Documentary Sourcebook* (London: Oceana Publications, 1983). It is not my purpose in this analysis to pass judgment on the merits of the arguments made on either side, merely to bear witness to their effects.

6 For a discussion and thinly veiled attack on this policy, see John Hickey, "Keep the Falklands British? The Principle of Self-Determination of Dependent Territories," *Inter-American Economic Affairs*, 31, No. 1 (Summer 1977), 77–88.

7 Hoffmann and Hoffmann, *Sovereignty Dispute*, 109.

8 The Rt. Hon. Lord Franks, Chairman, *Falkland Islands Review: Report of a Committee of Privy Counsellors* (London: Her Majesty's Stationery Office, 1983) (hereafter *Franks Report*), 6.

9 See Clive Ellerby, "The Role of the Falkland Lobby, 1968–1990," in Danchev, ed., *International Perspectives on the Falklands Conflict*, 85–108.

10 Hastings and Jenkins, *The Battle for the Falklands*, 23.

11 Tam Dalyell, *One Man's Falklands . . .* (London: Cecil Woolf, 1982), 10.

12 Hoffmann and Hoffmann, *Sovereignty Dispute*, 127.

13 Lord Shackleton, *Economic Survey of the Falkland Islands* (London: Economist Intelligence Unit, 1976). For a distillation of Shackleton's 400-page report, see Lord Shackleton, with contributions from R.J. Storey and R. Johnson, "Prospects of the Falkland Islands," *The Geographical Journal*, 143, Part 1 (March 1977), 1–13.

14 Hoffmann and Hoffmann, *Sovereignty Dispute*, 127–8. The two countries restored ambassadorial relations in 1979.

15 *Franks Report*, 75. On the nature of the military regime, see Charles Maechling, Jr., "The Argentina Pariah," *Foreign Policy*, No. 45 (Winter 1981–2), 69–83.

16 *Franks Report*, 20. Foreign Minister Lord Carrington sent a revised list of options to Thatcher and the other members of the Defence Committee in a minute on September 20, 1979. They were: (1) Fortress Falklands; (2) protracted negotiations with no concession on sovereignty; and (3) substantive negotiations on sovereignty. *Ibid.*, 20–1.

17 The two foreign ministries had apparently discussed the leaseback option as early as 1940. The index of Foreign Office files at the Public Record Office lists a 1940 file entitled, "Proposed offer by HMG to reunite [*sic*] Falkland Islands with Argentina and acceptance of lease." FO 93 14/4 (A 4514/2382/2, Public Record Office, London.) Britain also apparently offered Argentina the use of a harbor in the islands (FO 93 14/4 (A 3160/2382/2)). Unfortunately, the Foreign Office has embargoed both documents until 2016. It must be recalled, however, that these discussions were held in the middle of World War II, when Britain had a very strong immediate interest in improving relations with Argentina.

18 *Franks Report*, 23.

19 995 H.C. Deb. 5 s., cols. 128–9.

20 For the entire debate, see 995 H.C. Deb. 5 s., cols. 128–34.

21 Charlton, *The Little Platoon*, 74.

22 Russell Johnson, 995 H.C. Deb. 5 s., col. 130.

23 *Times of London*, December 3, 1980, 8. A lone dissenting voice complained that "the interests of 1,800 Falkland islanders [were taking] precedence over the interests of 55 million people in the United Kingdom." Frank Hooley, 995 H.C. Deb. 5 s., col. 130.

24 Hoffmann and Hoffmann, *Sovereignty Dispute*, 144.

25 Dobson *et al.*, *The Falklands Conflict*, 11; Eddy *et al.*, *The Falklands War*, 74; Hoffmann and Hoffmann, *Sovereignty Dispute*, 147.

26 Galtieri interview with Oriana Fallaci, *Times of London*, June 12, 1982, 4.

27 *Franks Report*, 25.

28 J. Iglesias Rouco, "La Ofensiva Exterior," *La Prensa*, January 24, 1982, 1, 4.

29 *Franks Report*, 38.

30 *Ibid.*, 36–7.

31 *Ibid.*, 37.

32 *Ibid.*, 41.

33 *Ibid.*, 42.

34 *Ibid.*, 45–6.

35 This finding suggested that the junta had decided to invade the Falklands if the British government did not present a constructive proposal by the end of the week. Such a proposal would have to include a concrete agreement to talk about the transfer of sovereignty within a set period of time. *Ibid.*, 71.

36 See generally the earlier works cited in n. 1 above. See also Jimmy Burns, *The Land that Lost its Heroes: The Falklands, the Post-War, and Alfonsin* (London: Bloomsbury, 1987), 2.

37 See Pym's very first statement as Secretary of State for Foreign and Commonwealth Affairs, April 7, 1982 (21 H.C. Deb. 6 s., col. 959); and Alexander M. Haig, Jr., *Caveat: Realism, Reagan, and Foreign Policy* (New York: Macmillan, 1984), 296.

38 Gustafson, *The Sovereignty Dispute over the Falkland (Malvinas) Islands*, 123.

39 *Economist*, April 10, 1982, 22; Burns, *The Land that Lost its Heroes*, 29.

40 Hastings and Jenkins, *The Battle for the Falklands*, 65.

41 *Franks Report*, 73. The Franks Commission's interpretations of events have been somewhat controversial. The commission sought to determine whether or not the British government should have been able to anticipate the Argentine invasion, and whether it had been derelict in its duties by not taking measures to forestall it. It answered both questions in the negative, prompting charges that the report was a whitewash of the Thatcher government. See, e.g., Lebow, "The Origins of the Falklands War," 249 n. 1. These charges are unfounded and unfair, as Alex Danchev demonstrates: "The Franks Report: a Chronicle of Unripe Time," in Danchev, ed., *International Perspectives on the Falklands Conflict*, 127–52. For an argument suggesting that the British government should have anticipated the Argentine move, see Eddy *et al.*, *The Falklands War*, 72–80.

42 Galtieri interview with Oriana Fallaci, *Times of London*, June 12, 1982, 4.

43 *Economist*, May 1, 1982, 21. Virginia Gamba insists in any case that "the 3-month regime of Galtieri was the least unpopular of all previous military governments," raising further questions on this score. Gamba, *The Falklands/Malvinas War*, 77.

44 *Ibid.*, 132–3.

45 The plan involved a surprise landing on the islands, and is thought to have also involved the removal of the existing population and its replacement by Argentine settlers – a mirror image of the British operation in 1833. Hastings and Jenkins, *The Battle for the Falklands*, 31.

46 Charlton, *The Little Platoon*, 116.

47 Haig, *Caveat*, 288.

48 *Times of London*, April 3, 1982, 3.

49 Gustafson, *The Sovereignty Dispute over the Falkland (Malvinas) Islands*, 147.

50 Oscar Raúl Cardosa, Ricardo Kirschbaum, and Eduardo van der Kooy,

Malvinas: The Secret Plot, unpublished ms., cited in Kinney, *National Interest/ National Honor*, 84; Hastings and Jenkins, *The Battle for the Falklands*, 46; Burns, *The Land that Lost its Heroes*, 30; Eddy *et al.*, *The Falklands War*, 27.

51 *Ibid.*, 27.

52 Freedman and Gamba-Stonehouse, *Signals of War*, 12–13.

53 Quoted in Charlton, *The Little Platoon*, 111.

54 Freedman and Gamba-Stonehouse, *Signals of War*, 23.

55 *Franks Report*, 37.

56 Quoted in Eddy *et al.*, *The Falklands War*, 28.

57 Burns, *The Land that Lost its Heroes*, 38.

58 Gustafson, *The Sovereignty Dispute over the Falkland (Malvinas) Islands*, 126.

59 For detailed analyses of Davidoff's visits, see Freedman and Gamba-Stonehouse, *Signals of War*, 39–48; and Moro, *The History of the South Atlantic Conflict*, 8–14. On the dispute within Argentina about Davidoff's role, see Kinney, *National Interest/National Honor*, 62.

60 Burns, *The Land that Lost its Heroes*, 41–8.

61 *Ibid.*, 44.

62 *Ibid.*, 46.

63 Gustafson, *The Sovereignty Dispute over the Falkland (Malvinas) Islands*, 126. Such was the opinion of British intelligence, which estimated that the episode "had not been contrived by the Argentine Government, but that the junta was taking full advantage of the incident to speed up negotiations on the transfer of sovereignty." *Franks Report*, 66. The Franks Report concluded that "Despite Sr. Davidoff's close contacts with some senior Argentine naval officers, the unauthorized landing was not considered to be part of the Navy's plans. There was no central coordination of Argentine policy and the Junta's intentions were not known, but it had a wide range of options open to it." *Ibid.*

64 Lawrence Freedman, "The Falklands War and the Concept of Escalation," in Danchev, ed., *International Perspectives on the Falklands Conflict*, 178. Britain's threat to remove Davidoff's men by force, in turn, may have been based on an incorrect report from the members of the British Antarctic Survey who discovered them, that the *Bahía Buen Suceso* had disembarked military personnel. Charlton, *The Little Platoon*, 113.

65 Galtieri interview with Oriana Fallaci, *Times of London*, June 12, 1982, 4.

66 Admiral Busser recalls that Argentina "had a very short period in which to act, and during that period Great Britain could *not* act. *After* that the position would be absolutely the opposite. The British *could* act, and Argentina would not be in any position to stop the scrap workers being removed from the Georgias . . . The overall situation, at the time, was set up in the following terms. British forces are heading south. Either we continue negotiations, which would not solve the problem but would give the British ships time to arrive. Or we could send our claim to the UN Security Council, but there the British had a veto and the prospect was dim. Third was the military solution which would *force* Britain to negotiate. The basic idea was to recover the islands with a small force, and leave a small force there. As we did. Of all these alternatives, only the military option offered the promise of a solution." Quoted in Charlton, *The Little Platoon*, 114–15.

67 Indeed, no British marines or civilians were killed in the initial Argentine invasion.

68 Freedman and Gamba-Stonehouse, *Signals of War*, 67.

69 Freedman, "The Falklands War and the Concept of Escalation," 178. A certain air of mystery surrounds the perception of a closing window of opportunity, for when the junta made its decision on March 26 to invade, the only hard information it had on British reinforcements heading toward the Falklands were reports that two unarmed ships attached to the British Antarctic Survey had departed for Port Stanley. One, the RRS *John Biscoe*, sailed from Montevideo with a detachment of marines on March 23; the other, the RRS *Bransfield*, left Punta Arenas on March 25. Hard information on the movement of frigates and nuclear submarines arrived only after the decision to invade had been made. Freedman and Gamba-Stonehouse, *Signals of War*, 76–7. Yet Anaya claimed that he was heavily influenced by a BBC announcement on March 17 suggesting that the nuclear-powered attack submarine HMS *Superb* had sailed from Gibraltar. He later told an American officer, Admiral Harry Train, who in 1982 was NATO's Supreme Allied Commander Atlantic, that he believed this was "his last opportunity to carry out his life's ambition to retake the Malvinas Islands for Argentina. He said, when this nuclear-powered submarine arrived on the scene, it would not be possible to execute the surface operations that would be required to place Argentine troops ashore at Port Stanley. The window of opportunity was limited by the steaming time it would take HMS *Superb* to get from Gibraltar to the vicinity of the Falklands." The BBC has no record of such a report; it first reported on the movement of British submarines on March 29. Charlton, *The Little Platoon*, 116. It is possible, of course, that the Junta decided on the basis of Argentine intelligence reports, the content of which we do not know at present.

70 Freedman and Gamba-Stonehouse, *Signals of War*, 68.

71 Haig, *Caveat*, 289. Cf. also *Times of London*, May 5, 1982, 10.

72 One of the few books that claims the islands have significant economic and strategic value is Alejandro Dabat and Luis Lorenzano, *Argentina: The Malvinas and the End of Military Rule*, trans. Ralph Johnstone (London: Verso, 1894), 45–50. Their argument is thin and unpersuasive.

73 *Economist*, April 24, 1982, 14.

74 See, e.g., Burns, *The Land that Lost its Heroes*, 45.

75 See p. 167, above.

76 The fact that National Security Directive 1/82 mentioned the exploration of resources at all is the primary reason why the Argentine evaluation in Table 6.1 is "very strong" rather than "conclusive."

77 See, e.g., Hoffmann and Hoffmann, *Sovereignty Dispute*, 123–6; Metford, "Falklands or Malvinas? The Background to the Dispute," 480; and Gustafson, *The Sovereignty Dispute over the Falkland (Malvinas) Islands*, 81–118.

78 Beck, *The Falkland Islands as an International Problem*, 185; citing Lord Shackleton, *Falkland Islands: Economic Study 1982*, Cmnd. 8653 (London: Her Majesty's Stationery Office, 1982).

79 Peter Calvert writes: "In the case of the Falkland Islands there is no evidence that their economic value as such was of any interest to Argentina

until United States speculation that their territorial waters might contain valuable oil reserves appeared to receive some confirmation from the Shackleton Report. The effect of this was to strengthen the determination of the military government that took power in 1976 to resist any attempt to exploit what it saw as part of the Argentine patrimony. It should be said that this was a purely negative sentiment. The military government were not, as far as it can be ascertained, motivated in any way by commercial considerations ... For their part, the islanders did not realise (and still have not realised) that the greater the economic development of the islands, the more nationalist sentiment would be generated on the mainland." Calvert, "The Malvinas as a Factor in Argentine Politics," 51.

80 Haig, *Caveat*, 268.

81 Kinney, *National Interest/National Honor*, 87.

82 In 1977, an International Court of Arbitration awarded the islands to Chile, but did not pronounce on the seaward extension of either side's claims. Argentina refused to acknowledge the award, and in 1978 the two nations came to the brink of war. The Pope appointed a mediator, who again favored Chile. Argentina delayed responding, and in 1982 announced its intention to abrogate a treaty with Chile that would have required the dispute to be referred to the International Court of Justice. *Franks Report*, 75.

83 Eddy *et al.*, *The Falklands War*, 29.

84 Freedman, *Britain and the Falklands War*, 112. Rubén Moro claims that the region is strategically important because of the volume of oil shipped around the Cape of Good Hope (30 percent of that consumed by Western Europe; 25 percent of that imported by the United States). Moro, *The History of the South Atlantic Conflict*, 17. The Falkland Islands, however, are thousands of miles from the Cape of Good Hope, and no force operating from them could hope to dominate the tip of Southern Africa. Moreover, it is difficult to imagine why either Britain or Argentina would wish to interdict oil traffic from the Persian Gulf to Europe and North America.

85 In 1982, the Chilean navy outnumbered the Argentine navy in combat vessels by a slight margin (20 to 16), but Argentina had an aircraft carrier, while Chile did not, which more than compensated for any numerical disadvantage. In addition, Argentina enjoyed important advantages in naval weaponry. *The Military Balance 1980–1981* (London: International Institute for Strategic Studies, 1981), 78, 80.

86 It is clear that the Malvinas were not considered an offset to the Beagle Channel islands symbolically or psychologically, because President Raúl Alfonsín held a referendum on the award of Chilean sovereignty on November 25, 1984, which the voters approved by a four-to-one margin. Gustafson, *The Sovereignty Dispute over the Falkland (Malvinas) Islands*, 183. Neither Alfonsín nor his successor, Carlos Menem, has relinquished Argentina's claim to the Malvinas.

87 Haig, *Caveat*, 277.

88 Galtieri interview with Oriana Fallaci, *Times of London*, June 12, 1982, 4. See also Destefani, *The Malvinas, the South Georgias and the South Sandwich Islands*, 7. The communiqué issued upon the capture of the islands on April 2 declared, "The military junta as the supreme organ of state, communi-

cates to the people of the Argentine nation that today ... the Republic, through the means of its armed forces, by means of the successful completion of a combined operation, have recovered the Islas Malvinas, Georgias and Sandwich del Sur for the national patrimony. In this manner, Argentine sovereignty has been assured over all the territory of the said islands and their respective sea and air spaces. May the entire country understand the profound and unequivocal national significance of this decision, in order that responsibility and collective effort might accompany this enterprise and permit, with God's help, the conversion into reality of a legitimate right of the Argentine people, held back patiently and prudently for almost 150 years." *The Falklands War: The Official History* (London: Latin American Newsletters, 1983), 11.

89 Haig, *Caveat*, 264.
90 See Burns, *The Land that Lost its Heroes*, 25.
91 Hoffmann and Hoffmann, *Sovereignty Dispute*, xiii.
92 *Ibid.*, 111.
93 Hastings and Jenkins, *The Battle for the Falklands*, 9.
94 Eddy *et al.*, *The Falklands War*, 49.
95 Hoffmann and Hoffmann, *Sovereignty Dispute*, 133.
96 Lebow, "Miscalculation in the South Atlantic," 98.
97 *Franks Report*, 28.
98 *Ibid.*
99 *Ibid.*, 29.
100 Haroldo Foulkes, *Las Malvinas, Una Causa Nacional*, 2nd edn. (Buenos Aires: Ediciones Corregidor, 1982).
101 *Franks Report*, 37–9.
102 Hoffmann and Hoffmann, *Sovereignty Dispute*, 149.
103 So also were the members of the Argentine foreign-policy establishment, who, according to David Gompert, Haig's assistant, were "more intense, though of course less frenzied" about the Malvinas issue than the throngs filling the streets of Buenos Aires. David C. Gompert, "American Diplomacy and the Haig Mission: An Insider's Perspective," in Coll and Arend, *The Falklands War*, 108.
104 Gustafson, *The Sovereignty Dispute over the Falkland (Malvinas) Islands*, 147. For a good critique of the view that Galtieri and Thatcher acted cynically in the Falklands/Malvinas episode, see *ibid.*, 144–68.
105 On the Argentine equation between sovereignty and holy sanction, and its institutional basis, see esp. Burns, *The Land that Lost its Heroes*, 68–73.
106 Argentine governments may have considered invading the islands several times in this century, only to be deterred. Burns reports that in 1942, the Argentine government reportedly instructed the military academy in Buenos Aires to study the feasibility of an invasion of the islands, and that in December 1966 an Argentine submarine conducted elaborate reconnaissance on East Falkland. *Ibid.*, 3–5. Hastings and Jenkins suggest that the Videla regime may have considered an invasion after the 1976 coup, and again after Argentina's World Cup victory in 1978, but that British submarine strength may have been a dissuading factor. *The Battle for the Falklands*, 32. The Franks Report acknowledges that, in 1977, Argentina

stepped up its military activities in the region, and that Britain responded by deploying a nuclear-powered submarine in the vicinity of the islands, and by ordering two frigates to stand by 1,000 miles away. The purpose of these deployments was to "be able to respond flexibly to limited acts of aggression." However, these deployments were shrouded in utmost secrecy, and the Franks Commission "found no evidence that the Argentine Government ever came to know" of them. *Franks Report*, 18.

107 Hastings and Jenkins, *The Battle for the Falklands*, 16.

108 Those who have criticized the British government for not perceiving Argentine intentions and not acting forcefully to forestall them point directly to this fact. As Tam Dalyell remarked in his testimony to Lord Franks, "the Foreign Office must have known that the Galtieri regime was much more determined than any of its predecessors over the 'Malvinas', and that the Argentinian people set considerable store by getting the islands back, before the 150th anniversary of their 'take-over' in 1833." Letter from Dalyell to Lord Franks, August 23, 1982; in Dalyell, *One Man's Falklands . . .*, Appendix A, 132.

The British attitude is well represented by the following exchange between Jeffrey Elliot and Marrack Goulding, former Counsellor and Head of Chancery of the British Mission to the United Nations (Reginald and Elliot, *Tempest in a Teapot*, 111):

> J.E.: Asked about the Argentine invasion, the Panamanian representative to the United Nations argued that invading the island [*sic*] was the only way Argentina could dramatize for the world a claim it has been making continuously for 150 years. Can you understand their frustration over the negotiating process and their ultimate decision to invade the islands?
>
> M.G.: The argument is rather like the argument about the chap who likes the look of the car next door, and so attempts to persuade the owner to part with it on his terms. When he fails, the chap pinches the car, claiming that he had exhausted all other avenues. The fact that you want something doesn't necessarily mean that you have a right to it.

109 See Gompert, "American Diplomacy and the Haig Mission," 109.

110 Haig, *Caveat*, 279. Whenever Haig felt he had made some progress toward softening the junta's intransigence, he would be rebuffed by a simple note such as that handed to him by Costa Méndez as he left for London on April 19: "It is absolutely essential and *conditio sine qua non* that negotiations will have to conclude with a result on December 31, 1982. This result must include a recognition of Argentinian sovereignty over the islands." *Ibid.*, 290.

111 According to Alexander Haig, who met repeatedly with the War Cabinet in London, the British simply would not move from the position that self-determination for the islanders was the "irreducible requirement for settlement." Haig, *Caveat*, 274, 283. The War Cabinet included the Prime Minister; her deputy, the Home Secretary, William Whitelaw; the Foreign Secretary, Francis Pym; the Defence Secretary, John Nott; and the Paymaster-

General and Chairman of the Conservative Party, Cecil Parkinson. Freedman, *Britain and the Falklands War*, 11.

112 Burns, *The Land that Lost its Heroes*, 2. A rare exception is the Marxist analysis of Dabat and Lorenzano: "the main objective of the Junta in 'recovering' the Malvinas was to forge a new basis for consensus and to relegitimize the state and the monopoly-finance fractions controlling it." *Argentina: The Malvinas and the End of Military Rule*, 76.

113 Burns, *The Land that Lost its Heroes*, 88–9. Peter Calvert writes, "It is certainly significant that, despite the flood of controversy about the military government and the war, no one in Argentina questioned either the validity or the value of the Argentine claim to the islands. Only one scholar was prepared to tell his fellow-countrymen that the grounds for the claim were even slightly less than proved beyond doubt ... [E]very qualification or reservation about any aspect of British policy expressed by a British writer or speaker was rapidly hailed in Buenos Aires as 'proof' of the essential rightness of the Argentine position." Calvert, "The Malvinas as a Factor in Argentine Politics," 58.

114 Gustafson, *The Sovereignty Dispute over the Falkland (Malvinas) Islands*, 121.

115 *Ibid.*, 130.

116 Quoted in Charlton, *The Little Platoon*, 102 (emphasis in the original).

117 Reginald and Elliot, *Tempest in a Teapot*, 124, 127.

118 Gamba, *The Falklands/Malvinas War*, 132.

119 Hastings and Jenkins, *The Battle for the Falklands*, 75.

120 Lebow, "Miscalculation in the South Atlantic," 109.

121 "Thoughts on the Late Transactions respecting Falkland's Islands," quoted in Eddy *et al.*, *The Falklands War*, 38.

122 See, e.g., Hastings and Jenkins, *The Battle for the Falklands*, 30: "The theory, widely held in Latin America and the USA, that Britain's attachment to the Falklands is based on the prospect of glowing oil riches has no foundation."

123 Gustafson notes that the Falklands' true strategic worth is well-indicated by Britain's decision to scrap *Endurance*. Gustafson, *The Sovereignty Dispute over the Falkland (Malvinas) Islands*, 141. British Minister of Defence Sir John Nott flatly stated after the war, "I've never been able to understand the global strategists' views of the importance of the South Atlantic, frankly." Charlton, *The Little Platoon*, 73.

124 Russell Johnson; April 3, 1982; 21 H.C. Deb. 6 s., col. 655.

125 April 14, 1982; 21 H.C. Deb. 6 s., col. 1155. Cf. also Metford, "Falklands or Malvinas? The Background to the Dispute," 480: "Britain would like to dispossess herself of the last remnants of an imperial past, especially when they are of no economic benefit, but she has an inescapable moral commitment to the Falkland Islanders who have no wish to be other than British."

126 "We cannot allow the democratic rights of the islanders to be denied by the territorial ambitions of Argentina ... The people of the Falkland Islands, like the people of the United Kingdom, are an island race. Their way of life is British; their allegiance is to the Crown. They are few in number, but they have the right to live in peace, to choose their own way of life and to determine their own allegiance ... It is the wish of the British people and

the duty of Her Majesty's Government to do everything that we can to uphold that right. That will be our hope and our endeavour and, I believe, the resolve of every member of the House." April 3, 1982; 21 H.C. Deb. 6 s., cols. 634, 638. "Our objective, endorsed by all sides of the House in recent debates, is that the people of the Falkland Islands shall be free to determine their own way of life and their own future. The wishes of the islanders must be paramount." April 14, 1982; 21 H.C. Deb. 6 s., col. 1146. See also April 7, 1982; 21 H.C. Deb. 6 s., col. 972.

127 "[T]he rights and the circumstances of the people in the Falkland Islands must be uppermost in our minds. There is no question in the Falkland Islands of any colonial dependence or anything of the sort. It is a question of people who wish to be associated with this country and who have built their whole lives on the basis of association with this country. We have a moral duty, a political duty and every other kind of duty to ensure that that is sustained." April 3, 1982; 21 H.C. Deb. 6 s., col. 638.

128 "I hope that the whole House supports the right of the Falkland Islanders to self-determination and to live in peace under a Government of their own choosing, as they have been able to do for the last 150 years. The right of self-determination is a fundamental human right that we are responsible for restoring ..." April 7, 1982; 21 H.C. Deb. 6 s., col. 965.

129 Carrington's letter of resignation said, "We must ... do everything we can to uphold the right of the islanders to live in peace, to choose their own way of life and to determine their own allegiance." April 7, 1982; 21 H.C. Deb. 6 s., col. 986.

130 "What matters is what the islanders want. It is their rights that have been taken away by naked aggression. It is their rights that we should restore." April 7, 1982; 21 H.C. Deb. 6 s., col. 1045.

131 See, e.g., the debates on April 3 (21 H.C. Deb. 6 s., cols. 633–68); April 7 (21 H.C. Deb. 6 s., cols. 959–1052); April 14 (21 H.C. Deb. 6 s., cols. 1146–208); April 19 (22 H.C. Deb. 6 s., cols. 21–8); April 21 (22 H.C. Deb. 6 s., cols. 271–80); April 26 (22 H.C. Deb. 6 s., cols. 609–17); and April 29 (22 H.C. Deb. 6 s., cols. 980–1060).

132 E.g., 77 percent in a MORI poll conducted on April 20–21; *Economist*, April 24, 1982, 27.

133 See Robert Harris, *Gotcha! The Media, the Government and the Falklands Crisis* (London: Faber and Faber, 1983), 38. The *Times of London* editorial of April 5 entitled, "We are all Falklanders Now," declared, "The objective therefore is the restoration of British sovereignty over the Falklands and the freedom for the Falklanders to choose what to do with their lives."

134 See Haig, *Caveat*, 267, 272.

135 On April 26, Thatcher declared that "unprovoked aggression must not be allowed to succeed. If it does, there will be no international law and many people will fear for their future." 22 H.C. Deb. 6 s., col. 613; cf. also May 20, 1982, 24 H.C. Deb. 6 s., col. 478.

136 See, e.g., Michael Foot's remarks on April 3 (21 H.C. Deb. 6 s., col. 639) and April 14 (21 H.C. Deb. 6 s., col. 1154). On April 7, Francis Pym declared, "If the world does not oblige Argentina to restore [the islanders'] rights, tomorrow it will be someone else's turn to suffer aggression and occu-

pation." 21 H.C. Deb. 6 s., col. 961. Cf. also the remarks of Sir Anthony Kershaw ("What is at stake is the credibility of this country – whether or not we intend to defend ourselves. If we do not defend the Falkland Islands, some may believe that we will not defend other territories and interests." April 7, 1982; 21 H.C. Deb. 6 s., col. 990); and Douglas Jay ("Effective action is necessary for two reasons. First, the rights of the people in the Falkland Islands are at stake. It does not matter how the British forces originally got there 150 years ago. What matters now is that these people wish to remain British, and that is the right of self-determination. Secondly, surely, as the whole history of this country has shown, if one gives way to this sort of desperate, illegal action, things will not get better, but will get worse." April 3, 1982; 21 H.C. Deb. 6 s., cols. 658–9).

137 *Economist*, May 15, 1982, 14; cf. also April 10, 1982, 11–13. In an editorial on April 14 (p. 9), the *Times of London* shifted the emphasis of its support for a forceful response in the direction of the credibility issue, proclaiming that "The principle of the matter is that aggression should be checked wherever and whenever it occurs by those best equipped to check it." In this instance, of course, this would have been the United States, not Great Britain.

138 See, e.g., the remarks of Patrick Cormack (Staffordshire, South-West): "I should think that there should be some anxious people in Gibraltar today. There will also be anxious people in Hong Kong." April 3, 1982; 21 H.C. Deb. 6 s., col. 652. Cf. also Denis Healey's remarks, April 7, 1982; 21 H.C. Deb. 6 s., col. 965.

139 *Economist*, April 17, 1982, 29, 64–5; *Times of London*, April 5, 1982, 4. Indeed, the two cases were very different: Gibraltar had been ceded to Britain in perpetuity by the Treat of Utrecht in 1713, whereas no Anglo-Argentine treaty existed with respect to the Falklands. The status of Hong Kong was likewise very different. There the British were simply tenants whose lease was due to expire in 1997. These various differences no doubt account for the rather surprising infrequency of the references to Gibraltar and Hong Kong during the Falklands crisis.

140 Dobson *et al.*, *The Falklands Conflict*, 206.

141 For a thorough discussion of British public opinion during the war, see Freedman, *Britain and the Falklands War*, 92–104.

142 As the crisis wore on, there was a slight tendency in the direction of increasing belligerence. (See the weekly reports in the *Economist*.) But the sinkings of the *General Belgrano* and the *Sheffield* in early May did not register a statistically significant change. "The 53 percent who said [loss of life] was worth it this week is less than the 58 percent who said the same last week before any loss of life, but is still up on the 44 percent who felt this way at the start of the crisis a month ago." *Economist*, May 8, 1982, 25. As British troops began landing on May 21, a poll indicated 76 percent of Britons favored the assault, and 53 percent considered a successful operation worth heavy casualties. Dobson *et al.*, *The Falklands Conflict*, 116.

143 For the British and Argentine orders of battle, see Middlebrook, *Operation Corporate*, 395–409.

144 See, e.g., Labour Party President Dame Judith Hart's speech, April 14,

1982; 21 H.C. Deb. 6 s., cols. 1160–2. A few Falklanders were evidently willing to acquiesce in Argentine rule and actively opposed a British military response out of fear for their lives. See the *Times of London*, April 10, 1982, 1. But the overwhelming majority remained hostile to the Argentine invaders and welcomed the British response. See John Smith, *74 Days: An Islander's Diary of the Falklands Occupation* (London: Century, 1984).

145 See, e.g., Hastings and Jenkins, *The Battle for the Falklands*, 337.

146 Gustafson, *The Sovereignty Dispute over the Falkland (Malvinas) Islands*, 150.

147 Reginald and Elliot, *Tempest in a Teapot*, 100–1.

148 Eddy *et al.*, *The Falklands War*, 172–3.

149 For the text of the British draft of the interim agreement, see Perl, *The Falkland Islands Dispute in International Law and Politics*, 487–8. The Argentine counterproposal follows, on p. 488.

150 Hastings and Jenkins, *The Battle for the Falklands*, 173.

151 924 H.C. Deb. 6 s., col. 479.

152 *Economist*, June 19, 1982, 34. Lawrence Freedman insists that by the mid-1980s, the cost of waging the war, replacing lost equipment, replenishing stores, and developing and maintaining the military garrison had reached £1.5 million per islander per year, a figure that was expected to rise to £2 million by the end of the decade. Freedman, *Britain and the Falklands War*, 66. For official estimates, see Dillon, *The Falklands, Politics and War*, 237–42.

153 As Hastings and Jenkins put it, Haig's mediation efforts might well have succeeded were it not for the fact that both sides "were entrenched on matters of principle in which the US had no leverage." Hastings and Jenkins, *The Battle for the Falklands*, 140.

154 This is not to suggest that all misperceptions in the Falklands/Malvinas war were value-driven, merely that philosophical incongruities aggravated them. Nor does this mean that an inability to sympathize with a normative commitment is the only reason to question its sincerity or power. Some in Britain, for example, shared with Argentina a deep suspicion of the British government's commitment to the principle of self-determination because of their reading of events in Diego Garcia just a few years before: "If the rights of islanders were sacred, let alone submission by Britain to the views or alleged views of islanders, why was it that a British Government could so readily be a party to the transportation of Diego Garcians from their own island in the Indian Ocean to Mauritius? The Diego Garcians were dumped on the quayside and told to make their own way as best they could. In fact, they were to languish and lead miserable lives in alien surroundings, simply because an Anglo-American military base was required in the British Indian Ocean territories." Dalyell, *One Man's Falklands . . .*, 12. A *possible* interpretation of the juxtaposition of these two events is that the British did not take the principle of self-determination seriously; another more likely interpretation is that they took it very seriously indeed, but applied it selectively. In race, language, place of origin, customs, mores, and sympathy, the Falkland Islanders were just like the British; in all these respects, the Diego Garcians were different. It is a regrettable fact of human existence that groups often give preferential treatment to those they consider their own, but the selective

application of a principle to an "in-group" does not necessarily detract from its sincerity in that specific circumstance.

155 Reginald and Elliot, *Tempest in a Teapot*, 111.

JUSTICE AND INJUSTICE IN A GLOBAL CONTEXT

1 When I speak of international society, I am referring to Hedley Bull's society of states. It is, of course, possible to speak of innumerable international societies, varying widely in purpose and membership; but since my subject is the nexus between armed international conflict and the justice motive, the members of the society with which I am concerned must be at once the actors chiefly associated with armed conflict, and the actors widely considered most competent to assert claims as to the justice or injustice of actions and arrangements: namely, sovereign states.

Bull defines a society of states as "a group of states, conscious of certain common interests and common values, [that] conceive themselves to be bound by a common set of rules in their relations with one another, and share in the working of common institutions." Hedley Bull, *The Anarchical Society* (London: Macmillan, 1977), 13. Bull's conception of society may be contrasted with Martin Wight's: a society is "a number of individuals joined in a system of relationships for certain common purposes." *Power Politics*, 105. Rawls defines a society as a scheme of cooperation for mutual advantage which is typically marked by shared as well as conflicting interests. John Rawls, *A Theory of Justice* (Cambridge, Mass.: Belknap, 1971), 4. Bull notes that the fairly minimal goals of the international society of states as we currently know it include (1) the preservation of the system; (2) the maintenance of the independence of individual states; (3) the maintenance of peace (for the most part); and (4) the limitation of violence, the keeping of promises, and the stabilization of possession by rules of property. *The Anarchical Society*, 16–20.

2 The degree to which international politics exhibits the virtue of order is commensurate with the level of cooperation in the system, especially in the management of disputes; a mark of order is the system's ability to evolve peacefully to meet the exigencies of changing circumstances. Cf. Stanley Hoffmann, *Primacy or World Order* (New York: McGraw-Hill, 1978), 188–9. On the various sources of order, see Bull, *The Anarchical Society*, 7, 48.

3 A "well-ordered society" is a society "effectively regulated by a public conception of justice" in which "everyone accepts and knows that the others accept the same principles of justice," and "the basic social institutions generally satisfy and are generally known to satisfy these principles." Rawls, *A Theory of Justice*, 4–5. Cf. Cicero: a political society is "not any collection of human beings brought together in any sort of way but an assemblage of people in large numbers associated in an agreement with respect to justice and a partnership for the common good." *De Republica*, Book I, XXV, trans. C.W. Keyes (Cambridge, Mass.: Loeb Classical Library, 1977), 65. It should be noted, however, that world order differs in several respects from domestic order, and that a global society differs also from a domestic society. While domestic order rests on a consensus on principles,

values, or the legitimacy of central authority, world order in rudimentary form may require merely a minimal consensus and "adequate institutions" – goals, not foundations. Cf. Hoffmann, *Duties Beyond Borders*, 194. And while a domestic society may be in part constituted by its members' commitment to a common purpose, a shared heritage, or a vision of community, a global society may be merely superstructural. Nevertheless, the relationship between order and justice may be understood the same way, if not in the same degree, *mutatis mutandis*.

4 Rawls, *A Theory of Justice*, 128. Cf. *ibid.*, 126–30.

5 It is possible to argue that the moral worth of a virtue is a function of the desirability of its consequences. Such a teleological account of the moral virtues, of course, would be philosophically controversial, and my intent is neither to assert its truth nor to spell out the argument in any detail. Rather, it is to note that the operation of each of the moral virtues does have a characteristic consequence that is widely acknowledged to be desirable whether or not the desirability of that consequence is taken to account for the moral worth of the virtue itself.

6 See, e.g., Hoffmann, *Primacy or World Order*, 12, 108.

7 See Morgenthau, *Politics Among Nations*, 8–10; George F. Kennan, *American Diplomacy: 1900–1950* (Chicago: University of Chicago Press, 1951), *passim*.

8 See n. 3, above.

9 By *cultural ethical relativism* I have in mind the doctrine sometimes referred to as *descriptive ethical relativism* – that is, the claim that different cultures in fact make different moral judgments – not *metaethical relativism* (the view that ethical terms mean different things to different cultures) or *normative ethical relativism* (the view that what is *actually morally right* in one cultural context may be *actually morally wrong* in another). Cultural ethical relativism is neutral on the question of what things actually are right or wrong; it is a sociological, not a philosophical doctrine.

10 John Locke, *An Essay Concerning Human Understanding*, I, III ("No innate Practical Principles"), §10; ed. Peter H. Nidditch (Oxford: Clarendon Press, 1982), 72.

11 William Graham Sumner, *Folkways: A Study of the Sociological Importance of Usages, Manners, Customs, Mores, and Morals* (Boston: Ginn, 1906); Edward Westermarck, *The Origin and Development of the Moral Ideas*, 2 vols. (London: Macmillan, 1906, 1908). See also F.S.C. Northrup, *The Meeting of East and West* (New York: Macmillan, 1946), chapt. 10; and Adda B. Bozeman, *The Future of Law in a Multicultural World* (Princeton, N.J.: Princeton University Press, 1971), ix–xvii, 14–33.

12 See Ginsberg, *Reason and Unreason in Society*, 346; Alexander MacBeath, *Experiments in Living: A Study of the Nature and Foundation of Ethics or Morals in the Light of Recent Work in Social Anthropology* (London: Macmillan, 1952); and May Edel and Abraham Edel, *Anthropology and Ethics: The Quest for Moral Understanding*, rev. edn. (Cleveland: Press of Case Western Reserve University, 1968).

13 "[T]he same act, being the same with regard to all meanings involved, has never been observed to incur different valuations. That is to say: within the same pattern of situational meanings only one of two contrary behaviours

can lay claim to the same ethical quality and valuation. There are, then, general *'inner laws'* of ethical valuation, the independent variables of which are meanings." Karl Duncker, "Ethical Relativity? (An Enquiry into the Psychology of Ethics)," *Mind*, new ser., 48, No. 189 (January 1939), 50.

14 See Richard B. Brandt, *Ethical Theory: The Problems of Normative and Critical Ethics* (Englewood Cliffs, N.J.: Prentice-Hall, 1959), 83–113; and *Hopi Ethics: A Theoretical Analysis* (Chicago: University of Chicago Press, 1954), 213–15, 245–6. Peter French, drawing on the work of Donald Davidson, argues against relativism that radical moral disagreement is impossible between cultures, simply because at some point it becomes impossible to know whether the parties to the debate mean the same things by the same terms. See Peter French, "Exorcising the Demon of Cultural Relativism," in Stephen Luper-Foy, ed., *Problems of International Justice* (Boulder, Colo.: Westview Press, 1988), 114–23.

15 Ronald Dworkin, *Taking Rights Seriously* (Cambridge, Mass.: Harvard University Press, 1977), 134.

16 Not only may conceptions of legitimate entitlement vary *between* cultures, they may also vary *within* a given culture over time, or even at any particular time. In the heyday of British imperialism, the principle of self-determination was not thought to carry any moral weight; today, it is taken very seriously indeed. Decolonization occurred in the interim, and was accelerated by the combination of external pressures and growing self-doubt about the ethics of imperial rule.

17 Luper-Foy, *Problems of International Justice*, 3. Cf. Rawls, who states that the "basic structure of society" is the primary subject of justice. By "basic structure," he means "the way in which the major social institutions distribute fundamental rights and duties and determine the division of advantages from social cooperation. By major institutions I understand the political constitution and the principal economic and social arrangements." Rawls, *A Theory of Justice*, 7.

18 *Treatise of Human Nature*, III, II, I; in Aiken, *Hume's Moral and Political Philosophy*, 69.

19 Terry Nardin, *Law, Morality, and the Relations of States* (Princeton, N.J.: Princeton University Press, 1983), 253, 257.

20 Contracts – legal promises – *are* enforced so as to ensure an even higher level of compliance. But this does not detract from the main point here, which is that contracts need not be enforced for the institution of contracting to exist and function tolerably well – well enough, at least, for the idea of "contract" to make sense.

21 A government that is legitimate *de facto*, according to Charles Beitz, is one that enjoys good standing among its citizens. A government that is legitimate *de jure* is one that has a moral right to be obeyed. De facto legitimacy can be determined empirically; de jure legitimacy is a normative notion. See Beitz, *Political Theory and International Relations*, 78 n. 26.

22 Rawls, *A Theory of Justice*, 580–1.

23 A plaintiff or a defendant in a court of law will undoubtedly be more interested in the particular right or obligation at issue; the judge, and society at large, will be more interested in the smooth functioning of the

judicial system itself. Ideally, the person who loses the suit or the trial will be persuaded by the judgment that the outcome is just; but this is not a necessary precondition for society as a whole to consider that justice has been done. If the loser cannot be persuaded that the outcome is consistent with socially or legally defined entitlements and obligations, he or she will not accept that it is just and may well enter into a state of war with society by becoming an outlaw. In such a case, the person advancing a claim can no longer advance a claim of *entitlement*, or a claim to a benefit that flows from an entitlement, because he or she has forsaken the institutional context in terms of which entitlements and obligations are defined. There is no justice in the state of war, just as there is no justice in the state of nature.

24 Nardin, *Law, Morality, and the Relations of States*, 145.
25 Some use the term "scope" to refer to what I have called "domain." See, e.g., D. Clayton Hubin, "The Scope of Justice," *Philosophy & Public Affairs*, 9, No. 1 (Fall 1979), 3–24. There does not appear to be a standard, and I have chosen to stipulate definitions that seem intuitive.
26 John Stuart Mill, *Utilitarianism*, ed. Oskar Piest (Indianapolis: Bobbs-Merrill, 1957), 6.
27 Nardin, *Law, Morality, and the Relations of States*, 60.
28 For a detailed discussion of a particular type of constructivism, see John Rawls, "Kantian Constructivism in Moral Theory: The Dewey Lectures 1980," *The Journal of Philosophy*, 77, No. 9 (September 1980), 515–72.
29 Rawls, *A Theory of Justice*, 13.
30 On reflective equilibrium, see *ibid.*, §4 (pp. 19–21) and §9 (pp. 48–51). See also Kai Nielsen, "World Government, Security, and Global Justice," in Luper-Foy, *Problems of International Justice*, 263–82; and Kai Nielsen, "In Defence of Wide Reflective Equilibrium," in Douglas Odegard, ed., *Ethics and Justification* (Edmonton, Alta.: Academic Printing & Publishing, 1988), 19–37.
31 Rawls, *A Theory of Justice*, 46–7.
32 "Whether justice as fairness can be extended to a general political conception for different kinds of societies existing under different historical and social conditions, or whether it can be extended to a general moral conception, or a significant part thereof, are altogether separate questions. I avoid prejudging these larger questions one way or the other." John Rawls, "Justice as Fairness: Political Not Metaphysical," *Philosophy & Public Affairs*, 14, No. 3 (Summer 1985), 224–5.
33 Nations have been defined historically in terms of common language, history, soul, spirit, destiny, race, culture, character, or some combination of these. Stanley French and Andres Gutman, "The Principle of National Self-Determination," in Virginia Held, Sidney Morgenbesser, and Thomas Nagel, eds., *Philosophy, Morality, and International Affairs* (New York: Oxford University Press, 1974), 139.
34 See Rawls, *A Theory of Justice*, §58, 377–82.
35 *Ibid.*, 378–9.
36 Rawls himself is very deferential to J.L. Brierly's treatment in *The Law of Nations*, 6th edn. (Oxford: Clarendon Press, 1963), chaps. IV–V. See Rawls, *A Theory of Justice*, 378n.
37 On the extension of Rawls's two principles globally, see Brian Barry, *The*

Liberal Theory of Justice (Oxford: Clarendon Press, 1973), 128–32; and Thomas Scanlon, "Rawls's Theory of Justice," *University of Pennsylvania Law Review*, 121, No. 5 (May 1973), 1066–7.

38 On hypothetical contract as the basis of (*de jure*) legitimacy, see Beitz, *Political Theory and International Relations*, 77–80.

39 Beitz is accordingly skeptical of the principle of "self-determination," especially when it is thrown up as an obstacle to cosmopolitan principles of justice. The very concept, he notes, is ambiguous: Who is the self? Does self-determination require mere political independence, or independent responsible government? What sort of independence is required – formal legal independence, or actual economic independence? *Political Theory and International Relations*, 95. But beyond the question of ambiguity, Beitz insists that "it is not clear why *any* moral importance should attach to common characteristics. Even if problems of territoriality could be settled, why should cultural, racial, tribal, or religious groups be eligible for self-determination?" *Ibid.*, 111. French and Gutman argue that "Nations do not possess any characteristic in common that distinguishes them from other populations. As a consequence, there is no apparent justification for restricting the principle of national self-determination to those populations which are ordinarily called nations." "The Principle of National Self-Determination," 140. Cf. Vernon Van Dyke, who argues that liberal theory is obsessively concerned with individual rights and duties, and that there is no reason *not* to treat ethnic communities as rights- and duties-bearing units, particularly since we do already. "The Individual, the State and Ethnic Communities in Political Theory," *World Politics*, 29, No. 3 (April 1977), 343–69. John Stuart Mill, less concerned with the question of whether common characteristics serve as the basis for political rights, occupies the simplest and most radical position on the issue: "One hardly knows what any division of the human race should be free to do if not to determine with which of the various collective bodies of human beings they choose to associate themselves," he writes; "the question of government ought to be decided by the governed." John Stuart Mill, *Considerations on Representative Government*, in J.M. Robson, ed., *Collected Works of John Stuart Mill*, 19 (Toronto: University of Toronto Press, 1977), 547.

40 *Political Theory and International Relations*, 65–6.

41 *Ibid.*, 138, 154. "If the societies of the world are now to be conceived as open, fully interdependent systems, the world as a whole would fit the description of a scheme of social cooperation, and the arguments for [Rawls's] two principles would apply, a fortiori, at the global level. The principles of justice for international politics would be the two principles for domestic society writ large ..." *Ibid.*, 132. "The state-centered image of the world has lost its normative relevance because of the rise of global economic interdependence. Hence, principles of distributive justice must apply in the first instance to the world as a whole, then derivatively to nation-states." Charles R. Beitz, "Justice and International Relations," *Philosophy & Public Affairs*, 4, No. 4 (Summer 1975), 383.

42 Charles R. Beitz, "Bounded Morality," *International Organization*, 33, No. 3 (Summer 1979), 417.

43 Beitz, *Political Theory and International Relations*, 128. Cf. Nardin, who notes that the suggestion that international society should be thought of as a means of realizing a substantive end, such as a global redistribution of wealth, is a recent one. Prior to this century, international society was exclusively thought of as a regulated order, what Nardin calls a "practical" rather than "purposive" association, governed simply by rules and restraints – the concept of "right" – rather than by a conception of the common good. It is difficult to see why an international society so conceived would embrace redistributive principles as a matter of justice rather than as a matter of mutual aid, because the whole point of practical principles of justice is to facilitate the independent pursuit of national aims by reducing outside interference. See, e.g., *Law, Morality, and the Relations of States*, 267.

44 Michael Walzer, *Spheres of Justice: A Defense of Pluralism and Equality* (New York: Basic Books, 1983), 312–13.

45 For Walzer's reply to Beitz's claim that global interdependence defeats claims to sovereignty, see Michael Walzer, "The Moral Standing of States," *Philosophy & Public Affairs*, 9, No. 3 (Spring 1980), 227.

46 *Ibid.*, 228.

47 Walzer, *Just and Unjust Wars*, 61–2. In the course of his disquisition, Walzer introduces and argues for a series of revisions to this paradigm that allow, *inter alia*, aid to secessionist movements that have demonstrated their representative character; intervention to balance the prior interventions of other powers; and military action to rescue peoples threatened with massacre. "In each of these cases we permit or, after the fact, we praise or don't condemn these violations of the formal rules of sovereignty, because they uphold the values of individual life and communal liberty of which sovereignty itself is merely an expression." *Ibid.*, 108.

48 The term "interpretive community" is a hermeneutical term designating a group of individuals who share a language of discourse, a pattern of situational meanings, and epistemic norms. The idea that meaning is relative to the structure and concerns of an interpretive community has established itself in a variety of disciplines. Ludwig Wittgenstein employed something like it in his reconsideration of the "picture theory" of language originally developed in the *Tractatus*; Thomas Kuhn employed it to describe how advances in science are accomplished by periodic and fairly rapid "paradigm shifts"; Stanley Fish, who coined the phrase, applied it to literary criticism; and Hilary Putnam has applied it to the study of truth itself, which, according to his theory of "Objective Relativism," is a notion somehow dependent upon standards of rational acceptability that may vary from community to community. Ludwig Wittgenstein, *Philosophical Investigations*, 3rd edn., trans. G.E.M. Anscombe (New York: Macmillan, 1968); Thomas Kuhn, *The Structure of Scientific Revolutions*, 2nd edn. (Chicago: University of Chicago Press, 1970); Hilary Putnam, *Reason, Truth and History* (Cambridge: Cambridge University Press, 1981); Stanley Fish, *Is There a Text in This Class? The Authority of Interpretive Communities* (Cambridge, Mass.: Harvard University Press, 1980). Although Karl Duncker did not employ the term, his argument against ethical relativism also turns on the notion of an interpretive community. See p. 195, above.

49 Examples of parochial conceptions of international justice include Henry Sidgwick's utilitarian treatment in *The Elements of Politics*, 4th edn. (London: Macmillan, 1919), 237–328, and the various rather poorly-specified cosmopolitan conceptions undergirding the World Order Models Project, or WOMP. See, e.g., Richard A. Falk, *The End of World Order: Essays on Normative International Relations* (New York: Holmes & Meier, 1983), 57–8.

50 See Alan H. Goldman, "Foreign Intervention," in Luper-Foy, *Problems of International Justice*, 196–204. Pollis and Schwab note that non-Western societies do not share the ideological and cultural underpinnings of individualism, and suggest that Western notions of human rights may not apply to them. Adamantia Pollis and Peter Schwab, eds., *Human Rights: Cultural and Ideological Perspectives* (New York: Praeger, 1979), 1.

51 Beitz, *Political Theory and International Relations*, 16–17.

52 *Ibid.*, 18–19.

53 *Ibid.*, 19. Cf. also p. 50.

54 "Perhaps the most problematic feature of my exposition is the use of the plural pronouns: we, our, ourselves, us. I have already demonstrated the ambiguity of those words by using them in two ways: to describe that group of Americans who condemned the Vietnam war, and to describe that much larger group who understood the condemnation (whether or not they agreed with it). I shall limit myself henceforth to the larger group. That its members share a common morality is the critical assumption of this book." Walzer, *Just and Unjust Wars*, xiv.

55 See Christopher Brewin, "Sovereignty," in James Mayall, ed., *The Community of States: A Study in International Political Theory* (London: George Allen & Unwin, 1982), 45.

56 Nardin, *Law, Morality, and the Relations of States*, 233.

57 David Luban, "Just War and Human Rights," *Philosophy & Public Affairs*, 9, No. 2 (Winter 1980), 161–2.

58 UN Charter Art. 2 [4], 55; Resolution 1514 (XX), December 14, 1960; Annex to Resolution 2625 (XXV), October 24, 1970. United Nations, General Assembly, *Official Records*, Fifteenth session, Supp. no. 16 (A/4, 684), 1961, 67; Twenty-fifth session, Supp. no. 28 (A/8, 028), 1971, 123–4.

59 Morgenthau, *Politics Among Nations*, 471–2.

60 Note the difference on this score between the cases of the Malvinas and the Beagle Channel islands. Argentina ultimately accepted an arbitrator's decision to award the Beagle Channel islands to Chile; thus it makes sense to say that Chile is *entitled* to the islands, because Chile and Argentina both considered such a procedure legitimate for deciding the question. At present, however, Argentina would not accept an arbitrator's decision to award the Malvinas to Britain. Until such time as Britain and Argentina can agree upon a *process* for determining rightful title that is independent of *outcome*, it does not make sense to say that either country can claim the islands as a matter of international justice.

61 Quoted in Waltz, *Man, the State, and War*, 113.

62 The progressive school would appear to be ascendant. See, e.g., Francis Fukuyama, *The End of History and the Last Man* (New York: Free Press, 1992); and Mueller, *The Obsolescence of Major War*.

63 Conceptions of justice change over time even within comparatively well-ordered societies: the dominant conception of justice in the United States, for example, has shifted over time from classical liberalism to welfare liberalism, from the pole of liberty to the pole of equality. See Louis Hartz, *The Liberal Tradition in America: An Interpretation of American Political Thought since the Revolution* (New York: Harcourt, Brace, 1955). Constitutional interpretation has followed this shift – again, with no appreciable damage to the moral authority of the American constitution. If the Reagan Revolution proves to be more than a temporary reaction, however, the pendulum may have started to swing back in the other direction.

64 On this point, Realists are univocal. "The most extensive society in which most men live and act in our times is the national society," writes Morgenthau. "The nation is ... the recipient of man's highest secular loyalties. Beyond it there are other nations, but no community for which man would be willing to act regardless of what he understands the interests of his own nation to be." Morgenthau, *Politics Among Nations*, 501. Osgood and Tucker agree: "The modern nation-state is, after all, the most inclusive, deep-seated popular institution of our time. It is the chief repository and guarantor of the very values that the deprecators of force exalt. Its overwhelming appeal, whether among the old and industrially advanced or the new and poor states is, if anything, increasing." Osgood and Tucker, *Force, Order, and Justice*, 7. See also Waltz, *Man, the State, and War*, 177. I refer in the text to *patriotism and nationalism* because sometimes a *nation* (as a group sharing common features or experiences) is the primary level of identification, and sometimes it is the *state* (or political community encompassed by a single state). Patriotism is loyalty to a society defined territorially and politically regardless of the cultural and ethnic backgrounds of its members. "This distinction is crucial because the primary ingredients of nationalism, such as myths or beliefs of common descent, are not available in multiethnic societies." R. Paul Shaw and Yuwa Wong, *Genetic Seeds of Warfare: Evolution, Nationalism, and Patriotism* (Boston: Unwin Hyman, 1989), 158. Not all multinational states succeed in cultivating patriotism; for an analysis of the United States's success and the Soviet Union's failure in this regard, see *ibid.*, 162–7. It should also be noted, of course, that although patriotism and nationalism generally take precedence in people's hierarchies of political loyalties, they do not necessarily do so to the exclusion of other loyalties. See H. Guetzkow, *Multiple Loyalties: Theoretical Approach to a Problem in International Organization* (Princeton, N.J.: Princeton University Press, 1955).

65 Ernest Gellner, "Scale and Nation," *Philosophy of the Social Sciences*, 3, No. 1 (March 1973), 10.

66 Nardin, *Law, Morality, and the Relations of States*, 273n. Cosmopolitanism may be an idea whose time has not yet come; but there are reasons to wonder whether it ever will. Alex Inkeles notes that although there are clear exponential patterns of growth in interconnectedness and interdependence between nations, there is no corresponding exponential growth of integration, and virtually nothing in the way of political transformation (in either structures or attitudes) toward cosmopolitanism. Alex Inkeles, "The Emerging Social Structure of the World," *World Politics*, 27,

No. 4 (July 1975), 467–95. See also Emile Durkheim, *Moral Education: A Study in the Theory and Application of the Sociology of Education*, trans. Everett K. Wilson and Herman Schnurrer (New York: Free Press, 1961), esp. 74–9.

67 Hedley Bull, "The State's Positive Role in World Affairs," in Richard A. Falk, Samuel S. Kim, and Saul H. Mendlovitz, eds., *Toward a Just World Order* (Boulder, Colo.: Westview Press, 1982), 61.

68 Hoffmann, *Duties Beyond Borders*, 147. "In the Third World, politics is about establishing the state, competing to control its apparatus and to administer its patronage; the idea of transcending or going beyond the state would seem to most Third World politicians a ludicrous fantasy. Nowhere indeed is it a serious issue." Mayall, *The Community of States*, 4. Nardin notes that decolonization has reaffirmed rather than challenged European concepts of statehood, sovereignty, and international society. *Law, Morality, and the Relations of States*, 321. But Hedley Bull detects an element of hypocrisy here. Third World statesmen, he argues, have been strong champions of sovereignty when their own domestic affairs are involved, advocates of intervention with respect to colonialist and white supremacist states, and cosmopolitans when it comes to the undeveloped global commons. Bull, "The State's Positive Role in World Affairs," 70–1.

69 Note that the concept of sovereignty does not exclude the idea of international obligations; thus sovereign states can be bound by international law. See Hidemi Suganami, "International Law," in Mayall, *The Community of States*, 64–5. Note also that formal state sovereignty does not necessarily put a check upon interdependence, and that the extent of sovereign prerogatives can change over time. In the post-Cold War world, for example, we may see the international community demonstrate increasing willingness to interfere in the domestic affairs of its members. See David A. Welch, "The New Multilateralism and Evolving Security Systems," in Fen Osler Hampson and Christopher Maule, eds., *Canada Among Nations 1992–1993: A New World Order?* (Ottawa: Carleton University Press, 1992), 67–93.

70 On varying conceptions of "human rights" – Western, socialist, and Third World – see Fouad Ajami, "Human Rights and World Order Politics," in Falk, Kim, and Mendlovitz, *Toward a Just World Order*, 371–99. On competing conceptions of economic justice – Western (regulative, negative obligations) and Third World (purposive; positive obligations) – see James Mayall, "The Liberal Economy," in Mayall, *The Community of States*, 107, who notes that many Third World claims to redistribution are not motivated by a sense of justice but the drive for economic security.

71 Don MacNiven, *Bradley's Moral Psychology*, Studies in the History of Philosophy, 3 (Lewiston, N.Y.: Edwin Mellen Press, 1987), 210.

72 Stephen D. Krasner, "Structural Causes and Regime Consequences: Regimes as Intervening Variables," in Krasner, ed. *International Regimes* (Ithaca, N.Y.: Cornell University Press, 1983), 2.

73 *Ibid.*, emphasis added.

74 Robert O. Keohane, *After Hegemony* (Princeton, N.J.: Princeton University Press, 1984), 244–5. It is widely acknowledged that regimes matter; they alter the climate, substance, and processes of world politics. But regimes have had the greatest impact in a restricted domain – the "low politics" of

trade, finance, oceans, aviation, communications, energy, sports, and culture. Regimes have had a less obvious effect on the "high politics" of security, though there is reason to believe that even committed adversaries may successfully employ regimes to stabilize their political and military competition when they share an overriding interest in avoiding serious confrontation. Though it is difficult to know the magnitude of the effect, the sign, it seems, is clear: regimes promote order. Order, in turn, promotes peace. See the summary in David Welch, "Internationalism: Contacts, Trade, and Institutions," in Joseph S. Nye, Graham T. Allison, and Albert Carnesale, eds., *Fateful Visions: Avoiding Nuclear Catastrophe* (Cambridge, Mass.: Ballinger, 1988), esp. 190–5. See also Joseph S. Nye, Jr., "Nuclear Learning and US-Soviet Security Regimes," *International Organization*, 41, No. 3 (Summer 1987), 371–402. It should be noted that, while regimes are generally acknowledged to influence international affairs in the ways mentioned, relatively little is yet known about how and why, and under what circumstances they are more (or less) likely to matter. See Stephan Haggard and Beth A. Simmons, "Theories of International Regimes," *International Organization*, 41, No. 3 (Summer 1987), 491–517, esp. 513–17.

75 See, e.g., *Treatise of Human Nature*, III, II, §I; in Aiken, *Hume's Moral and Political Philosophy*, 49–69.

76 Durkheim suggested that social norms have three defining characteristics: regularity of behavior; the sense that it is obligatory; and the support of social sanctions. But most people "obey" norms not out of fear of sanctions, but because of internal motivation. See Robert T. Hall, *Emile Durkheim: Ethics and the Sociology of Morals* (New York: Greenwood Press, 1987), 48, 54.

77 Thomas Pogge, "Moral Progress," in Luper-Foy, *Problems of International Justice*, 295.

78 Jan Narveson, "Justifying a Morality," in Odegard, *Ethics and Justification*, 270.

79 A regime governing such an issue might be based upon a conception of imperfect procedural justice or a conception of pure procedural justice. In the case of the former, a just outcome in a dispute is known only in the abstract, and a fairly reliable procedure is designed to reach it (such as a trial). In the latter case, there is no antecedent criterion for the result, and the procedure itself determines the fairness of the outcome (such as arbitration). See Rawls, *A Theory of Justice*, §14, 85–8. Provided the conception enjoyed legitimacy and functioned adequately, it is a matter of indifference which form the regime would take. The latter may seem more likely, if Evan Luard is correct to argue that order in international society as we know it depends upon a procedural consensus, not a consensus on ends and values. Evan Luard, *Types of International Society* (New York: Free Press, 1976), 378.

80 Thomas W. Pogge, "Liberalism and Global Justice: Hoffmann and Nardin on Morality in International Affairs," *Philosophy & Public Affairs*, 15, No. 1 (Winter 1986), 81.

81 Hoffmann, *Primacy or World Order*, 250.

CONCLUSION

1 Nardin, *Law, Morality, and the Relations of States*, 28–9.
2 It is possible, of course, to speak of leadership sub-cultures. British policy in the years prior to World War II may have been heavily influenced by the fact that British leaders generally belonged to a class, and were the products of an educational system, that stressed the importance of "fair play." The postwar foreign policy establishment in the United States, in contrast, is a sub-culture heavily influenced by Realism.

BIBLIOGRAPHY

PRIMARY SOURCES, COLLECTIONS OF DOCUMENTS, REFERENCE WORKS

Bonnin, Georges, ed. *Bismarck and the Hohenzollern Candidature for the Spanish Throne: The Documents in the German Archives*. Trans. Isabella M. Massey. London: Chatto & Windus, 1957.

British Documents on the Origins of the War. Vol. VI. Ed. G.P. Gooch and Harold Temperley. London: His Majesty's Stationery Office, 1930.

Collected Diplomatic Documents Relating to the Outbreak of the European War. London: His Majesty's Stationery Office, 1915.

France. Commission de Publication des Documents Relatifs aux Origines de la Guerre 1939–1945. *Documents Diplomatiques Français 1932–1939*. Paris: Imprimerie Nationale, 1963–1986.

Ministère des Affaires Étrangères. *The French Yellow Book: Diplomatic Documents (1938–1939): Papers Relative to the Events and Negotiations which Preceded the Opening of Hostilities between Germany on the One Hand, and Poland, Great Britain and France on the Other*. New York: Reynal & Hitchcock, 1940.

Geiss, Imanuel, ed. *July 1914: The Outbreak of the First World War: Selected Documents*. New York: Charles Scribner's Sons, 1967.

Germany. Auswärtiges Amt. *Documents on German Foreign Policy, 1918–1945*. Washington, D.C.: United States Government Printing Office, 1949– .

Great Britain. Cabinet Papers. Public Record Office, London.

Foreign Office. *Documents on British Foreign Policy, 1919–1939*. London: His Majesty's Stationery Office, 1946–1986.

Foreign Office Papers. Public Record Office, London.

Hansard's Parliamentary Debates, 3rd Series.

Japan. Foreign Office. *Correspondence Regarding the Negotiations between Japan and Russia (1903–1904)*. Washington, D.C.: Gibson, 1904.

Lord, Robert Howard. *The Origins of the War of 1870: New Documents from the German Archives*. New York: Russell & Russell, 1966.

Noakes, Jeremy, and Geoffrey Pridham. *Documents on Nazism, 1919–1945*. New York: Viking, 1975.

Official German Documents Relating to the World War. Vol. II. New York: Oxford Univ. Press, 1923.

Les Origines Diplomatiques de la Guerre de 1870. 29 vols. Paris: Imprimerie Nationale, 1910–1932.

Parliamentary Debates Official Report. Fifth and Sixth Series, Commons.

Pribram, Alfred Franzis. *The Secret Treaties of Austria-Hungary, 1879–1914*. 2 vols. Trans. J.G. d'Arcy Paul and Denys P. Myers. New York: Howard Fertig, 1967.

The Treaty of Peace Between the Allied and Associated Powers and Germany, The Protocol thereto, the Agreement respecting the military occupation of the Rhine, and the Treaty Between France and Great Britain respecting Assistance to France in the event of unprovoked aggression by Germany, Signed at Versailles, June 28th, 1919. London: His Majesty's Stationery Office, 1919.

United Nations. General Assembly. *Official Records*. Fifteenth, Seventeenth, Twentieth, and Twenty-fifth Sessions; Sixth special session. New York: United Nations, 1961, 1963, 1966, 1971, 1974.

NEWSPAPERS AND PERIODICALS

The Economist
Morning Chronicle (London)
La Prensa (Buenos Aires)
The Times of London

BOOKS AND ARTICLES

Acton, John Emerich Edward Dalberg-Acton, First Baron. "The Causes of the Franco-Prussian War." *Historical Essays and Studies*. Ed. John Neville Figgis and Reginald Vere Laurence. London: Macmillan, 1908.

Adamthwaite, Anthony. *France and the Coming of the Second World War*. London: Frank Cass, 1977.

Adler, Selig. "The War Guilt Question and American Disillusionment, 1918–1928." *Journal of Modern History*, 23, No. 1 (March 1951), 1–28.

Aiken, Henry D., ed. *Hume's Moral and Political Philosophy*. New York: Hafner Press, 1948.

Albertini, Luigi. *The Origins of the War of 1914*. 3 vols. Trans. and ed. Isabella M. Massey. London: Oxford Univ. Press, 1952.

Anderson, Paul, and Timothy J. McKeown. "Changing Aspirations, Limited Attention, and War." *World Politics*, 40, No. 1 (October 1987), 1–29.

Argentina. Ministerio de Educación. *Bibliografía Sobre Las Islas Malvinas*. Buenos Aires: Centro Nacional de Documentación e Información Educativa, 1982.

Aristotle. *The Politics*. Trans. Carnes Lord. Chicago: Univ. of Chicago Press, 1984.

Asquith, Rt. Hon. Herbert Henry. *The Genesis of the War*. New York: George H. Doran, 1923.

Aster, Sidney. *1939: The Making of the Second World War*. New York: Simon and Schuster, 1973.

Atkinson, J.W. *An Introduction to Motivation*. Princeton, N.J.: Princeton Univ. Press, 1964.

Balfour, Michael. *The Kaiser and His Times*. Boston: Houghton Mifflin, 1964.

Barker, A.J. *The War Against Russia, 1854–1856*. New York: Holt, Rinehart and Winston, 1970.

310

Barnes, Harry Elmer. *In Quest of Truth and Justice: De-Bunking the War Guilt Myth*. Chicago: National Historical Society, 1928.

The Genesis of the World War: An Introduction to the Problem of War Guilt. New York: Knopf, 1929.

Barry, Brian. *The Liberal Theory of Justice*. Oxford: Clarendon Press, 1973.

Baumgart, Winfried. *The Peace of Paris, 1856: Studies in War, Diplomacy, and Peacemaking*. Santa Barbara, Calif.: ABC-Clio, 1981.

Baumont, Maurice. "The Role of Foreign Policy in the Success of the National-Socialist Party." In *The Third Reich*. Ed. Maurice Baumont, John H.E. Fried, and Edmond Vermeil. New York: Praeger, 1955, 456–78.

Beck, Peter. *The Falkland Islands as an International Problem*. London: Routledge, 1988.

Beitz, Charles R. "Bounded Morality." *International Organization*, 33, No. 3 (Summer 1979), 405–24.

"Justice and International Relations." *Philosophy & Public Affairs*, 4, No. 4 (Summer 1975), 360–89.

Political Theory and International Relations. Princeton, N.J.: Princeton Univ. Press, 1979.

Bell, P.M.H. *The Origins of the Second World War in Europe*. London: Longman, 1986.

Benedetti, Le Comte. *Ma Mission en Prusse*. Paris: Henri Plon, 1871.

Bernstein, Paul. "The Economic Aspects of Napoleon III's Rhine Policy." *French Historical Studies*, 1, No. 3 (Spring 1960), 335–47.

Bertier de Sauvigny, Guillaume de. *The Bourbon Restoration*. Trans. Lynn M. Case. Philadelphia: Univ. of Pennsylvania Press, 1967.

Bethmann Hollweg, Theobald von. *Reflections on the World War*. Trans. George Young. London: Thornton Butterworth, 1920.

Bismarck, Otto Fürst von. *Bismarck, the Man and the Statesman: Being the Reflections and Reminiscences of Otto, Prince von Bismarck, Written and Dictated by Himself after His Retirement from Office*. Vol. II. Trans. A.J. Butler. New York: Harper & Brothers, 1898.

Blainey, Geoffrey. *The Causes of War*. New York: Free Press, 1973.

Blight, James G. *The Shattered Crystal Ball: Fear and Learning in the Cuban Missile Crisis*. Savage, Md.: Rowman and Littlefield, 1990.

Blight, James G., and David A. Welch. *On the Brink: Americans and Soviets Reexamine the Cuban Missile Crisis*. 2nd edn. New York: Noonday, 1990.

Bloch, Camille. *The Causes of the World War: An Historical Summary*. London: George Allen & Unwin, 1935.

Bogitshevich, M. *Causes of the War: An Examination into the Causes of the European War with Special Reference to Russia and Serbia*. Amsterdam: C.L. Van Langenhuysen, 1919.

Bolsover, G.H. "Nicholas I and the Partition of Turkey." *Slavonic and East European Review*, 27, No. 68 (December 1948), 115–46.

Bozeman, Adda B. *The Future of Law in a Multicultural World*. Princeton, N.J.: Princeton Univ. Press, 1971.

Brandenburg, Erich. *From Bismarck to the World War: A History of German Foreign Policy, 1870–1914*. Trans. Annie Elizabeth Adams. London: Oxford Univ. Press, 1927.

Brandt, Richard B. *Ethical Theory: The Problems of Normative and Critical Ethics*. Englewood Cliffs, N.J.: Prentice-Hall, 1959.

Hopi Ethics: A Theoretical Analysis. Chicago: Univ. of Chicago Press, 1954.

Breslauer, George W., and Philip E. Tetlock, eds. *Learning in U.S. and Soviet Foreign Policy*. Boulder, Colo.: Westview, 1991.

Brierly, J.L. *The Law of Nations*. 6th edn. Oxford: Clarendon Press, 1963.

Broad, C.D. *Broad's Critical Essays in Moral Philosophy*. Ed. H.D. Lewis. London: George Allen & Unwin, 1971.

Brodie, Bernard. *War and Politics*. New York: Macmillan, 1973.

Brook-Shepherd, Gordon. *Royal Sunset: The European Dynasties and the Great War*. Garden City, N.Y: Doubleday, 1987.

Bull, Hedley. *The Anarchical Society*. London: Macmillan, 1977.

Bullock, Alan. *Hitler: A Study in Tyranny*. Abr. edn. New York: Harper & Row, 1971.

Bülow, Bernhard Heinrich Martin Karl, fürst von. *Memoirs of Prince von Bülow*. Vols. I and III. Boston: Little, Brown, 1931–32.

Imperial Germany. Trans. Marie A. Lewenz. New York: Dodd, Mead, 1917.

Burns, Jimmy. *The Land that Lost its Heroes: The Falklands, the Post-War, and Alfonsin*. London: Bloomsbury, 1987.

Butler, Rohan d'O. *The Roots of National Socialism, 1783–1933*. New York: Howard Fertig, 1968.

Calleo, David P. *The German Problem Reconsidered: Germany and the World Order, 1870 to the Present*. Cambridge: Cambridge Univ. Press, 1978.

Calvert, Peter. *The Falklands Crisis: The Rights and the Wrongs*. London: Frances Pinter, 1982.

Cardosa, Oscar Raul, Ricardo Kirschbaum, and Eduardo van der Kooy. *Malvinas: The Secret Plot*. Unpublished ms.

Carr, E.H. *International Relations Between the Two World Wars (1919–1939)*. London: Macmillan, 1963.

What Is History? London: Macmillan, 1961.

Carroll, E. Malcolm. "French Public Opinion on War with Prussia in 1870." *American Historical Review*, 31, No. 4 (July 1926), 679–700.

Case, Lynn M. *French Opinion on War and Diplomacy during the Second Empire*. Philadelphia: Univ. of Pennsylvania Press, 1954.

Cerf, Barry. *Alsace-Lorraine since 1870*. New York: Macmillan, 1919.

Chamberlain, Houston Stewart. *Foundations of the Nineteenth Century*. 2 vols. Trans. John Lees. New York: John Lane, 1913.

Charlton, Michael. *The Little Platoon: Diplomacy and the Falklands Dispute*. London: Basil Blackwell, 1989.

Chateaubriand, François-René, vicomte de. *Congrès de Vérone; Guerre d'Espagne; Negociations: Colonies Espagnoles*. Vol. I. Paris: Delloyé, 1838.

Christensen, Thomas J. "Threats, Assurances, and the Last Chance for Peace: The Lessons of Mao's Korean War Telegrams." *International Security*, 17, No. 1 (Summer 1992), 122–54.

Churchill, Winston S. *The World Crisis*. Vol. I. New York: Charles Scribner's Sons, 1923.

Cicero. *De Republica*. Trans. C.W. Keyes. Cambridge, Mass.: Loeb Classical Library, 1977.

Clark, Chester W. "Bismarck, Russia, and the War of 1870." *Journal of Modern History*, 14, No. 2 (June 1942), 195–208.

Cohen, Raymond. *Threat Perception in International Crisis*. Madison: Univ. of Wisconsin Press, 1979.

Coll, Alberto R., and Anthony C. Arend, eds. *The Falklands War: Lessons for Strategy, Diplomacy, and International Law*. Boston: George Allen & Unwin, 1985.

Crampton, R.J. *The Hollow Detente: Anglo-German Relations in the Balkans, 1911–1914*. London: George Prior, n.d.

Curtiss, John Shelton. *Russia's Crimean War*. Durham, N.C.: Duke Univ. Press, 1979.

Dabat, Alejandro, and Luis Lorenzano. *Argentina: The Malvinas and the End of Military Rule*. Trans. Ralph Johnstone. London: Verso, 1894.

Dacier, Michel. "La Candidature Hohenzollern." *Écrits de Paris*, No. 295 (September 1970), 3–12.

Dalyell, Tam. *One Man's Falklands . . .* London: Cecil Woolf, 1982.

Danchev, Alex, ed. *International Perspectives on the Falklands Conflict*. New York: St. Martin's, 1992.

Darmstaedter, F. *Bismarck and the Creation of the Second Reich*. New York: Russell & Russell, 1965.

Daus, Federico A., and Raúl C. Rey Balmaceda. *Islas Malvinas: Geografía-Bibliografía*. Buenos Aires: OIKOS, Asociación para la Promoción de los Estudios Territoriales y Ambientales, 1982.

Dent, N.J.H. *The Moral Psychology of the Virtues*. Cambridge: Cambridge Univ. Press, 1984.

De Rivera, Joseph H. *The Psychological Dimension of Foreign Policy*. Columbus, Oh.: Merrill, 1968.

Destefani, Laurio H. *The Malvinas, the South Georgias and the South Sandwich Islands: The Conflict with Britain*. Buenos Aires: Edipress, 1982.

Deutsch, Karl W. *Political Community and the North Atlantic Area: International Organization in the Light of Historical Experience*. Princeton, N.J.: Princeton Univ. Press, 1957.

Diehl, Paul F., and Gary Goertz. "Territorial Changes and Militarized Conflict." *Journal of Conflict Resolution*, 32, No. 1 (March 1988), 103–22.

Dillon, G.M. *The Falklands, Politics and War*. London: Macmillan, 1989.

Dobson, Christopher, John Miller, and Ronald Payne. *The Falklands Conflict*. London: Coronet, 1982.

Douglas, Roy. *In the Year of Munich*. New York: St. Martin's, 1977.

Doyle, Michael. "Liberalism and World Politics." *American Political Science Review*, 80, No. 4 (December 1986), 1151–69.

Duncker, Karl. "Ethical Relativity? (An Enquiry into the Psychology of Ethics.)" *Mind*, new ser., 48, No. 189 (January 1939), 39–57.

Dupuy, Aimé. *1870–1871: La Guerre, la Commune, et la Presse*. Paris: Armand Colin, 1959.

Durkheim, Emile. *Moral Education: A Study in the Theory and Application of the Sociology of Education*. Trans. Everett K. Wilson and Herman Schnurrer. New York: Free Press, 1961.

Duroselle, Jean-Baptiste. "France and the Crisis of March 1936." In *French*

Society and Culture Since the Old Regime. Ed. Evelyn M. Acomb and Marvin L. Brown, Jr. New York: Holt, Rinehart and Winston, 1966, 244–68.

Dworkin, Ronald. *Taking Rights Seriously*. Cambridge, Mass.: Harvard Univ. Press, 1977.

Echard, William E., ed. *Foreign Policy of the French Second Empire: A Bibliography*. New York: Greenwood Press, 1988.

Eckstein, Harry. "Case Study and Theory in Political Science." In *Strategies of Inquiry*. Handbook of Political Science, VII. Ed. Fred I. Greenstein and Nelson W. Polsby. Reading, Mass.: Addison-Wesley, 1975, 104–13.

Eddy, Paul, and Magnus Linklater, Peter Gillman, and The Sunday Times Insight Team. *The Falklands War*. London: André Deutsch, 1982.

Edel, May, and Abraham Edel. *Anthropology and Ethics: The Quest for Moral Understanding*. Rev. edn. Cleveland: Press of Case Western Reserve Univ., 1968.

Ekstein, Michael G., and Zara Steiner. "The Sarajevo Crisis." In *British Foreign Policy Under Sir Edward Grey*. Ed. F.H. Hinsley. Cambridge: Cambridge Univ. Press, 1977, 397–410.

Ember, Carol R., Melvin Ember, and Bruce M. Russett. "Peace Between Participatory Polities: A Cross-Cultural Test of the 'Democracies Rarely Fight Each Other' Hypothesis." *World Politics*, 44, No. 4 (July 1992), 573–99.

Evans, Peter B., Dietrich Rueschemeyer, and Theda Skocpol, eds. *Bringing the State Back In*. Cambridge: Cambridge Univ. Press, 1985.

Falk, Richard A. *The End of World Order: Essays on Normative International Relations*. New York: Holmes & Meier, 1983.

Falk, Richard A., Samuel S. Kim, and Saul H. Mendlovitz, eds. *Toward a Just World Order*. Boulder, Colo.: Westview, 1982.

The Falklands War: The Official History. London: Latin American Newsletters, 1983.

Favre, Jules. *The Government of the National Defence, from the 30th of June to the 31st of October 1870*. Trans. H. Clark. New York: AMS Press, 1974.

Fay, Sidney Bradshaw. *The Origins of the World War*. 2 vols. 2nd edn. New York: Free Press, 1966.

Feaver, Peter Douglas. *Guarding the Guardians: Civilian Control of Nuclear Weapons in the United States*. Ithaca, N.Y.: Cornell Univ. Press, 1992.

Feiling, Keith. *The Life of Neville Chamberlain*. London: Macmillan, 1947.

Fischer, Fritz. *Germany's Aims in the First World War*. New York: Norton, 1967.
War of Illusions: German Policies from 1911 to 1914. Trans. Marian Jackson. London: Chatto & Windus, 1975.
World Power or Decline: The Controversy Over Germany's Aims in the First World War. Trans. Lancelot L. Farrar, Robert Kimber, and Rita Kimber. New York: Norton, 1974.

Fish, Stanley. *Is There a Text in This Class? The Authority of Interpretive Communities*. Cambridge, Mass.: Harvard Univ. Press, 1980.

Fleming, Nicholas. *August 1939: The Last Days of Peace*. London: Peter Davies, 1979.

Fogel, Robert William, and G.R. Elton. *Which Road to the Past? Two Views of History*. New Haven: Yale Univ. Press, 1983.

Folger, Robert, ed. *The Sense of Injustice: Social Psychological Perspectives*. New York: Plenum Press, 1984.

Foulkes, Haroldo. *Las Malvinas, Una Causa Nacional.* 2nd edn. Buenos Aires: Ediciones Corregidor, 1982.

Franks, The Rt. Hon. Lord, Chairman. *Falkland Islands Review: Report of a Committee of Privy Counsellors.* London: Her Majesty's Stationery Office, 1983.

Freedman, Lawrence. *Britain and the Falklands War.* Oxford: Basil Blackwell, 1988.

Freedman, Lawrence, and Virginia Gamba-Stonehouse. *Signals of War: The Falklands Conflict of 1982.* London: Faber and Faber, 1990.

French, Stanley, and Andres Gutman. "The Principle of National Self-Determination." In *Philosophy, Morality, and International Affairs.* Ed. Virginia Held, Sidney Morgenbesser, and Thomas Nagel. New York: Oxford Univ. Press, 1974.

Friedman, Milton. *Essays in Positive Economics.* Chicago: Univ. of Chicago Press, 1953.

Frolich, Norman, and Joe Oppenheimer. "Beyond Economic Man: Altruism, Egalitarianism, and Difference Maximizing." *Journal of Conflict Resolution,* 28, No. 1 (March 1984), 3–24.

Fryer, W.R. "The War of 1870 in the Pattern of Franco-German Relations." *Renaissance and Modern Studies,* 18 (1974), 77–125.

Fukuyama, Francis. *The End of History and the Last Man.* New York: Free Press, 1992.

Gamba, Virginia. *The Falklands/Malvinas War: A Model for North–South Crisis Prevention.* Boston: Allen & Unwin, 1987.

Gatzke, Hans W., ed. *European Diplomacy Between Two Wars, 1919–1939.* Chicago: Quadrangle Books, 1972.

Gay, Albert Carl, Jr. "The Daladier Administration, 1938–1940." Diss. Univ. of North Carolina 1970.

Gellner, Ernest. "Scale and Nation." *Philosophy of the Social Sciences,* 3, No. 1 (March 1973), 1–17.

George, Alexander L. "Case Studies and Theory Development: The Method of Structured, Focussed Comparison." In *Diplomacy: New Approaches in History, Theory, and Policy.* Ed. Paul Gordon Lauren. New York: Free Press, 1979, 43–68.

Gilpin, Robert. "The Theory of Hegemonic War." *Journal of Interdisciplinary History,* 18, No. 4 (Spring 1988), 591–613.

War and Change in World Politics. Cambridge: Cambridge Univ. Press, 1981.

Ginsberg, Morris. *Reason and Unreason in Society: Essays in Sociology and Social Philosopy.* Cambridge, Mass.: Harvard Univ. Press, 1948.

Giraudeau, Fernand. *La Verité sur la Campagne de 1870: Examen Raisonné des Causes de la Guerre et de Nos Reverses.* Marseille: Typographie Marius Olive, 1871.

Glaser, Charles L. "Political Consequences of Military Strategy: Expanding and Refining the Spiral and Deterrence Models." *World Politics,* 44, No. 4 (July 1992), 497–538.

Goldmann, Kjell. "The Concept of 'Realism' as a Source of Confusion." *Cooperation and Conflict,* 23, No. 1 (1988), 2–14.

Gooch, Brison D. "A Century of Historiography on the Origins of the Crimean War." *American Historical Review,* 62, No. 1 (October 1956), 33–58.

Gooch, G.P. *Before the War: Studies in Diplomacy.* 2 vols. London: Longmans, Green, 1936.

Recent Revelations of European Diplomacy. London: Longmans, Green, 1927.

Gramont, Le Duc de. *La France et la Prusse Avant la Guerre.* Paris: E. Dentu, 1872.

Great Britain. Foreign and Commonwealth Office. *The Disputed Islands: The Falkland Crisis: A History & Background.* London: Her Majesty's Stationery Office, 1982.

The Falkland Islands: The Facts, rev. edn. London: Her Majesty's Stationery Office, 1982.

Greenberg, Jerald, and Ronald L. Cohen, eds. *Equity and Justice in Social Behavior.* New York: Academic Press, 1982.

Grey of Fallodon, Edward, Viscount. *Twenty-Five Years, 1892–1916.* 2 vols. New York: Frederick A. Stokes, 1925.

Grieco, Joseph M. "Anarchy and the Limits of Cooperation: A Realist Critique of the Newest Liberal Institutionalism." *International Organization,* 42, No. 3 (Summer 1988), 485–507.

Cooperation Among Nations: Europe, America, and Non-Tariff Barriers to Trade. Ithaca, N.Y.: Cornell Univ. Press, 1990.

Guetzkow, H. *Multiple Loyalties: Theoretical Approach to a Problem in International Organization.* Princeton, N.J.: Princeton Univ. Press, 1955.

Gustafson, Lowell S. *The Sovereignty Dispute over the Falkland (Malvinas) Islands.* New York: Oxford Univ. Press, 1988.

Gutmann, Emanuel. "Concealed or Conjured Irredentism: The Case of Alsace." In *Irredentism and International Politics.* Ed. Naomi Chazan. Boulder, Colo.: Lynne Rienner, 1991, 37–50.

Haggard, Stephan, and Beth A. Simmons. "Theories of International Regimes." *International Organization,* 41, No. 3 (Summer 1987), 491–517.

Haig, Alexander M., Jr. *Caveat: Realism, Reagan, and Foreign Policy.* New York: Macmillan, 1984.

Hall, Robert T. *Emile Durkheim: Ethics and the Sociology of Morals.* New York: Greenwood Press, 1987.

Halperin, S. William. "The Origins of the Franco-Prussian War Revisited: Bismarck and the Hohenzollern Candidature for the Spanish Throne." *Journal of Modern History,* 45, No. 1 (March 1973), 83–91.

Hamilton, Richard F. *Who Voted for Hitler?* Princeton, N.J.: Princeton Univ. Press, 1982.

Hamley, Gen. Sir Edward. *The War in the Crimea.* 7th edn. London: Seeley, 1986.

Haraszti, Éva H. *The Invaders: Hitler Occupies the Rhineland.* Trans. Zsófia László; translation revised by Brian McLean. Budapest: Akadémiai Kiadó, 1983.

Harris, Robert. *Gotcha! The Media, the Government and the Falklands Crisis.* London: Faber and Faber, 1983.

Hartz, Louis. *The Liberal Tradition in America: An Interpretation of American Political Thought since the Revolution.* New York: Harcourt, Brace, 1955.

Hastings, Max, and Simon Jenkins. *The Battle for the Falklands.* New York: Norton, 1984.

Hazen, Charles Downer. *Alsace-Lorraine under German Rule.* New York: Henry Holt, 1917.

Henderson, Gavin Burns. *Crimean War Diplomacy and Other Historical Essays.* New York: Russell & Russell, 1975.

Herkless, J.L. "Stratford, The Cabinet, and the Outbreak of the Crimean War." *Historical Journal*, 18, No. 3 (September 1975), 497–523.

Hermann, Margaret G. "Leader Personality and Foreign Policy Behavior." In *Comparing Foreign Policies: Theories, Findings, and Methods.* Ed. James N. Rosenau. New York: Sage, 1974, 201–34.

Hertz, John. "Idealist Internationalism and the Security Dilemma." *World Politics*, 2, No. 2 (January 1950), 157–80.

Hickey, John. "Keep the Falklands British? The Principle of Self-Determination of Dependent Territories." *Inter-American Economic Affairs*, 31, No. 1 (Summer 1977), 77–88.

Hiden, John, and John Farquharson. *Explaining Hitler's Germany: Historians and the Third Reich.* Totowa, N.J.: Barnes & Noble, 1983.

Hill, Leonidas. "Three Crises, 1938–39." *Journal of Contemporary History*, 3, No. 1 (January 1968), 113–44.

Hitler, Adolf. *Hitler's Secret Book.* Trans. Salvator Attanasio. New York: Grove Press, 1961.

——. *Mein Kampf.* New York: Reynal & Hitchcock, 1939.

——. *My New Order.* Ed. Raoul de Roussy de Sales. New York: Reynal & Hitchcock, 1941.

Hobbes, Thomas. *Leviathan.* Ed. C.B. Macpherson. Harmondsworth: Penguin, 1968.

Hoffman, Martin L. "Affect, Cognition, and Motivation." In *Handbook of Motivation and Cognition.* Ed. Richard M. Sorrentino and E. Tory Higgins. New York: Guilford Press, 1986, 254–80.

Hoffmann, Fritz L., and Olga Mingo Hoffmann. *Sovereignty Dispute: The Falklands/Malvinas, 1493–1982.* Boulder, Colo.: Westview, 1984.

Hoffmann, Stanley. *Duties Beyond Borders.* Syracuse, N.Y.: Syracuse Univ. Press, 1981.

——. *Primacy or World Order.* New York: McGraw-Hill, 1978.

Houweling, Henk, and Jan G. Siccama. "Power Transitions as a Cause of War." *Journal of Conflict Resolution*, 32, No. 1 (March 1988), 87–102.

How the War Began in 1914: Being the Diary of the Russian Foreign Office from the 3rd to the 20th (Old Style) of July, 1914. Trans. Maj. W. Cyprian Bridge. London: George Allen & Unwin, 1925.

Howard, Michael. *The Franco-Prussian War: The German Invasion of France, 1870–1871.* New York: Macmillan, 1962.

Hubin, D. Clayton. "The Scope of Justice." *Philosophy & Public Affairs*, 9, No. 1 (Fall 1979), 3–24.

Hugo, Grant. *Appearance and Reality in International Relations.* New York: Columbia Univ. Press, 1970.

Hume, Martin A.S. *Modern Spain, 1788–1898.* New York: G.P. Putnam's Sons, 1903.

Hurewitz, J.C. "Ottoman Diplomacy and the European State System." *Middle East Journal*, 15, No. 2 (Spring 1961), 141–52.

——. "Russia and the Turkish Straits: A Reevaluation of the Origins of the Problem." *World Politics*, 14, No. 4 (July 1962), 605–32.

Inkeles, Alex. "The Emerging Social Structure of the World." *World Politics*, 27, No. 4 (July 1975), 467–95.

Janis, Irving. *Groupthink: Psychological Studies of Policy Decisions and Fiascoes.* New York: Houghton Mifflin, 1982.

Janis, Irving L., and Leon Mann. *Decision Making: A Psychological Analysis of Conflict, Choice, and Commitment.* New York: Free Press, 1977.

Jarausch, Konrad H. "The Illusion of Limited War: Chancellor Bethmann Hollweg's Calculated Risk, July 1914." *Central European History*, 2, No. 1 (March 1969), 48–76.

Jardin, André, and André-Jean Tudesq. *Restoration and Reaction, 1815–1848.* Trans. Elborg Forster. Cambridge: Cambridge Univ. Press, 1983.

Jervis, Robert. "Hypotheses on Misperception." In *Power, Strategy, and Security.* Ed. Klaus Knorr. Princeton, N.J.: Princeton Univ. Press, 1983, 152–77.

Perception and Misperception in International Politics. Princeton, N.J.: Princeton Univ. Press, 1976.

"Realism, Game Theory, and Cooperation." *World Politics*, 40, No. 3 (April 1988), 317–49.

Jervis, Robert, Richard Ned Lebow, and Janice Gross Stein, with contributions by Patrick M. Morgan and Jack L. Snyder. *Psychology & Deterrence.* Baltimore: Johns Hopkins Univ. Press, 1985.

Joll, James. *The Origins of the First World War.* London: Longman, 1984.

Kagan, Donald. *The Outbreak of the Peloponnesian War.* Ithaca, N.Y.: Cornell Univ. Press, 1969.

Kahneman, Daniel, Jack L. Knetsch, and Richard H. Thaler. "Fairness and the Assumptions of Economics." *Journal of Business*, 59, No. 4 (October 1986), S285-S300.

"The Endowment Effect, Loss Aversion, and the Status Quo Bias." *Journal of Economic Perspectives*, 5, No. 1 (Winter 1991), 193–206.

Kahneman, Daniel, and Amos Tversky. "Prospect Theory: An Analysis of Decisions under Risk." *Econometrica*, 47, No. 2 (March 1979), 263–91.

Kahneman, Daniel, Paul Slovic, and Amos Tversky, eds. *Judgment under Uncertainty: Heuristics and Biases.* Cambridge: Cambridge Univ. Press, 1982.

Kaiser, David E. "Germany and the Origins of the First World War." *Journal of Modern History*, 55, No. 3 (September 1983), 442–74.

Kajima, Morinosuke. *The Diplomacy of Japan 1894–1922.* II. Tokyo: Kajima Institute of International Peace, 1978.

Kautsky, Karl. *The Guilt of William Hohenzollern.* London: Skeffington & Son, n.d.

Kehr, Helen, and Janet Langmaid. *The Nazi Era, 1919–1945: A Select Bibliography of Published Works from the Early Roots to 1980.* London: Mansell, 1982.

Keiger, John F.V. *France and the Origins of the First World War.* London: Macmillan, 1983.

Kennan, George F. *American Diplomacy: 1900–1950.* Chicago: Univ. of Chicago Press, 1951.

The Fateful Alliance: France, Russia, and the Coming of the First World War. Manchester: Manchester Univ. Press, 1984.

Kennedy, Paul M. *The Rise of the Anglo-German Antagonism 1860–1914.* London: Allen & Unwin, 1980.

Keohane, Robert O. *After Hegemony.* Princeton, N.J.: Princeton Univ. Press, 1984.

Keohane, Robert O., ed. *Neorealism and its Critics*. New York: Columbia Univ. Press, 1986.

Keohane, Robert O., and Joseph S. Nye, Jr. *Power and Interdependence: World Politics in Transition*. Boston: Little, Brown 1977.

Keynes, John Maynard. *The Economic Consequences of the Peace*. New York: Harcourt, Brace and Howe, 1920.

Kinglake, Alexander William. *The Invasion of the Crimea: Its Origin and an Account of Its Progress Down to the Death of Lord Raglan*. 3rd edn. Vol. I. Edinburgh: W. Blackwood and Sons, 1863.

Kinney, Douglas. *National Interest/National Honor: The Diplomacy of the Falklands Crisis*. New York: Praeger, 1989.

Knetsch, Jack L. "The Endowment Effect and Evidence of Nonreversible Indifference Curves." *American Economic Review*, 79, No. 5 (December 1989), 1277–84

Koch, H.W. *The Origins of the First World War: Great Power Rivalry and German War Aims*. 2nd edn. Basingstoke, Hampshire: Macmillan, 1984.

Kolb, Eberhard. *Der Kriegsausbruch 1870: Politische Entscheidungsprozesse und Verantworlichkeiten in der Julikrise 1870*. Göttingen: Vandenhoeck & Ruprecht, 1970.

Krasner, Stephen D., ed. *International Regimes*. Ithaca, N.Y.: Cornell Univ. Press, 1983.

Kuhn, Thomas S. *The Structure of Scientific Revolutions*. 2nd ed. Chicago: Univ. of Chicago Press, 1970.

Lafore, Laurence. *The Long Fuse: An Interpretation of the Origins of World War I*. Philadelphia: Lippincott, 1965.

La Gorce, Pierre de. *Histoire du Second Empire*. Vol. VI. Paris: Librairie Plon, 1912.

Langer, William L. "Bismarck as a Dramatist." In *Studies in Diplomatic History and Historiography in Honour of G.P.Gooch*. Ed. A.O. Sarkissian. London: Longman's, 1961, 199–216.

Laqueur, Walter, and George L. Mosse, eds. *1914: The Coming of the First World War*. New York: Harper & Row, 1966.

Lebow, Richard Ned. *Between Peace and War: The Nature of International Crisis*. Baltimore: Johns Hopkins Univ. Press, 1981.

Lebow, Richard Ned, and Janice Gross Stein. "Afghanistan, Carter, and Foreign Policy Change: The Limits of Cognitive Models." In *Force, Diplomacy, and Statecraft: Essays in Honor of Alexander L. George*. Ed. Timothy J. McKeown and Dan Caldwell. Boulder, Colo.: Westview, in press.

"Deterrence: The Elusive Dependent Variable." *World Politics*, 42, No. 3 (April 1990), 336–69.

"Rational Deterrence Theory: I Think, Therefore I Deter," *World Politics*, 61, No. 2 (January 1989), 208–24.

We All Lost the Cold War. Princeton, N.J.: Princeton Univ. Press, forthcoming.

Lee, Dwight E., ed. *The Outbreak of the First World War: Who Was Responsible?* Boston: D.C. Heath, 1958.

Le Goff, Jacques, and Pierre Nora, eds. *Constructing the Past: Essays in Historical Methodology*. Cambridge: Cambridge Univ. Press, 1985.

Lehautcourt, Pierre (Général Palat). *Les Origines de la Guerre de 1870: La Candidature Hohenzollern, 1868–1870*. Paris: Berger-Levrault, 1912.

Lentin, A. *Lloyd George, Woodrow Wilson and the Guilt of Germany: An Essay in the Pre-history of Appeasement*. Leicester: Leicester Univ. Press, 1984.

Lerner, Melvin J. "The Justice Motive in Social Behavior: Introduction." *Journal of Social Issues*, 31, No. 3 (1975), 1–19.

"The Justice Motive: Some Hypotheses as to its Origins and Forms." *Journal of Personality*, 45, No. 1 (March 1977), 1–52.

Lerner, Melvin J., and Sally C. Lerner, eds. *The Justice Motive in Social Behavior: Adapting to Times of Scarcity and Change*. New York: Plenum Press, 1981.

Levy, Jack S. "Declining Power and the Preventive Motive for War." *World Politics*, 40, No. 1 (October 1987), 82–107.

"Domestic Politics and War." *Journal of Interdisciplinary History*, 18, No. 4 (Spring 1988), 653–73.

"Misperception and the Causes of War: Theoretical Linkages and Analytical Problems." *World Politics*, 36, No. 1 (October 1983), 76–99.

"Organizational Routines and the Causes of War." *International Studies Quarterly*, 30, No. 2 (June 1986), 193–222.

War in the Modern Great Power System, 1495–1975. Lexington: Univ. Press of Kentucky, 1983.

Lieven, D.C.B. *Russia and the Origins of the First World War*. New York: St. Martin's, 1983.

Lijphart, Arend. "The Comparable Case Strategy in Comparative Research." *Comparative Political Studies*, 8, No. 2 (July 1975), 158–77.

Lindzey, Gardner, ed. *Assessment of Human Motives*. Westport, Conn.: Glenwood Press, 1979.

Lloyd George, David. *War Memoirs of David Lloyd George*. Vol. I. Boston: Little, Brown, 1933.

Locke, John. *An Essay Concerning Human Understanding*. Ed. Peter H. Nidditch. Oxford: Clarendon Press, 1982.

London, Kurt. *Backgrounds of Conflict: Ideas and Forms in World Politics*. New York, Macmillan, 1945.

Luard, Evan. *Types of International Society*. New York: Free Press, 1976.

Luban, David. "Just War and Human Rights." *Philosophy & Public Affairs*, 9, No. 2 (Winter 1980), 160–81.

Luper-Foy, Stephen, ed. *Problems of International Justice*. Boulder, Colo.: Westview, 1988.

Lynn-Jones, Sean M. "Détente and Deterrence: Anglo-German Relations, 1911–1914." *International Security*, 11, No. 2 (Fall 1986), 121–50.

MacBeath, Alexander. *Experiments in Living: A Study of the Nature and Foundation of Ethics or Morals in the Light of Recent Work in Social Anthropology*. London: Macmillan, 1952.

Macleod, Iain. *Neville Chamberlain*. London: Frederick Muller, 1961.

MacNiven, Don. *Bradley's Moral Psychology*. Studies in the History of Philosophy, Vol. III. Lewiston, N.Y.: Edwin Mellen Press, 1987.

Madsen, K.B. *Theories of Motivation*. Cleveland: Howard Allen, 1961.

Maechling, Charles, Jr. "The Argentina Pariah." *Foreign Policy*, No. 45 (Winter 1981–82), 69–83.

Mandel, Robert. "Psychological Approaches to International Relations." In *Political Psychology*. Ed. Margaret G. Hermann. San Francisco: Jossey-Bass, 1986, 251–78.

Maoz, Zeev. *National Choices and International Processes*. Cambridge: Cambridge Univ. Press, 1990.

"Revisionism or Misinterpretation? A Reply to Professor Walker." *Political Psychology*, 8, No. 4 (December 1987), 623–36.

Maoz, Zeev, and Anat Shayer. "The Cognitive Structure of Peace and War Argumentation: Israeli Prime Ministers Versus the Knesset." *Political Psychology*, 8, No. 4 (December 1987), 575–604.

Maringer, H. *Force au Droit: Le Problème d'Alsace-Lorraine*. Paris: Berger-Levrault, 1913.

Marriott, J.A.R. *The Eastern Question: An Historical Study in European Diplomacy*. 4th edn. Oxford: Clarendon Press, 1940.

Martel, Gordon, ed. The Origins of the Second World War *Reconsidered: The A.J.P. Taylor Debate after Twenty-Five Years*. Boston: Allen & Unwin, 1986.

The Origins of the First World War. London: Longman, 1987.

Matthias, Eric. "The Influence of the Versailles Treaty on the Internal Development of the Weimar Republic." In *German Democracy and the Triumph of Hitler*. Ed. Anthony Nicholls and Eric Matthias. New York: St. Martin's, 1971, 13–28.

Maxwell, Mary. *Morality Among Nations: An Evolutionary View*. Albany: State Univ. of New York Press, 1990.

Mayall, James, ed. *The Community of States: A Study in International Political Theory*. London: George Allen & Unwin, 1982.

Nationalism and International Society. Cambridge: Cambridge Univ. Press, 1990.

Meléndez, Federico. *The Falklands: A Study in International Confrontation*. Carlsbad, Calif.: Arcadia Publications, 1984.

Metford, J.C.J. "Falklands or Malvinas? The Background to the Dispute." *International Affairs*, 44, No. 3 (July 1968), 463–81.

Meyerhoff, Hans, ed. *The Philosophy of History in Our Time*. New York: Doubleday, 1959.

Middlebrook, Martin. *Operation Corporate: The Falklands War, 1982*. London: Viking, 1985.

Middlemas, Keith, and John Barnes. *Baldwin: A Biography*. New York: Macmillan, 1969.

Midlarsky, Manus I., ed. *Handbook of War Studies*. Boston: Unwin Hyman, 1989.

Mikula, Gerold, ed. *Justice and Social Interaction: Experimental and Theoretical Contributions from Psychological Research*. New York: Springer-Verlag, 1980.

The Military Balance 1980–1981. London: International Institute for Strategic Studies, 1981.

Mill, John Stuart. *Considerations on Representative Government*. In *Collected Works of John Stuart Mill*. Vol. XIX. Ed. J.M. Robson. Toronto: Univ. of Toronto Press, 1977, 371–577.

Utilitarianism. Ed. Oskar Piest. Indianapolis: Bobbs-Merrill, 1957.

Miller, Steven E., ed. *Military Strategy and the Origins of the First World War*. Princeton, N.J.: Princeton Univ. Press, 1985.

Moltke, Helmuth von. *The Franco-German War of 1870–71*. Trans. Clara Bell and Henry W. Fischer. New York: Harper & Brothers, 1901.

Monnier, Luc. *Étude sur les Origines de la Guerre de Crimée*. Geneva: Librairie Droz, 1977.

Montgelas, Count Max. *The Case for the Central Powers: An Impeachment of the Versailles Verdict*. Trans. Constance Vesey. New York: Knopf, 1925.

Morgenthau, Hans J. *Politics Among Nations: The Struggle for Power and Peace*. 5th ed. New York: Knopf, 1978.

Moro, Rubén O. *The History of the South Atlantic Conflict*. Trans. Michael Valeur. New York: Praeger, 1989.

Moses, John A. *The Politics of Illusion: The Fischer Controversy in German Historiography*. London: George Prior, 1975.

Most, Benjamin A., and Harvey Starr. "International Relations Theory, Foreign Policy Substitutability, and 'Nice' Laws." *World Politics*, 36, No. 3 (April 1984), 383–406.

Mueller, John. *Retreat from Doomsday: The Obsolescence of Major War*. New York: Basic Books, 1989.

Mundo Lo, Sara de. *The Falkland/Malvinas Islands: A Bibliography of Books (1619–1982)*. Urbana, Ill.: Albatross, 1983.

Murray, Williamson. *The Change in the European Balance of Power, 1938–1939: The Path to Ruin*. Princeton, N.J.: Princeton Univ. Press, 1984.

Nardin, Terry. *Law, Morality, and the Relations of States*. Princeton, N.J.: Princeton Univ. Press, 1983.

Newman, Simon. *March 1939: The British Guarantee to Poland: A Study in the Continuity of British Foreign Policy*. Oxford: Clarendon Press, 1976.

Nicholson, Graeme. *Seeing and Reading*. London: Macmillan, 1984.

North, Robert C. *War, Peace, Survival: Global Politics and Conceptual Synthesis*. Boulder, Colo.: Westview, 1990.

Northedge, F.S., and M.D. Donelan. *International Disputes: The Political Aspects*. London: Europa, 1971.

Northrup, F.S.C. *The Meeting of East and West*. New York: Macmillan, 1946.

Nye, Joseph S., Jr. *Bound to Lead: The Changing Nature of American Power*. New York: Basic Books, 1990.

Nuclear Ethics. New York: Free Press, 1986.

"Nuclear Learning and U.S.-Soviet Security Regimes." *International Organization*, 41, No. 3 (Summer 1987), 371–402.

Odegard, Douglas, ed. *Ethics and Justification*. Edmonton, Alta.: Academic Printing & Publishing, 1988.

Ollivier, Émile. *The Franco-Prussian War and its Hidden Causes*. Trans. George Burnham Ives. London: Sir Isaac Pitman & Sons, 1913.

Oncken, Hermann. *Napoleon III and the Rhine: The Origin of the War of 1870–1871*. Trans. Edwin H. Zeydel. New York: Russell & Russell, 1967.

Osgood, Robert E., and Robert W. Tucker. *Force, Order, and Justice*. Baltimore: Johns Hopkins Univ. Press, 1967.

Paléologue, Maurice. *An Ambassador's Memoirs*. 6th edn. Vol. I. Trans. F.A. Holt. New York, George H. Doran, 1924.

Palmer, Alan. *The Banner of Battle: The Story of the Crimean War*. New York: St. Martin's, 1987.

Pares, Bernard. *A History of Russia*. New York: Knopf, 1953.

Pasquier, Etienne Denis, duc. *Histoire de Mon Temps: Mémoires du Chancelier Pasquier*. Vol. V. Paris: E. Plon, Nourrit, 1894.

Perl, Raphael. *The Falkland Islands Dispute in International Law and Politics: A Documentary Sourcebook*. London: Oceana Publications, 1983.

Phillipson, Coleman. *Alsace-Lorraine: Past, Present, and Future*. New York: E.P. Dutton, 1918.

Pogge, Thomas W. "Liberalism and Global Justice: Hoffmann and Nardin on Morality in International Affairs." *Philosophy & Public Affairs*, 15, No. 1 (Winter 1986), 67–81.

Poincaré, Raymond. *Les Origines de la Guerre*. Paris: Librairie Plon, 1921.

Pollis, Adamantia, and Peter Schwab, eds. *Human Rights: Cultural and Ideological Perspectives*. New York: Praeger, 1979.

Prazmowska, Anita. *Britain, Poland, and the Eastern Front, 1939*. Cambridge: Cambridge Univ. Press, 1987.

Pribram, Alfred Francis. *Austrian Foreign Policy, 1908–1918*. London: George Allen & Unwin, 1923.

Przeworski, Adam, and Henry Teune. *The Logic of Comparative Social Inquiry*. New York: Wiley-Interscience, 1970.

Puryear, Vernon John. *England, Russia and the Straits Question, 1844–1856*. Berkeley: Univ. of California Press, 1931.

Putnam, Hilary. *Reason, Truth, and History*. Cambridge: Cambridge Univ. Press, 1981.

Putnam, Robert. "Diplomacy and Domestic Politics: The Logic of Two-Level Games." *International Organization*, 42, No. 3 (Summer 1988), 427–60.

Rawls, John. "Justice as Fairness: Political Not Metaphysical." *Philosophy & Public Affairs*, 14, No. 3 (Summer 1985), 223–51.

"Kantian Constructivism in Moral Theory: The Dewey Lectures 1980." *The Journal of Philosophy*, 77, No. 9 (September 1980), 515–72.

A Theory of Justice. Cambridge, Mass.: Belknap, 1971.

Reginald, R., and Dr. Jeffrey M. Elliot. *Tempest in a Teapot: The Falkland Islands War*. San Bernardino, Calif.: Borgo Press, 1983.

Remak, Joachim. *The Origins of World War I, 1874–1914*. New York: Holt, Rinehart & Winston, 1967.

Renouvin, Pierre. *The Immediate Origins of the War (28th June – 4th August 1914)*. Trans. Theodore Carswell Hume. New Haven: Yale Univ. Press, 1928.

Riasanovsky, Nicholas V. *Nicholas I and Official Nationality in Russia, 1825–1855*. Berkeley: Univ. of California Press, 1959.

Rich, Norman. *Why the Crimean War? A Cautionary Tale*. Hanover [N.H.]: Univ. Press of New England, for Brown Univ., 1985.

Richardson, Louise. "Avoiding and Incurring Losses: Decision-Making in the Suez Crisis." *International Journal*, 47, No. 2 (Spring 1992), 370–401.

RIO: Reshaping the International Order: A Report to the Club of Rome. New York: Dutton, 1976.

Ritter, Gerhard. *The Schlieffen Plan: Critique of a Myth*. London: Oswald Wolff, 1958.

Robertson, E.M. *Hitler's Pre-war Policy and Military Plans, 1933–1939*. London: Longmans, 1963.

Robertson, E.M., ed. *The Origins of the Second World War: Historical Interpretations*. London: Macmillan, 1971.

Rock, William R. *British Appeasement in the 1930s*. London: Edward Arnold, 1977.

Rousseau, Jean Jacques. *A Lasting Peace through the Federation of Europe and the State of War*. Trans. C.E. Vaughan. London: Constable, 1917.

Saab, Ann Pottinger. *The Origins of the Crimean Alliance*. Charlottesville: Univ. Press of Virginia, 1977.

Saint Marc, Pierre. *Émile Ollivier*. Paris: Plon, 1950.

Sampson, Edward E. *Justice and the Critique of Pure Psychology*. New York: Plenum Press, 1983.

Sartori, Giovanni. "Concept Misformation in Comparative Politics." *American Political Science Review*, 64, No. 4 (December 1970), 1033–53.

Sazonov, Serge. *Fateful Years, 1909–1916: The Reminiscences of Serge Sazonov*. New York: Frederick A. Stokes, 1928.

Scanlon, Thomas. "Rawls's Theory of Justice." *Univ. of Pennsylvania Law Review*, 121, No. 5 (May 1973), 1020–69.

Schlatter, Richard, ed. *Hobbes's Thucydides*. New Brunswick, N.J.: Rutgers Univ. Press, 1975.

Schmitt, Bernadotte Everly. *The Coming of the War, 1914*. 2 vols. New York: Charles Scribner's sons, 1930.

    "The Diplomatic Preliminaries of the Crimean War." *American Historical Review*, 25, No. 1 (October 1919), 36–67.

Schoen, Freiherr von. *The Memoirs of An Ambassador: A Contribution to the Political History of Modern Times*. Trans. Constance Vesey. London: George Allen & Unwin, 1922.

Schroeder, Paul W. *Austria, Great Britain, and the Crimean War: The Destruction of the European Concert*. Ithaca, N.Y.: Cornell Univ. Press, 1972.

Seabury, Paul, and Angelo Codevilla. *War: Ends and Means*. New York: Basic Books, 1989.

Seaton, Albert. *The Crimean War: a Russian Chronicle*. London: Batsford, 1977.

Seton-Watson, R.W. *German, Slav, and Magyar: A Study in the Origins of the Great War*. London: Williams and Norgate, 1916.

    Sarajevo: A Study in the Origins of the Great War. London: Hutchinson, 1926.

    The Southern Slav Question and the Hapsburg Monarchy. New York: Howard Fertig, 1969.

    "William II's Balkan Policy." *The Slavonic and East European Review*, 7, No. 19 (June 1928), 1–29.

Seymour, Charles. *The Diplomatic Background of the War, 1870–1914*. New Haven: Yale Univ. Press, 1916.

Shackelton, Lord. *Economic Survey of the Falkland Islands*. London: Economist Intelligence Unit, 1976.

    Falkland Islands: Economic Study 1982. Cmnd. 8653. London: Her Majesty's Stationery Office, 1982.

Shackleton, Lord, with contributions from R.J. Storey and R. Johnson. "Prospects of the Falkland Islands." *The Geographical Journal*, 143, Part 1 (March 1977), 1–13.

Shaw, R. Paul, and Yuwa Wong. *Genetic Seeds of Warfare: Evolution, Nationalism, and Patriotism*. Boston: Unwin Hyman, 1989.

Shklar, Judith N. *The Faces of Injustice*. New Haven: Yale Univ. Press, 1990.

Sidgwick, Henry. *The Elements of Politics*. 4th edn. London: Macmillan, 1919.

Sinden, Jack L., and J.A. Sinden. "Willingness to Pay and Compensation Demanded: Experimental Evidence of an Unexpected Disparity in Measures of Value." *Quarterly Journal of Economics*, 99, No. 3 (August 1984), 507–21.

Small, Melvin, and J. David Singer. *Resort to Arms: International and Civil Wars, 1816–1980*. Beverly Hills, Calif.: Sage Publications, 1982.

Smith, John. *74 Days: An Islander's Diary of the Falklands Occupation*. London: Century, 1984.

Smith, Michael Joseph. *Realist Thought from Weber to Kissinger*. Baton Rouge: Louisiana State Univ. Press, 1986.

Smith, Willard A. "The Background of the Spanish Revolution of 1868." *American Historical Review*, 55, No. 4 (July 1950), 787–810.

"Napoleon III and the Spanish Revolution of 1868." *Journal of Modern History*, 25, No. 3 (September 1953), 211–33.

Snyder, Jack. *The Ideology of the Offensive: Military Decision Making and the Disasters of 1914*. Ithaca, N.Y.: Cornell Univ. Press, 1984.

Myths of Empire: Domestic Politics and International Ambition. Ithaca, N.Y.: Cornell Univ. Press, 1991.

Snyder, Louis Leo. *The Third Reich, 1933–1945: A Bibliographical Guide to German National Socialism*. New York: Garland, 1987.

Sofer, Sasson. "International Relations and the Invisibility of Ideology." *Millennium: Journal of International Studies*, 16, No. 3 (Winter 1987), 489–521.

Sorel, Albert. *Histoire Diplomatique de la Guerre Franco-Allemande*. 2 vols. Paris: E. Plon, 1875.

Spencer, Frank. "Historical Revision No. 122: Bismarck and the Franco-Prussian War." *History*, 40, No. 140 (October 1955), 319–25.

Stachura, Peter D. *The Weimar Era and Hitler, 1918–1933: A Critical Bibliography*. Oxford: Clio Press, 1977.

Staudinger, Hans. *The Inner Nazi: A Critical Analysis of* Mein Kampf. Ed. Peter M. Rutkoff and William B. Scott. Baton Rouge: Louisiana State Univ. Press, 1981.

Steefel, Lawrence D. *Bismarck, the Hohenzollern Candidacy, and the Origins of the Franco-German War of 1870*. Cambridge: Harvard Univ. Press, 1962.

Stein, Janice Gross. "The Arab–Israeli War of 1967: Inadvertent War Through Miscalculated Escalation," in *Avoiding War: Problems of Crisis Management*. Ed. Alexander L. George. Boulder, Colo.: Westview, 1991, 126–59.

"Building Politics into Psychology: The Misperception of Threat." *Political Psychology*, 9, No. 2 (June 1988), 245–71.

"Deterrence and Compellence in the Gulf, 1990–91: A Failed or Impossible Task?" *International Security*, 17, No. 2 (Fall 1992), 147–79.

"International Co-operation and Loss Avoidance: Framing the Problem." *International Journal*, 47, No. 2 (Spring 1992), 202–34.

Stein, Janice Gross, and Louis W. Pauly, eds. *Choosing to Co-operate: How States Avoid Loss*. Baltimore: Johns Hopkins Univ. Press, 1993.

Stein, Janice Gross, and David A. Welch. "Entitlement and Legitimacy in Decision Making." Unpublished paper, October 1991.

Steiner, Zara S. *Britain and the Origins of the First World War*. New York: St. Martin's, 1977.

Stengers, J. "Aux Origines de la Guerre de 1870: Gouvernement et Opinion Publique." *Revue Belge de Philologie et d'Histoire*, 34, No. 3 (1956), 701–47.

Sterling, John Ewart Wallace. "Diplomacy and the Newspaper Press in Austria-Hungary, Midsummer 1914." Diss. Stanford 1937.

Sumner, William Graham. *Folkways: A Study of the Sociological Importance of Usages, Manners, Customs, Mores, and Morals*. Boston: Ginn, 1906.

Taylor, A.J.P. *The Origins of the Second World War*. New York: Atheneum, 1962.

Temperley, Harold. *England and the Near East: The Crimea*. [Hamden, Conn.]: Archon Books, 1964.

Thaler, Richard. "Toward a Positive Theory of Consumer Choice." *Journal of Economic Behavior and Organization*, 1, No. 1 (March 1980), 39–60.

Thomas, Laurence. *Living Morally: A Psychology of Moral Character*. Philadelphia: Temple Univ. Press, 1989.

Thucydides. *The Peloponnesian War*. Trans. Rex Warner. Harmondsworth: Penguin, 1983.

Tirpitz, Grand Admiral Alfred von. *My Memoirs*. Vol. I. New York: Dodd, Mead, 1919.

Toland, John. *Adolf Hitler*. Garden City, N.Y.: Doubleday, 1976.

Trachtenberg, Marc. "The Meaning of Mobilization in 1914." *International Security*, 15, No. 3 (Winter 1990/91), 120–50.

Treitschke, Heinrich von. *Germany, France, Russia, & Islam*. Trans. George Haven Putnam. New York: G.P. Putnam's Sons, 1915.

Trevor-Roper, H.R. "The Mind of Adolf Hitler." Introductory essay to *Hitler's Secret Conversations 1941–1944*. New York: Farrar, Straus & Young, 1953, vii–xxx.

Tuchman, Barbara W. *The Guns of August*. New York: Macmillan, 1962.

Turner, L.C.F. *Origins of the First World War*. New York: Norton, 1970.

Tversky, Amos, and Daniel Kahneman. "The Framing of Decisions and the Psychology of Choice." *Science*, 211 (30 January 1981), 453–8.

Van Dyke, Vernon. "The Individual, the State and Ethnic Communities in Political Theory." *World Politics*, 29, No. 3 (April 1977), 343–69.

Vital, David. "Czechoslovakia and the Powers, September 1938." *Journal of Contemporary History*, 1, No. 4 (October 1966), 37–67.

Waite, Robert G.L. "Adolf Hitler's Anti-Semitism: A Study in History and Psychoanalysis." In *The Psychoanalytic Interpretation of History*. Ed. Benjamin B. Wolman. New York: Basic Books, 1971, 192–230.

Walker, Stephen G. "Personality, Situation, and Cognitive Complexity: A Revisionist Analysis of the Israeli Cases." *Political Psychology*, 8, No. 4 (December 1987), 605–21.

Wallach, Jehuda L. *The Dogma of the Battle of Annihilation: The Theories of Clausewitz and Schlieffen and their Impact on the German Conduct of Two World Wars*. Westport, Conn.: Greenwood Press, 1986.

Walster, Elaine, G. William Walster, and Ellen Berscheid. *Equity: Theory and Research*. Boston: Allyn and Bacon, 1978.

Walt, Stephen M. *The Origins of Alliances*. Ithaca, N.Y.: Cornell Univ. Press, 1987.

Waltz, Kenneth N. *Man, the State and War: A Theoretical Analysis*. New York: Columbia Univ. Press, 1959.

"The Origin of War in Neorealist Theory." *Journal of Interdisciplinary History*, 18, No. 4 (Spring 1988), 615–28.

Theory of International Relations. Reading, Mass.: Addison–Wesley, 1979.

Walzer, Michael. *Just and Unjust Wars*. New York: Basic Books, 1977.

"The Moral Standing of States: A Reply to Four Critics." *Philosophy & Public Affairs*, 9, No. 3 (Spring 1980), 209–29.

Spheres of Justice: A Defense of Pluralism and Equality. New York: Basic Books, 1983.

The War Diary of the Emperor Frederick III, 1870–1871. Trans. and ed. A.R. Allinson. New York: Howard Fertig, 1988.

Watt, Donald Cameron. "German Plans for the Reoccupation of the Rhineland." *Journal of Contemporary History*, 1, No. 4 (October 1966), 193–9.

How War Came: The Immediate Origins of the Second World War, 1938–1939. New York: Pantheon, 1989.

Weinberg, Gerhard L. *The Foreign Policy of Hitler's Germany: Diplomatic Revolution in Europe, 1933–36*. Chicago: Univ. of Chicago Press, 1970.

The Foreign Policy of Hitler's Germany: Starting World War II, 1937–1939. Chicago: Univ. of Chicago Press, 1980.

Welch, David A. "Internationalism: Contacts, Trade, and Institutions." In *Fateful Visions: Avoiding Nuclear Catastrophe*. Ed. Joseph S. Nye, Graham T. Allison, and Albert Carnesale. Cambridge, Mass.: Ballinger, 1988, 171–96.

"The New Multilateralism and Evolving Security Systems." In *Canada Among Nations 1992–1993: A New World Order?* Ed. Fen Osler Hampson and Christopher Maule. Ottawa: Carleton University Press, 1992, 67–93.

"The Organizational Process and Bureaucratic Politics Paradigms: Retrospect and Prospect." *International Security*, 17, No. 2 (Fall 1992), 112–46.

Welschinger, Henri. *La Guerre de 1870: Causes et Responsabilités*. 2nd edn. Vol. II. Paris: Plon–Nourrit, 1910.

Wertheimer, Mildred S. *The Pan–German League, 1890–1914*, Columbia Univ. Studies in History, Economics and Public Law, Vol. CXII, No. 2. New York: Longmans, Green, 1924.

Westermarck, Edward. *The Origin and Development of the Moral Ideas*. 2 vols. London: Macmillan, 1906, 1908.

Wetzel, David. *The Crimean War: A Diplomatic History*. East European Monograph No. CXCIII. New York: Columbia Univ. Press, 1985.

Wheaton, Eliot Barculo. *Prelude to Calamity: The Nazi Revolution, 1933–35*. Garden City, N.Y.: Doubleday, 1968.

Wight, Martin. *Power Politics*. Ed. Hedley Bull and Carsten Holbraad. London: Royal Institute of International Affairs, 1978.

Williamson, Samuel R., Jr. *The Politics of Grand Strategy: Britain and France Prepare for War, 1904–1914*. Cambridge, Mass.: Harvard Univ. Press, 1969.

Wittgenstein, Ludwig. *Philosophical Investigations*. 3rd edn. Trans. G.E.M. Anscombe. New York: Macmillan, 1968.

Wolfers, Arnold. *Britain and France Between Two Wars: Conflicting Strategies of Peace since Versailles*. New York: Harcourt, Brace, 1940.

Yoder, Amos. *World Politics and the Causes of War since 1914*. Lanham, Md.: Univ. Press of America, 1986.

Zeldin, Theodore. *Émile Ollivier and the Liberal Empire of Napoleon III*. Oxford: Clarendon Press, 1963.

INDEX

Dundas, Admiral Sir James Whitley
Deans, 56–7
Durkheim, Emile, 195
Dušan the Great of Serbia, 107
Dworkin, Ronald, 196

Economic Consequences of the Peace, The
(Keynes), 141
Economist, The, 179, 184
Ekstein, Michael, 122, 123
Elliott, Jeffrey, 175–6, 181–2
empirical-normative gap, 3–4
Ems Telegram, 86, 87, 88, 91
endowment effect, 24
errors in judgement, and the justice
motive, 25–9
Essay Concerning Human Understanding
(Locke), 194–5
Eulenburg, Count Philipp, 97
European Community, 212–13
evoked set, 27–8
expected utility theory, and the justice
motive, 22–3

Falklands/Malvinas war, 25, 27–8, 30–1,
36, 37, 155–85
and international justice, 207–10, 214,
216
and the justice motive, 155, 174–7, 188,
190, 191
Fallaci, Oriana, 160, 164
Faure, François, 105
Favre, Jules, 79
Fay, Sidney Bradshaw, 97, 102
Feiling, Keith, 145
Ferdinand of Saxe-Coburg-Gotha, 81
Figueroa, Gustavo, 167
First World War, 7, 34, 37, 95–126
and the justice motive, 95–6, 97, 118,
119, 186–7, 188, 189
and Serbian nationalism, 106–12
Foot, Michael, 178
forbearance-demanding perceptions of
injustice, 42, 44
Foulkes, Haroldo, 173
foundationalist theory of justice, 201, 206
France
and Alsace-Lorraine, 25, 100, 102–5, 187
and the approach to the Second World
War, 147–50
and the Crimean war, 50, 58, 59, 72–3,
73, 75, 197

and the First World War, 119–21, 124–5,
126, 187
and the Franco-Prussian war, 78–81,
83, 87–90
and German remilitarization of the
Rhineland, 140, 142
and German reunification, 79–81
and Hitler, 132, 142–3
and the Treaty of Versailles, 141, 143
Francis Ferdinand, Archduke of Austria,
112, 117
Francis Joseph, Emperor of Austria, 107
Franco-Prussian war, 18, 35, 37, 40, 45,
76–94, 192
peace settlement, 92–3
Franks Report, 170
Freedman, Lawrence, 168–9
Friesen, Richard von, 90

Galtieri, General Leopoldo, 160–1, 164–6,
167, 168, 169, 170, 171, 173, 174
Gamba-Stonehouse, Virginia, 168–9, 176
Gambetta, Leon, 79
General Agreement on Tariffs and Trade,
213
Germany, *see also* Hitler; Versailles,
Treaty of
and Alsace-Lorraine, 25, 102–6, 187
and the First World War, 97–102, 123–5,
126, 187; motivations, 117–19
and the Treaty of Versailles, 127–9,
131–2
Gibraltar, 179
Gilpin, Robert, 12
Gladstone, William, 123
Gooch, G. P., 121
Goremykin, I. L., 117
Göring, Hermann, 135
Gorchakov, Prince Mikhail, 66
Goschen, Sir Edward, 124
Goulding, Marrack, 181–2, 185
governments, legitimacy of, and the
justice motive, 43–4
Gramont, Antoine-Alfred-Agénor, duc de,
83, 84–5, 86, 90
Great Depression, and Nazism, 137, 138
Great Power wars, 32–40
Greenwood, Arthur, 151
Grey, Sir Edward, 99–100, 121–2, 122–3,
125
Grieco, Joseph, 13
Grotius, Hugo, 1, 201, 210